VISION and REVISION

VISION and REVISION

The Process of Reading and Writing

Sally Sullivan
The University of North Carolina Wilmington

Macmillan Publishing Company
New York

Macmillan Publishing Company
866 Third Avenue, New York, New York 10022

Library of Congress Cataloging-in-Publication Data
Sullivan, Sally.
  Vision and revision.

  Includes bibliographies and index.
  1. English language—Rhetoric.   2. College readers.
I. Title.
PE1408.S7796   1988   808'.0427   86-28538

Printing: 1 2 3 4 5 6 7   Year: 8 9 0 1 2 3 4

ISBN 0-02-418363-6

This book is dedicated to the memory of my father, William Goodman Sullivan, and with love to Mother, Cam, Kathleen, and Jim.

Preface

To the Instructor

At this moment, you might be thinking that another composition text is not exactly what the world needs. On the other hand, perhaps like me, you have not been entirely satisfied with any of the texts you have used or examined. Because of my dissatisfaction with the approaches used in other texts, I had several aims in mind when I began *Vision and Revision*. Above all, I wanted to level with students about the way writers really write. I especially wanted to stress both the individuality and recursiveness of the writing process, and I wanted to emphasize the interrelatedness of the processes of reading and writing as processes of "vision" and "revision," of "seeing" and "re-seeing." Most important, I wanted to use plenty of real student writing to illustrate every one of the writing concepts and skills discussed in the text. Because of these aims and others, *Vision and Revision* differs from other rhetoric texts in a number of significant ways.

1. *It clearly and amply illustrates the interrelatedness of the processes of reading and writing.* In the second chapter ("The Process of Reading"), students are introduced to reading as a process of vision and revision, of "seeing" and "re-seeing" a text in an attempt to derive meaning from it. Because deriving meaning from a text is a process, in *Vision and Revision* students are asked to read each assigned essay twice, responding in writing after each reading. These written responses to reading demonstrate that, like writing, reading is a process that differs from reader to reader. Furthermore, because no two readers derive identical meanings from a text, a reader essentially "writes" his or her own text. Finally, readers are literally writers when they respond to a text in writing.

In the third chapter ("The Process of Writing"), students are introduced to the recursive process of writing and revision, which demands that writers assume the role of their readers when they look back at what they have written, "re-see" it from their readers' point of view, and recompose. *Vision and Revision* further connects reading and writing in these ways: students are told that as readers they can unconsciously absorb the uses of language but that they can also accelerate the acquisition of writing skills by *consciously* noting how professional writers use these skills. For this reason I recommend that students read assignments a third time, paying attention to the professional writers' use of the skills under discussion.

The questions under the heading "Development and Style," which follow each professional essay and the two sample student essays in each writing chapter, ask students how each particular writer has used the skills discussed up to that point in the text. Besides reinforcing current knowledge, some of these questions prepare students for future learning by asking them to note a particular skill that they will encounter in a succeeding chapter. Last, the interrelatedness of reading and writing is underscored by the sequence of chapters: reading chapters precede writing chapters, and the suggestions in each writing chapter for finding topics are derived largely from the professional essays in the previous reading chapter.

2. *Vision and Revision emphasizes that writers begin with something to say, not with a particular rhetorical mode or pattern in mind.* As we all know, no professional writer arises on a Tuesday morning and says, "I think I'll write a persuasive essay today" or "I think I'll write a comparison/contrast essay today." Writers write because they have something they want to say. Furthermore, no professional essay I ever read used only one rhetorical pattern. If students are asked to put the cart before the horse, so to speak—to choose a rhetorical strategy before they have something to say—they will generally use that pattern exclusively. Such an approach to teaching exposition gives students the false idea that writing exposition is the mysterious and arduous task of finding content to plug into a particular prescribed form, instead of what it is: the process of a creative mind attempting to make meaning on paper, an attempt that results in an organic unity of form and content.

3. *Although* **Vision and Revision** *never asks students to use a particular rhetorical pattern, it gives them plenty of practice writing exposition and persuasion.* These two rhetorical modes are the most important ones to both college and professional writers. I level with students about the differences between themselves and professional writers, about the artificiality of a course in writing, and about the fact that college writing and writing in the world after college will most often demand that they write exposition or persuasion. Half of the essay assignments in the text ask students to write either exposition or persuasion (Chapters 10 12, and 14). In addition, your students will probably choose an expository mode in Chapter 6.

4. *Vision and Revision gives students a great deal of help in discovering both topics to write about and ideas to develop their*

chosen topics. Each assignment permits a wide range of subjects for writing, and each writing chapter begins by reminding students to reread their responses to the professional essays in the previous chapter and to scan their personal journals (if they are keeping one) for possible ideas. After checking these two valuable sources for interesting ideas, students can brainstorm in a group or make individual lists under a series of headings derived either directly or indirectly from the readings in the previous chapter.

Headings for brainstorming (listing) are provided in each chapter, and following them are two final drafts of good student writing. These essays serve several purposes: to illustrate the range of possibilities for handling the assignment; to stimulate further ideas for writing; and to illustrate how these two particular writers have used the writing skills that students have learned by that point in the text. Besides serving these purposes, the questions under the heading "Ideas and Meaning," which follow each student essay, also help students discover ideas for writing by asking them to relate their own experiences to the writer's. Using this text, you should find that many of your students already have a number of ideas for writing even before the assignment is made.

Vision and Revision introduces students to a number of invention techniques. In Chapter 2 students are introduced to brainstorming (listing) and freewriting. In Chapter 8 students are introduced to cubing, another useful technique for discovering ideas about the subject of any essay. And in Chapter 10 I present traditional rhetorical strategies as a list of seven questions that students can use to discover ideas about the subjects of expository or persuasive essays.

5. *In a number of ways,* **Vision and Revision** *demonstrates that the writing process differs from writer to writer and that both the writing process and the acquisition of writing skills are recursive rather than linear.* Since every writing chapter of *Vision and Revision* contains one student essay in draft form, students see that no two writers' processes are identical. Also the recursiveness of the writing process is demonstrated in many ways. In Chapter 10, for instance, after she composes two drafts of her essay, Cynthia returns to freewriting to discover another topic.

In addition, *Vision and Revision* consistently asks students to revise "old" writing in order to practice a particular new skill before applying it in a new assignment. In Chapter 4, for example, students write one objective and two subjective descriptions of a person or a place. Later, in Chapter 6, where they learn about coherence, they are asked to revise one of their subjective descriptions, making it more coherent. Then in Chapter 8, where students learn how to vary sentence beginnings and how to rearrange sentences for emphasis, they are asked to revise the other subjective description using this new knowledge to improve their sentence structure. This method encourages and motivates students in these ways: (1) It encourages students to revise because it is usually much easier to "re-see" old writing in a new light than it is to re-see writing under way. (2) As a consequence of having practiced a new skill once in old writing, students are generally more successful at revising present writing using that particular new skill. (3) Last, and most important, students are encouraged and motivated because they see from reviewing earlier efforts how much their writing has improved. Invariably, when students revise their subjective descriptions, I hear statements like this: "I can't *believe* I really wrote like this. These sentences are so choppy!"

Vision and Revision also demonstrates that the acquisition of writing skills is both recursive and cumulative. Supporting this idea are two regular features of the text—"The Critic's Guide" and the questions listed under the heading "Development and Style," which follow all professional and student essays. Because both lists of questions cover all those skills that students have learned by a particular point in the text, each list grows longer as the text progresses and students learn additional skills.

6. *Because in each writing chapter a new writing skill is introduced between the first and final drafts of a student essay,* Vision and Revision *ensures that students will be successful in their efforts to revise.* They will improve their essays at least in regard to the specific new skill they have learned. As a result of their success at revision, students are both encouraged and motivated to continue to revise their writing.

7. ***Vision and Revision*** *introduces students to the idea of writing as a collaborative effort.* Since no professional writer publishes anything without collaborating with one or more reviewers and one or more editors, *Vision and Revision* emphasizes peer criticism. In each writing chapter there is at least one critic's guide for students to use, and in each of these chapters the student essay that demonstrates process is shown with a critic's remarks in the margins. Also, I recommend collaboration as a way of discovering ideas for writing. In several chapters I suggest that students might brainstorm in groups since it is likely that each of them will mention at least one idea that the others would not have thought of, and I also suggest that they share any ideas they have for additional headings for brainstorming.

8. ***Vision and Revision*** *contains more student writing than any other similar text on the market.* Every writing concept and skill taught in this text is illustrated by at least one student's writing. In most instances, two or more student examples are used because I want to demonstrate the options that writers always have in every writing situation. In addition to the student writing that illustrates process and the two final drafts of good student writing in each writing chapter, with the exception of Chapter 2, each reading chapter contains two responses by a student after each of the professional essays. In the second chapter I use the responses of two students after each of the readings to illustrate that no two readers derive identical meanings from a text and that no two writers have identical voices.

9. ***Vision and Revision*** *reinforces the idea that usage instruction should not be divorced from writing.* At the end of each of the six writing chapters there is a proofreading tip that explains a usage or punctuation error commonly found in college students' writing. Since there is space for only six, some of the errors that we see in students' writing had to be omitted. As nearly as possible, these particular tips were chosen because they related somehow to the material in the preceding chapter. For example, avoiding the dangling modifier is the tip at the end of Chapter 8, in which students are taught that beginning sentences with verbal phrases is one way to avoid starting with the subject.

10. ***Vision and Revision*** *contains two helpful instructional aids in addition to the features outlined thus far.* At the end of each writing chapter there is a list of ideas for other writing assignments. In addition, there is an appendix with instruction on sentence combining. Part I of this appendix shows students how to combine sentences using adverb and adjective clauses, and Part II shows students how to combine sentences using the appositive, prepositional, participial, infinitive, and absolute phrasal constructions. Since each part of the appendix is further divided into sections devoted to particular constructions, you can direct individual students to a specific section or sections, or you can assign a specific section or sections to your whole class, depending on the needs of your students.

Vision and Revision is a text that does not ask students to choose a rhetorical pattern before they have something to say; that, as nearly as possible, allows student writers the freedom that professional writers enjoy, despite the constraints and artificiality of a course in writing; that contains plenty of examples of real student writing as well as professional writing; and that, above all, clearly explains and illustrates the interrelatedness of reading and writing. In addition to the particular aims outlined thus far, my ultimate aim in *Vision and Revision* was to write a text that would never end for students; I want them to become so excited about writing and reading that their course never ends. For some or for many of your students this may indeed happen. I sincerely hope so. Whether or not this particular aim is realized, I believe that *Vision and Revision* will help your students become competent, enthusiastic writers equipped with the knowledge necessary to succeed at college writing and beyond—in the writing that the world demands.

Note: *In this text, the usage, mechanical, and spelling errors made by students in the sample writings have been retained for several reasons. One reason is that the student writing is authentic, and real student writers make mistakes. Another reason is that I wanted to encourage students who use the text by showing them that others, even good student writers, make errors. And, most important, the retention of these writers' errors, which are ones that we commonly find in our students' writing, will give you the opportunity to bring them to the attention of your students.*

To the Student

You are probably somewhat, or decidedly, anxious about taking a course in college composition. Because I was once a freshman composition student myself, I think I know how you may be feeling right now. Even though it was a long time ago, I vividly recall the elevator ride up to my composition class on the fifteenth floor in the tower of the library at the University of Texas. My knees really did feel a little weak as I leaned against the back wall, and I kept staring at a spot on my glossy, new grasshopper-green notebook where the dim elevator light fell in a thumbnail-sized sliver of pale yellow. I was nervous and scared as I rode to that first meeting of my composition class. And, probably similar to your feelings now, I was frightened generally at the prospect of being a college student; but, more specifically, I was appalled at the idea of *writing*, of actually taking a college course in composition. What would I write, for heaven's sake?! Would the professor give me F's for writing *one* comma splice, as Ms. Jenkins, my high school teacher said would happen? Well, I had a lot of surprises in store for me, and I'm certain that you do too—a lot of *pleasant* surprises.

For one thing, whether you are the typical age of a college freshman—eighteen or nineteen—or whether instead you are a nontraditional student of thirty-five who is returning to school, some of the things that you may have heard about writing (which make you so nervous) just may not be true. For example, you may have heard that all writers make outlines before they write. *Not true.* Or, have you heard that you had better be careful not to end a sentence with a preposition? *Also not true.* These are but two of the myths about writing that many college students have heard and unfortunately believe. Now let's consider some things that you may *not* have heard about writing that *are* true. Have you heard, for instance, that sometimes writers discover what they want to say as they write, that in other words, by writing, writers actually discover thoughts that they didn't know they had? This is true, absolutely true. Make you feel better? Let's try one more: Did you ever hear that you could start a sentence with a conjunction like *and* or *but?* No—you've heard just the opposite? Well, this is also absolutely true—you certainly may begin a sentence with a conjunction. In fact, one of the surprises in store for you is this fact: There is *no* statement that either I or anyone else could make about either writers or writing that would hold true for every writer and every composition. Indeed, the truth is that there is no "proper" way, no *one* way, to write. Hence, as a writer, you have total freedom: there just simply are no "rules" for the composing process.

By now, I hope that you're feeling much better. There is nothing so comforting or inviting to the human spirit as freedom. And that is precisely what this textbook and your composition course promise you—freedom.

But, perhaps, like me in the past, you have one primary fear: What will I write about? Let me set your mind at rest. In this text you will be shown several methods you can use to find topics to write about. And if experience is the teacher that I think it is, you, like my students, will have too many ideas instead of none, so that you will have to choose a topic from a number of subjects that interest you. Furthermore, besides showing you how to find topics to write about, *Vision and Revision* will show you a number of invention techniques that you can use to discover ideas about the topics you choose. Thus, you need never worry again about having nothing to write about.

In addition to learning how to discover ideas, you will learn that reading can be a very valuable source of ideas to a writer and that both reading and writing are ways of seeing, discovering, and knowing yourself, others, and the world. Moreover, you will learn that both reading and writing are processes that involve "re-vi-sion," or "re-seeing," so that as you write and *revise*, read and reread, your insights will deepen and your perceptions grow keener.

And besides learning these things about reading and writing, there are many skills that you will learn to help you become a better writer, reader, and thinker.

When you get near the end of this course and the text, maybe you could let me know if I was right on both counts: your free-dom as a writer and the surprises you had in store. If you keep a personal journal throughout the semester, you could write a letter to me care of Macmillan as one of your last entries of the semes-ter and send me a photocopy. In addition, you might tell me what you think of *Vision and Revision*, perhaps what worked well for you and what didn't. As you will learn from this text, all writers need criticism to help them improve their writing. And that goes for professional writers just as much as it does for you.

Besides learning about the value of criticism to a writer, above all, I hope you will learn that writing can be a way of truly living. And I think you will discover one other fact as well: that a text-book about writing can be fun to read. But beyond "fun," and more important, is one last promise I feel comfortable making to you: It is almost a certainty that you will never take a course that adds to the quality of your life more than this one.

I hope I have accomplished my principal aims here: to allay your fears and to let you know what to expect from your compo-sition course and from this text. There remains only one more thing to be said: *Bon voyage.*

S.S.

Acknowledgments

Initially, I would like to thank every composition student that I've taught over the years because I learned so much from each of them, especially about how to teach writing. Second, I would like to thank specifically those students whose wonderful writing appears in this book under various pseudonyms. To each of you I can only say that I could never thank you adequately for what you have added to this text: Nancy Barclay, Julie Buffaloe, Lisa M. Butler, Camela Carstarphen, Anita Clark, Eric Cole, Menzetter Donahue, Matt Doyle, Art Giverson, David Harvey, Susan V. Headrick, Margaret Humphrey, Debra Jackson, Don Johnson, Vickie Lennon, Paula Nemser, Terry Proctor, Bill Thomas, Joan Travis, Pam Weaver, Sonia Weiss, and Dare Wicker.

In addition to these special students' contributions to *Vision and Revision*, other people have contributed as well. I wish to express my gratitude to my editor, Jennifer Crewe, for her astute advice and to editorial assistant, Sara Steen, for her help when Jennifer was away. I would also like to express my gratitude to Pat Cabeza, the production supervisor. Besides these professionals, I am indebted to the reviewers of *Vision and Revision*, who offered such expert advice and criticism. They are William Pierce, Prince George's Community College; Carl Singleton, Fort Hays State University; Richard Liba, Michigan Technological University; T. Ella Strother, Madison Area Technical College; A. Leslie Harris, Georgia State University; Mary Rosner, University of Louisville; Catharine B. Kloss, University of Pittsburgh at Johnstown; Duane H. Roen, University of Roen; Nancy Barry, University of Iowa; Jill Dix Ghanssia, University of Hartford. To each of you I am grateful for helping me to make *Vision and Revision* the best book it could be.

I am also immensely indebted to Christi Prentice, who kindly agreed to type my manuscript even though, as secretary to the chair of our department, she is a very busy person.

Finally, I want to thank my daughters, Camela Carstarphen and Kathleen McMurrey, for their devotion, love, and encouragement through the years.

Contents

CHAPTER 3   **The Process of Writing   59**

PART II   **Reading and Writing About Language   89**

CHAPTER 4   **Using the Power of Language   91**

CHAPTER 5   **Reading About Language: Its Uses and Misuses   105**

CHAPTER 6   **Writing About Language   127**

PART IV Reading and Writing Exposition   227

CHAPTER 9   The Act of Saying "I": Writers Exploring and Explaining Their Ideas   229

PART V **Reading and Writing Persuasion   375**

CHAPTER 13 **The Critical "I": Reading About What's Wrong with Our World 377**

CHAPTER 14 **The Critical "I": Writing About What's Wrong with Our World 411**

Reading
And Writing:
Interrelated
Processes

I

C H A P T E R

Writing As a Way of Seeing, Exploring, And Knowing

1

Like some college freshmen, you may dread the prospect of taking one or more courses in composition. Also, like many others, you may wonder why you must learn to write. After all, you say, my major is engineering. Why do I need to learn to write? And, furthermore, why can't I communicate with speech alone?

There are several answers to your questions, but the first and foremost response is that through writing, a writer gains power over himself and others. Personal writing, simply recording what you see, hear, think, and feel in a journal, for instance, allows you to examine your thoughts and feelings and, thus, to discover new insights into yourself or to realize perhaps for the first time what your thoughts and feelings really are. For example, when he was incarcerated, Eldridge Cleaver began a journal that he subsequently entitled *Soul on Ice*. Near the beginning of his journal, Cleaver explained why he began writing:

> After I returned to prison, I took a long look at myself. . . . My pride as a man dissolved and my whole fragile moral structure seemed to collapse, completely shattered. That is why I started to write. To save myself.
> . . . I had to find out who I am. . . .

As Cleaver indicates here, knowing yourself is where you begin, and writing is a way of finding out who you are. In other words, knowing yourself is a kind of power that neither Cleaver nor you, nor anyone else can do without. If you do not know who you are and what you think or feel, how can others know you, your thoughts or feelings? They cannot since you cannot express to them what you yourself do not know. Personal writing can definitely help you discover yourself and thereby gain the self-knowledge that you need in order to communicate your ideas to others. As the poet John Ciardi has put it, "The artist writes compulsively *as a way of knowing himself*. . . . The drunkard hopes to lose himself in his bottle, whereas the writer hopes *to find himself on the page."* In addition to Ciardi and Cleaver, many other writers have said much the same thing: writing is a way of knowing yourself—who you are and what you think.

That's where you begin—finding out who you are and what you think. Then, if you learn how to express better what you think, if you can communicate clearly in writing, you will get the satisfaction that we all feel when we write a letter or an essay, and our audience really understands what we mean. Furthermore, if you learn how to express yourself better in writing, you'll be able to write clear answers on essay exams, and you'll get the material reward of a passing grade. That's the power you need to get through college.

Last, the reason you cannot communicate just with speech is that the spoken word evaporates, the sound waves eventually dissipate and are gone forever. On the other hand, the written word remains forever. Its power to communicate or to persuade endures through the centuries. Without the written word, there would be no history, and people would have to discover over and over what their predecessors already learned.

Besides giving us history, the power of the written word has molded men's and women's minds and hearts, sometimes for the better, other times for the worse. No doubt, many examples come to your mind: the Holy Bible, *Mein Kampf, Das Kapital,* the Declaration of Independence, "Letter From a Birmingham Jail"; the list is endless. If Adolph Hitler had merely spoken his words, his power would have died with him. Unfortunately, he still has the power to sway men's minds, but, fortunately, so, too, does Martin Luther King, Jr.

Maybe you have never really thought about it, but all politicians and leaders of nations gained their political power and leadership by making their thoughts known to others, by *writing their beliefs* and persuading others to accept them. But perhaps you do not want to change the world or to rule it. As I have noted, learning to write well will result in many material, as well as immaterial, rewards as you pursue your college career.

And what about beyond college? How is being able to write going to help you as your pursue your career in computer science, chemistry, or engineering? The truth is that in almost any job that you take after college, when you demonstrate your ability to write well, you will be promoted to higher and higher positions that require you to write more and more. The inescapable truth is that corporate executives are writers. They spend most of their time thinking and writing their thoughts, as well as the thoughts of others occasionally.

Thus, learning to write well can insure your success after college, as well as in college. But above all, as a writer, you will know yourself better: you will have the power of self-knowledge, and there's no success or power greater than this.

Not only power, but joy and delight are the results of writing. You are about to take one of the most creative courses you have even taken or are likely ever to take, unless you are an art major or an English major who plans to take creative writing courses. Think about it: Every essay you write, every sentence even, never existed until you wrote them. And, furthermore, no other writer will ever create sentences or essays exactly like yours. When E. B. White, the noted American writer, tried to define the essayist, he said the following: "Each new excursion of the essayist, each new 'attempt,' differs from the last and takes him into new country. This delights him." As White indicates here, not only will no one else create essays like yours, but each essay you write will differ from all the others that you have created.

White put quotations marks around the word *attempt* because the noun *essay* means "an attempt" or "an endeavor." Thus, like any artist, the writer of essays is making an attempt to say what he wants to say, using the medium of language in the creation of something whole, his essay. And the result of such attempts is delight, as E. B. White says. As you will discover, the joy of creating something entirely new is like no other joy you have ever experienced.

Don't misunderstand me. I have said that the creation of something new is joyful; I have *not* said that the *process* of creating is always joyful. Often it is not. In fact, the process may sometimes be painful, more painful for some than for others. Furthermore, the labor pains that any one writer experiences will differ in length and intensity with each essay he or she composes.

Nevertheless, despite whatever pains you endure, you have the joy at the end when you have created your essay, your thoughts alive on paper. Because this course offers you the indescribable delight of creation, instead of approaching it with dread, you should approach it with eager anticipation.

The Writer's Journal

To begin the process that will lead to the birth of many good essays, you can start by keeping a journal. Many professional writers use journals to record their experiences and what they think and feel as a result of these experiences. For example, Annie Dillard, whose essays you will read later, has said that "[s]eeing is of course very much a matter of verbalization. Unless I call my attention to what passes before my eyes, I simply won't see it." In other words, if you do not write down what you see, you haven't really seen it. The implication of this statement is that writing is a way of really living. If we lose what we have experienced through our senses, we have lost life.

Noticing what you experience through your senses is not only a way to catch hold of life and keep it but also a way to become a good writer. All good writers want their readers to see what they saw, hear what they heard, smell what they smelled. Stating his aims as a writer, Joseph Conrad, the novelist, had this to say: "My task . . . is by the power of the written word, to make you hear, to make you feel—it is, before all, to make you *see.*"

Because good writing relies on the "power of the written word" to evoke images in the reader's mind, all good writers pay attention to sensory data. Since sensory data are so important to a writer, you might begin your journal by writing about the data you gather through your senses. In addition, you would want to write your reactions to what you hear, smell, or see and also the associations you make with some of these sounds, odors, and sights. To begin noticing more of what you experience through your senses, you might want to work on one sense at a time. Thus, one day you would record what you hear, the next what you taste, and so on until you have recorded data taken in by all five senses. A good way to do this is to carry a small, pocket-sized notebook and record in words or phrases the data that you gather through the particular sense you are working on. Don't forget to record your reactions and associations also.

At the end of the day, read over your list and then put it aside. Next, write down the data as you remember them, recording reactions or associations as you go. You can freewrite these responses, which means that you do not stop writing for a given period of time. Generally, most people can write continually for ten minutes without tiring. If you want to rest after you have written ten minutes, do so, and when you resume writing, write without stopping for another period of ten minutes or more, repeating this process until you have finished. Also, besides writing continually, when you freewrite you do not reread or cross out words, phrases, or sentences. Nor do you worry about correct spelling, punctuation, or usage. If you should get stuck and your thoughts quit coming, repeat the last word that you wrote. Your mind will associate and you'll be off again. Also, you can pay attention to what your senses are taking in at the moment and record those data if you get stuck.

Follow this same procedure each of the four days that you spend paying attention to the senses of hearing, smell, taste, and touch. You may order these senses any way you like, but save the sense of sight for the fifth day. At the end of the day that you spend noticing what you see, read over your list and check the sight that most impressed you, perhaps because of the associations you made with it. For example, suppose you saw two people arguing. The girl kept running her hands through her short, jet-black hair. The guy was leaning against a pine tree, and as she talked excitedly, gesticulating, he kept looking down at his feet, where he was making little circles with the toes of his sneakers, first one foot, then the other. Almost at once, you remember the particularly disturbing argument you had over dinner at Luigi's. Immediately you smell the pepperoni and cheese; you remember Lisa's green eyes, how you kept twisting your napkin in your lap, until it was reduced to a shredded heap that looked like confetti. These, and other details that your other senses were taking in, flood your brain. After you have chosen a sight such as this that prompted the strongest reactions in you, freewrite just as you have been doing, only this time, use detail that you gathered from your other senses as you try to re-create this experience. As best you can, try to capture in words the images of this experience that remain so vividly in your mind.

So that you can get a clear idea of what you can do, the following are examples from several students' efforts to notice what their senses took in and what their reactions and associations were. Except for the last example using the sense of sight, the others are only *excerpts* from these students' freewriting. Most of the freewrites were three, four, or more pages long. One last thing: Many of these students titled their freewrites, using such titles as "Catcher in the Eye," "Try Being Nosey," and "Are You Listening? Are you Really Listening?" for example. You may do whatever you like: give your freewrites titles or merely head them Smell, Taste, and so on. However, for the last one you might want to supply a title that suits your subject. Giving titles to your journal entries not only helps you to remain on focus but provides you with practice thinking of appropriate, short, and interesting titles.*

Paying Attention to Your Senses

Sound

The alarm clock ushers in the day with the brashness of bricks dragging across concrete. I reach for the button to silence it and hear the grinding crunch of bone against bone in my right shoulder. It is 7:00 a.m. and I lie in bed, wondering if

---

*In the following student examples, *and in all other student writing in this text,* you will find errors in usage, punctuation, and spelling. These errors have been retained for several reasons: The student writing is authentic, and "real" student writers make errors. I wanted you to see that other writers, even good ones, make errors. Last, I hoped that you might more readily correct the errors you make by noticing similar ones in other students' writing.

it is Saturday yet. The fan roars in my ear and I hear the drip, drip, dripping of the leaky bathroom faucet. . . .

My elbow hits the side of the tub with a hollow, echoing thump. I muse upon what sounds a fetus must hear in the womb. Maybe this is why I take baths instead of showers. Perhaps it is my way of returning momentarily to the security of prenatal life. . . .

Cupcake is ready to eat and the Gravy Train falls like marbles into her bowl. . . .

Hearing a familiar "Meow," I open the front door to see Smoky and Alex with hunger in their eyes. Their food pelts like hail into their dishes. . . . Tongues lap like sandpaper at their fur. I think of Eddie, my missing cat, and wonder what happened to him. . . .

Classes change in a cacophony of footsteps. Sandals slap and flip-flop at the pavement. Sneakers pad softly, and high heels fire rapidly at the sidewalk with a serious and decided rhythm. Spokes whirr like roulette wheels. . . .

Low conversation turns to whispers as the roll is called. Zup-Zup-Zup! Bookbags are opened. . . .

The cashier totals our bill on an adding machine that chatters "chtt-chtt-chtt," like an angry squirrel. . . .

Turning my house key in the door lock, I hear a thump-thump-thump inside. It is the familiar cadence of Cupcake's wagging tail against the floor in honor of my homecoming.

Smell

8:00 a.m.

Of all the senses, smell wakes the latest. The first distinctive aroma I detected was the medicinally minty smell of my shaving cream. It's like mint-flavored rubbing alcohol. The towel I used to wipe my face was dirty. It was a dark print so I couldn't tell by looking, but it smelled dirty, like stale socks.

The bar of Irish Spring in the shower has a great smell. I love it. The shampoo has an herbal scent, but I think it smells more like a weed than an herb. . . .

Mounted on my motorcycle heading for class, I smell the exhaust of every car and truck on the road. It's not very appetizing. It brings to mind committing suicide by sitting in a running car in a closed garage. Pleasant thought.

Campus isn't as alive with smells as it is with noise and sights, but there are a few. I guess you could get a wide range of smells if you walked up to people and sniffed. Not my bag. The girl in front of me in class uses Body on Tap shampoo. I like the smell of that stuff. . . .

On the way home I smell the cooking in the Chinese restaurant near my house. I smell it everytime I pass the place and it always makes me hungry. The aroma of pork, shrimp, chicken, soy sauce, and vegetables mingling in the olfactory makes my mouth water. I'll have to go eat there again soon. If restaurants could devise a way to broadcast smells along with their TV ads, sales would rocket. Interesting idea. I'll check the feasability with an electronics expert. . . .

Touch

. . . I touch my toes horizonitically so there is a space between each toe and kick the top sheet off my feet. The fan at the end of the bed gives only small relief and then only to my web-like toes. . . .

Running naked down the stairs for the relief of the AC, my breasts juggle a little and it hurts. That's just one other thing a woman has to put up with. It's too cold down here so I put on John's old blue T-shirt. Comfortable and reassuring.

Later we go to the Piney Woods Festival at Hugh MacRae park. I touch no one and no one touches me but yet I feel compressed, almost claustrophobic. There are too many people milling around. Is it possible not to actually be touched but still feel as though hands and bodies are all over you? Of course—since that's the way I feel. But, I wonder if I'm not just a little "loony tunes" for feeling this way. . . .

We have to wait in line at the Pilot House for lunch so I half sit half lean on the porch railing outside. As my hands grab the railing for balance they feel concaved warpedness of the wood and my fingers run the length of a tiny crack. I look down at the rail and am caught suddenly by the acute reality of it. The things that tree must have gone through just to end up as a railing on this porch! Quickly I glance around me to see if anyone has caught me fondling and examining the wood.

A branch from a small spindly tree hangs over my shoulder, one leaf scratching my face whenever I turn just the right way. Reaching up to pull the leaf off I'm reminded of my mother when I was little. She would make my brothers and I pick our own switches with which she would handily whip us. We had to strip the leaves off ourselves and the switches had to be good and skinny or else she'd send us back to pick a better one. She almost always did that—make us pick another one, I mean—so that we'd have plenty of time to agonize over our fate. It was always such a humbling experience to offer my self-made punishing rod to my mother, hoping it would be just the right thickness (or should I say thinness?) to satisfy her so that she might take some small measure of pity on me. She rarely did, though, and I would end up dancing and hopping around on one foot then another, turning circles and screaming bloody murder. Boy—this kid knew how to pick a switch that could really burn and sting.

Taste

Immediately I think of the mouthwash commercial where the husband and wife wake up, turn their heads away from one another, say good morning, run to the bathroom and rinse with mouthwash, and then greet each other with a smile and kiss. My mouth feels as theirs does, I'm sure. Dry, harsh, harsh, harsh, harsh, harsh, harsh, harsh, crude sort of feeling. Next, Carnation Instant Breakfast rolls over my taste buds leaving a distinct taste of chocolate behind. Also, an after taste is left which really tastes indescribable. . . .

Another break—another chance to use my taste buds. The chicken is hot—so are the french fries. The salt on the fries makes my lips feel old and shriveled. . . .

For supper—cream corn and ham and cheese rolled up in dough. . . . The cream corn looks like baby food. That starts me thinking about babies. . . . It always seems anything of value, anything of true worth, must be born of love and pain. Life would be too easy if we just had love and no pain. We human race—would become so spoiled—so soft—so useless—so fruitless. Life with pain only, would be hell. The two together make a great combination, producing, if allowed to, characters of true worth and integrity. So much for my philosophical speech.

Popcorn at the movies. . . . It was perfect. Most of the time when I go to the movies and get popcorn my lips become dry and feel swollen from excessive salt. Tonight the popcorn is just right. . . . You know, it seems I rush so much through life I really don't take the time to appreciate what I taste. Sometimes, though, my tastebuds control me. They control me. I don't even know what a tastebud looks like. Makes you feel kind of weak, small, to have something that's a part of you, that you can't even see, control you. Taste—I wonder where it starts. I wonder where it begins.

Sight

The Shell

As I stand at the waters edge waiting for some miracle, some seed of inspiration to permeate within, I notice a small band of sandpipers just ahead of me playing tag with the ebb and flow of the waves.

Intrigued with these tiny birds on stilt-like legs skittering along the shoreline, I forget my own limbs which carry me stumbling knee deep into a cold, clear tidal pool. I recover my balance and begin searching the pool for shells, but find nothing more than a few common oyster shells.

But the collector's blood runs through my veins, and I am compelled to pick up one and examine it.

Though oyster shells are not prized for their beauty so much as for the meat they house, and are often overlooked by collectors for more showy species, I am impressed by the shape of this representative which I hold in my hand. It is like the worn and withered foot of an old, old woman.

Bone white with mottled grey, it has ceased to house its maker for quite some time. In the porcelain-smooth underside, a bruise of color mars the virginal white-arched instep of the shell, vestige of the soft-bodied inhabitant's attachment.

Subtle ridges emerge along the top of the shell like hardened veins. They run the length of the surface and swell prominently into three toes, capped with splitting layers of calcium carbonate resembling the yellow, thick toenails of the aged.

Bringing the shell close for inspection, I notice that it has taken on the smell of its environment. The clean, salty smell of the ocean mingles with slight traces of the dank odor of kelp and mud, imparting to its surface a fungal, but pleasant scent.

I turn the skeleton in my hand and feel its cold, bony-hard surface. My grandmother's feet felt this way when she died.

Mother and I went into the hospital room where she lay with so many whirring and beeping machines converging on her body. I remember thinking that she seemed the source of their life, rather than they the source of hers. She was in so much pain. Mother and I took turns massaging her small, tired feet in a futile attempt to make her comfortable. They felt so hard and cold, like this oyster shell I hold in my hand.

As you have seen, most of these students, while recording sensory data, recorded their associations as well. In the first freewrite on the sense of hearing, however, Tina makes few associations. Nevertheless, she does something very good: she uses a number of comparisons to help make her writing concrete. When a writer is concrete, the reader will get images, pictures in his or her mind, as you no doubt did as you read Tina's freewrite. For example, her comparison of the unpleasant sound of an alarm to bricks dragging on concrete is so effective that the reader almost gets goose bumps as a result of the vivid image. Other good comparisons are the sounds her pets' food makes when she pours it into their bowls. The dog's food sounds like marbles, whereas the cats' food sounds like hail. In addition, she has compared the sound of high heels on a sidewalk to the sound of roulette wheels. Last, she has attempted to duplicate actual sounds through spelling: Zup-Zup-Zup for the sound of bookbags opening and chtt-chtt-chtt for the sound of an adding machine likened to the sound of an angry squirrel. (Spelling words that sound like what they stand for is called onomatopoeia.) Although Tina makes only one association, it is an interesting one that causes her to reflect on herself. In her second paragraph, the hollow sound of her elbow hitting the tub causes her to wonder about the sounds a fetus might hear from the womb.

Like Tina, Gregg makes few associations, except in his third paragraph where the exhaust fumes he smells from cars and trucks make him think of suicide by carbon monoxide and in his last paragraph where the appetizing odors of Chinese food prompt the idea that if we could smell the television ads of restaurants, they might do more business. This is an interesting idea, and what is more, it is likely to become a reality in the future. In his first paragraph Gregg makes the odor of his shaving cream fairly concrete by using a comparison to the odor of mint-flavored alcohol. In the remainder of his freewrite, Gregg has used several specific nouns, which help the reader to experience more nearly what he did. In the last paragraph he has listed the odors of specific foods—pork, shrimp, chicken, and soy sauce, for example. Also, Irish Spring soap and Body on Tap shampoo are further examples. However, instead of the general noun *vegetables,* he could have been more specific by naming them—broccoli, snow peas, water chestnuts, and so on. Likewise, in his second paragraph he could have named a particular weed that his shampoo smelled like. And in his fourth paragraph he could have used a comparison of the fragrance of Body on Tap shampoo to a fragrance we are familiar with. Nevertheless, Gregg has begun to notice sensory data, and in his final paragraph he uses a nice pun on the word *olfactory,* as if it were spelled *ol factory,* like *shoe factory.* The implications of his pun are quite true: our sense of smell manufactures a great deal—memories, thoughts, feelings.

In the freewrite following Gregg's, Meredith attempts to make her claustrophobia concrete when she says that it is similar to feeling "hands and bodies all over you." Near the end of her freewrite, she makes a rather sad association with a leaf that scratches her cheek. Meredith's ensuing narration of her experience picking switches for her own punishment makes the reader want to know more; thus, she has material here that might be developed into an interesting essay.

In her freewrite on taste Gretta also has some thoughtful responses to her experiences. As you see, in her first paragraph she got stuck for awhile and repeated the word *harsh.* Then she mentions the aftertaste of Carnation Instant Breakfast, which she writes is indescribable. To be more concrete, Gretta might have compared it to the metallic taste of a copper penny. She is more concrete in her next paragraph when she uses the verb *shriveled*. Later, when she associates cream corn with baby food, Gretta reflects on life's mixture of pleasure and pain, an observation that she might want to expand into an essay at a later time. Again, in her last paragraph, Gretta reflects on her experiences, this time noting that something that she can't even see—her taste buds—controls her in a limited way. Still, even though taste buds control only part of Gretta's life experiences, think what she would lose if she had no sense of taste. For all of us life would indeed be diminished if we could never taste pizza, lemon pie, or anything else again.

These four excerpts are examples of what you can do. Noting sensory data, along with your associations, thoughts, and feelings is obviously the most productive way to record your experiences. If Tina had associated more, and Louise had been more concrete, both would have profited even more from their writing.

The fifth freewrite, Tina's observation of an oyster shell, is a very good example of the combination of concrete detail and association. The first paragraph ends with the image of sandpipers "playing tag" with the waves. In her second paragraph Tina makes this image even more concrete with her accurate comparison of sandpipers' legs to stilts and with the concrete verb *skittering*, which so accurately describes the way these birds walk. At the end of paragraph four Tina compares the shell to a foot, specifically that of an old woman. In her next two paragraphs she extends this comparison, noting the "virginal white-*arched instep*" and the *"hardened veins"* along the top that end with "three *toes*." In these paragraphs she also uses such descriptive phrases as "bone white with mottled grey"; "bruise of color"; and "the yellow, thick toenails of the aged."

In the next paragraph Tina uses her sense of smell to describe the shell, noting that its odor is a pleasant combination of the salty smell of the ocean, mingled with the odor of kelp and mud.

In the paragraph following this one Tina uses her sense of touch, describing the cold, bony-hard surface which reminds her of her dying grandmother's feet, the original image of the shell that she began with.

Tina then ends her freewrite describing the sight of her grandmother hooked up to "whirring and beeping" machines as she and her mother attempted to ease her grandmother's pain by massaging her feet that felt like the oyster shell.

Tina's writing here is very good, primarily as a result of her use of concrete, specific words and comparisons.

Making Use of Concrete/Specific Words

Like Conrad, all good writers want to make their readers see what they saw, hear what they heard. In order to do this they use words that appeal to the senses and thus evoke images. Words that evoke images are either concrete or specific. Some words fall into both categories, as you will see. Words that do not evoke definite images in a reader's mind are abstract words and general words.

For example, if I said that I had a dependable vehicle, would you know what that vehicle was? Would your image of it be the same as mine or one of your classmates? Probably not. Such a coincidence would be very unlikely because *vehicle* is a very general word: it names a *category of items* (nouns). In addition, general words can name a *category of actions* (verbs). For instance if I said that Jane *walked* into the room, would you get a particular image of Jane's movement that coincides with mine or one of your classmates? Not very likely since *walked* is a very general verb. People walk many different ways. On the other hand, if I were to use *specific nouns* and *verbs* that name individual members of a category of items or actions, you would have an image similar to mine and to your classmates' images.

To illustrate, if I said that I have a dependable *car*, I would be less general than when I used the more general noun *vehicle*, but still you would not know what kind of car. What if I said that I have a Toyota? Still not specific enough for you to have the image that matches mine. And if I said Toyota Corolla Deluxe, your image might be closer to mine, but you would still need to know the color and year: a 1979, red Toyota Corolla Deluxe. Although there may be few writing situations that would require this degree of specificity, this example illustrates that general nouns can be made more and more specific, as Figure 1 also makes clear.

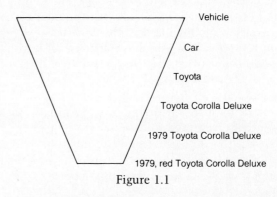

Figure 1.1

General nouns can be made more and more specific like this, but general verbs are made specific by choosing words that denote a particular way of acting that the general word encompasses. For example, suppose I said that Jane *strutted* into the room. You have a picture now that coincides more closely with mine because I have used a word that describes a particular way of walking, just as Tina did previously when she chose the verb *skittering* to describe the way that sandpipers walk. There are many other specific verbs for the way people or animals walk: *lope, sidle, stagger, slither, limp, stroll, saunter, amble, stride, march, stomp, glide, meander, lilt, waltz, trudge, traipse, lumber, plod, trot, sway,* and *lurch,* to name a few.

Some of these specific verbs, *stomp, lope, slither, stagger, stride, lilt, trudge,* and *lurch,* for example, are also *concrete* words. Concrete words *appeal to any one or more of the five senses,* and to the sixth sense, *kinesis,* the sense of motion. Thus, words like *stomp, lope,* and *stagger,* for example, are concrete because they appeal to our sense of *sight.* Each verb evokes a definite image that differs from the images evoked by the other two. For instance, the verb *lope* prompts the image in my mind of someone walking with a long and rhythmical stride, whereas the verb *stagger* prompts an image of the unsteady wavering of a drunk. For most of us the verb *stomp* appeals not only to our sense of sight but to our sense of hearing as well. With this verb, do you get the image of someone walking heavily, slapping feet to the floor with a loud thud? If so, then you *hear* the sound of *stomp* as well as see it! Like these specific verbs, some specific nouns can also be concrete, as well as specific. Such a word as *avocado,* for instance, both names an individual member of the category fruit and appeals to the senses of sight, taste, touch, and smell. In addition to being nouns and verbs, concrete words can be adjectives or adverbs. Some concrete words are *horseshoe, apple* (nouns); *lisp, stutter, gyrate* (verbs); *sticky, gummy, sour, syrupy, bumpy, jerky* (adjectives); *jerkily* and *gingerly* (adverbs).

It is important to note that besides evoking specific images in our minds, concrete words have the power of prompting memories and thus of arousing emotions. For example, when I read the noun *coconut,* I see myself at eight years of age sitting beneath a coconut tree in Dania, Florida, with a hammer and screwdriver, desperately using both in my efforts to remove the husk. Such frustration and labor, I remember, and such joy when I succeeded in removing the husk and cracked the nut with my hammer, revealing the succulent white meat inside. This particular power of concrete words means that when you use them, you can count on truly *involving* your reader. Look at what happens to me with the simple word *coconut!* Why does this happen? The reason concrete words have the power to arouse memories and emotions is that we record life through our senses. Thus, memories are dependent on sensory experience. Just imagine: What life would you experience if you were numb all over, having lost all sensation through your skin, and, in addition, you were blind, deaf, and could neither smell nor taste anything?

In contrast to concrete words are *abstract* words, which do not appeal to the senses. Instead, they name *qualities, ideas, concepts,* or *states of being.* Like concrete words, abstract words can be nouns, verbs, adjectives, or adverbs. Such words as *good, bad, beautiful, hopeful* (adjectives); *well, badly, beautifully, wonderfully, hopefully,* (adverbs); *goodness, evil, beauty, wonder, hope* (nouns); *become, be, hope,* and *wonder* (verbs) are all abstractions. These words denote nothing that we can see, taste, hear, smell, or touch.

Neither general nor abstract words will help your reader get the images of your subject that you have. Although you can avoid using general words, you cannot avoid using abstractions altogether. Therefore, when you use them, you will need to define them somehow, perhaps by giving examples of what you mean. Or, you can define abstractions the way many writers do—by comparing them to something concrete.

Using Metaphors and Similes

Besides using concrete, specific words to help their audiences see, hear, and smell what they see, hear, and smell, writers often use metaphors or similes to make their abstractions concrete. In the quotation I used earlier, Joseph Conrad mentioned that his aim was also to make his audience *feel;* that is, his aim was to convey emotions so that his audience felt them. As you know, emotions are abstract: what exactly is feeling good, bad, happy, sad? In her book *Pilgrim at Tinker Creek,* for example, Annie Dillard writes about a moment of ecstatic revelation. In her attempt to define exactly what she *felt,* Dillard uses several metaphorical statements: "I filled up like a new wineskin. I breathed an air like light; I saw a light like water. I was the lip of a fountain the creek filled forever; I was ether, the leaf in a zephyr; I was fleshflake, feather, bone."

Using these comparisons, Dillard concretely conveys the emotions she felt as a result of her revelatory experience with nature, a moment during which she really "saw." If you analyze the statements she uses here, you will see that *metaphors* and *similes* are *comparisons between two essentially dissimilar objects.* A *metaphor* is *an implied comparison,* whereas a *simile* is *an ex-*

plicit comparison using the prepositions like or as. A person is not really like a wineskin or the lip of a fountain. Nor can a person really be ether, a leaf, a feather, a bone, or a "fleshflake."

Thus, because they suggest surprising similarities between two essentially different items, metaphors have a startling effect. For example, when Dillard says that she filled up "like a new wineskin," we get an image of a wineskin slowly expanding, and also we may feel the headiness that comes from drinking wine. The simile implies that Dillard's experience gave her a full, heady feeling. But if she had said just that—"I felt full and heady"—look at what she would have lost. None of her readers would have similar images; none of them would know exactly how Dillard felt.

Earlier in her book Dillard uses another effective comparison to describe the color of a frog that she saw. She says there that the frog was the color of "wet hickory bark." If Dillard had not used this metaphor, she might have described the color as "a shiny, brownish green," or something similar. Surely such a description does not evoke the image in a reader that "wet hickory bark" does.

Especially when you attempt to describe feelings or emotions, metaphors can be helpful, but they are also helpful when you attempt to describe almost anything—the color of a frog included.

When you use metaphors or similes, you need to be sure that they are fresh ones, not the instant, ready-made kind you've heard before: "a complexion like sugar and cream"; "soft as velvet"; "hard as a rock"; "slow as a turtle"; "busy as a bee"; "lips like cherries"; "cheeks like roses"; and "white as snow," for example. These are similes that we have heard over and over; they are trite and hackneyed. As a result, they will surprise no one; they have definitely lost their punch. In addition, because a trite comparison has been used by many others, it cannot express your own, unique impressions. If a comparison comes instantly to mind, chances are that it is one you've heard before. Examine it first, and if it is a trite comparison, throw it out. You're better off not using a metaphor than you are using a trite one.

Another problem you may encounter is called the *mixed metaphor,* such as this: "His dark eyes, like two lumps of coal, drilled his opponent." The problem here is that there are two comparisons "mixed together," not just one. First the person's eyes are compared to lumps of coal, then to drills (both of them also fairly trite comparisons).

Finally, the last consideration when you use a metaphor or a simile is whether or not it is appropriate for your purpose. For example, suppose you compared a friend's small, dark eyes to a rat's eyes. If your purpose was to convey a positive image of this person, you would not choose such a comparison. It would be inappropriate because in our culture most people make many negative associations with rats—filth, pestilence, and so on.

To summarize: When you use metaphors or similes, make sure that they are fresh, that they are appropriate, and that they make only one comparison. Perhaps at this point you think that using metaphors is a risky business. All good writers take risks and sometimes they succeed; other times they fail. Using metaphors may be risky, but what if you succeed? Look what your reader gains as a result—a frog the color of "wet hickory bark," a feeling of being filled "like a new wineskin." Since your business as a writer is to show, not merely to tell, and to make your reader "see," above all, then use not only concrete, specific words, but metaphors, as well. Take the risks involved. If you succeed, you have truly made your reader *see;* if you fail, it is no great catastrophe—scratch out what you have written and try again. That's what writing is about. It is the continual process of trying, of "attempting," and of trying again.

Practice Using Concrete/Specific Words

The skills involved in writing are best learned a few at a time, and to master these skills, you need practice using them. You might first want to practice what you have learned by doing the following exercises before you try practicing the use of concrete, specific words and metaphors in your own writing.

Making Nouns More Concrete/Specific

Make the following general nouns gradually more specific: person, animal, clothing. *An example making the general noun* furniture *more specific follows.*

I. Furniture
   a. appliance
   b. electric appliance
   c. electric stove
   d. Kenmore electric stove
   e. Kenmore Deluxe electric stove
   f. 1980 Kenmore Deluxe electric stove
   g. 1980 Sunset Gold Kenmore Deluxe electric stove

Making Verbs More Concrete/Specific

List as many specific verbs as you can think of for the general verbs, talk, move, *and* take. *Then choose a specific verb from each of the three lists and write a sentence using each one. The following is an example using the general verb* sing.

Sing: *warble, croon, bellow, wail, trill, yodel, tweet, hum, chirp, cheep, peep, chant, carol, serenade*

Example: Janis Joplin *wailed* the blues.

Making General Statements More Concrete/Specific

Rewrite the general statements that follow, replacing them with sentences containing concrete/specific words and phrases. Follow this example:

General: Josie is a *very busy* student.

Concrete/specific: Josie is chairperson of the debate team, and she is also president of the student government. An outstanding competitor on the women's swim team, Josie manages to do all this while working part-time at J. C. Penney's and taking a full course load at school.

If you prefer, you may retain the general statement and follow it with concrete/specific statements that make it clearer.

Example: Josie is a very busy student. She is chairperson. . .

1. Some of my classes are interesting.
2. My roommate (housemate, husband, wife) is a nice person.
3. My hometown was a good place to grow up.
4. _____ is an interesting television series. (Put in your choice.)
5. Our campus is beautiful.
6. _____ is a bad habit. (Substitute for any one of the preceding statements, and put in you choice of habits.)

Using Metaphors

In the following sentences, try to write fresh metaphors or similes.

1. The sky was the color of _____.
2. The road looked like _____.
3. I felt as _____ as _____.
   or I felt like _____.
4. With heavy backpacks, we trudged up the mountainside like _____.

5. Through the mist the sun looked like _____ .
6. The hallway smelled like _____ .
7. The surface of the polluted pond looked like _____ .
8. The mashed potatoes tasted like _____ .
9. The avocado feels like _____ .
10. The machines tearing up the sidewalk sounded like _____ .

After finishing these exercises, you may find it helpful to share your writing in small groups and to choose some writing to share with the whole class when you reassemble. You will probably find that each of you made the general nouns more specific in slightly different ways. Also, some of you may have thought of more concrete/specific verbs for *talk, move,* and *take* than others did. Because of these differences, you can learn a great deal from each other by sharing.

Revision: "Re-Seeing" and Recomposing

Unfortunately, writing is not a one-step endeavor. Unlike Athena, who sprang full-blown from the head of Zeus, essays do not spring from the heads of writers in final-draft form. Instead, writing is a multidrafting process.* Virginia Woolf, for example, often wrote as many as seven drafts of a single essay. In fact, in the history of English and American literature, the only known instance of a professional first-draft publication is Samuel Johnson's *Rasselas,* which was published right away because Johnson needed money. With the exception of Johnson, the truth is that no professional writer publishes without having revised his or her work at least once.

From its Latin derivatives *re –*, meaning, "again" or "back," and the verb *videre,* meaning "to see," *revision* literally means "to see again." Thus, as a stage in the writing process, revision occurs whenever a writer looks back at what he or she has written, sees it in a new light, and consequently recomposes part or all of it. If you look in a dictionary, you will also find that the verb *revise* means "to read over carefully and to correct or improve." Certainly, improvement is what all writers desire when they revise, but "to see again" unfortunately does not always mean "to see again better." Consequently, sometimes writers' revisions, especially those of beginning writers, do not always result in a great deal of improvement. It is important, however, that you not be discouraged if you fail to improve a piece of writing significantly when you revise it. Because in this text you will learn at least one writing skill between beginning drafts and later ones,

---

* The writing process will be discussed at greater length in Chapter 3.

you are almost assured of improving your essay in regard to that one skill at least, and it is equally certain that as the semester progresses, you will find that your revisions become more and more successful. Since you have now learned one writing skill—how to be concrete and specific—you are equipped with the knowledge necessary to try your hand at revising something you have written, trying "to see it again" in a new light in order to make it more concrete.

Revising Writing for Concreteness

Now that you have a clear understanding of abstract/general and concrete/specific words, as well as of metaphors, you can practice what you have learned in your own writing. Because you were to use all your senses in the last journal assignment describing a sight that impressed you, you might choose that particular writing, especially if you were more or less abstract/general. You might also consider any one of the other four journal assignments that could be made more concrete/specific. Or, you could choose to describe a new subject: a person, a local hangout, or another narrowed topic.

Even though her description of the oyster shell she found at the beach was concrete and specific more often than it was not, Tina noticed that there were words and phrases that she could revise to be more concrete or specific. Because her original description was fairly concrete and specific, Tina began her revision by making it more abstract and general. Then, she again revised her original description, making it even more concrete and specific, as you will see in the following paragraphs.

Abstract/General Description

When I was at the beach, I looked at the birds running back and forth on the shore as the waves came and went. Wading into a pool of water, I began looking for shells. I saw some oyster shells, and even though they are commonly found, I picked one up.

It felt hard and it smelled salty and dank.

Its hard surface reminded me of my dying grandmother's feet which my mother and I had massaged to try to relieve her pain.

Revised Concrete/Specific Description

As I loll at the edge of the ocean at Topsail Beach, waiting for some miracle, some seed of inspiration to sprout within, I notice a small band of sandpipers just ahead of me playing tag with the ebb and flow of the waves.

Intrigued with these tiny birds on stiltlike legs skittering along the shoreline, I forget my own legs, stumbling knee deep into a cold, clear tidal pool. Recovering my balance, I scan the pool for shells, but glimpse nothing more than a few common oyster shells.

But the collector's blood pumps through my veins and I am compelled to grasp one and examine it.

Though oyster shells are not prized for their beauty so much as for the meat within and are often overlooked by collectors for more exotic and delicate species, I am impressed by the shape of this specimen that I clench in my hand. It is like the worn and withered foot of an old, old woman.

Bone-white with mottled grey, it has ceased to house its maker for quite some time. In the porcelain-smooth underside, bruise-purple mars the virginal white-arched instep of the shell, vestige of the soft-bodied inhabitant's attachment.

Subtle ridges, like hardened veins, emerge along the top of the shell. They ripple the length of the surface and swell prominently into three toes, capped with splitting layers of calcium carbonate resembling the thick, yellow toenails of the aged.

Clasping the shell and bringing it closer for inspection, I notice that it is permeated with the odors of its environment. The clean, salty smell of the ocean mingles with slight traces of the dank odor of kelp and mud, imparting to its surface a fungal, but pleasant scent.

Revolving the skeleton in my hand, I feel its cold, bony-hard surface. My grandmother's feet felt this way when she died.

Mother and I tip-toed into the hospital room where she lay with so many whirring and beeping machines converging on her body. I remember thinking that she seemed the source of their life, rather than they being the source of hers. She was in agonizing pain. Taking turns, mother and I massaged her small, tired feet in a futile attempt to make her more comfortable. They felt so hard and cold, like this oyster shell I hold in my hand.

It is evident from her abstract/general description that Tina clearly understands what abstract/general language is. Also evident from her revised description is that she clearly understands how to make writing more concrete and specific. Tina has revised her good writing, making it even better. In her first sentence, for example, she has made several changes, resulting in a more concrete/specific description. She has replaced the general verb *stand* with the specific verb *loll;* she has replaced the general phrase "the water's edge" with the specific phrase "the edge of the ocean at Topsail Beach;" and, last, in this sentence, she has replaced the mixed metaphor "some seed of inspiration to permeate" with a metaphor that now works: "some seed of inspiration to sprout." Seeds sprout; they do not permeate. Odors permeate; water can permeate, but seeds cannot. In addition to these revisions, Tina has replaced the general noun *limbs* with *legs* and the general phrase "a bruise of color" with "bruise-purple." Also, she has used such specific verbs as *scan, glimpse, pump, grasp, clench, ripple, clasping, revolving,* and *tip-toed.* More specific adjectives she has used are "exotic and delicate" in place of *showy,* and *agonizing* in place of the phrase "so much."

Tina's revision of her good writing illustrates an important point about the writing process and about the craft of writing. The poet Allen Tate once remarked that to talk of "good" poetry is to imply that there is "better" poetry and "best" poetry. This is true not only for poets but for all writers. To talk of "good" writing is certainly to imply that there is "better" writing and "best" writing. Indeed, it is not only a possibility but a certainty that a serious writer can make his "good" writing better, as you have seen here in Tina's revision.

Other Uses of a Journal

In Chapter 9 Joan Didion observes in her essay "On Keeping a Notebook" that keeping a notebook is a way of keeping in touch with herself. Like Didion, many professional writers keep journals to record their experiences, such as their memories of the past, people from the past or places or events from the past, in an attempt to explore what these past experiences meant, to reevaluate them, or even to understand them for the first time. For example, in her essay "Why I Write," Joan Didion explains that she writes "entirely to find out what I'm thinking, what I'm looking at, what I see and what it means." She has also said in her essay "On Keeping a Notebook" that she gave up keeping a diary that recorded her daily activities because such a record was not only boring but meaningless:

> So the point of my keeping a notebook has never been, nor is it now, to have an accurate factual record of what I have been doing . . . and on those few occasions when I have tried dutifully to record a day's events, boredom has so overcome me that the results are mysterious at best. . . . In fact, I have abandoned altogether that kind of pointless entry.

If you decide to keep a personal journal, take a tip from Didion and don't make it a boring and meaningless record of what you did that day: "Got up at 8:00, had breakfast," and so on. Make it a meaningful writer's journal in which you do not merely record what you did but instead explore your reactions to what you did, you thoughts, your feelings, your fears. You will discover that Didion is correct about the value of writing: it is a means of discovering all sorts of knowledge. In addition, you will find that what Virginia Woolf wrote in her diary is also true. Several days before her death, in the final entry of her *Writer's Diary*, these were Virginia Woolf's last words:

> I find that it's seven; and must cook dinner. Haddock and sausage meat. I think it is true that one gains a certain hold on sausage and haddock by writing them down.

How very true. You will discover that writing can give you a hold on everything important—yourself, your ideas, "what you see and what it means." Even haddock and sausage.

You will find that keeping a journal is a very profitable endeavor for other reasons as well. For one thing, such a record often results in ideas that can be developed later and made public in an essay. But even if you never use ideas from a journal entry in an essay, you will find that daily writing in a journal can help you to become a better writer more quickly because the more you write, the more you learn about writing, and the easier it becomes. If you keep a journal, writing becomes a habit, a way of living, a way of examining your life, and, as Socrates once noted, the unexamined life is not worth living.

In addition to writing about present or past experiences to help you examine your life, you can write many other things in your journal that will result in insights into yourself and others. For example, you could write letters to people you wish you could talk to but cannot, for one reason or another. Because there are so many things that you can write in a journal, at the end of this chapter you will find some suggestions about the various kinds of writing you might have in your journal. Although this list certainly does not exhaust the possibilities for you as a journal writer, it should make you aware of just how limitless those possibilities are. There is simply no freedom like the freedom a writer has, for, as William Stafford has put it, "Working back and forth between experience and thought writers have more than space and time can offer." Just think of it: Your physical notebook itself may exist in time and space, but what you write in it—your thoughts and the limitless possibilities you have for expression of them—transcends both time and space.

Guidelines for Keeping a Journal

When you focus on one particular subject, give your journal entry an appropriate title, such as "A Time of Trouble" (or something more specific, like "Going to Jail"), and when you write unfocused entries, entitle them "Wandering" or something else that seems apropos.

Always be sure to date each entry, and you might also note where you are by putting down the city and state, since you will probably write in several locales—at school and at home or at other places on vacations. You might head each entry something like this, for instance:

January 10, 1987
5:00 p.m. (This is optional, but it is a habit of mine to note the time.)
at VPI (or "at home" "at school," and so on)

When you begin keeping your journal, it is best to write at the same time and in the same place every day. This kind of regularity helps you establish the habit of writing. My own preference is to write in the mornings at my kitchen table while I have my morning coffee. If I write in the evenings, I do so at the same table while my dinner cooks. Whenever you leave school, take your journal with you and try to establish some kind of regularity wherever you go.

I have found that a thick, looseleaf notebook works best for me, and I also keep a separate notebook in which I write letters to writers that I have read and feel compelled to respond to for one reason or another. In the next chapter you will be asked to keep a similar journal in which you write responses to the readings you are assigned. Like me, you might also like to have a separate notebook for these writings, or if you like, you could put them in a separate section of the notebook you use for your personal writing. Whichever decision you make—one notebook or two—I think you will find, like Didion, that keeping a notebook is an invaluable way of keeping in touch with yourself.

Conclusion

At this point, you have learned one very important way to make your writing better, and that is by being concrete. Keep in mind that all good writers want their writing to evoke images similar to their own in their readers' minds. To do this, writers continually observe the life around them; they pay attention to what their senses take in; to what they see, hear, smell, touch, and taste: how Ms. Smith's face wrinkles like an accordian when she smiles; how wet pine needles have a musky, fungal odor; how grief is a long, dark tunnel and joy is as yellow as a daffodil.

You have made a good beginning now. Like all good writers,

continue to pay attention to what your senses record of the world around you.

Ideas for Journal Writing

Ideas for Dialogues

Write a dialogue:

1. With yourself about a decision you need to make. You might label the participants various ways, depending on the subject of the dialogue: Me and Myself; Me and My Devil; Me and My Conscience, and so on.
2. With yourself about something that bothers you about yourself: something you did or didn't do; a habit you have that you don't like.
3. With yourself and someone else, telling him or her what you have been unable to face to face.
4. With a person whom you wish you could talk to.
5. With a famous person, past or present, whom you wish you could talk to.
6. With your instructor about anything that concerns you that you wish you could say.

Ideas for Letters

Write a letter:

1. To someone saying what you'd like to say face to face but cannot.
2. To a writer, deceased or living, about anything—something pertaining to his or her writing or something else, for example, to Annie Dillard about why you'd like to meet her.
3. To anyone with whom you are angry but unable to express your feelings.
4. To a person you admire, but to whom you have not expressed, or cannot express, your feelings.
5. To a famous person, past or present, for any reason, such as a letter to Benjamin Franklin expressing your admiration for his accomplishments.
6. To a character in a story, novel, film, or drama.
7. To a director or producer of a film that you liked or disliked (or to an actor or actress you like or dislike).
8. To a historical person you consider evil, telling him or her why you feel as you do.
9. To Americans, the world, or future generations.
10. To one or both of your parents, explaining something that they have not understood about you or your actions.

11. To yourself as though from someone you would especially like to have a letter from.
12. A letter of complaint to anyone—a sales clerk, your parents, your roommate, the dean of students, and so on.

Memories of the Past and Other Ideas

Write about:

1. Something in your past that you wish you could forget.
2. Something in your past that you like to remember.
3. Something in your past that you're ashamed of.
4. Something in your past that you're proud of.
5. Past experiences with individual family members, friends, neighbors, teachers, bosses, and so on.
6. Past experiences you didn't understand at the time but do now.
7. A question you have been unable to answer about life, love, relationships, and so on.
8. A conflict you had with someone, told first from your point of view and then from the other person's point of view.
9. Why you like or do not like a character in a film, a novel, a story, a drama, or a television series.
10. A bad habit you have, and explore the causes of it and/or the effects of it on your life.
11. A good habit you have, and explore the causes of it and/or the effects of it on your life.
12. A prejudice you have and explore the causes and effects of it on your life.
13. Something you wish would happen to you.
14. Something you wish had *not* happened to you.
15. Dreams you have that interest you for various reasons.

Plan also to:

16. Continue to observe the data your senses record; describe the things you see, hear, taste, smell, and so on. In all entries be sure to use the sensory detail that you recall.
17. Use the following titles (and others you think of) for journal entries: A Bad Memory; Lies; Truth; Disappointment; Success; A Change of Heart; What I Like about ____ ____; What I Don't Like about ____; Being Lonely; Being Angry; Being ____; Falling out of Love; Ways to Get over a Broken Heart; Changes I'd Like to Make in Myself.

CHAPTER

2

The Process of Reading

Having revised your own descriptive writing, you have discovered for yourself that writing is not a one-step activity but, instead, an ongoing process. The same is true of reading; furthermore, reading and writing are very closely related activities.

The process of writing is a process of discovering thoughts and feelings and then translating them into written symbols. Because of the difficulty of such a translation, the writer's intended meaning is probably never exactly translated. For example, if his meaning is designated A, his translation is at best A_1. On the other hand, the process of reading is the reverse. The reader translates written symbols into thoughts and feelings, from which he or she derives meaning. Therefore, depending on any number of factors, the translation of written symbols into meaning by a given reader is likely, at best, to be A_2. For instance, look at this passage from Virginia Woolf's novel *Mrs. Dalloway:*

> Such fools we are, she thought, crossing Victoria Street. For Heaven only knows why one loves it so, how one sees it so, making it up, building it round one, tumbling it, creating it every moment afresh; but the veriest frumps, the most dejected of miseries sitting on doorsteps (drink their downfall) do the same; can't be dealt with, she felt positive, by Acts of Parliament for that very reason: they love life.

There is no doubt that in this passage Woolf's attempt is to convey Mrs. Dalloway's exuberance, her *joie de vivre.* And although we feel Mrs. Dalloway's love of life, her joy in the moment, we probably do not feel exactly what Woolf felt and intended to convey, for several reasons. One is that it is really impossible to convey in language exactly what one *feels.* Another reason is that it is doubtful that you, the reader, have felt *exactly* what Woolf felt and attempted to translate into language. Even though you have experienced moments of great joy in life and in living, your precise sensations at such times differ from those of everyone else.

Despite the impossibility of deriving all of an author's intended meaning from a text, you have probably observed that the more times you read an essay, a story, or a novel, the more meaning you derive. In addition, meanings derived from one reading of a text may be altered by successive readings. To illustrate, read the preceding passage again. Did you discover a word or a phrase that you simply hadn't noticed on the first reading? Chances are you did. Or perhaps a word or phrase that you had noticed on the first reading resulted in a different feeling or idea this time. As readers, we can assume that if we overlook any word, phrase, or passage on a first, second, or third reading, we will certainly miss part of the author's intended meaning.

Also, probably the most important factors in the process of reading and deriving meaning from a text are life experience and reading experience. Because a reader brings to the text his or her own life experiences in addition to his or her own reading experiences, any two readers, Tony and Josie, reading any given text, will derive various meanings from it.

However, it is also true that more experienced readers are more likely to see more and thus to translate closer to the writer's intended meaning than inexperienced readers are likely to. Furthermore, if Tony and Josie are people who have read quite a bit, their two readings of a text are more likely to be similar to each other than they are to the meanings derived by an inexperienced reader.

Because of all the variables, both in the writer's translation of thought into written symbols and the reader's reverse translation, it is almost absurd to assume that any text may be translated only one way, deriving only one "correct" set of meanings from it. If not absurd, such an assumption is irrelevant. Although they may differ, the meanings that Tony derives from a text are just as valuable to him as the meanings that Josie derives are to her. Both readers have gained knowledge that they did not have before—both have met another's mind through the medium of written symbols, translated, and discovered new thoughts, new ideas as a result.

It seems clear that deriving meaning from a text is the consequence of a reading process—of multiple readings and responses, resulting in additional and modified meanings as the process continues.

There are several conclusions that can be drawn as a result of the relationship between writing and reading. The first is that the experienced reader is more likely to become a better writer because he has had more experience with written symbols. Also, people who have read a great deal unconsciously absorb the uses of language; they absorb knowledge of coherence, rhythm, and concreteness, to name a few writing skills that readers become acquainted with. That is why Richard Wright, the noted black novelist, wrote in his book *Black Boy* that when he decided to become a writer, he read everything he could get his hands on. Not only Wright, but every writer I know of is an avid reader who began reading at an early age.

If you read essays by good or excellent writers, consciously noting how these writers get your attention, how they develop their thoughts, how they evoke images, or how they achieve coherence, you can speed up the acquisition of these skills in your own writing. But before conscious analysis of any writer's particular writing skills, you need to read a text solely as a reader attempting to derive meaning. One way to become a better reader (and writer) is to write your responses to a text after you have read it.

Keeping a Response Journal

good idea

?

!

great

The process you might follow is this: read an essay all the way through in one sitting. Be sure that you read with a pen or pencil so that you can underline words, phrases, or sentences that you do or do not like, that you do not understand, or that prompt a particular idea or emotion. Also, you can make various notations in the margins: you might write a question mark by a passage that you don't understand; you might put exclamation marks by passages that excite you or that you disagree with, or you might write words or phrases that express your reactions such as "great!" "No!" or "Don't get it," just as I have annotated this passage, for example. Once you have completed a first reading of an essay, freewrite a response to it immediately. In this response you can write what you feel, what you think about the meaning, what associations you make with the text—anything. But you should write at least one full page. Next, read the essay a second time. Again, upon completion, write a response of at least one page. You may change your mind about something you said in your first response; you may write about something you noticed this time that you did not the first time; you may write about another association with the text. You are absolutely free to do whatever you like in these responses to writing as a reader. Above all, you are not restricted to writing about what the text means.

The only restriction is this: You should read the text and respond to it in one sitting. Furthermore, it is to your advantage to complete both readings and both responses in one sitting. If you cannot do both readings and both responses in one sitting, do the second reading and response as soon as possible after the first.

Since writing is a process of discovering what you think, that is, of discovering knowledge, writing responses to various texts allows you to discover your thoughts about what you have read and to explore them. When you put your thoughts on paper, you

can look at them, contemplate them, and perhaps conclude sometimes that one or more of your ideas are not really what you think
or to discover other ideas as a result of having written a particular
thought.

Besides allowing you to discover what you think, writing responses to essays that you read can help you in other ways. Because you will make associations with a writer's text, you may
often write about an experience that could become the topic of
one of your own essays. Also, as you read, write, and associate,
no doubt you will discover knowledge of yourself that you did not
have before.

Above all, you will become a better writer as a result both of
reading and writing your responses to a text. After you have read
a text twice and responded, you can learn a great deal by reading
it a third time, paying attention to the particular writing skill or
skills that you are in the process of acquiring. For example, in a
third reading of the Dillard essay that follows, you might underline the concrete, specific words and phrases that she uses. In addition, you might note the metaphors and similes she has employed to help give her readers clear images of the subject she is
describing. In succeeding chapters, try to read each essay you are
assigned a third time, underlining examples of whatever skills you
have learned at that point in the semester. In fact, even on your
first reading of Dillard's essay, you might find yourself noting examples of concrete/specific language. If so, by all means respond—underline them or write in the margin "great image" or
whatever expresses your particular reaction.

After "Scorpions in Amber" are two students' responses to the
essay that illustrate the points I have made about the reading process and about the divergent meanings any two readers will derive from a text. They also illustrate the various ways that a reader
can respond to a text. Because nothing should intervene between
your reading of a text and your response to it, you may want to
read these students' responses as examples before you read Dillard's essay. After you have read and responded to her essay, you
can discuss these two students' responses and compare your reactions and ideas with theirs. In addition, you and your classmates might share your responses, so that you have the advantage
of other readers' ideas and associations.

ANNIE DILLARD

Scorpions in Amber

1 A couple of summers ago I was walking along the edge of the
island to see what I could see in the water, and mainly to scare
frogs. Frogs have an inelegant way of taking off from invisible

positions on the bank just ahead of your feet, in dire panic, emitting a froggy "Yike!" and splashing into the water. Incredibly, this amused me, and, incredibly, it amuses me still. As I walked along the grassy edge of the island, I got better and better at seeing frogs both in and out of the water. I learned to recognize, slowing down, the difference in texture of the light reflected from mudbank, water, grass, or frog. Frogs were flying all around me. At the end of the island I noticed a small green frog. He was exactly half in and half out of the water, looking like a schematic diagram of an amphibian, and he didn't jump.

2 He didn't jump; I crept closer. At last I knelt on the island's winterkilled grass, lost, dumbstruck, staring at the frog in the creek just four feet away. He was a very small frog with wide, dull eyes. And just as I looked at him, he slowly crumpled and began to sag. The spirit vanished from his eyes as if snuffed. His skin emptied and drooped; his very skull seemed to collapse and settle like a kicked tent. He was shrinking before my eyes like a deflating football. I watched the taut, glistening skin on his shoulders ruck, and rumple, and fall. Soon, part of his skin, formless as a pricked balloon, lay in floating folds like bright scum on top of the water: it was a monstrous and terrifying thing. I gaped bewildered, appalled. An oval shadow hung in the water behind the drained frog; then the shadow glided away. The frog skin bag started to sink.

3 I had read about the giant water bug, but never seen one. "Giant water bug" is really the name of the creature, which is an enormous, heavy-bodied brown beetle. It eats insects, tadpoles, fish, and frogs. Its grasping forelegs are mighty and hooked inward. It seizes a victim with these legs, hugs it tight, and paralyzes it with enzymes injected during a vicious bite. That one bite is the only bite it ever takes. Through the puncture shoot the poisons that dissolve the victim's muscles and bones and organs—all but the skin—and through it the giant water bug sucks out the victim's body, reduced to a juice. This event is quite common in warm fresh water. The frog I saw was being sucked by a giant water bug. I had been kneeling on the island grass; when the unrecognizable flap of frog skin settled on the creek bottom, swaying, I stood up and brushed the knees of my pants. I couldn't catch my breath.

4 Of course, many carnivorous animals devour their prey alive. The usual method seems to be to subdue the victim by downing or grasping it so it can't flee, then eating it whole or in a series of bloody bites. Frogs eat everything whole, stuffing prey into their mouths with their thumbs. People have seen frogs with their wide jaws so full of live dragonflies they couldn't close them. Ants don't even have to catch their prey: in the spring they swarm over newly hatched, featherless birds in the nest and eat them tiny bite by bite.

5 That it's rough out there and chancy is no surprise. Every live thing is a survivor on a kind of extended emergency bivouac. But at the same time we are also created. In the Koran, Allah asks, "The heaven and the earth and all in between, thinkest thou I made them *in jest?*" It's a good question. What do we think of the created universe, spanning an unthinkable void with an unthinkable profusion of forms? Or what do we think of nothingness, those sickening reaches of time in either direction? If the giant water bug was not made in jest, was it then made in earnest? Pascal uses a nice term to describe the notion of the creator's, once having called forth the universe, turning his back to it: *Deus Absconditus.* Is this what we think happened? Was the sense of it there, and God absconded with it, ate it, like a wolf who disappears round the edge of the house with the Thanksgiving turkey? "God is subtle," Einstein said, "but not malicious." Again, Einstein said that "nature conceals her mystery by means of her essential grandeur, not by her cunning." It could be that God has not absconded but spread, as our vision and understanding of the universe have spread, to a fabric of spirit and sense so grand and subtle, so powerful in a new way, that we can only feel blindly of its hem. In making the thick darkness a swaddling band for the sea, God "set bars and doors" and said, "Hitherto shalt thou come, but no further." But have we come even that far? Have we rowed out to the thick darkness, or are we all playing pinochle in the bottom of the boat?

6 Cruelty is a mystery, and the waste of pain. But if we describe a world to compass these things, a world that is a long, brute game, then we bump against another mystery: the inrush of power and light, the canary that sings on the skull. Unless all ages and races of men have been deluded by the same mass hypnotist (who?), there seems to be such a thing as beauty, a grace wholly gratuitous. About five years ago I saw a mockingbird make a straight vertical descent from the roof gutter of a four-story building. It was an act as careless and spontaneous as the curl of a stem or the kindling of a star.

7 The mockingbird took a single step into the air and dropped. His wings were still folded against his sides as though he were singing from a limb and not falling, accelerating thirty-two feet per second per second, through empty air. Just a breath before he would have been dashed to the ground, he unfurled his wings with exact, deliberate care, revealing the broad bars of white, spread his elegant, white-banded tail, and so floated onto the grass. I had just rounded a corner when his insouciant step caught my eye; there was no one else in sight. The fact of his free fall was like the old philosophical conundrum about the tree that falls in the forest. The answer must be, I think, that beauty and grace are performed

whether or not we will or sense them. The least we can do is try
to be there.

8 Another time I saw another wonder: sharks off the Atlantic
coast of Florida. There is a way a wave rises about the ocean horizon, a triangular wedge against the sky. If you stand where the
ocean breaks on a shallow beach, you see the raised water in a
wave is translucent, shot with lights. One late afternoon at low
tide a hundred big sharks passed the beach near the mouth of a
tidal river in a feeding frenzy. As each green wave rose from the
churning water, it illuminated within itself the six- or eight-foot-
long bodies of twisting sharks. The sharks disappeared as each
wave rolled toward me; then a new wave would swell above the
horizon, containing in it, like scorpions in amber, sharks that roiled
and heaved. The sight held awesome wonders: power and beauty,
grace tangled in a rapture with violence.

9 We don't know what's going on here. If these tremendous events
are random combinations of matter run amok, the yield of millions of monkeys at millions of typewriters, then what is it in us,
hammered out of those same typewriters, that they ignite? We
don't know. Our life is a faint tracing on the surface of mystery,
like the idle, curved tunnels of leaf miners on the face of a leaf.
We must somehow take a wider view, look at the whole landscape, really see it, and describe what's going on here. Then we
can at least wail the right question into the swaddling band of
darkness, or, if it comes to that, choir the proper praise.

10 At the time of Lewis and Clark, setting the prairies on fire was
a well-known signal that meant, "Come down to the water." It
was an extravagant gesture, but we can't do less. If the landscape
reveals one certainty, it is that the extravagant gesture is the very
stuff of creation. After the one extravagant gesture of creation in
the first place, the universe has continued to deal exclusively in
extravagances, flinging intricacies and colossi down aeons of emptiness, heaping profusions on profligacies with ever-fresh vigor.
The whole show has been on fire from the word go. I come down
to the water to cool my eyes. But everywhere I look I see fire;
that which isn't flint is tinder, and the whole world sparks and
flames.

Ideas and Meaning

1. Does Dillard come to any conclusion about the entanglement of beauty and violence in nature? Why does she ask so
   many questions? Does she provide any answers?
2. What generalization about nature and life does the frog's death
   exemplify? The mockingbird's fall? The sharks' feeding?
3. How does the simile comparing the sharks to "scorpions in

amber" exemplify the generalization Dillard makes in this paragraph (8)?

4. In paragraph 9 what does Dillard mean by "really seeing" our world? What examples has she provided? Why does she think that "really seeing" is important?

5. In paragraph 10, Dillard makes the generalization that the universe deals in "extravagances." What examples has she provided?

6. What does Dillard mean by her generalization that "cruelty is a waste of pain"? What examples has she given? How can pain *not* be a waste?

7. Could you supply examples from your own experiences with nature similar to the frog's death? The mockingbird's fall? The sharks' feeding?

Development and Style

1. What concrete, specific words and metaphors does Dillard use to evoke clear images of the frog, the mockingbird, and the sharks?

2. How do the similes she uses in paragraph 2 convey both a clear image of the frog and Dillard's attitude towards the scene she witnesses?

3. The similes "like a deflating football" and "like a pricked balloon" could be considered trite in other contexts. In what contexts would they be trite? What saves them from being trite here in Dillard's essay?

4. Discuss the effects of the concrete/specific verbs that Dillard uses in paragraphs 2 and 8. How do they convey clear images of her subjects, and how do they support the ideas Dillard presents in each paragraph?

5. How is the simile at the end of paragraph 6 appropriate to the generalization she has made in this paragraph? How does it clarify her generalization?

6. How does Dillard's metaphor in the last paragraph clarify her concluding idea? Is it an appropriate comparison? Why? Why not?

7. In paragraph 2 Dillard uses the concrete/specific verbs *ruck* and *rumple*. Supply other concrete/specific verbs synonymous to these that she could have used. Are they as effective?

8. Besides using many metaphors and similes in her writing, Dillard also uses the poetic devices of *alliteration* and *assonance*. Alliteration is the repetition of the initial sounds of two or more consecutive words, such as "ruck and rumple." Assonance is the repetition of a vowel sound in two or more

consecutive words, such as "reduced to juice." What are the effects of alliteration and assonance? Identify other examples of these devices in the essay, and discuss the effects each has.

9. How does Dillard's beginning sentence get your attention?

Pat's Two Responses

Reading Journal: "Scorpions in Amber" First Response

I'm not sure, but I don't think Dillard comes to any definite conclusions concerning her questions in this essay. She seems to resolve her questions by accepting the fact that life is full of bad things and good things.

I received this impression because of the three examples that she gives. The first one was a frightening terrible example of "survival of the fittest." The second example was a beautiful description of a mockingbird. I loved the example she uses about the sharks. Sharks are frightening, but they are beautiful to watch in the sunlight.

I'm glad that Dillard resolves her feelings in this way. It seems that sometimes I just get so frustrated with life. Maybe I'm just going through a "stage," but ever since about the age of fifteen, I have tried to figure out the meaning of life. Well this just leads to frustration, tears, and anger, so I'm just going to say "to Hell with it." Life is good and Life is bad, and we experience life in three stages. The first is innocent, unreflective childhood. The second is "stormy" youth. And the third is a mature stage in which we acquire reflective contemplative powers.

Maybe I am straying too far from the point, but the essay reminded me of this because we experience different stages when we move from one environment to another.

Second Response

Annie Dillard's essay "Scorpions in Amber" was just as interesting the second time as it was the first. The one basic theme concerning this essay which touched me most was the cruelty of Nature. Nature is an element in our world which can be beautiful as well as frightening at the same time. This was indeed a vivid contrast in Dillard's essay.

This reminds me of an experience I had the last time I went back home. I am from a very small shrimping community on the coast which is situated next to a sound known as Core Sound. The sound is very near my house (within walking distance), and I always loved to sit by the shore and watch the sun go down. The pounding of the surf and the beauty of the scenery always lull me into a meditative mood. The wind would run its icy fingers through my hair as the seagulls laughed above my head.

I always loved to watch the seagulls as they soared gracefully above my head. I always thought they were some of the most beautiful creatures I had ever seen when they were in flight.

Well, one particular evening when I was at the shore, I noticed a skirmish in the bushes. I spotted a tiny seagull that was almost dead, and buzzards were picking at it. This was a pitiful, shocking sight to behold. The tiny creature was obviously in deep pain. Its wings were battered and bloody, and its tiny chest heaved in painful attempts to breathe. Its head was smeared with dirty blood, and it lolled back and forth on its neck like a pendulum. Its head was also covered with a layer of ants. Every time one of the buzzards picked at its wounds, it would give a pitiful little croak.

I became very angry at the buzzards and I did everything I could to chase them away. I wanted to do something to help the baby gull. It was just to cruel.

An old man came along and after seeing my efforts to chase the birds away, came back with a gun and offered to put the gull out of its misery. I didn't want him to shoot it, but he said it was simply too far gone to help.

I was very upset. This poor baby gull was suffering and those ugly bastards (the buzzards and ants) couldn't even wait for it to do die before they started eating it. This is much like what Dillard described in her essay.

Frieda's Two Responses

Reading Journal: "Scorpions in Amber" First Response

In this essay, Dillard seems to be getting at the grandeur of the universe—those amazing things that are always happening, whether they're terrifying or joyful and inspiring. She questions what these various sights mean, ~~and do~~ if they even have meaning. Did God create everything with a specific purpose in mind and then disappear with that purpose, or was everything randomly thrown in and sort of happened this way?

Dillard's recollections of the amazing things she's seen are easy to relate to. Last winter I was hiking around the Susquehanna River. It was especially beautiful because there was a fresh snow covering everything. Suddenly I noticed some movement, and a huge deer leaped across the path. ~~it~~ It moved so silently, and seemed to be dancing along on the clouds.

When I think back on it, and how afterwards I trudged noisily on through the snow stepping on branches and twigs, I realize that there really are some beautiful and amazing things in this world. There are also cruel and vicious things, and the mixture of the two make for confusing ~~and~~ yet interesting thought.

In fact, I recall a flood I was in when I was ten or eleven, I've forgotten which. Anyhow, that experience was terrifying and the result was that I saw life in a different way after that. That flood washed away some beliefs I had about human control over nature and my own place in the scheme of things.

It's hard to believe that all of this could be the result of chaos and chance, especially when we can view such events and be stunned by them. Something sets them apart from all other experience, and it's interesting to note that more often than not the people who see these things are those who take notice of the world, not those who stay tied down to jobs, houses, bars, or whatever. It always makes me mad to think of how much I'm missing by being here in school, but then I suppose I reconcile that in some other way. The questions are some we'll never know answers to, but ~~they~~ the events will always be there to awe.

Second Response

After my second reading of this essay I can appreciate the message that I think Dillard was trying to project. Toward the end, she indicates that because the existence of these "extravagances" is such a mystery, we must learn to really watch for them. Then we can take in all the data and at least ask the right question—who knows, maybe someday the answer will come. Beyond that, there's really not a whole lot more to do, except observe and interpret.

I always wanted to believe that the philosophical tree in the woods would make a noise as it fell, even if no one was there to perceive it. But then again something tells me that because we're relying on the senses to tell us these things, they may be all false images. Its not a pleasant thought, and false isn't a pleasant word—but neither is temporary, and we do know that that tree will only fall once—the animal will die, and so on.

I like Dillard's idea that perhaps God has just spread out as our vision and understanding have spread. This seems to create something beyond the human experience, something far more vast and elusive. That would certainly make my own confusion about a God somehow clearer, because he would obviously be something we couldn't understand in this form of life. But, who wants to live forever in a state of confusion? I'd prefer, as Dillard says, to watch all the "fires" in life, and draw from them what I can. Hopefully that could produce contentment for enough of the time that the confusion wouldn't seem quite as weighty.

(After reading this second response again,—maybe I was in a state of confusion when I wrote it!)

Responding to Reading: Exploration and Discovery

Both Pat's and Frieda's responses contain some good examples from their own experiences of both the cruelty and beauty of nature. Pat's description of the baby seagull as an example of nature's cruelty and Frieda's description of the deer as an example of its grace and beauty are vivid and thought-provoking. In addition, Frieda mentions a flood as an example of the terror she experienced at the hands of nature. Both writers might want to expand these examples into subjects of future essays or use them as examples in an essay on a related topic. As you will see later on, Frieda chose to use the flood as a topic for her first essay.

Although both Frieda and Pat have expressed various meanings that they derived from "Scorpions in Amber," Frieda sticks more closely than Pat to analysis of meaning, and in contrast to her own perception of her second response, Frieda does not seem the least bit confused about Dillard's questions and final conclusion concerning our ignorance of "what is going on here."

Even though these two writers express similar notions of Dillard's central idea in the essay, you may find that your perception or some of your classmates' perceptions were not the same as theirs. Also, you may find that your interpretations coincide with those of your classmates on some points and diverge on others. However, such divergent readings of this or any other essay can lead to a greater understanding of the text. Thus, you should consider divergence an opportunity to learn, not a cause for concern.

On the other hand, you may have had a problem that should concern you, one that neither Pat nor Frieda had since each one wrote well over one page. Your aim in these responses is to put down all the thoughts, feelings, and questions you have as a result of your readings. Therefore, if you cannot fill at least one full page, you are not fully exploring your reactions—your thoughts, ideas, feelings, and questions. Also, perhaps you are not making associations that you could make, such as those that both Pat and Frieda made.

In addition, resist the temptation to write a generalization that will not hold up, such as "I don't understand this essay at all."

There will never be an essay that fails in *every sentence* to communicate with you. However, there may be a few or many statements that you do not understand. If there are, write them down one by one, and after each one *explore* the possible reasons for your lack of understanding. Thus, the less you understand an essay, the more you have to write about. Let's assume that you did not understand what Dillard meant when she wrote that cruelty was a waste of pain. As you explored your confusion, you might have written something like this:

I don't understand what Dillard's first sentence in paragraph 6 means. I can see that cruelty is a waste of pain, perhaps, because cruelty is a waste of life; it's a waste of everything. But I can't understand how pain is not a waste. That is, how is it that pain can be useful? Since she says that cruelty wastes pain, she must think that pain can be useful. Let's see . . . well, pain can keep you from hurting yourself really bad. If you burn your finger on a stove, you won't touch a hot burner again. How else? What about emotional pain? Could she mean that, too? My friend's father was (is) an alcoholic. He lost his job, his wife, his family. Then he quit drinking. I suppose the pain he felt when he lost everything was responsible for making him well. In that case, he didn't waste his pain. Maybe she does mean something like that. . . . I don't know . . . And another thing I don't understand is . . .

The idea, as you see, is always to explore possible meanings, explore the reasons for your lack of understanding, explore your reactions, explore, explore, in the way that only writing allows you to do.

And since you are concentrating on exploration, not on composition, you do not want to worry about organization, spelling, punctuation, or usage. Your objective is to write as rapidly as you can in order to keep up with the thoughts you have and the associations you make. Both Pat and Frieda crossed out words, but not very often. Furthermore, it seems evident that they made these corrections right away since the sentences that follow them make sense with the new words, not with the omitted ones. The point is that you want neither to worry about mechanics nor to tarry too long, crossing out words. If you do, some important thoughts you had may flit across your mind and escape forever.

The following is a second essay by Dillard, "The Death of a Moth." As suggested previously, you might read the text a third time, underlining the concrete/specific words and the metaphors that Dillard uses.

ANNIE DILLARD

The Death of a Moth

1 I live alone with two cats, who sleep on my legs. There is a yellow one, and a black one whose name is Small. In the morning I joke to the black one, Do you remember last night? Do you remember? I throw them both out before breakfast, so I can eat.

2 There is a spider, too, in the bathroom, of uncertain lineage, bulbous at the abdomen and drab, whose six-inch mess of web works, works somehow, works miraculously, to keep her alive and me amazed. The web is in a corner behind the toilet, connecting tile wall to tile wall. The house is new, the bathroom immaculate, save for the spider, her web, and the sixteen or so corpses she's tossed to the floor.

3 The corpses appear to be mostly sow bugs, those little armadillo creatures who live to travel flat out in houses, and die round. In addition to sow-bug husks, hollow and sipped empty of color, there are what seem to be two or three wingless moth bodies, one new flake of earwig, and three spider carcasses crinkled and clenched.

4 I wonder on what fool's errand an earwig, or a moth, or a sow bug, would visit that clean corner of the house behind the toilet; I have not noticed any blind parades of sow bugs blundering into corners. Yet they do hazard there, at a rate of more than one a week, and the spider thrives. Yesterday she was working on the earwig, mouth on gut; today he's on the floor. It must take a certain genius to throw things away from there, to find a straight line through that sticky tangle to the floor.

5 Today the earwig shines darkly, and gleams, what there is of him: a dorsal curve of thorax and abdomen, and a smooth pair of pincers by which I knew his name. Next week, if the other bodies are any indication, he'll be shrunk and gray, webbed to the floor with dust. The sow bugs beside him are curled and empty, fragile, a breath away from brittle fluff. The spiders lie on their sides, translucent and ragged, their legs drying in knots. The moths stagger against each other, headless, in a confusion of arcing strips of chitin like peeling varnish, like a jumble of buttresses for cathedral vaults, like nothing resembling moths, so that I would hesitate to call them moths, except that I have had some experience with the figure Moth reduced to a nub.

6 Two summers ago I was camped alone in the Blue Ridge Mountains of Virginia. I had hauled myself and gear up there to read, among other things, *The Day on Fire,* by James Ullman, a novel about Rimbaud that had made me want to be a writer when I was

sixteen; I was hoping it would do it again. So I read every day sitting under a tree by my tent, while warblers sang in the leaves overhead and bristle worms trailed their inches over the twiggy dirt at my feet; and I read every night by candlelight, while barred owls called in the forest and pale moths seeking mates massed around my head in the clearing, where my light made a ring.

7   Moths kept flying into the candle. They would hiss and recoil, reeling upside down in the shadows among my cooking pans. Or they would singe their wings and fall, and their hot wings, as if melted, would stick to the first thing they touched—a pan, a lid, a spoon—so that the snagged moths could struggle only in tiny arcs, unable to flutter free. These I could release by a quick flip with a stick; in the morning I would find my cooking stuff decorated with torn flecks of moth wings, ghostly triangles of shiny dust here and there on the aluminum. So I read, and boiled water, and replenished candles, and read on.

8   One night a moth flew into the candle, was caught, burnt dry, and held. I must have been staring at the candle, or maybe I looked up when a shadow crossed my page; at any rate, I saw it all. A golden female moth, a biggish one with a two-inch wingspread, flapped into the fire, dropped abdomen into the wet wax, stuck, flamed, and frazzled in a second. Her moving wings ignited like tissue paper, like angels' wings, enlarging the circle of light in the clearing and creating out of the darkness the sudden blue sleeves of my sweater, the green leaves of jewelweed by my side, the ragged red trunk of a pine; at once the light contracted again and the moth's wings vanished in a fine, foul smoke. At the same time, her six legs clawed, curled, blackened, and ceased, disappearing utterly. And her head jerked in spasms, making a spattering noise; her antennae cripsed and burnt away and her heaving mouthparts cracked like pistol fire. When it was all over, her head was, so far as I could determine, gone, gone the long way of her wings and legs. Her head was a hole lost to time. All that was left was the glowing horn shell of her abdomen and thorax—a fraying, partially collapsed gold tube jammed upright in the candle's round pool.

9   And then this moth-essence, this spectacular skeleton, began to act as a wick. She kept burning. The wax rose in the moth's body from her soaking abdomen to her thorax to the shattered hole where her head should have been, and widened into flame, a saffron-yellow flame that robed her to the ground like an immolating monk. That candle had two wicks, two winding flames of identical light, side by side. The moth's head was fire. She burned for two hours, until I blew her out.

10 She burned for two hours without changing, without swaying or kneeling—only glowing within, like a building fire glimpsed through silhouetted walls, like a hollow saint, like a flame-faced

virgin gone to God, while I read by her light, kindled, while Rimbaud in Paris burnt out his brain in a thousand poems, while night pooled wetly at my feet.

11 So. That is why I think those hollow shreds on the bathroom floor are moths. I believe I know what moths look like, in any state.

12 I have three candles here on the table which I disentangle from the plants and light when visitors come. The cats avoid them, although Small's tail caught fire once; I rubbed it out before she noticed. I don't mind living alone. I like eating alone and reading. I don't mind sleeping alone. The only time I mind being alone is when something is funny; then, when I am laughing at something funny, I wish someone were around. Sometimes I think it is pretty funny that I sleep alone.

Ideas and Meaning

1. What similarities does Dillard imply between herself and the moth? Between the moth and Rimbaud?
2. Why does Dillard say that she would like someone around when she is laughing at something funny?
3. In her last sentence does Dillard use the word *funny* to mean "laughable" or "strange"? Could both meanings apply?
4. Why was Dillard in the Blue Ridge Mountains when she saw the moth burn? What was she doing when it burned? Is there any significance in these circumstances?
5. How does the spider in the bathroom contribute to the meaning of the essay?
6. Could you consider this an essay about creative genius? About loneliness? About the connection between the two?

Development and Style

1. How does Dillard evoke clear images of the burning moth?
2. In paragraphs 9 and 10, what are the similes that Dillard uses for the burning moth? What do they have in common? How do they suggest Dillard's attitude towards the death of the moth?
3. Discuss the effects of the concrete/specific words (nouns, verbs, and adjectives) that Dillard uses in paragraphs 3 and 5. What examples of alliteration can you find?
4. What words or phrases does Dillard use to connect herself with the moth? To connect Rimbaud with the moth? As a result of these connections, what does Dillard imply about writing and writers?
5. In the burning scene, how is Dillard a contrast to the moth?
6. What word in the last sentence of paragraph 8 is repeated in

the last sentence of paragraph 10? What are the effects of this repetition? What are the images created in each sentence?

7. What details in paragraph 8 make readers experience the moment the moth ignites as if they were present?

8. Why does Dillard have breaks between paragraphs 5 and 6 and between 10 and 11?

9. How does Dillard get your attention in the first sentence?

Amy's Two Responses

Reading Journal: "The Death of a Moth" First Response

The moth and its death—a tragedy of "aloneness". I wonder what the connection between the moth's death and the author's state of being alone is? Is she perhaps implying that all of life may be filled with people and connections; but the final act—the most spectacular—is spent mentally, physically (perhaps), and spiritually alone? And what of this continuity of life—this invisible lifeline—"while I read by her light, kindled, while Rimbaud in Paris burnt out his brain on a thousand poems, while night pooled wetly at my feet."

What are these connections? How does the moth's death affect her life, the aging of Rimbaud, and the death of day into night. Without changing the moth affects the growth of Dillard's mind and is connected to the life cycle of humans and that of natural day and night. A cycle.

What does the spider have to do with the story. Thinking of the spider slowly killing its prey made me think of an incident that occurred a couple of years ago. I was playing tennis one spring day, and I noticed that passers by were stopping and looking at the sidewalk. The spot was hidden from my view by a hedge. After 15 minutes or so, I decided to investigate. This indeed was a tragic sight. A baby bird had fallen from its nest, high in the trees, and landed on its head, thus breaking its neck, but not completely killing it. It was truly a heartbreaker to watch it die slowly.

Second Response

My brain is as empty as those poor moths carcasses. Is her (Dillard's) life empty? Empty as those carcasses? Is it funny—strange—that she sleeps alone, or laughable? Does she see herself like this moth, whose light is shining through, yet only observed and appreciated by an outsider. Are we, the readers, Dillard's outsiders?

I also question the black and orange cats. Is the black one

night and the orange one day—or black = doubt. For she asks
the black one of the night. Almost directly suggesting that her
nights are meaningless—"Do you remember last night?" Is
she saying something of the process of life—sharing creates
validity? Why does she throw them out in the morning so that
she can eat? In the morning is the remembrance of loneliness
so great that the cats only increase her awareness? Or am I
perhaps digging too deep. I certainly sense an emptiness in
Dillard's life.

At times when I have been lonely in my life, odd things in-
tensified my loneliness—especially seeing two companions.
This brings me to the "two of a kind" idea. Dillard's cats are
companions—"two of a kind." Dillard has no one of her kind,
she relates and interacts with domestic animals and those of
nature. As Dillard watches the light of the moth, she is the
only observer. Does she see herself—a light to give—yet only
those who receive and appreciate are those she does not
know?

Linda's Two Responses

Reading Journal: "The Death of a Moth" First Response

Candles. Another of man's ingenious fire products, invented
in line with matches and hurricane lamps. Without them,
moths would have better chances, save for spiders and sharing webs in bathroom corners.

It's cliche now—"drawn like a moth to a flame." But what is
it about fire and light that so obsessively attracts the moth?
Is it warmth they crave? Or are their tiny eyes like ours, requiring light to see? Perhaps, they strive for something spiritual in their flaming suicide—private moth rituals that only
they in their mute flutterings share.

Lightbulbs seem to frustrate moths. Caught under a lamp-
shade, ricocheting off the sides, they try desperately to penetrate the thin glass to reach the inner core. They bang and
pound their fragile bodies against the bulb time and time
again to no avail. Finally, exhausted, they either drop to the
desktop or the floor or they go off in search of a more attain-
able fire. Or a wool sweater.

Whatever the reasons moths do what they do, Dillard successfully conveys the spiritual possibility of a moth's death
with incredible descriptions—"She burned for two hours without changing, without swaying or kneeling . . . like a hollow
saint, like a flame-faced virgin gone to God."

My cats prey on moths—Banjo especially, the lithe, quick

one, loves to catch them under lampshades or against the screen door. I often find traces of a moth's demise on her whiskers, like Dillard finds in her pots and pans; pieces of wings, or the silvery-gold wingdust they wear, cling to Banjo's face. She looks at me with unknowing eyes and I brush the debris of death from her whiskers. Our lights burn at night, attracting without malice the searching moth.

Second Response

A second reading and I drifted to the past week when we retraced his lonely footsteps all over the farm on the mountain. It was the morning before the funeral, and October color crackled beneath our feet.

The land was like a spouse to him, yet he struggled against it also, but there was nothing Pop could do about the wild growth of his wife's mind. Her schooling and her efforts toward a doctorate planted seeds of intelligent growth in her mind that created in her a desire to spread far beyond the confines of the isolated farm high on a mountain in Tennessee.

He is dead now and before the casket was lowered into the gaping hole in the ground, we dropped below a few choice leaves of October color. Pop and the farm will be together in death as they were in life.

Dillard's talking about death and immortality, and so much more. She was alone like Pop. Alone with the land and nature. Alone reading, alone trying to write, to create. And the moth was alone; its burning brightness lit up Dillard's sweater, but more than that—it lit up Dillard's mind.

Finding Your Own Voice

You probably noticed when you read "The Death of a Moth" that the voice you heard speaking was the same voice that you had heard as you read "Scorpions in Amber." And sometime in the future, if you happen to read an essay without the author's name, if it is written by Dillard, you will probably know immediately; you will recognize her voice. In order to test this idea, read the passage below and decide whether or not the voice speaking is Dillard's.

Mr. Sweet was a diabetic and an alcoholic and a guitar player and lived down the road from us on a neglected cotton farm. My older brothers and sisters got the most benefit from Mr. Sweet, for when they were growing up he had quite a few years ahead of him and so was capable of being called back from the brink of death any number of times—whenever the voice of my father reached him as he lay expiring.

If you decided that this is not Dillard's voice, you are correct. This is the voice of Alice Walker, whose account of Mr. Sweet is printed later on in this chapter. Now consider the following passage. Is this voice Dillard's?

Everything I see—the water, the log-wrecked beach, the farm on the hill, the bluff, the white church in the trees—looks overly distinct and shining. . . . It all looks staged. It all looks brittle and unreal, a skin of colors painted on glass, which if you prodded it with a finger would powder and fall. A blank sky, perfectly blended with all other sky, has sealed over the crack in the world where the plane fell, and the air has hushed the matter up.

No doubt you correctly identified this voice as Dillard's. This paragraph is from her book *Holy the Firm*. Just as no two speakers have identical speaking voices, so no two writers have identical writing voices. Every writer's voice is distinctly different from every other writer's voice.

You might define the writer's voice as the voice you hear speaking through a writer's words. As you have noted, Dillard's way of speaking through her words is different from the way that Alice Walker speaks through hers. Another way of putting it is that the writer's voice is the result of the writer being himself or herself on paper. For example, you have probably noticed that the students whose responses you have read have had distinctly different voices. Pat's voice is different from Frieda's, Tony's, and Silvia's.

The importance of voice in writing is this: If a writer is not himself on paper, if he uses someone else's voice, readers will detect deception and distrust the writer. Or readers may become bored by a writer who uses everyone else's voice, not his own. For instance, read the following passage and note your reactions to it.

In the modern world of today with its fast-paced living and modern technology, it is clear that our young people hold the future in their hands. They will need to put their shoulders to the wheel and continue to put their heads together if they want to solve the world's problems. If they want to succeed, they will need to try, try again, without expecting everything to be lily white or smooth as glass.

This writer is using everyone's else's voice, not his or her own. He or she has written one cliché after another, phrases that we have heard or read over and over, such as "modern world of today," "fast-paced living and modern technology," "put their shoulders to the wheel," and so on. I don't want to read this; you don't want to read this. Clichés are a great deal like dehydrated, instant soup. They are quick and easy; they come ready-made to the mind; they are "instant" language. And like every package of instant onion soup, they always taste the same, not like home-made onion soup that tastes slightly different from cook to cook or even slightly different from batch to batch prepared by the same cook. Even though you can "warm up" a pot of instant onion soup, you can never "warm up" a cliché. It will lie there on your page, cold and dead, and nothing can revive it.

Thus, as a beginning writer, you want to be wary of any phrase that comes immediately to mind. Chances are that this "instant" phrase is a cliché. Discard it and struggle to find your own way of saying what you want to say. If you do, your distinctly different voice will come through your words.

Because you probably have not written very much, you may need to find your writer's voice, and at first, it may seem to stammer or stutter, to sound a little squeaky, rusty, or hoarse. But that's what happens to a voice when it isn't used—it gets a little squeaky or hoarse. Furthermore, it may sound a little stilted, perhaps, or sometimes falsetto, hitting high notes a little off key. But don't let this bother you, for after you have written only a little while, attempting to be yourself on paper, you *will* find your own voice, just as Annie Dillard, Alice Walker, and every other professional and student writer have found theirs.

It is probably a relief for you to know that as a writer you can be yourself. Not only can you be yourself, but, in fact, your readers demand that you are yourself and that the voice they hear is yours alone, no one else's.

To find your own voice, you will discover that frequent writing, especially in a journal, is very useful. Journal writing can be helpful because you are likely to be less self-conscious when you write for yourself than when you write for an audience. The responses that you have written and will write to various texts are written for yourself. Even though you may share some of these responses with classmates, you did not write them for your classmates. You wrote them, instead, to discover the ideas and feelings you had and the associations you made as a result of your reading. In these responses you are a voyager seeking discovery of yourself through writing, and one of your discoveries will be your own writer's voice.

Whereas the essays you have read by Annie Dillard presented subjects from nature, the subject of Alice Walker's essay below is a person, Mr. Sweet—a very important person in Walker's life. However, like Dillard, Walker uses a great many concrete, specific words that give her readers vivid images of her subject. And also like Annie Dillard, Alice Walker uses her own voice.

ALICE WALKER

To Hell with Dying

1 "To hell with dying," my father would say. "These children want Mr. Sweet!"

2 Mr. Sweet was a diabetic and an alcoholic and a guitar player and lived down the road from us on a neglected cotton farm. My older brothers and sisters got the most benefit from Mr. Sweet, for when they were growing up he had quite a few years ahead of him and so was capable of being called back from the brink of death any number of times—whenever the voice of my father reached him as he lay expiring. "To hell with dying, man," my father would say, pushing the wife away from the bedside (in tears although she knew the death was not necessarily the last one unless Mr. Sweet really wanted it to be). "These children want Mr. Sweet!" And they did want him, for at a signal from Father they would come crowding around the bed and throw themselves on the covers, and whoever was the smallest at the time would kiss him all over his wrinkled brown face and begin to tickle him so that he would laugh all down in his stomach, and his moustache, which was long and sort of straggly, would shake like Spanish moss and was also that color.

3 Mr. Sweet had been ambitious as a boy, wanted to be a doctor or lawyer or sailor, only to find that black men fare better if they are not. Since he could become none of these things he turned to fishing as his only earnest career and playing the guitar as his only claim to doing anything extraordinarily well. His son, the only one that he and his wife, Miss Mary, had, was shiftless as the day is long and spent money as if he were trying to see the bottom of the mint, which Mr. Sweet would tell him was the clean brown palm of his hand. Miss Mary loved her "baby," however, and worked hard to get him the "li'l necessaries" of life, which turned out mostly to be women.

4 Mr. Sweet was a tall, thinnish man with thick kinky hair going dead white. He was dark brown, his eyes were very squinty and sort of bluish, and he chewed Brown Mule tobacco. He was constantly on the verge of being blind drunk, for he brewed his own liquor and was not in the least a stingy sort of man, and was always very melancholy and sad, though frequently when he was "feelin' good" he'd dance around the yard with us, usually keeling over just as my mother came to see what the commotion was.

5 Toward all of us children he was very kind, and had the grace to be shy with us, which is unusual in grown-ups. He had great respect for my mother for she never held his drunkenness against him and would let us play with him even when he was about to fall in the fireplace from drink. Although Mr. Sweet would some-

times lose complete or nearly complete control of his head and neck so that he would loll in his chair, his mind remained strangely acute and his speech not too affected. His ability to be drunk and sober at the same time made him an ideal playmate, for he was as weak as we were and we could usually best him in wrestling, all the while keeping a fairly coherent conversation going.

6 We never felt anything of Mr. Sweet's age when we played with him. We loved his wrinkles and would draw some on our brows to be like him, and his white hair was my special treasure and he knew it and would never come to visit us just after he had had his hair cut off at the barbershop. Once he came to our house for something, probably to see my father about fertilizer for his crops because, although he never paid the slightest attention to his crops, he liked to know what things would be best to use on them if he ever did. Anyhow, he had not come with his hair since he had just had it shaved off at the barbershop. He wore a huge straw hat to keep off the sun and also to keep his head away from me. But as soon as I saw him I ran up and demanded that he take me up and kiss me with his funny beard which smelled so strongly of tobacco. Looking forward to burying my small fingers into his woolly hair I threw away his hat only to find he had done something to his hair, that it was no longer there! I let out a squall which made my mother think that Mr. Sweet had finally dropped me in the well or something and from that day I've been wary of men in hats. However, not long after, Mr. Sweet showed up with his hair grown out and just as white and kinky and impenetrable as it ever was.

7 Mr. Sweet used to call me his princess, and I believed it. He made me feel pretty at five and six, and simply outrageously devastating at the blazing age of eight and a half. When he came to our house with his guitar the whole family would stop whatever they were doing to sit around him and listen to him play. He liked to play "Sweet Georgia Brown," that was what he called me sometimes, and also he liked to play "Caldonia" and all sorts of sweet, sad, wonderful songs which he sometimes made up. It was from one of these songs that I learned that he had had to marry Miss Mary when he had in fact loved somebody else (now living in Chi-ca-go, or De-stroy, Michigan). He was not sure that Joe Lee, her "baby," was also his baby. Sometimes he would cry and that was an indication that he was about to die again. And so we would all get prepared, for we were sure to be called upon.

8 I was seven the first time I remember actually participating in one of Mr. Sweet's "revivals"—my parents told me I had participated before, I had been the one chosen to kiss him and tickle him long before I knew the rite of Mr. Sweet's rehabilitation. He had come to our house, it was a few years after his wife's death, and was very sad, and also, typically, very drunk. He sat on the

floor next to me and my older brother, the rest of the children were grown up and lived elsewhere, and began to play his guitar and cry. I held his woolly head in my arms and wished I could have been old enough to have been the woman he loved so much and that I had not been lost years and years ago.

9 When he was leaving, my mother said to us that we'd better sleep light that night for we'd probably have to go over to Mr. Sweet's before daylight. And we did. For soon after we had gone to bed one of the neighbors knocked on our door and called my father and said that Mr. Sweet was sinking fast and if he wanted to get in a word before the crossover he'd better shake a leg and get over to Mr. Sweet's house. All the neighbors knew to come to our house if something was wrong with Mr. Sweet, but they did not know how we always managed to make him well, or at least stop him from dying, when he was often so near death. As soon as we heard the cry we got up, my brother and I and my mother and father, and put on our clothes. We hurried out of the house and down the road for we were always afraid that we might someday be too late and Mr. Sweet would get tired of dallying.

10 When we got to the house, a very poor shack really, we found the front room full of neighbors and relatives and someone met us at the door and said that it was all very sad that old Mr. Sweet Little (for Little was his family name, although we mostly ignored it) was about to kick the bucket. My parents were advised not to take my brother and me into the "death room," seeing we were so young and all, but we were so much more accustomed to the death room than he that we ignored him and dashed in without giving his warning a second thought. I was almost in tears, for these deaths upset me fearfully, and the thought of how much depended on me and my brother (who was such a ham most of the time) made me very nervous.

11 The doctor was bending over the bed and turned back to tell us for at least the tenth time in the history of my family that, alas, old Mr. Sweet Little was dying and that the children had best not see the face of implacable death (I didn't know what "implacable" was, but whatever it was, Mr. Sweet was not!). My father pushed him rather abruptly out of the way saying, as he always did and very loudly for he was saying it to Mr. Sweet, "To hell with dying, man, these children want Mr. Sweet"—which was my cue to throw myself upon the bed and kiss Mr. Sweet all around the whiskers and under the eyes and around the collar of his nightshirt where he smelled so strongly of all sorts of things, mostly liniment.

12 I was very good at bringing him around, for as soon as I saw that he was struggling to open his eyes I knew he was going to be all right, and so could finish my revival sure of success. As soon as his eyes were open he would begin to smile and that way I knew that I had surely won. Once, though, I got a tremendous

scare, for he could not open his eyes and later I learned that he had had a stroke and that one side of his face was stiff and hard to get into motion. When he began to smile I could tickle him in earnest because I was sure that nothing would get in the way of his laughter, although once he began to cough so hard that he almost threw me off his stomach, but that was when I was very small, little more than a baby, and my bushy hair had gotten in his nose.

13 When we were sure he would listen to us we would ask him why he was in bed and when he was coming to sec us again and could we play with his guitar, which more than likely would be leaning against the bed. His eyes would get all misty and he would sometimes cry out loud, but we never let it embarrass us, for he knew that we loved him and that we sometimes cried too for no reason. My parents would leave the room to just the three of us; Mr. Sweet, by that time, would be propped up in bed with a number of pillows behind his head and with me sitting and lying on his shoulder and along his chest. Even when he had trouble breathing he would not ask me to get down. Looking into my eyes he would shake his white head and run a scratchy old finger all around my hairline, which was rather low down, nearly to my eyebrows, and made some people say I looked like a baby monkey.

14 My brother was very generous in all this, he let me do all the revivaling—he had done it for years before I was born and so was glad to be able to pass it on to someone new. What he would do while I talked to Mr. Sweet was pretend to play the guitar, in fact pretend that he was a young version of Mr. Sweet, and it always made Mr. Sweet glad to think that someone wanted to be like him—of course, we did not know this then, we played the thing by ear, and whatever he seemed to like, we did. We were desperately afraid that he was just going to take off one day and leave us.

15 It did not occur to us that we were doing anything special; we had not learned that death was final when it did come. We thought nothing of triumphing over it so many times, and in fact became a trifle contemptuous of people who let themselves be carried away. It did not occur to us that if our own father had been dying we could not have stopped it, that Mr. Sweet was the only person over whom we had power.

15 When Mr. Sweet was in his eighties I was studying in the university many miles from home. I saw him whenever I went home, but he was never on the verge of dying that I could tell and I began to feel that my anxiety for his health and psychological well-being was unnecessary. By this time he not only had a moustache but a long flowing snow-white beard, which I loved and combed and braided for hours. He was very peaceful, fragile, gentle,

and the only jarring note about him was his old steel guitar, which he still played in the old sad, sweet, down-home blues way.

17 On Mr. Sweet's ninetieth birthday I was finishing my doctorate in Massachusetts and had been making arrangements to go home for several weeks' rest. That morning I got a telegram telling me that Mr. Sweet was dying again and could I please drop everything and come home. Of course I could. My dissertation could wait and my teachers would understand when I explained to them when I got back. I ran to the phone, called the airport, and within four hours I was speeding along the dusty road to Mr. Sweet's.

18 The house was more dilapidated than when I was last there, barely a shack, but it was overgrown with yellow roses which my family had planted many years ago. The air was heavy and sweet and very peaccful. I felt strange walking through the gate and up the old rickety steps. But the strangeness left me as I caught sight of the long white beard I loved so well flowing down the thin body over the familiar quilt coverlet. Mr. Sweet!

19 His eyes were closed tight and his hands, crossed over his stomach, were thin and delicate, no longer scratchy. I remembered how always before I had run and jumped up on him just anywhere; now I knew he would not be able to support my weight. I looked around at my parents, and was surprised to see that my father and mother also looked old and frail. My father, his own hair very gray, leaned over the quietly sleeping old man, who, incidentally, smelled still of wine and tobacco, and said, as he'd done so many times, "To hell with dying, man! My daughter is home to see Mr. Sweet!" My brother had not been able to come as he was in the war in Asia. I bent down and gently stroked the closed eyes and gradually they began to open. The closed, wine-stained lips twitched a little, then parted in a warm, slightly embarrassed smile. Mr. Sweet could see me and he recognized me and his eyes looked very spry and twinkly for a moment. I put my head down on the pillow next to his and we just looked at each other for a long time. Then he began to trace my peculiar hairline with a thin, smooth finger. I closed my eyes when his finger halted above my ear (he used to rejoice at the dirt in my ears when I was little), his hand stayed cupped around my cheek. When I opened my eyes, sure that I had reached him in time, his were closed.

20 Even at twenty-four how could I believe that I had failed? that Mr. Sweet was really gone? He had never gone before. But when I looked up at my parents I saw that they were holding back tears. They had loved him dearly. He was like a piece of rare and delicate china which was always being saved from breaking and which finally fell. I looked long at the old face, the wrinkled forehead, the red lips, the hands that still reached out to me. Soon I felt my father pushing something cool into my hands. It was Mr. Sweet's

guitar. He had asked them months before to give it to me; he had known that even if I came next time he would not be able to respond in the old way. He did not want me to feel that my trip had been for nothing.

21 The old guitar! I plucked the strings, hummed "Sweet Georgia Brown." The magic of Mr. Sweet lingered still in the cool steel box. Through the window I could catch the fragrant delicate scent of tender yellow roses. The man on the high old-fashioned bed with the quilt coverlet and the flowing white beard had been my first love.

Ideas and Meaning

1. In what ways was Mr. Sweet different from other grown-ups?
2. Why was it that Mr. Sweet was on the brink of death many times? How did the Walkers save him?
3. Why was his relationship with Alice Walker special?
4. When Mr. Sweet dies, Walker writes that because of all their "revivals" of him in the past, she could not believe that she had failed and that he was gone. In what concrete ways is Mr. Sweet *not* "gone"?
5. Does Walker imply possible reasons for Mr. Sweet's overindulgence in alcohol?
6. Even though this essay is about Mr. Sweet, what do you learn about the Walker family? About Alice Walker in particular?
7. Is this essay about Mr. Sweet, death, or immortality? Is it about all three?

Development and Style

1. Discuss the concrete and specific words and phrases used throughout the essay to describe Mr. Sweet. How is the simile at the end of paragraph 2 particularly effective? What specific words or phrases are repeated? What is the effect of this repetition?
2. How does Walker imply criticism of the racist culture that Mr. Sweet lived in?
3. Does Walker use the guitar symbolically? If so, how does the symbolism add to the effectiveness of the essay?
4. What are the effects of the repetition of the odor of the yellow roses in paragraphs 18 and 21?
5. Are the yellow roses used symbolically? If so, what do they symbolize? What are yellow roses traditionally used to symbolize?
6. The title of the essay is repeated in the beginning sentence

and later on in the essay. What is the effect of this repetition? Does the title take on added significance beyond the essay?

7. How does the first sentence get your attention?

Gloria's Two Responses

Reading Journal: "To Hell With Dying" First Response

As I got to the end of this essay by Alice Walker, I felt the familiar tingling sensation of goose bumps that I get when I am deeply moved but won't let myself cry. I was moved; I wanted to cry, but I didn't.

I'm sorry that Mr. Sweet died, but he was a lucky man to have had a family like Alice Walker's for friends. They were very kind to a man who apparently brought a lot of pleasure to the children in the Walker family. That was an important gift he had to make the children feel that they deserved respect from a grown-up. I believe that's the way Ms. Walker put it.

I got a wonderful picture of his beard when she compared it to the color of Spanish moss, and of his eyes, so old the whites looked blue, and the last image, his death bed where she put her head on his pillow and looked into his eyes, before he closed them and died. And a detail I'll always remember—the yellow roses in bloom when Ms. Walker got to the house. I imagine that when she smells the fragrance of yellow roses, she always recalls the day that Mr. Sweet really died.

Oh, this essay is about so much, so much more than Mr. Sweet—love, friendship, death. It's also about a realization for the first time that death is irrevocable. That time passes, and at twenty-four, when Mr. Sweet died, Ms. Walker looks at her own parents and realizes that they look old.

And the subtle hint of the destructiveness of racism in Mr. Sweet's life. He had wanted to be a doctor, a lawyer, but couldn't be because he was black. You wonder—did these stifled ambitions have something to do with his drinking? And, too, the loss of his "real" love? Did that contribute to Sweet Little's enduring sadness? And I have written way too long on this first response.

Second Response

This time as I read, I remembered the last time that I saw my grandfather alive. It was also the first time that I had felt close to him. It was a special day for me, one I'll always remember. And at the end of that day he played his mandolin that my brother plays now. Also, like Mr. Sweet, he had a woman in his past, one he'd played his mandolin for years before.

It was in the fall that we travelled the dusty road to grandfather's—but I'm getting too much into my own past now and leaving behind this very touching essay.

I'm glad I read this; I'll never forget it, just as I'll never forget Annie Dillard's essays either. And how different these women's voices are from each other. For me, Ms. Walker is easier to understand, but I am tremendously grateful to Annie D. for opening my seeing eyes more and my mind's eyes also. I am grateful to Alice Walker, too, for letting me know that it's all right to let people know that you cry. And to both writers I am grateful for encouraging me to think that I can write my own way and be beautiful, too, in a different way from them.

I wish I had known Mr. Sweet. I feel now as if I <u>do</u> know him, and I suppose I'm a little angry that I never really knew him like Alice Walker did and now he's gone. Gone forever and yet not gone forever because he's here in these four pages of print. Here forever. That's a nice thing to do for somebody. Make them immortal, annihilate death. I'd like to do that sometime for someone.

Jake's Two Responses

Reading Journal: "To Hell With Dying" First Response

In reading this essay the first thing that really affected me was a memory from my own childhood that the essay prompted.

There was an old man we used to call "Bill the Clown" mainly because of his mixed manner of dress—color, stripes, and plaids. As children, we didn't know "Bill the Clown" was in actuality a derelict. He shuffled when he walked, and he always smelt bad, yet he always seemed to have gumballs and funny anecdotes for us children. Then one day—I was around five—"Bill the Clown" disappeared. My father sat my two sisters and me down and explained that the man who taught us how to pitch pennies and play freeze tag had frozen to death in a Dempsy Dumpster.

Needless to say, my views of life changed. I realized that even the lowest of society could be kind and humane, but it also seems that these type of people are always closer to children because children are still innocent of the ways of the world. They don't look down on people like "Bill" or Mr. Sweet. Instead, they find room in their hearts for them. Children like adults who treat them as equals, and in turn there are some people who are lost and alone, needing love from somewhere, if only from a child. These people don't expect society to open up and take them in, but a child is more likely to because society often ignores the views and opinions of children, much as they do the undesirables.

But life goes on and children grow up and understand. Children learn to conform, while all the Mr. Sweets of the world cry wolf for the last time. Children conform while all the "Bills" are found in the trash. Someday maybe children will conform to society less, and retain a child's natural compassion more.

Second Response

After a second reading, I thought perhaps I should clarify myself from my first response. I do realize the difference in the relationship between Ms. Walker and Mr. Sweet and the way I felt about "Bill the Clown."

Mr. Sweet was an unfortunate victim of society. Racial prejudices probably placed him in his predicament. Plus I think that black families of the late 1940s early 1950s, and even still, feel a closeness that others couldn't understand unless they had been oppressed as blacks have.

The essay is readable, believable and moving. A lesson in human nature can be learned from this essay. People in general are a cold species. It is fortunate that wilder animals aren't capable of being racially, socio-economically prejudiced. There is an old philosophy "I think therefore I am." From this essay about Mr. Sweet we should be able to find a new philosophy: "Others think so I am what they ~~want~~ limit me to be." Without question Mr. Sweet was being the best person he was capable—or allowed—to be. The reason, society had set limits or expectations for him. Until someone cared. Other children in Ms. Walker's family probably at one time cared for Mr. Sweet, but they soon grew up and viewed him as just another drunk. Ms. Walker heard his cries for help. She realized he needed love and understanding, even if it meant faking death.

I wonder what would have happened if no one had cared enough, years before he died, whether or not he was dying. I wonder if it is possible for society to separate a person so much that they eventually die of loneliness.

Conclusion

As you have seen, the voices of Dillard and Walker differ from each other, as do the voices of the six students who responded to the essays. Besides illustrating how writers' voices differ from each other, professional writing demonstrates the ways various writers use the skills that you are in the process of acquiring. In this chapter, for example, you focused on noticing how Dillard and Walker used metaphors and concrete/specific words and phrases to evoke images in their readers' minds. Therefore, reading professional writing reinforces your knowledge of various writing skills as you learn them, and responding to professional writing allows you not only to practice using your own voice but also to discover new thoughts and feelings as you attempt to discover a writer's meaning. Thus, reading and responding to reading can give you many new ideas for your own writing.

Furthermore, you undoubtedly will find that the students' responses in the text, as well as your classmates' responses, if you share them in class, will often act as catalysts to a compound of your own ideas. As a result of such stimuli to your own thinking, when it comes time for you to write, you will probably already have several ideas in mind.

C H A P T E R

The Process of Writing

3

In the last chapter you discovered that reading is a process and that writers' voices differ from each other. Besides the difference in voice among writers, there is also a difference in the process writers go through as they compose. Nevertheless, it is equally true that for all writers, *writing is a process.* For Annie Dillard, perhaps writing starts in her head, where she may draft the beginnings of an essay. Or perhaps she does her prewriting by writing whatever comes to mind, discarding some ideas, keeping others. Maybe Alice Walker does something similar or entirely different. Also, for every writer certain props differ. Some writers prefer to write with a pen, others prefer pencils. Still others prefer to compose on a typewriter or a word processor. Some want music in the background, others want dead silence. Some writers compose in the morning, others write in the evening, preferring the cloak of darkness and quiet of night. But, despite these differences in the props that writers prefer, most writers have a favorite place where they write, where all their props are assembled and ready to go. Generally speaking, there is only one place a writer feels comfortable, and it is there he or she retires to compose.

In addition, there is one other similarity among writers: Although their props and composing processes may differ, all writers revise and edit. The number of drafts writers compose, however, varies not only from writer to writer, but also from essay to essay written by the same writer. Thus, the process of writing is not a linear one, but a recursive one. Furthermore, it is never predictable. For example, you can label the various stages of the writing process, as you see in the following diagram. The arrows indicate one possible example of the recursiveness of the process.

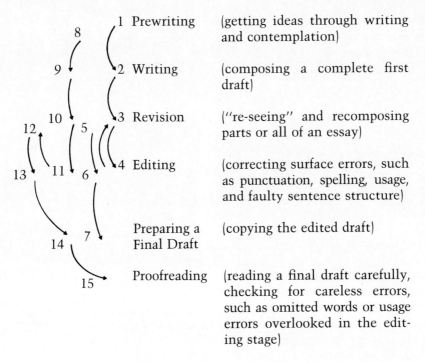

1 Prewriting (getting ideas through writing and contemplation)

2 Writing (composing a complete first draft)

3 Revision ("re-seeing" and recomposing parts or all of an essay)

4 Editing (correcting surface errors, such as punctuation, spelling, usage, and faulty sentence structure)

Preparing a Final Draft (copying the edited draft)

Proofreading (reading a final draft carefully, checking for careless errors, such as omitted words or usage errors overlooked in the editing stage)

The recursiveness of the composing process is evident: for one thing, a writer may revise an essay as many as seven or more times, or as few as two or even one, although that is rare. Moreover, a writer may complete a revision and discover that he or she does not like at all what the essay says or that he or she is really not interested in the subject. Thus, the writer begins again at step one: prewriting. As the previous diagram illustrates, going back to the first step is a possibility even after the completion of a final draft. In Chapter 10 you will see such a likelihood demonstrated by Cynthia's writing. After completing at least two drafts of her essay, Cynthia abandoned it and returned to the prewriting stage because she felt that what she had written lacked freshness and originality. This may also happen to you, and if, for any reason, you lose enthusiasm for your subject, by all means begin again. The worst thing you can do is to write about a subject that doesn't interest you. If you are not interested in what you say, your lack of involvement and enthusiasm will show in your writing, and the result will be a dull, dull essay—a chore both to write and to read.

Just as each writer's process differs from another's, so does each writer's process of revision. Some writers revise previously written parts of their essays as they write a first draft. Others write a complete draft before they begin the task of "re-seeing" what they have written. An example of an unusual method of revision is provided by D. H. Lawrence, who revised *Lady Chatterley's Lover* by rewriting the whole text from beginning to end, putting aside the first version altogether! Generally, however, writers revise by recomposing parts of their text, retaining some of it unchanged. And which part of his or her essay a writer revises first is also a matter of choice that differs with each writer and with each text written by the same writer.

At this point you are probably wondering, "All this is fine, but *how will I know what to revise, what needs to be changed?*" The answer is probably obvious: The revisions you make depend on the writing skills you have. At this time you have learned to use concrete/specific language and figures of speech so that these skills will be ones that you will use when you revise your first essay. That is, after you complete a first draft, you will read it, looking for words or statements that could be made more concrete or specific. In addition, between your first and final drafts you will learn another skill that you can use when you revise this first essay.

As you will see in the following description of her writing process, Marcia revises as she writes a first draft. Both Gail's and Marcia's descriptions of their writing processes clearly illustrate how the composing process differs from writer to writer. After you have written the final draft of your first essay, you might also write a description of the specific props you used and the particular process you went through while composing it. If you and your classmates write such descriptions and share them, you will see how vastly writers differ, both in their writing processes and in the props they require to get the job done. And further, as you continue to write essay after essay, you will be surprised at how much your own process will differ from essay to essay—although your props are likely to remain the same.

Gail's Writing Process

Whenever I plan to write an essay of more than several typed pages, I have a system that I follow.

After a topic is chosen nothing is done until my mind has had time to think about it, to decide how the essay is to be written.

Sometimes during this period of contemplation a sentence or phrase will come to mind and it is immediately written down on whatever paper happens to be close by.

The next step—the big step—is to start writing, any and everything that comes to my mind. It can be sifted out later. After that I type it, for seeing the typed words enables me to picture more clearly just what I have composed.

From the typed pages, for me, begins the difficult job of revision. It is here many of the sentences are reworded, trying to put my thought into as few words as possible.

Gail has begun the description of her writing process after she has a topic, whereas in the following description Marcia begins by telling how she discovers a subject to write about.

Marcia's Writing Process

I would have to say that the process I follow differs depending on what I'm writing. The process of writing a poem differs from the process of writing an essay. If it's an essay, I generally brainstorm for a topic by writing down a list of ideas. Then, if I have the time, I think about various things I've listed as I go about my daily routine. After I choose an idea, I begin writing as rapidly as I can, getting down everything that comes to mind. Sometimes I don't like what I come up with, so I choose another topic and write on it as rapidly as I can. When I've gotten something down that seems workable, I may cross out some things that are off the focus and try to clarify the statements I made.

Sometimes I know the point I want to make before I begin the first rapidly written draft. Other times I have a hazy idea or none at all, and I discover the point by writing. Even when I think I know the point I want to make, it changes as I write. So I never worry about having a point before I write. Even if I do have one, I know it's going to change—sometimes a lot, other times slightly.

When I begin a second draft, I stop periodically to read what I've written to that point, crossing out words and sentences and rewriting. I may even insert whole paragraphs on another sheet of paper. By the time I get to the end of this draft, the first few paragraphs may have been read perhaps ten times or more because every time I stop, I read from the beginning to the point where I stopped. Sometimes the first few paragraphs are barely decipherable because of all the crossing out. Even though I write with a pencil, I cross out until I can't any more because it's quicker than erasing.

After this, I type, editing and revising words and sentences and sometimes adding material as I type. Then there's more revising and editing. Generally I revise sentence structure and transitions at this point. I may also rewrite whole paragraphs, omit some, or add new ones. Next, I type again and revise words and sentences as I type. This is usually the final draft until I get someone else's advice.

Because Marcia revises as she writes her second draft, parts of this draft have been revised six, seven, or more times. Not only do many writers edit and revise as they write, but like Marcia, they often discover what they want to say as they write.

Audience, Purpose, and Point

Besides discovering what they want to say as they write, some writers may also discover an audience and a purpose after they begin writing. On the other hand, before they begin to write, some writers have a clear idea not only of the point they'd like to make, but also of their audience and their purpose. Nevertheless, as these writers write, their points may alter a great deal or slightly. If a writer's point changes considerably, he or she may even decide to write for another audience with yet another purpose from the original one.

The important thing is that finally a writer arrives at a clear idea of audience and purpose, as well as a point to make, either explicit (stated) or implied. To understand the importance of audience, purpose, and point, consider Annie Dillard's and Alice Walker's essays. To whom is Dillard writing? What kind of person did she have in mind as she wrote the two essays you read? For both, she probably had similar audiences in mind: intelligent and sensitive people who are fairly well educated or who, like you, are in the process of getting an education. What seems to be her purpose in each essay? In "Scorpions in Amber," Dillard presents some questions for which there are no clear-cut answers; her purpose seems to be to describe and narrate her experience with nature and to convince her audience that they should be more observant of life and nature so that they ask the right questions about life's mysteries. Her point is that the entanglement of cruelty and beauty in nature is perplexing and that if we want to ask the right questions about such mysteries, we need to be more observant.

On the other hand, in "The Death of a Moth," Dillard's purpose is not to convince us of anything but to describe and narrate a personal experience. The point she implies is that creativity and loneliness are connected.

In contrast to Dillard's audience, Alice Walker's audience could be any adult or young adult in our society. Since she illuminates a man who was more or less a victim of a racist society, she might particularly like a white audience to read her essay, but it is not written exclusively for a white audience. Because of Mr. Sweet's victimization, Walker's purpose may have been to illuminate both his worthiness and the destructiveness of racism. The point implied in her essay is that even though as a black man Mr. Sweet could not be what he wanted to be, he was a worthy, loving person who gave a great deal.

To summarize: A particular audience affects what a writer says and how he or she says it. For example, would Annie Dillard write the previous essays for an elementary school magazine? Yet another example: Would you write an essay about women's hairstyles for *Esquire* magazine? As for the importance of purpose, suppose you needed some money in order to visit a friend over the weekend. Would you write a letter to your parents asking for money and tell them that you flunked your tests in math and chemistry the past week? Last, having a point to make is most important. For instance, can you imagine what your reaction would be if Annie Dillard had described the frog's death and said nothing more? Or even if she had then described the bird's fall and said nothing more? Your reaction would be to say "So what? Why did you describe these scenes?" Even if you enjoyed the vividness of Dillard's descriptions, your question would be what's the point? If there is no point, readers feel as if they've wasted their time.

For the essay you are about to begin, if you have a hard time envisioning an audience for yourself, you might imagine that you are writing your essay for publication in the local newspaper in a column entitled "Our Personal Worlds." Or you could imagine that you were writing for a similar column in your school newspaper.

Your purpose you must decide for yourself, but if you write on a subject suggested by Dillard's or Walker's writing, you will most likely have purposes similar to theirs: to narrate and to describe; to narrate, describe, and explain; or to narrate, describe, and convince. Whoever your audience and whatever your purpose, you will want to make sure that in your final draft you have a point to make.

Purpose and Traditional Rhetorical Modes

To define Dillard's and Walker's purposes, I used the phrases "to narrate," "to describe," "to explain," and "to convince." Traditionally, rhetoricians have classified nonfiction prose as narration, description, exposition, or persuasion, according to a writer's purpose.

Narration: The writer's purpose is to relate a series of events.
Description: The writer's purpose is to describe a subject.
Exposition: The writer's purpose is to explain his or her views on a subject.
Persuasion: The writer's purpose is to persuade readers to accept his or her views on a subject, usually a controversial one.

Even though these particular modes are distinguished from each other according to purpose, in Walker's essay, for example, you saw that a writer may use a great deal of description in a narrative. Furthermore, in her essay "Scorpions in Amber," Dillard uses a great deal of narration and description to help her explain her point and to convince her readers to accept it. Given this mixture, how would you classify her essay? Is it primarily descriptive, narrative, expository, or persuasive? The truth is that, like Dillard's, any given essay may contain a mixture of modes.

However, despite the fact that these traditional rhetorical modes seem arbitrary and overlapping, there is a clear distinction in purpose between narration/description and exposition/persuasion. Because narration often contains a great deal of description, both terms together oftentimes describe a writer's purpose better than either one alone, and because good exposition has an arguable point, both terms often more nearly describe a writer's purpose than either term alone.

For instance, no doubt you would agree that Dillard's primary purpose in "Scorpions" seems to be expository/persuasive rather than descriptive/narrative. Clearly, her intent is to explain her views of the beauty and cruelty in nature and to persuade us to accept the point she makes about this inexplicable mixture.

In the essay you are about to write, you will determine your purpose yourself. Like Walker, you may want to write a narrative, or like Dillard, you may want to explain your views and persuade your readers to accept them also. Like both writers, you will want to use concrete/specific words and phrases to help your readers see what you saw and hear what you heard.

But before you discover a purpose, like all professional writers, you must first discover *what you want to say.* All professional writers begin with something they want to say, and from that they discover a purpose. Below are several suggestions to help you find a subject, and, finally, to discover what you want to say about it.

Suggestions for Writing and Getting Started

In your responses to Annie Dillard's two essays and to Alice Walker's essay, you may have related a personal experience that could be the nucleus of an essay. In addition, if you have continued to keep a personal journal, even though you have not been at it long, you might find the seed of a good idea there. Also, you can get a number of ideas by "brainstorming," that is, by listing ideas in words and phrases as quickly as you can. You might brainstorm under the following headings, suggested by the essays you have read:

Beliefs I Question
Beliefs I've Lost
Beliefs I've Gained
People and Actions Hard to Give Up
Past Experiences with Nature

In addition to listing under these or other headings you think of, you might like to spend several hours in a wooded area, perhaps near a pond, a lake, or a stream, observing and writing what you see, hear, smell, and what your reactions and associations are. The following are Frieda's brainstorming ideas under each of the suggested headings. Although she wrote a description of an afternoon she spent in the woods, she preferred two of the subjects from her listing. After she completed her listing, she put checkmarks by the two topics that she thought she'd like to write about.

Beliefs I Question
Wisdom comes with age
Technology is for the better
Art should exist solely for the sake of art
Art can't exist merely for itself—it must always say something
School is the best place for me right now—it'll make me a better, happier person
You're only as old as you feel

Beliefs I've Lost
The only way to improve something is to change it
Friends stay friends forever
Time heals all wounds
If you work hard all your life you'll be happy and have a lot to show for it

Beliefs I've Gained
A person can't be judged from one meeting
Mexican food tastes good
American films can be as good as foreign

Things, People, Actions Hard to Give Up
Parents when you move out
Privacy when moving in with others
My mean, stubborn, careless, loving grandfather who died of cancer
Sniffy, my dog who went on many hiking trips with me
√ All my favorite hot, spicy foods I had to give up because of digestion problems

Past Experiences with Nature
Watching my grandfather's cow give birth and then die
Seeing deer while walking near Susquehanna River [from one of her responses]
Several beautiful sunsets while camping at the Peaks of Otter
√ The flood in Pennsylvania when I was a child [from one of her responses]
Many wonderful things in the fields when I worked as a field hand a couple of summers ago

After Frieda decided on two subjects that she preferred over the others, she freewrote a draft of each one. She tried to write as rapidly as possible, getting down all her thoughts without discarding any at that point. In class, she read both drafts to two class-mates, who decided that they liked better her narrative of the flood, which you can read later on.

Now, so that you can get a clearer idea of what kind of essay you might write, you can read the final drafts of two of Frieda's classmates, Gregg and Andrea. Also, reading these essays now might give you further ideas for topics of your own.

Last, you can see how both Gregg and Andrea have used sensory data to make their writing concrete and to help them convey to their readers the images of their experiences that remain in their minds. In addition to being concrete, both writers have taken the risks of using metaphors and their own voices—and how different from each other they truly are. Above all, you will see that both students have attained Conrad's aim: You will hear what they heard, feel what they felt, and *see* what they saw.

Gregg's Final Draft

Adventures in the Forest of Knowledge

1 Beyond the highways and by-ways of human expansion there lies another world, a world of beauty and yet a world in which the weak die very young. This world is the unadulterated outdoors. Within the grandeur of nature there exists a delicate balance between life and death, a harsh reality often forgotten by those enjoying the rapture of natural splendor. Yet, these perils inherent in nature are most often beautiful in themselves.

2 As a young child I was spellbound by nature's world of wonder. Oaks, pines, and elms, ants and spiders, meadowlarks, robins, and rabbits—all made the forest a joyful experience. But we must all learn to respect the outdoors, and nature has many subtle ways of gaining that respect. She taught me at the tender age of ten.

3 It was a spectacular October Saturday, with a gentle nip in the air that only October Saturdays can have. The sky was a delicate blue that made a perfect backdrop for the explosion of autumn golds, reds, and yellows ablaze in the treetops. I was in the woods with my father, helping him cut wood for our winter comfort. I must admit that at that age I was not much help to my father, perhaps even a burden as he was continuously having to locate me. But the forest was in rare form, alive with a thousand playmates for me to chase—a brilliant red cardinal here, a fleet-footed rabbit slicing through the leaves there—and I was loving every minute.

4 At one point I was told to return to the car for chain-saw oil. As I strolled back into the woods, eyes alert for a new playmate, I heard a rustling to my left. It was a soft swishing

in the underbrush, like a grass skirt on an extremely agile hula dancer. Always ready for new things I jerked my head around to catch a glimpse of the cause, hoping to see a playful bunny.

5 It wasn't a rabbit. Standing six feet from my inquisitive stare were two of the largest snakes I had ever seen. They were copperheads, although that made little or no difference to me at the time, and their copper, golden, and brown hues melted into the autumn backdrop. These great reptiles were standing up off the ground like cobras, swaying to and fro to some mystic rhythm. I was frozen, not knowing whether to faint or run, too terrified to do either.

6 The snakes were weaving and swinging like two ropes attached to earth, extended upwards and oblivious to gravity, with each sway there was a rustling sound when their skins touched like suede being rubbed against itself, and their tongues flicked in rhythm with their dance.

7 Now totally white, I knew I had to do something. So I screamed. The sound of my own voice broke the mesmerizing spell which had been cast on me by the entwining reptiles and my very cold feet came alive. Green, golds, yellows, reds, and browns blurred past as I ran for my protector, Dad.

8 Later, back in Chapel Hill, a professor of zoology informed us that the snakes had been engaged in their mating ritual and that we were very lucky to witness the sight. I remember thinking that he was off his rocker.

9 Now, however, after the fear is gone, I heartily agree with him. The snakes were dangerous, it is true, but there was a majesty about them, entwined in each other, consumating their ritual of new life. That incident showed me for the first time the perilous side of nature, but even those dangerous reptiles were beautiful in their dance. From that time on I have looked at nature with respect as well as awe. Nature, in all her splendor and grace, holds many treasures for us all. We must remember, however, that in Nature's beauty there can be danger, so that we must respect the outdoors before we can truly enjoy it.

Ideas and Meaning

1. What is Gregg's point? Is it explicit or implicit?
2. After his experience seeing the snakes, how did Gregg change his mind?
3. Do you agree that he was lucky?
4. Have you had any experiences with nature that illustrate its simultaneous beauty and danger?

Development and Style

1. What concrete/specific words and phrases does Gregg use in paragraphs 2 through 7?
2. In paragraph 4, what simile does Gregg use to make the sound he heard more concrete? Is it effective? How? Why not?
3. In paragraph 6 he uses two similes, "like two ropes" and "like suede being rubbed against itself." How is each effective in creating images? To which sense or senses does each appeal?
4. Are there any places in Gregg's essay where you think he needs to be more concrete or specific? Are there any places where you would remove some of the specific details?

Andrea's Final Draft

Salt Lick Song

1 The last time I saw my Grandpa Vaunt alive was the first time, in all the twelve years that I had known him, that I felt very close to him. It was 1972—a balmy, long-shadowed day in late August, summer's soft amber end—and Michigan was beginning its transition into the season of cooler nights and browner leaves of trees. I retain a whirlwind of strong images from this day with sharp clarity. Everything seemed brighter, greener, fuller, more vivid and essential to memory.

2 The day began with a long drive down wood-lined Dean Lake Road—a narrow, winding paved lane that seemed as if it would reach the end of forever. Three canopies overhead created a filtering sunscreen on the windshield, scattering and flashing pieces of early sunlight. And rabbits were everywhere. Peter Cottontail and Beatrix Potter were there; it was Watership Down Land and rabbits were hopping, playing and cajoling all along the roadside. Nature's morning entertainment special—rockin' rabbits, happy and wild with their rightful freedom.

3 Nearing my grandfather's property, we turned onto "Shadowlane"—a dusty, gravelly road that he named himself when he built his home back in the thick Michigan woods. Indeed, it was Shadowlane; the brush was deep and full, and trees were old and enormous with great masses of dense leaves darkening the lane as if it were always dusk. I remember feeling as if I were traveling in Sherwood Forest.

4 Reaching the end of the lane, his home loomed before us, large, warm and intriguing. Its Tudor style took me back again to picture books of Old Europe with fairy-tale gingerbread structures. Pulling in the drive, I saw my Grandpa

emerge from his garden shed, rake and bucket in hand. As I watched him, I felt a nervous twinge of fear in my stomach, anxious about facing this grand stranger I both loved and respected. When he noticed our car, his drooping eyelids suddenly lifted, and young life twinkled in the eyes of the old face. He had very smiling, sincere eyes when he was happy, and he seemed genuinely happy to see us. Maybe this was because we were older, too. My grandfather wasn't too terribly fond of small children. My mother later remarked that he had patiently tolerated our earlier diapered visits and that he enjoyed us much more as older, thinking individuals. This helped me to understand why my father was an only child. I felt extra love and extra lucky for my brothers that day.

5 The day was delightful. One of the most vivid recollections I have of it was that after lunch my grandfather and I somehow ended up alone, standing side by side at a huge window that looked out onto his back acreage of field and garden. There was the salt lick.

6 The salt lick had always been a curious source of wonderment for me. It sat out in the clearing, stark white and about the size of a cinder block. I had never seen anything around it until that day my grandfather and I watched together in silence. Almost as if she knew we waited there, a timid tawny doe stepped gingerly out of the woods, her ears twitching and attentive, her haunches taut and muscular. She cautiously sniffed at the salty offering, then ventured forth a long pink tongue for a lick. Turning toward the woods, she motioned just slightly with her delicate head. A small fawn with fragile, spindly, trembling legs emerged, shy and uncertain. The doe put her nose under his ribs and nudged him, almost uplifting him, toward the salt lick. Together they stood, silent and peaceful like my grandfather and me, and licked at the white block.

7 Then my grandfather reached for me, lifted me up in his arms for a better view and, in a gentle voice older and barely audible, called me his little fawn. I felt so close to him then, and all previous fears and reservations melted away like wet salt. I wanted time to stand still, freezing the deer and us in time like a photograph. It did, in my mind, and there it hangs—a favorite mental snapshot I glance at often for comfort.

8 Another clear, captured picture of time hangs there next to it in my memory's gallery. It was later the same day and my grandfather gathered us all on the screened porch for a little night music and togetherness. He carefully lifted his mandolin from the wall pegs and comforted himself in a high fan-backed wicker chair—a rustic throne for a rustic, musical

king. Candles cast liquid orange shadows, creating movement where there was none. Outside, the blackest night whirred with chirping, clicking crickets, providing a deep, steady back-up rhythm to the mandolin's clear, harp like melody.

9 He looked prime, my grandfather did, with the old instrument cradled gently in his sensitive hands. Around the mandolin's neck, an old red silk ribbon was carefully threaded under the upper strings. That tattered piece of material held secrets.

10 While in Europe during World War I, my grandfather, then a handsome young soldier, stopped in an all-night Parisian bistro to escape the cold rain and lonely blues. Sitting alone at another table was a pretty lady of the evening, down and out because of an "uneventful" night. Sympathetic and kind-hearted as he was, my grandfather bought her a glass of rosé and proceeded to serenade the sad woman with the lovely music of his mandolin. As the hours passed, he so lifted her spirits that, when he rose to leave, she pulled a red silk ribbon from her golden hair and tied it around the mandolin's slender neck. It has been there ever since.

11 As my grandfather recounted this story while quietly strumming and frailing the strings, it kindled in me a feeling I felt so deeply it hurt. The intense love of music and romanticism was instilled in my heart that enchanted night and is growing constantly. At times I feel that's all I'll ever want or need of life.

12 My grandfather made me a dreamer that day and that night. His glistening eyes, the soft, sentimental melodies, the deer, the salt lick, the red silk ribbon, the magical Michigan air—these all lump together in my throat now, especially when I hear my own talented brother play the same mandolin. Though barely intact, the ribbon is still there holding secrets that I, overwhelmingly grateful, have the privilege of knowing. Whenever the memory chooses to surface as memories unpredictably do, my grandfather is here and there, in dreams and candlelight and sounds of music. Together we stand in silence, watching the world and the open back field, waiting for deer at the salt lick, and sharing quiet secrets.

Ideas and Meaning

1. What kind of person was Andrea's grandfather?
2. Of what importance is the anecdote about how her grandfather got the red ribbon on his mandolin? Should it be deleted from the essay? Why? Why not?
3. Why had Andrea not felt close to her grandfather before this visit when she was twelve?

4. What is Andrea's point? Is it stated explicitly or is it implicit?
5. Have you ever had an experience similar to Andrea's when you felt especially close to a relative? Like Andrea, do you retain vivid images of the occasion? What are they?

Development and Style

1. Throughout her essay Andrea has used concrete/specific words and phrases. Discuss the effectiveness of each example, from paragraphs 1 through 12.
2. In her first paragraph Andrea uses the metaphor "a whirlwind of strong images." To which sense or senses does this metaphor appeal? Is it effective? Why? Why not?
3. In paragraph 8 Andrea uses the metaphor "memory's gallery." How is this metaphor effective and appropriate to her context? To which sense does it appeal? Is it trite?
4. Are there any places that you think Andrea needs more concrete/specific detail? Is there any such detail that you would omit? What and why?

You should keep in mind that these were Gregg's and Andrea's *final* drafts, not their first, second, or even third, perhaps. Frieda also wrote a very successful, concrete essay, and you can see how it evolved from first to final draft as you write your own composition. Frieda's freewritten first draft follows.

Frieda's First Draft

I can't remember the exact year of this flood, but it seems that I was nine or ten at the time. I was with my family, visiting my grandparents up in Laceyville, Pennsylvania. The mountains up there have always seemed to have a certain age or maturity that I don't associate with mountains in Virginia and North Carolina. The trees are thicker, the cliffs seem higher, and the animals more apparent. Everywhere you go, the remnants of a past life are apparent—arrowheads, old Indian dwellings, etc. But, while age may make things wiser, it doesn't make them invulnerable. It was during this year that water buried the entire northern section of the state, leaving only the tips of mountains gasping for air.

My sister and I stood with our faces and hands pressed to the glass of grandma's front parlor. Everything on the other side of the window pane was a dark gray color with absolutely no promise of ever being blue again. The rain began as a trickle, bunches of tiny little drops forming mists of water all through the air. The water drops got bigger and bigger, until I believed I had never seen a raindrop quite that large.

The rain continued unceasingly for a few days. An amazing

thing happened on about the third night of the heavy rains. My grandfather went out to the porch with his big spotlight and illuminated the yard and there were about six deer out there. They were moving slowly through the rain, I imagine heading for higher ground. There was no panic here—they just went. The next few mornings all sorts of animals showed up on the front and back porches of the house.

As each hour went by on the last night of our occupation of the house, the water reached eagerly for the front steps. Its such a feeling of helplessness to see this happening and know that nothing can stop it. We moved all the furniture to the upper floors and once it was out, I felt I knew why it didn't want to go. The empty rooms weren't just empty—they were shockingly empty. It knew and we knew that we were going perhaps for the last time. As if to confirm this, I looked outside again and saw a clear, bright light moving toward the house. It was dad coming up in a rowboat through the front yard. His arrival was our departure, and we went slowly out the back and up the mountain where the deer had gone.

As you can see, Frieda does not yet have a point, although she does have a focus. After she and her groupmates had helped each other choose a subject, they reread their chosen drafts and helped each other further by suggesting where more concrete or specific detail was needed. They also pointed out where a metaphor or a simile might be used to advantage, and they questioned each other about what their points might be. Between this draft and the next Frieda concentrated on adding concrete/specific detail, and she also discovered a point she wanted to make. Revising and editing her own writing, she wrote two drafts before preparing the following draft.

Frieda's Revised Draft for In-Class Criticism

title?
good

1 I can't remember the exact year of the flood, but it seems that I was about eleven years old at the time, and when I said jump, all the world jumped. I was probably very happy then because I knew that I, my family, and every other human being was in control of the situation. Well, the flood smashed straight through that fallacy and left me trembling on the wayside.

2 Whenever I think of Laceyville, Pennsylvania, I think of the huge mountains and the Susquehanna River. The mountains form a jagged, indomitable relief against the sky, and I rest assured that when everything else is gone, those old coal mountains will still stand. They rise above everything, and rolling and gurgling through everything is the Susquehanna River. Its a wide river, its deep, and its full of life. The river and

Don't you mean the contraction it's for it is?

How did they, both provide "food, fun, and peace"? Could you give some examples?

good image

good clear image

what things? Could you name some specific items?

?

What do you mean here?

Was the light their eyes? (

good image

Could you add some description of those animals?

What specific items? furniture is a general word

mountain have been <u>providers of food, fun and peace</u> for the folks in Laceyville for a long, long time. More than likely, they will continue to do so for a long, long time to come.

3 Time seemed to stand still as my sister and I stood with our faces and hands pressed to the glass on grandma's parlor. Grandma stood back away from the glass and watched from behind me. Everything on the other side of that window pane was a dark gray color. It was a <u>gray like dead earthworms,</u> and it was a gray with absolutely no promise of ever being blue again. I looked over at Grandma and she seemed to have become a mirror of what lay outside. Her hair was gray, her skin was gray, and even her expression was gray. She'd seen all this before; she knew what it meant; I didn't. I glanced over at my sister who was nine at the time, and <u>her blond hair contrasted sharply with the misty</u> grayness outside; her pink cheeks looked unnaturally healthy. I followed her widened eyes back out the window to the bunches of tiny little drops, water reflecting water, all through the air. The drops got bigger and bigger, like a rolling snowball, and they gradually took over our world like a raging fire. But there was no cold or hot—only that awful in-between grayness.

4 On the third night of the heavy downpour, an amazing thing happened. My grandfather went out to the porch to get <u>some things,</u> and when he turned on the outside light, <u>tiny sparkles began to come up</u> from the yard. It was like watching fireflies as they float about in the night air; and then I realized, no, it was more like a cat's eyes when headlights find them—those beautifully clear marbles that glow in the light, and mysteriously move about of their own accord. Grandpa got his spotlight and illuminated the yard, and we discovered that there were about six deer out there. They were moving slowly through the rain, I imagine heading for higher ground. <u>They drifted like spectres</u> in the darkness and managed to keep the same pace while trudging up the mountain. There was no panic here—they just did it. The next few mornings were to hold similar scenes, as all sorts of animals showed up on the front and back porches of the house. <u>Tiny mice, possums, chipmunks, squirrels, rabbits</u>—they were all huddled on the porches, forgetting that in any other situation, some would have been meals to others.

5 As each hour went by on our last night there, the water reached eagerly for the front steps. The Susquehanna overflowed her banks, lashed out at the mountains, and roared through the valley. <u>Its</u> such a feeling of helplessness to see this happening and know that nothing can stop it. We moved all the <u>furniture</u> to the upper floors, and it was like moving pieces of lead—none of it wanted to go. Once the furniture was out, I felt I knew why it didn't want to go. The empty rooms

weren't just empty. There was a silence and stillness that awakened in me a feeling of desperation. This was how the house would look if no one lived there. It knew, and we knew, that we were going—perhaps for the last time.

6 As it turned out, it wasn't to be the last time. The house had suffered some damage, but it survived. So did I, so did my relatives. The year that only mountaintops were left <u>gasping for air</u> was the year <u>things quit jumping for me.</u> I guess I left that <u>whole notion</u> down at the house when we slowly trudged up the mountain, the way the deer had gone.

This is a very good essay. You have used some good concrete words & metaphors. I particularly like "gray as dead earthworms."

good
What do you mean? This phrase usually means that things quit being very lively. Don't you mean something else?

What notion?

Critical Analysis

As you see, her reader has noted that Frieda needs a title for her final draft. You will discover that sometimes a good title comes automatically, whereas at other times, finding a title poses quite a problem. In general, a good title is short, suggestive of content, and arresting. Besides needing a title Frieda needs to add some concrete, specific details here and there and some examples. In paragraph 2 she needs examples of the food, fun, and peace that the mountains and rivers provided. In paragraph 4 she needs to clarify what she means in the sentence "tiny sparkles began coming up from the yard." And at the end of that paragraph she could add some concrete adjectives to give a more vivid picture of the animals that came to the porches. In paragraph 5 she needs to replace the general noun *furniture* with specific items, and finally, in the last paragraph, Frieda's sentence "things quit jumping for me" is unclear. Even though we know what she means because of what she wrote in her first paragraph, we are puzzled at first since the idomatic sentence "things quit jumping" means that things were no longer lively. Last, in this paragraph, Frieda needs to clarify what she means by "that whole notion." From beginning to end, Frieda's classmate has offered her some very helpful suggestions for revision.

Learning to Criticize Writing

There are many ways that you can criticize each other's essays, but no matter how you and your classmates handle it, there are several advantages to peer criticism. For one thing, reviewing*

---

* Since the terms *reviewer* and *critic, to review* and *to criticize* are synonymous, they will be used interchangeably to avoid awkwardness or unnecessary repetition.

classmates' essays will help to reinforce your understanding of whatever skill or skills you are learning or have already learned. For example, when you review the essays you are writing now, you will note when a writer needs to be more concrete or specific and when he or she might use a metaphor or a simile to advantage. Furthermore, you can point out whether or not the writer's first sentence gets the reader's attention since this is another skill that you noted in Dillard's and Walker's essays. If you criticize each other's writing for only the skills that you have learned or are learning, you will feel more competent as a critic. That is, you are not expected to criticize writing for skills you have not learned. As far as mechanics, such as spelling, punctuation, and usage, you may note such an error, and thus assume the role of editor as well, if you are certain that you are correct, but it would be best to point out only one or two at most. You want to concentrate, instead, on how well a writer shows you his subject, on how well he or she creates vivid images in the reader's mind through the use of concrete or specific words and metaphors.

Besides helping to reinforce your own understanding of certain writing skills, peer criticism allows you to collaborate, to share ideas, and to learn from each other. It also allows you as a writer to get immediate feedback from an audience. Even professional writers get ideas from their critics and editors, and any published textbook, novel, or essay has been more or less a collaborative effort involving reviewers and editors.

As critics you may find that you occasionally disagree with one another. This is both inevitable and acceptable. Even professional critics sometimes disagree. Because you are novices, the spirit in which you criticize is important: even though you know that you may give unsound advice sometimes, each of you should keep in mind that you are trying as best you can to help each other improve your writing. If you should have two readers who offer conflicting advice, you as writer must finally be the judge. Also, if you ever disagree with a peer critic's advice, follow the dictates of your own understanding or ask your instructor for guidance.

In any event, peer criticism allows you both to share and to reinforce your understanding of the writing skills you have learned.

The following is the guide that Frieda's reviewer used and that you may also find helpful.

The Critic's Guide

Note: Before you use any guide for criticism, always read an essay from beginning to end before you begin to criticize it.

1. Does the writer have a title yet? If not, suggest one if you can.
2. Does the writer's first sentence get the reader's attention? If

it could be more effective, write a query in the margin, such as "Could you think of a better beginning sentence?"

3. Are there any places in the essay where the writer needs more development of his or her ideas? If so, write in the margin, "Could you supply an example or two here?"; "Could you use more descriptive details or a metaphor here?"; "Could you use a more concrete (or specific) word here?" If you can, make suggestions, such as a metaphor that might work or a more concrete or specific word. If more descriptive details are needed, ask questions concerning the particular details that you wish you had: "color?", "How long?", "What did he look like?", and so forth.

4. What is the writer's point? If it is explicit, underline the sentence in which it is made and in the margin write "Is this your point? If the point is implicit, at the end of the essay write "Is your point that _____?" If the writer did not have a point, at the end of the essay write "What is your point? I did not get it."

5. Are there any sentences or phrases that you did not understand? If so, underline them and in the margin write "unclear" or "I don't understand."

6. At the end of the essay tell the writer what you particularly liked about his or her composition.

When you have finished your review, return the essay to the writer. Take this opportunity to explain further any suggestions you have made or to ask him or her about anything that you did not understand. Also, take this opportunity to answer any questions the writer has concerning your suggestions for revision.

Getting the Reader's Attention

Readers are hungry people. They expect hearty fare; furthermore, if the appetizers are stale, bland, or tasteless, they, like most diners, are not likely to wait around for the main course. Instead, they are more likely to leave. The main course you offer may indeed be zesty and satisfying, but a reader isn't going to stick around to find out. If you do not snare his interest in the beginning of your essay, he may quit reading.

For example, in her essay "Scorpions in Amber," Annie Dillard gets her readers' attention by making a startling statement. We are surprised that a grown-up likes to scare frogs. In "The Death of a Moth," however, Dillard begins with a sentences that arouses her readers' curiosity. We wonder why she sleeps alone with cats on her legs. On the other hand, Alice Walker gets the reader's attention by neither of these means, but, instead, by quoting her father, using a quotation that not only gets the readers' attention but also introduces the subject of her essay, Mr. Sweet. In addition, Walker's quotation arouses our curiosity about who "these children" are and who Mr. Sweet is. Her beginning sentence illustrates that a writer may use a sentence that gets the reader's attention in a number of ways.

Besides the three ways illustrated by Dillard and Walker, there are other means writers can use to interest their readers. The list that follows contains some additional methods of enticing your readers to continue reading. Some of the examples were written by the professional writers in this text. Other methods not illustrated by the professional writing in this book are exemplified by sentences from students' essays.

Methods of Getting the Reader's Attention

1. Make a startling statement:

   A couple of summers ago I was walking along the edge of the island to see what I could see in the water, and mainly to scare frogs.

   (Annie Dillard, "Scorpions in Amber")

2. Use a startling statistic:

   Nearly 85 percent of the nation's youth have experimented with drugs by the age of thirteen.

3. Make a paradoxical statement:

   To win is to lose.

4. Make a statement that arouses curiosity:

   I never learned hate at home, or shame.
   (Dick Gregory, "Pain and Growth")

5. Use a comparison:

   Working a typewriter by touch, like riding a bicycle or strolling on a path, is best done by not giving it a glancing thought.
   (Lewis Thomas, "Autonomy")

6. Use a quotation pertinent to your subject:

   "To hell with dying," my father would say. "These children want Mr. Sweet!"

   (Alice Walker, "To Hell with Dying")

7. Use a vividly descriptive statement:

   It was a moonlit August evening, filled with the ratchety calls of crickets, the whirring croon of locusts, and the raucous cacophony of tree frogs off in the distance.

8. Use a dramatic statement:

The bulky shadow up ahead, like a crouching bear, moved closer, closer still.

9. Use a command:

Stop paying attention to others and pay attention to yourself.

10. Make a statement of promise:

If you want the truth about fraternities, read on.

11. Use any short, vigorous, or pithy statement:

It is easier to see the beginnings of things, and harder to see the ends.

> (Joan Didion, "Goodbye to All That")

12. Use a short dialogue pertinent to your subject:

"Can I watch the horror movie tonight?" ten-year-old Johnny asked his mother.

"Sure," was his mother's insouciant reply.

13. Begin with an anecdote, a short tale that illustrates a point:

The other day I ran into a former classmate who had recently been released from prison. When I asked him what had happened, he replied, "Oh, the usual: dealing."

14. Use dramatic form:

The year: 1984. The place: Asheville, North Carolina. The event: The trial of a fifteen-year-old and a sixteen-year-old accused of murder by a prosecutor asking for the death penalty.

15. Ask a thought-provoking question:

Do Americans really believe that beauty is only skin deep?

Note: A rhetorical question that invites an obvious yes or no is not very effective. For example, "Do you want to be successful?" Also, using a question as a means of getting attention has been slightly overused, so try to use another method.

Sometimes a good beginning sentence will come to mind effortlessly. Other times you may need to write several sentences before you find one that works well for your particular subject, audience, and purpose. You might try several different means of getting attention before you write another draft of your essay. Frieda, for example, tried four different methods before she discovered a sentence that she liked. The following are the four sentences that Frieda composed, and as you will see in her final draft, she chose the last one.

Cascading from the skies, the rain began as tiny pinpoint drops that pierced my childhood beliefs.

Control does not stay long with people.

To lose one belief is to gain another.

The rain came and it didn't stop coming until a small bit of my world drowned beneath it.

All these sentences are good, as was the sentence that began Frieda's previous draft. Her final draft, which follows, is a successful revision with a good title that fits her content and that also interests the reader.

Frieda's Final Draft

Staying Afloat

1 The rain came and it didn't stop coming until a small bit of my world drowned beneath it. I guess I was about eleven years old at the time, and when I said jump, all the world jumped. I was probably very happy then because I knew that I, my family, and every other human being was in control of the situation. Back then, control was no mere word, it was what gave people their superiority over every other element in the universe. Well, the flood smashed straight through that fallacy and left me trembling on the wayside.

2 Whenever I think of Laceyville, Pennsylvania, I think of the huge mountains and the Susquehanna River. The mountains form a jagged, indomitable relief, black against the sky, and I rest assured that when everything else is gone, those old coal mountains will still stand. They rise above everything, and rolling and gurgling through everything is the Susquehanna River. It's a wide river, it's deep, and it's full of life—all kinds of fish, crawfish, frogs, and muskrats. The river and mountains have been providers of food, fun, and peace for the folks in Laceyville for a long, long time. From the mountains, we got rabbits, deer, quail, and dove, and from the river, there was always plenty of fish. Often we had fun in the mountains, hiking and picnicking, and many Sunday afternoons in spring and summer we spent canoeing on the river. Last, both the mountains and the river could provide serenity for a troubled mind. Even in the aftermath of the flood, we believed they would continue to provide these things for a long, long time.

3 Time seemed to stand still as my sister and I stood with faces and hands pressed to the cold, glass window panes in Grandma's parlor. Grandma stood back from the glass and watched from behind me. Everything on the other side of that

window pane was a dark gray color. It was a gray like dead earthworms, and it was a gray with absolutely no promise of ever being blue again. I looked over at Grandma, and she seemed to have become a mirror of what lay outside. Her hair was gray, her skin was gray, and even her expression was gray. She'd seen all this before; she knew what it meant. I didn't. She knew a sense of loss and utter destruction that I had no conception of. I glanced over at my nine-year-old sister, and her blonde hair contrasted sharply with the mist outside; her pink cheeks looked unnaturally healthy. I followed her widened eyes back out the window to the bunches of tiny drops, water reflecting water, all through the air. The drops got bigger and bigger, gradually taking over our world like a raging fire.

4   On the third night of the heavy downpour, an amazing thing happened. My grandfather went out to the porch, and when he turned on the outside lamps, tiny orbs of phosphorescent light floated in the air like fireflies. And then I realized that they were more like cat's eyes when headlights find them—those beautifully clear marbles that glow in the light and mysteriously move about of their own accord. Grandpa got his spotlight and illuminated the yard, and we discovered that the floating lights were the eyes of approximately six deer. They were moving slowly through the rain, heading for higher ground. Like spectres drifting in the darkness, they managed to keep the same pace while trudging up the mountain. There was no panic there—they just did it. The next few mornings were to bring similar scenes, as all sorts of animals showed up on the front and back porches of the house. Tiny mice, pale-faced possums, shivering chipmunks, red squirrels, white-tailed rabbits—all were huddled on the porches, clinging to a life raft that we ourselves would soon abandon.

5   As each hour went by on our last night there, the water reached eagerly for the front steps. The Susquehanna overflowed her banks, lashed out at the mountains, and roared through the valley. It's such a feeling of helplessness to see this happening and know that nothing can stop it. We moved the dining room table, the sofa, the overstuffed chairs—everything—to the upper floors, and it was like moving pieces of lead. None of it wanted to go. Once the furniture was out, I felt I knew why it didn't want to go. The empty rooms weren't just empty. There was a silence and stillness that awakened in me a feeling of desperation. This was how the house would look if no one lived there. It knew, and we knew, that we were going—perhaps for the last time.

6   As it turned out, it wasn't to be the last time. The house had suffered some damages, but it survived. So did I; so did my rel-

atives. The year that only the mountain tops were left gasping for air was the year I realized that the world would no longer jump at my every command. I guess I left that whole notion down at the house when we slowly trudged up the mountain, the way the deer had gone.

Proofreading: The Last Step

Although Frieda, Gregg, and Andrea have a few technical errors, which you may have noted, they all carefully proofread their final drafts and the errors they have made are the result not of overlooking them, but of misunderstanding.

First of all, when you proofread, you look for words you may have omitted as you copied from your previous draft. Secondly, you check for spelling, punctuation, and usage errors. At the end of each chapter in this text there will be a proofreading tip that explains either a punctuation or usage error commonly found in essays written by college freshmen. These tips can help you eliminate a particular punctuation or usage error from your writing, one at a time, which is probably the best way to understand and correct any such errors that you may make.

To be successful at catching omitted words or technical mistakes, you should read your essay aloud to yourself. This will help you more than if you read silently. The reason for this is that you are so familiar with your text from having drafted it several times that if you read silently, you may overlook errors. The tape in your mind plays on and you don't pay attention, whereas if you must articulate each word, reading from the text, you will be more likely to notice omissions, misspellings, and faulty punctuation. Many times when students read their essays aloud in class, they correct errors that they hadn't seen previously. If you can coax someone—a friend, roommate, or parent—into being an audience, that would be even better than reading aloud to yourself.

Even more productive is to have a classmate or a friend proof your essay a second time, after your own proofreading. Because semesters and quarters are so short, your instructor may not be able to allow a second proofreading session in class. If not, you can arrange a second proofreading on your own. You might agree to proofread a classmate's essay if he or she will proof yours a second time.

Whatever arrangement you come up with, proofreading is an important last step in the composing process. If you turn in an essay with a number of careless omissions or careless misspellings, you will give the impression that you don't care very much about your composition. Since your essay is your own creation, such carelessness is like a parent's allowing his or her child to go out into the world sloppily and haphazardly dressed.

The proofreading tip that follows explains proper use of the comma in joining two or more sentences. After you read it, as you proofread your essay, you can be on the lookout for the error known as the comma fault or the comma splice.

Proofreading Tip:
Asyndeton and the Comma Fault

Greek rhetoricians defined the omission of the conjunction where ordinarily there would be one as *asundeton.* We use the word *asyndeton* for the same kind of construction. Asyndeton is illustrated in this series of short, parallel (the repetition of the same parts of speech in the same order) sentences: "She screamed, she cried, she raged."

In addition to this permissible construction, it is also correct to use a comma between a series of independent clauses joined by a coordinate conjunction:

She screamed, she cried, and she raged. I could run, I could scream for help, or I could fight.

You probably noticed that there were two examples of this grammatical construction in Freida's last draft:

It's a wide river, it's deep, and it's full of life—all kinds of fish, crawfish, frogs, and muskrats.

Her hair was gray, her skin was gray, and even her expression was gray.

In this last series of independent clauses, Frieda could also have used asyndeton effectively:

Her hair was gray, her skin was gray, even her expression was gray.

Even though *asyndeton* is not only permissible but preferable in constructions using short, parallel sentences, separating two sentences with only a comma is not permissible when the sentences are long or when there are internal commas in one or both sentences. In these cases, misreading is often the result, and the use of a comma in such a construction is called a *comma fault* or *comma splice.*

In Gregg's essay you may have noticed a comma fault, because it probably caused you to misread his sentences at first:

The snakes were weaving and swinging like two ropes attached to earth, extended upwards and oblivious to gravity, with each sway there was a rustling sound when their skins touched, like suede being rubbed against itself, and their forked tongues flicked in rhythm with their dance.

Gregg has four options that he can use to correct his comma fault: He can add a coordinate conjunction (*and, but, or, nor, for, so, yet*) after his comma, or he can replace the comma with a period, a semicolon, or a colon. Since Gregg has already used the coordinate conjunction *and* to join his last two independent clauses, he would not want to use another one. Stringing independent clauses together with a coordinate conjunction is a stylistic feature of grade-school children's writing. Of the three options remaining to Gregg— the colon, the semicolon, and the period—usually one will be preferable, depending upon the relationship between the two sentences. The colon is used between two sentences when the second is an effect or a consequence of the first; when the second restates or interprets the first; or when the second is in apposition to a word in the first. The following three pairs of sentences illustrate each of these three relationships.

Jason's mother was elected to the board of trustees: his father was ecstatic. (consequence)

It rained during the entire four-hour trip home: all in all, it was a gloomy, exhausting day. (interpretation)

When I was seven I learned the truth: my father was not infallible. (apposition)

As you can see, the colon is another option that Gregg cannot use, because his second sentence is not related to the first in any one of these three ways.

The two options now remaining are the semicolon, which is used between two closely related sentences, and the period, which is used to cause a definite break or to separate sentences not very closely related. Following are Gregg's sentences using each of these two options.

The snakes were weaving and swinging like two ropes attached to earth, extended upwards and oblivious to gravity; with each sway, there was a rustling sound when their skins touched, like suede being rubbed against itself, and their forked tongues flicked in rhythm with their dance.

The snakes were weaving and swinging like two ropes attached to earth, extended upwards and oblivious to gravity.
With each sway, there was a rustling sound when their skins
touched, like suede being rubbed against itself, and their
forked tongues flicked in rhythm with their dance.

If you analyze the effect of each mark, you see that the period
provides a longer and more definite break between the two sentences. Because of the length of Gregg's sentences, the period is
probably better. However, since they are closely related sentences, if they were shorter, the semicolon would work as well or
perhaps even better. When writers choose among options, the determining factor is always the entire writing context—subject, audience, purpose, and the effect the writer wants.

Here is another example from Joan's writing. Which option
would you choose to correct her comma fault?

When I first came to school, I was so lonely that I almost left,
I didn't know a soul here.

Even though we do not know the context of Joan's sentences
or her purpose, through analysis we can eliminate three of her
four options—the coordinate conjunction, the colon, and the period. Let's see why. Since the relationship between Joan's two
sentences is causal, the conjunction *for,* meaning "because," is
the only one she can use.

When I first came to school, I was so lonely that I almost left,
for I didn't know a soul here.

There are two reasons this option does not work well: The sentence is rather long, and it sounds unnatural because the conjunction *for* is commonly used in more formal contexts. With the colon, I think you will readily see the problem:

When I first came to school, I was so lonely that I almost left:
I didn't know a soul here.

As you have learned, the colon is used between two sentences
that follow a logical cause/effect sequence. Therefore, the colon
does not work here because the second sentence is a *cause,* not
an *effect* of the first one. The last mark that will not work well
for Joan is the period, which is used between sentences that are
not closely related.

When I first came to school, I was so lonely that I almost left. I
didn't know a soul here.

With these three options eliminated, Joan has but one left—the semicolon.

When I first came to school, I was so lonely that I almost left; I didn't know a soul here.

In both Joan's and Gregg's sentences, you have seen that usually one of the four options for correcting a comma fault will be superior to the other three.

In the exercise that follows, you can practice what you have learned about asyndeton and the comma fault.

Exercise: Recognizing and Correcting the Comma Fault

In the space provided, correct Lori's comma fault in the following sentence by using all four options. Then, put a checkmark by the option you prefer, and write the reason for your choice.

Most people go to these other towns to grocery shop too, just try buying a bottle of table wine in Grifton.

Now, read the sentences that follow and determine whether or not the use of the comma to separate independent clauses is acceptable. If it is not, rewrite the sentence in the space provided.

1. Jacob is an education major with a minor in English, after he gets his degree, he will travel to Rome, Italy.

2. The box fell, the lid flew open, and out spilled hundreds of quarters.

3. When Alicia was in sixth grade, she sprained her ankle, in the seventh grade, she broke her arm.

4. Last summer several students toured Spain, Italy, and Portugal, when they came home in August, each of them had journals filled with memorable experiences.

5. Bill felt lost, he felt alone, but he felt no fear.

6. In time I came to realize that suffering brings growth, it took a long time, however, for me to come to this realization.

7. I felt truly alive, I was happy, and I was satisfied.

8. When I first came to college, I was lonely, I was even thinking of going back home.

9. I decided to visit Jody and talk over our problems, if I had known how she was going to react, I never would have gone.

10. I could hit the ball, I could place it, and I could serve—all after only four lessons.

The separation of long sentences with only a comma results in a lack of clarity and should be avoided. Using a comma without a conjunction is not only permissible but preferable, however, when separating short, parallel sentences. As you proofread your essay, make sure that you have not used a comma alone between two or more sentences, unless those sentences are short and closely related.

Suggestions for Further Writing

Note: *For the following writing assignments and for all those in subsequent chapters, assume that your classmates are your audience unless either your instructor or the particular assignment specifies another one. You may, of course, specify a particular audience of your own choosing.*

1. From your own experience, describe a time you were a witness to nature's cruelty.

2. From your experience, describe one or more examples of the beauty to be found in nature.

3. Write an essay about a particular time, perhaps the first time, when you felt especially close to someone, a relative or a friend.

4. Write an essay describing the death of one of nature's creatures that you happened to see.

5. Write about a person other than a relative who was particularly important in your life as you grew up.

6. Write about a time that you were in danger as a result of the forces of nature or of one or more of her creatures.

7. Describe a favorite activity you enjoy in nature, such as Dillard's scaring frogs or reading beneath trees by candlelight.

8. Write about a time you were with someone you know well whom you fear or feel uncomfortable with.

9. Write an essay about why you no longer have a belief that you used to have. Use examples as well as concrete/specific details to help clarify your general statements.

10. Write an essay about why you believe or do not believe that "time heals all wounds." Use examples as well as concrete/specific details to help clarify your generalizations.

11. Describe a time when you or someone you know was harmed by the prejudice of others. This may be an illustration of racism, sexism, or any other prejudice people have.

12. Write an essay telling why you believe or do not believe that "wisdom comes with age." Use examples as well as concrete/specific details to help clarify your general statements.

13. Write an essay about a prejudice that you have, and tell why you have it. Use examples in addition to concrete/specific details to help clarify your generalizations.

14. Write about a prejudice you had, but no longer have. Tell how or why you came to lose this prejudice. Besides concrete/specific details, use examples to help clarify your general statements.

15. Write a letter to Dillard about one of her essays or to Walker about hers, telling the writer about your reactions to her essay. You may want to ask questions about her writing or about something you did not understand.

16. Suppose that you were asked to judge a literary contest in which Frieda's, Gregg's, and Andrea's essays were entered. Which composition would you judge superior to the other two? Based on what you know about good writing, write why you chose the essay you did.

Reading and Writing About Language

Using the Power of Language

4

Denotation and Connotation

No doubt you can recall at least one time in your life when you shouted defensively at a name-calling adversary, "Sticks and stones may break my bones, but words can never hurt me." But the truth is that words *can* hurt us, and ironically, we use this shibboleth when we have been hurt, diminished, or insulted by someone who has called us a liar, a cheat, or some other derogatory term.

Words hurt us not only because of their meanings, known as their *denotations*, but also because of the associations we make with them, known as their *connotations*. For example, if you are a person who is sure of yourself, you would prefer to be called *confident* or even *assertive* rather than *aggressive, pushy,* or *dominant*. All these adjectives have similar denotations, but the connotations of *aggressive, pushy,* and *dominant* are more negative than the connotations of *assertive* and *confident*. With the adjective *aggressive*, for instance, we associate violence or belligerence; with *pushy* we associate effusive and offensive advances, lacking propriety. With the adjective *dominant* we think of someone who insists on his or her opinions over those of others, who presides over others, diminishing their importance. On the other hand, the more positive connotations of *assertive* call to mind someone who is unafraid to voice his or her opinions, who knows what his or her convictions are and voices them. Unlike the dominant person, the assertive individual would allow others to assert themselves also. Even more positive than the connotations of *assertive*, however, are those of the adjective *confident*. Furthermore, we associate a certain calm and stability with confidence. The person who is confident has the "right stuff" to cope unruffled with the demands of the occasion at hand.

As you might surmise from this analysis of the connotations of these five adjectives, because of connotation and precise denotative differences, there are no true synonyms in our language. Instead, so-called synonyms are like twins, triplets, quadruplets, quintuplets, and so on, who, despite their similarities on the outside, are quite different, or slightly different, inside. Such duplicates may "look alike," but they have different attitudes, they produce various reactions in others, and they associate with different people. That is, synonymous words produce various degrees of positive, negative, or neutral reactions. In addition, they may be found in certain contexts and not in others. For instance, you would not want to use the verb *stroll* in this context: "The wounded soldier *strolled* through the battlefield amongst the dead bodies of hundreds of comrades." Meaning "to walk slowly," the verb *stroll* is most commonly found in contexts that imply that the person walking is enjoying his or her surroundings. Thus, lovers *stroll* hand in hand through the park; people *stroll* down the sidewalk, looking in store windows. But a wounded soldier wouldn't *stroll* through a battlefield strewn with dead bodies. He might *stumble, trudge,* or *stagger,* but he wouldn't *stroll.*

Thus, words, especially synonyms, are like people: you must get to know them, who they hang around with, and what their attitudes are, before you can properly judge them. This means that a thesaurus is a risky helpmate, at best. You get to know words through reading, through seeing them in context, through seeing the words they hang around with. Jonathan Swift, the eighteenth-century English satirist, wrote an aspiring young author that the art of writing was "putting the proper word in the proper place." Largely as a result of convention or connotation, only your first-hand acquaintance with words can help you with this difficult task.

Exercise: Synonyms and Connotation

If most of the words in our language did not have similar associations for all speakers, we could not communicate very well. As you have seen with the adjectives *confident, assertive, pushy,* and *dominant,* words have *relatively* positive or negative connotations. And, of course, some words have relatively neutral connotations, such as the nouns *chair, table,* or *eraser,* for example.

For practice, list all the synonyms you can think of for the adjective shy. *Then, put them in columns labeled* Positive, Neutral, *and* Negative. *After each word, jot down the associations you make with it. The following is a sample from Lisa's listing of synonyms for the adjective* intelligent.

Positive	**Neutral**	**Negative**
clever—like a fox; thinks of unusual solutions; witty		*sly*—smart to be up to no good; untrustworthy
		shrewd—smart to get the most from others; may cheat or lie

If you compare your lists with your classmates' lists, you will find that most of you agreed on the relatively positive, neutral, or negative connotations of the many synonyms for the adjective *shy*. You will find, too, that some of you thought of more synonyms than others did. Also, you may find that your own and others' specific associations with each word vary widely, although you have similar reactions to each word.

Connotation and Tone

In the last chapter you learned the importance of using your own voice in writing. All your life you have used your own voice when speaking to others, and, no doubt, the tone of your voice varied with the occasion. When you discovered that your sister had taken your favorite flannel shirt, your tone of voice was angry. When you were trying to convince your little brother to take out the garbage for you, it was wheedling. When you explained the causes of World War II in history class, your voice was calm and deliberate. And when you told your mother about the 100 grade you made on the chemistry exam, your voice was exultant or jubilant.

These are but a few examples of the various tones of voice you use when you speak. In writing, your choice of words helps establish your tone of voice, and although denotation plays a role, connotation is also important. In order to illustrate the importance of connotation in establishing your tone of voice, let's assume that you have an acquaintance Joel, who is outgoing and rather talkative. In addition, he is very conscientious about his studies. Joel is also slender, slightly underweight. Further, let's assume that you have invited Tonya, a friend from a nearby college, for the weekend. You have arranged a date for her with Joel. Your propose is to write Tonya a letter that describes Joel in such a way that she will be eager to meet him. Given such a purpose, you would probably write something like this:

Dear Tonya:

I can't wait for you to get here, and, boy, have I fixed you up with a great guy. Joel is his name, and he's a svelte six-footer who is very outgoing, never at a loss for words; I guess you'd call him a very fluent conversationalist. On top of all this, Joel is a dedicated student; he's nearly always on the dean's list. . . .

Here Joel's characteristics are described in words with extremely positive connotations: "svelte," "outgoing," "fluent conversationalist," and "dedicated." The tone is definitely enthusiastic. Now, let's change the situation and the purpose somewhat. Your friend Tonya is still coming for a visit, but you have recently discovered that another mutual friend has arranged a date for her with Joel, whom you do not like at all. This time your purpose is to present Joel's characteristics negatively so that Tonya will change her plans. As a result, you might write something like this:

Dear Tonya:

I can't wait for you to get here, but I'm writing because Lee told me that she'd gotten you a date with Joel Newton for Saturday night. I'm afraid I've got bad news for you. Joel is an excruciating bore. In fact, he's a garrulous, loud-mouthed bore. He thinks he knows everything. And that's because he's a bookworm. All he does when he's not showing off what he knows is study. And I mean that's all he cares about—grades, grades, grades. But that's not all, you should see what he looks like—cadaverous. I mean, he's emaciated. Six feet of nothing but bones and mouth, that's Joel.
Do anything, but get out of this date. . . .

The tone here? Definitely not enthusiastic. This letter is serious, critical, and urgent in tone. Instead of "svelte," we have "emaciated" and "cadaverous"; in place of "dedicated," we have "bookworm," and instead of "fluent conversationalist," we have "garrulous bore." If you were Tonya, after receiving this letter, you would probably waste no time phoning your friend Lee to change your plans for Saturday night.

As you have just seen in these letters, paying attention not only to the denotations of words, but to their connotations as well, helps establish your tone of voice, which conveys your attitude towards your subject and persuades your reader to adopt a similar one.

Connotation and Metaphors

Because connotations help indicate your attitude towards your subject, the connotations of the comparisons you make when using similes and metaphors determine their appropriateness. You may remember from the discussion of appropriateness in the first chapter that comparing a friend's eyes to a rat's, for example, would not be appropriate if you wished to convey a positive attitude toward your friend.

In the following list of comparisons, designate the connotations as positive or negative:

dark as a coal mine
dark as a cathedral
trees like fascist guards
trees like graceful ballerinas
smoke like wisps of angel hair
smoke trails like uncoiled serpents

Always, of course, the appropriateness or inappropriateness of any comparison depends upon what the writer's purpose is and upon the attitude he wishes to convey. In his novel *Hard Times*, Charles Dickens used a metaphor similar to the last one just cited because he wanted to convey the evil of industrialization. This is how he described Coketown:

It was a town of machinery and tall chimneys, out of which interminable *serpents of smoke* trailed themselves forever and ever, and *never got uncoiled.* (emphasis added)

Connotation: Advertising and Propaganda

Because the connotations of words convey writers' attitudes towards their subjects and therefore have the power to influence their readers to adopt a similar attitude, advertisers and politicians have used the powerful persuasive force of connotation to help them sell their products or ideologies. Automobile manufacturers, for instance, use the power of connotation when they name a vehicle. One example is the Cougar, manufactured by Ford Motor Company. The name of this automobile suggests that it has the speed, grace, and wild, untamed glamor that we associate with the jungle animal. To emphasize the metaphor and its connotations, Ford Motor Company used ads with a cougar stretched atop the hood of the automobile.

Besides the importance connotation plays in naming commercial products of all kinds, it is very important also in advertise-

What good is a car that could make it to the next century, if you can't get past the first payment.

The new Volkswagen Jetta offers the longevity European road cars are famous for. At a price mere mortals can afford. It's sporty, roomy and as reliable as a VW. We tested it through 3.7 million miles of hell and high water. To prove its durability, we back it with our new 2-year Unlimited-mileage Protection Plan.*

Jetta. Because a car can't get you to the next city, let alone the next century, if you can't afford the car.

The new Jetta $7,995.** It's not a car. It's a Volkswagen.

Seatbelts save lives.

ment copy for these products. If you read the magazine or newspaper copy of several ads for various kinds of products, you will discover how carefully the writers have chosen words and phrases with positive connotations. In the accompanying Volkswagen advertisement (see Figure 4.1), underline the important words and phrases. What are their connotations? What are the connotations of *Jetta*, the name of the automobile? What selling point does the copy emphasize? What does the background suggest to you?

Like manufacturers who use connotation to woo consumers, politicians and demagogues have likewise employed its persuasive power. As Haig Bosmajian, a professor at the University of Washington, pointed out in the introduction to his book *The Language of Oppression*, Adolph Hitler used the persuasive power of connotation in the derogatory terms he used for the Jewish people: *bacilli, plague,* and *vermin* were a few of these terms. The associations we make with all these words are extremely negative. Through the power of association the word *vermin* reduces human beings to microscopic "worms," the image evoked in most people by the word, which is derived from the Latin adjective *verminus,* meaning "wormy," and the noun *vermi(s),* meaning "worm." Unfortunately, the political history of our civilization provides a long lesson in the use of language as a tool of oppression. In our own country, of course, we have used racist language to oppress the black man and sexist language to denigrate the female. If we call a man a "boy" or "coon," we have diminished him first to an immature male and then to an animal. If we call a woman a "chick," she is reduced to the status of a female barnyard animal, and the associations we make with the word *chicken* are brainlessness and obnoxious cackling. Further, a chicken's primary uses are to breed and to produce eggs.

Clearly, the connotation of language plays an important role in our everyday lives. We may be persuaded to buy a Jetta because of it, and, unfortunately, we employ its power when we use sexist or racist language to degrade and diminish others.

Choosing a Level of Diction

In addition to having denotations and connotations, together with degrees of specificity and concreteness, or abstraction and generality, words also have degrees of formality. That is, there are words that we label formal, such as the noun *domicile.* Less formal is the word *residence,* and even more informal is the noun *home.* Most informal are the slang expressions *digs* or *pad.* Also informal are colloquialisms, which are local or regional dialectal expressions; for example, the verb *stay* is used by some southeastern North Carolinians to mean "to live in." Thus, you will occasionally hear someone in this part of the country say, "I stay in Burgaw" to mean that he or she *lives* there.

Generally speaking, the level of diction appropriate for the real audience you have—your classmates—is the middle ground between very formal and slang, the word *home,* for example, instead of *domicile* or *residence* on the formal end of the scale and *pad* on the slang end. Your audience is the determining factor in choosing a level of diction. However, no matter who your audience is, you should never use slang or curse words unless you are quoting dialoguc.

Besides using midlevel diction, you need to be sure that you use that level consistently. Mixing levels of diction has the same effect on the ear as hitting a wrong note on the piano. And sometimes, besides being cacophonous, mixed diction can also be humorous. Therefore, unless your intent is to be funny, don't mix levels of diction. For example, suppose that you received an invitation to a wedding reception that you could not attend. Would you write a note like this?

I regret that I must decline the invitation to your bash.

Funny, as well as jarring to the ear, isn't it? The following are examples of a formal reply and a more informal, midlevel reply like one you would probably write:

Formal: I regretfully must decline the invitation to your wedding reception on October 30, 1987.

Midlevel: I am sorry that I cannot come to your wedding reception next Friday.

Diction and the Image You Convey

Since diction means "choice of words," and the words you choose convey your own, distinct writer's voice, the level of diction you use helps to formulate an image of you in your reader's mind. For instance, consider the following excerpts written by Meg and Margo, whose entire essays you will read in Chapter 14. What are the images you have of each writer? Which one uses more sophisticated words? How do these words contribute to the image you have of this writer?

Meg's Voice and Diction

Indeed, "destruction" is a very harsh term to use in order to describe the fate of my own generation. Is it, perhaps, too harsh? I don't think so. By "destruction" I don't necessarily mean that we are all going to kill ourselves physically. Maybe we will. But more specifically, we are going to kill ourselves mentally and emotionally because of our attitudes. . . .

Margo's Voice and Diction

Actually, I don't particularly care what anyone puts into his or her own body, or how they go about it. And I don't have a thing in the world against vegetarians, as long as they don't castigate me for my choice of a diet somewhat different from theirs. It's the ones who are always on the defensive, always ready to condemn others for what they see as a less than wholesome or "natural" lifestyle that rub me the wrong way.

In just these two short paragraphs Meg and Margo convey distinctly different voices, tones, and diction. As a result, your images of the two writers are also distinctly different.

Even though "what you say is what you are" to your readers, do not get uptight over the importance of word choice. For one thing, the truth is that in your everyday speech you use a more or less midlevel diction quite naturally when you converse with people whom you do not know well. Let me prove my point: You would never use slang or curse words when conversing with a salesclerk at Sears or with the dean of students, would you? You wouldn't say to a salesclerk, "This sweater's too damned tight" or to Dean Smith, "I've been bashing it too much, that's the problem." No, you would say, "This sweater's too tight" and "I think I've been partying too much." You see, slang, like jargon (the vocabulary of a particular profession or group), is used among people who belong to a particular group. On the other hand, with people outside any select groups we may belong to, all of us use more or less midlevel diction. So, you can relax. Use your own language, the words you know. And if you haven't already done so, throw out your thesaurus because the only problem you are likely to have with diction is inconsistency, which often results from choosing an unknown, sophisticated "synonym" from a thesaurus.

To summarize: Use a natural, midlevel diction in your writing and do not use slang, vulgarisms, or curse words unless they appear in dialogue. Finally, your audience determines your level of diction, but no matter which level you use, *be consistent*—unless your aim is to be humorous.

Using Connotation in Objective and Subjective Writing

When you are objective, you do not reveal either a positive or a negative attitude towards your subject. You are unbiased, and therefore you choose words with more or less neutral connotations. In subjective writing, on the other hand, you reveal your personal (subjective) feelings and attitudes. In order to find a topic for this writing assignment, make a list of persons you do not care for or places you have been that you do not like. From your listing, choose one subject and write an objective description of this person or place. Be sure to use words with more or less neutral connotations. Such an objective description would be similar to a newspaper article in which only the facts are reported. Once you have completed this unbiased description, write two others, one employing words with negative connotations, the other employing words with positive connotations. The following are Lori's three descriptions of her hometown, a small, rural community.

Lori's Objective and Subjective Descriptions of a Place

Objective Description

Grifton, North Carolina has a population of about a thousand and most of its people commute to larger towns to work. The town consists of a bank, a post office, two grocery stores, a drugstore, a dime store, and a hardware store. Grifton also has its own primary and secondary schools but the high school is combined with another town. As for religion, the town has all denominations except Catholic and Lutheran but those two can be found in Kinston which is only eleven miles away. The town is small with no crime to speak of except DWI's.

Positive Connotation

I am from a lovely little town called Grifton. Grifton is the ideal place to raise an all-American family. The elementary school is within walking distance of all the children in town. You don't have to worry about dirty old men trying to pick up your children because crime in Grifton is virtually unknown. Why, we don't even have a jailhouse.

The scenery of Grifton is beautiful. There are no dump sites or factory pollution anywhere around Grifton. All the houses in Grifton have lovely lawns that usually have flower beds. There is also a park which in the summers has recreational activities for all the kids. We also have several beautiful churches to show Grifton has deep religious roots.

There is everything necessary for everyday living right in Grifton. The town has two grocery stores right across from one another. We have a post office, dime store, hardware store, a bank, and of course a feed and fertilizer place. What is so unique about all these places is that they're on the same street and you only have to drive one place. Not only are these places conveniently located but parking is no problem at all.

Yes, for stress-free living, clean air and quiet nights Grifton is the place to be. The people are so friendly and just love to talk. If you would like the "Father Knows Best" type of life-style Grifton is the place to find it.

Negative Connotation

I am from a small dinky town called Grifton. The town is so small that it only has one stoplight and two public phones. We also have one bank with whom I would not bank if you know what I mean. As far as shopping goes there are no clothes stores unless you count the dime store. To shop you have to go to Kinston or Greenville. Most people go to these other towns to grocery shop too, just try buying a bottle of table wine in Grifton. All the wine in Grifton is corkless. We don't even have a Krogers or a Food Lion. But, no fear we do have a Piggly Wiggly and a Red and White.

If going to church isn't enough, you have to go to the larger towns for entertainment. There is not a movie theater in Grifton much less a nice restaurant or bar. Don't fret though because we do have a pool room with a jukebox of all your favorite country songs. I feel this is the reason for all those DWI's in Grifton, you have to drive fifteen miles to get drunk so you can come back to Grifton and handle the boredom. If sitting on the benches downtown on a Saturday night drunk and stoned is not your idea of fun, Grifton is not the place for you.

If you like privacy, forget it. Grifton has a healthy supply of Gossips who never get the truth exactly right. They gossip at their quilting gatherings during the week and after church on Sundays. I was really shocked when I heard that I had been in a horrible accident, but it's fun to call home and find out what a mess my life is. The gossips are really Grifton's only source of entertainment so we can't be too mean to them.

Well, that's about all I have to say about Grifton. I could tell you about the stills, the revivals and the few families of snobs but I won't bore you with all that. Besides if this gets back to the gossips they will kill me off like a soap-opera star except the murderer would probably be some dreadful venereal disease or something like that.

Lori has done a fine job maintaining a consistently objective point of view in her objective description and in consistently using words with positive or negative connotations in her other two versions. In fact, if you did not know otherwise, you certainly could not tell from her description using positive connotations that Lori does not like her hometown. It read as if it were written by the town's Chamber of Commerce (if it has one).

So that you have an idea of what you might do with descriptions of a person, you can read Gretchen's various views of a person she knows.

Gretchen's Objective and Subjective Descriptions of a Person

Objective Description

Rebecca Ann Brown is a young, white female who lives in Atlanta, Georgia. Miss Brown is approximately five feet ten inches tall and weighs around 135 pounds. Her hair is a brownish color with red highlights. Miss Brown, who will be twenty-three next month, works as a telephone switchboard operater. She is presently residing with her mother, but the green-eyed graduate of ECU aspires to become a model in the future. Miss Brown received a degree in physical education.

Positive Connotation

Becky Brown is a young outgoing twenty-three-year-old with long, flowing, bouncy auburn curls. Her soft, silky hair is a beautiful mixture of brown which is highlighted with deep, golden streaks of red. Her fair complexion is a gorgeous contrast with her dark hair, and a pair of deep green eyes speckled with blue make her picture-perfect. Becky is tall, and a set of voluptuous hips emit a sensual aura from her body as she gracefully floats into a room.

Becky has become a dedicated switchboard operator since obtaining a degree at East Carolina University. While attending ECU, Becky became involved in the activities of her school. She was an outstanding cheerleader with a bubbly personality. Becky was also popular in an elite group of fashionable students attending the university.

Because Becky is such a devoted young daughter, she lives with her mother and refuses to abandon her in her old age. She also has ambitions to become a model, and with her looks, she could be bigger than Brooke Shields.

Becky also proved that a healthy mind deserves a healthy body by obtaining a degree in physical education.

Negative Connotation

Rebecca Brown is a young, loud-mouthed woman with dry, stringy unkempt carrot-colored hair, streaked with dull mousy brown from years of chemical dyes. Her pale white, ghostly complexion produces a horrid clash with her hair, and a pair of squinty, green eyes make her looks even more ridiculous.

Rebecca's lanky body seems to wobble as she stomps into a room because of her unusually large hips.

Rebecca lucked out and snagged a cushy job as a switchboard operator because she was too lazy to pursue a career in physical education, her major. While attending college at ECU, her only ambition was to have fun. Because of this, she became a stereotypical, bubble-headed cheerleader. When she was at school, Becky hung out with a bunch of snobs with a tacky preference for pink and green preppie clothes.

Rebecca still insists upon living with her mother and being a burden because she is too spoiled even to think of getting her own place. She fantasizes about becoming a model, but with her looks, she couldn't even make the advertisements in Hustler.

Conclusion

Despite their originally negative attitudes towards their subjects, both Gretchen and Lori were remarkably successful at presenting their subjects favorably using positive connotation. Also, both writers successfully maintained an objective point of view in their first descriptions. Such objectivity is suitable not only for factual newspaper articles but also for scientific and business report writing, types of compositions that you may be required to write sometime during the course of your college career.

The only problem that you are likely to encounter with this assignment is consistency, a problem that neither Lori nor Gretchen had. That is, the objective account must be free from any subjective words or phrases, and both subjective accounts must be consistently negative or positive. For example, in her objective description, if Gretchen had written that Ms. Brown has a "cushy" job as a telephone operator, the word *cushy* would have prevented the description from being consistently objective since "cushy' is a subjective judgment. Likewise, in her description using positive connotation, Lori could not have said that Grifton was a town of "friendly gossips." No matter what the adjective preceding it may be, the word *gossips* remains a noun with negative connotations.

One last reminder before you begin writing your three descriptions: In you subjective accounts, try to be as concrete and specific as Gretchen was in her two. As you will see later on in the text, when Lori revised her negative account of Grifton to improve her coherence, she also improved her description by adding concrete, specific details she does not have in the draft just presented.

After you have completed the assignment, it would be beneficial to share your writing in small groups, choosing some good examples to be read aloud to the entire class. Just be sure that the writing you choose is consistent—that the objective description contains no subjective judgments and that the subjective descriptions contain words with consistently negative or positive connotations.

The professional writing in the next chapter will make you even more aware not only of the power of connotation but of various other uses and misuses of our language as well. As Edwin Newman once put it, "we have no more valuable possession" than our language, and, furthermore, to paraphrase the poet Czeslaw Milosz, you can leave your homeland, but never your language. That is a possession you have always.

Reading about Language: Its Uses and Misuses

5

Having become acquainted with the power of connotation, you will be introduced to various other aspects of language in the reading selections that follow.

First, in an advertisement for Marsteller, Inc., an advertising agency, the writers explore the similarity between words and people, making associations with which you may agree or disagree.

Next, in his article "How to Speak without an Accent," Melvin Maddocks calls attention to what we really lose when we lose our own particular dialects, when we try to speak like others, especially those of the media, without a regional dialect. You should be aware that the term *accent* correctly refers to the stressing of one syllable over another, so that linguists would use the term *dialect* rather than *accent* in this context. Therefore, properly speaking, one does not have an "accent" using one's own language. Instead, one speaks a dialect of his or her language. Thus, southerners speak a dialect, whereas foreigners have an "accent"—a French, German, or Polish "accent," for example.

Last, in her essay "From the Poets in the Kitchen," fiction writer Paule Marshall discusses the concrete and metaphorical language of her mother and her mother's Barbadian friends who suffered in racist America, but who triumphed and rose above their alienation through the use of their own language.

All of these writers will no doubt convey opinions with which you will agree and disagree. In any event, they discuss several aspects of language that you may not have thought about before.

MARSTELLER, INC.

The Wonderful World of Words

1 Human beings come in all sizes, a variety of color, in different ages, and with unique, complex and changing personalities.

2   So do words.

3   There are tall, skinny words and short, fat ones, and strong ones and weak ones, and boy words and girl words.

4   For instance, title, lattice, latitude, lily, tattle, Illinois and intellect are all lean and lanky. While these words get their height partly out of "t's" and "l's" and "i's", other words are tall and skinny without a lot of ascenders and descenders. Take, for example, Abraham, peninsula and ellipsis, all tall.

5   Here are some nice short-fat words: hog, yogurt, bomb, pot, bon-bon, acne, plump, sop and slobber.

6   Sometimes a word gets its size from what it means but sometimes it's just how the word sounds. Acne is a short-fat word even though pimple, with which it is associated, in a puny word.

7   Puny words are not the same as feminine words. Feminine words are such as tissue, slipper, cute, squeamish, peek, flutter, gauze and cumulus. Masculine words are like bourbon, rupture, oak, cartel, steak and socks. Words can mean the same thing and be of the opposite sex. Naked is masculine, but nude is feminine.

8   Sex isn't always a clear-cut, yes-or-no thing and there are words like that, too. On a fencing team, for instance, a man may compete with a sabre and that is definitely a masculine word. Because it is a sword of sorts, an épée is also a boy word, but you know how it is with épées.

9   Just as feminine words are not necessarily puny words, masculine words are not necessarily muscular. Muscular words are thrust, earth, girder, ingot, cask, Leo, ale, bulldozer, sledge and thug. Fullback is very muscular; quarterback is masculine but not especially muscular.

Words Have Colors, Too

10   Red: fire, passion, rape, explode, smash, murder, lightning, attack.

11   Green: moss, brook, cool, comfort, meander, solitude, hammock.

12   Black: glower, agitate, funeral, dictator, anarchy, thunder, tomb, somber, cloak.

13   Beige: unctuous, abstruse, surrender, clerk, conform, observe, float.

14   San Francisco is a red city, Cleveland is beige, Asheville is green and Buffalo is black.

15   Shout is red, persuade is green, rave is black and listen is beige.

One of the More Useful
Characteristics of Words is Their Age

16   There's youth in go, pancake, hamburger, bat, ball, frog, air, surprise, morning and tickle. Middle age brings moderate, agree,

shade, stroll and uncertain. Fragile, lavender, astringent, fern, velvet, lace, worn and Packard are old. There never was a young
Packard, not even the touring car.

17 Mostly, religion is old. Prayer, vespers, choir, Joshua, Judges,
Ruth and cathedral are all old. Once, temple was older than ca-
thedral and still is in some parts of the world, but in the United
States, temple is now fairly young.

18 Saturday, the seventh day of the week, is young, while Sunday,
the first day of the week, is old. Night is old, and so, although
more old people die in the hours of the morning just before dawn,
we call that part of the morning, incorrectly, night.

19 Some words are worried and some radiate disgusting self-con-
fidence. Pill, ulcer, twitch, itch, stomach and peek are all worried
words. Confident, smug words are like proud, major, divine, stare,
dare, ignore, demand. Joe is confident; Horace is worried.

Now about Shapes

20 For round products, round companies or round ideas use dot,
bob, melon, loquacious, hock, bubble and bald. Square words are,
for instance, box, cramp, sunk, block and even ankle. Ohio is round
but Iowa, a similar word, is square but not as square as Nebraska.
The roundest city is, of course, Oslo.

21 Some words are clearly oblong. Obscure is oblong (it is also
beige) and so are platter and meditation (which is also middle-
aged). The most oblong lake is Ontario, even more than Michigan, which is also surprisingly muscular for an oblong, though
not nearly as strong as Huron, which is more stocky. Lake
Pontchartrain is almost a straight line. Lake Como is round and
very short and fat. Lake Erie is worried.

22 Some words are shaped like Rorschach ink blots. Like drool,
plot, mediocre, involvement, liquid, amoeba and phlegm.

23 At first blush (which is young), fast words seem to come from
a common stem (which is puny). For example, dash, flash, bash
and brash are all fast words. However, ash, hash and gnash are all
slow. Flush is changing. It used to be slow, somewhat like sluice,
but it is getting faster. Both are wet words, as is Flushing, which
is really quite dry compared to New Canaan, which sounds drier
but is much wetter. Wilkinsburg, as you would expect, is dry,
square, old and light gray. But back to motion.

24 Raid, rocket, piccolo, hound, bee and rob are fast words. Guard,
drizzle, lard, cow, sloth, muck and damp are slow words. Fast
words are often young and slow words old, but not always. Hamburger is young and slow, especially when uncooked. Astringent
is old but fast. Black is old, and yellow—almost opposite on the
spectrum—is young, but orange and brown are nearly next to each
other and orange is just as young as yellow while brown is only

middle-aged. Further, purple, though darker than lavender, is not as old; however, it is much slower than violet, which is extremely fast.

25 Lavender is actually a rather hard word. Not as hard as rock, edge, point, corner, jaw, trooper, frigid or trumpet, but hard nevertheless. Lamb, lip, thud, sofa, fuzz, stuff, froth and madam are soft. Although they are the same thing, timpani are harder than kettle drums, partly because drum is a soft word (it is also fat and slow), and as pots and pans go, kettle is one of the softer.

There Is a Point to All This

26 Ours is a business of imagination. We are employed to make corporations personable, to make useful products desirable, to clarify ideas, to create friendships in the mass for our employers.

27 We have great power to do these things. We have power through art and photography and graphics and typography and all the visual elements that are part of the finished advertisement.

28 And these are great powers. Often it is true that one picture is worth ten thousand words.

29 But not necessarily worth one word.

30 It it's the *right* word.

Ideas and Meaning

1. What is the point of the Marsteller ad? If it is stated explicitly, where is it?
2. What is the purpose of the ad? Who is the audience?
3. What are the various characteristics of people that the writers claim are also characteristic of words?
4. On what bases do the writers judge words fat, skinny, feminine, masculine, and so on? With which words do you make associations that differ from those that the writers make?
5. In paragraph 7, are the writers being sexist in their labeling of feminine and masculine words? Why? Why not?
6. In paragraph 7 the writers claim that the word *naked* is masculine and the word *nude* is feminine. Do you agree or disagree? Why? Robert Graves's poem "The Naked and the Nude" follows. How are the associations Graves makes with each word similar to and different from those the writers of the ad make? How are your associations similar to or different from those Graves makes?

The Naked and the Nude

For me, the naked and the nude
(By lexicographers construed
As synonyms that should express
The same deficiency of dress

or shelter) stand as wide apart
As love from lies, or truth from art.
Lovers without reproach will gaze
On bodies naked and ablaze;
The hippocratic eye will see
In nakedness, anatomy;
And naked shines the Goddess when
She mounts her lion among men.

The nude are bold, the nude are sly
To hold each treasonable eye.
While draping by a showman's trick
Their dishabille in rhetoric,
They grin a mock-religious grin
Of scorn at those of naked skin.

The naked, therefore, who compete
Against the nude may know defeat;
Yet when they both together tread
The briary pastures of the dead,
By Gorgons with long whips pursued,
Now naked go the sometime nude!

7. How would you classify the following words according to sex? Explain the associations you make with each.

strict   ball   fluffy   boat
lenient   kitten coarse   rock
soft   tweed   car   grass
hard   linen   rocket   lawnmower

8. Why is *épée* a "boy" word, and *sabre* a masculine word?
9. Do you agree that Lake Erie is "worried"? Why? Why not?
10. Make a list of one or more words to fit each of the characteristics of words that are presented in the ad. Explain your choices.
11. Are there words you do not like? Why? Are they a particular size? Color? Age? Texture? Sex? What are their connotations?
12. What are your favorite words? Why? Do they have a color? Size? Sex? What are the connotations of each?
13. Would you agree that this essay is an effective advertisement? Why? Why not?

Development and Style

1. How do the first two sentences get the reader's attention?
2. How would you describe the writer's voice?
3. What are the connotations of the metaphor on which the article is based?
4. Which words and phrases in paragraphs 26 through 28 have positive connotations? What are the connotations of each?

5. How do the writers support their statements that words are puny, short, fat, masculine, and so on?

6. What is the effect of writing the second sentence by itself as a paragraph? Would the effect have been the same had it been written as the second sentence of the first paragraph?

7. Which words or phrases in the first sentences of paragraphs 4, 5, 6, 7, and 8 make a connection with the paragraphs preceding them?

8. What word or phrase in the first sentence of paragraph 25 makes a connection with paragraph 24? How could the connection be made stronger?

9. What would be the results if the headings in the essay were removed?

Rebecca's Two Responses

Reading Journal: "The Wonderful World of Words"
First Response

After reading "The Wonderful World of Words," I wonder about the success of Marsteller, Inc. While it's true words have the power to convey, almost at will, whatever the author wants, I think they got a little carried away in driving this point home. While I guess it could be used as a reference piece, I'm not sure I could even use it for that because I did not agree with some of their associations. Rage is definitely red in my book. Brood is black.

Words with their associations and connotations are surely important tools for every writer. They help create an atmosphere, a mood, a feeling. They paint a picture, a person, or a place. You interpret the piece as the writer wants you to. You see everything through his or her eyes.

And so it is even more important for the writer of advertisements to choose his words wisely. He has the power to sell, and how well a product sells depends on him. Unfortunately, I was not sold on this article. I think it would have been much more effective if they had chosen a different approach, one that was less boring. At any rate, the point was well taken.

Second Response

Upon reading this a second time, I was a little more tolerant of the article and able to reach beyond the mere words written on paper.

I still disagree with a lot of their associations, particularly with the tall, skinny words and the words having to do with shapes. I am assuming that their tall skinny words are categorized so because of the tall, skinny letters involved in their spelling. My association is determined by the interpretation or meaning of the word. And so I believe a lot of words and associations are relative.

My vocabulary is a lot more limited than I'd like it to be so maybe the fault lies therein. I must rely on words that I have become familiar and comfortable with, more like a friend than an acquaintance. Based on my personal observations, I daresay the general public is probably more tuned in to words that I associate with rather than some of Marsteller's associations. In fact, who edited their list? . . .

Words. Who invents them? How long are they used before they become a bona fide part of the language? Who sits on the committee that approves and rejects them?

We've come a long way from those first guttural sounds issued by the cave men and yet our speech is not quite as eloquent as in times past. I guess it's become streamlined to meet the needs of a fast-paced generation.

Now read Melvin Maddocks's humorous treatment of the results of losing one's individual dialect in order to speak "nowhere" English.

MELVIN MADDOCKS

How to Speak without an Accent

1 In England accent is the gold stripe on the sleeve, the outward sign of one's rank—or so the people with non-U accents never tire of telling us.

2 A Mayfair accent is not without its power of command in the United States either, and many a poor wretch who has mastered a Harvard accent has been lost in mid-Atlantic, pushing toward the ultimate: an Oxbridge sound.

3 But for the most part, the American ideal of speech is no accent at all. Speech, like water, should be colorless, odorless, tasteless.

4 The final compliment to be paid an American is: "I can't tell where you come from."

5 Or even: "You sound as if you come from nowhere at all."

6 Unispeech—could anything be more democratic? The stuff that TV announcers are made of.

7 Alas, in certain parts of the country speech is still pungent, unmistakable. Immigrants to California, where unispeech is a passion if not a prejudice, can be in trouble if they bear with them the stigmata of old-country speech—a Georgia drawl or perhaps a severe case of Beacon Hill nasals.

8 What to do if "Boston" come out "Bahston" or terminal g's keep goin' away?

9 There is now, it seems, an industry in California made up of "accent therapists" who will meet you at the border of Los Angeles and erase the identifying East Coast curse. With tapes and enough electronic gadgetry to make a Len Deighton novel look primitive, these accent-washers will launder the last regional color out of your mouth, or your foreign currency back.

10 One of them, Dr. Morton Cooper, has dramatized the social service rendered: "There was this fellow from New York with a heavy accent. People reacted to him like he was someone to be suspicious of. He lived all his life like this until one day he walked in and said, 'I want you to change this. I can afford therapy, and I want you to help me.' "

11 Well, sir, accent or no accent, these were the words Dr. Cooper wanted to hear, and a couple of months and a couple of thousand dollars later the New York toad turned into a California prince, speaking perfect jewels of nowhere English.

12 "An accent stamps you," Dr. Cooper argues. "We give greater acceptability."

13 A lot of amateur sociologists might growl glibly that the table grape, not to mention white bread, has been given "greater acceptability" too by packaging in plastic—after removing the flavor. But Dr. Cooper speaks of the "pain" felt by the person who speaks differently, and we are not prepared to sneer "1984!" in the face of that.

14 Still, a nightmarish Orwellian fantasy does haunt us. After a year, two years, maybe five, the ex-New Yorker, the Prince of Nowhere wakes up, bends over his swimming pool before his morning dip, and, as usual, recites: "The rains in Spain fall mainly in the plains—and certainly not in southern California." The words ring as true as the readout from a computer—flawlessly neutral.

15 But, for the first time, our hero takes no pleasure in being, verbally, the Invisible Man. On the contrary, he suddenly feels as if part of himself is missing. He has had his plastic surgery, and now, perversely, he longs for that old crook-nose, snaggletooth look.

16 The man-without-an-accent takes up his homeless post at gas stations along the California border, waiting for another immigrant to roll in from the Bronx or Brooklyn and sing out for a quart of "erl."

17 The new "pain" grows worse than the old.

18 Then one day the answer hits our ever-so-ex-New Yorker. He buys back his deprogramming tapes from his old therapist and starts playing them in reverse.

19 What music! Bit by bit, he regains his original accent, and maybe a little more.

20 Soon he is helping others do the same—a "counter-accent therapist." Next, native-born Californians are flocking to him with

their thousands of dollars, begging to be taught how to pronounce "bird" as "boid."

21 All right, all right. Our fantasies have a way of going too far. But so do American fads.

22 In any case, for the moment we're standing pat. Thanks all the same, Dr. Cooper, but we'd fill up the holes in our wormwood furniture before we'd give up the r-r-r we choose to pronounce at the end of the word "idea."

Ideas and Meaning

1. What is Maddocks's point? If it is explicit, where is it?
2. Who is his audience? What is his purpose?
3. What is Maddocks criticizing? The speech of television and radio announcers? Accent therapists? The desire to speak "nowhere" English?
4. How does your speech reflect your identity? If you were to lose your dialect or certain expressions you use, how would you feel? Would you feel invisible? Explain.
5. In paragraph 10, Maddocks implies that we suspect people with accents or dialects different from our own. In your experience, is this true or not? Explain.
6. Are there any dialects or accents that you do not like? Explain.
7. Do you react negatively or positively to foreign speakers of English? Explain.
8. In paragraph 3, Maddocks compares unispeech to water—colorless, odorless, and tasteless. Is this an effective analogy? Why? Why not?
9. How could Dr. Cooper's first name be symbolic? (Hint: Look up the words *mortuary* and *mortician*.)
10. How does an "accent" or a dialect stamp a person? For example, what sterotypical characteristics do you associate with the following: a southern dialect, Yiddish, a Boston dialect, a German accent, an Italian accent, a French accent, a British accent?
11. In a recent Associated Press article Marcus Eliason quoted the British actor Peter Bowles, who said that " 'part of him wished that he had kept his Nottingham brogue' " because he felt that " 'the backbone of my identity had been interfered with.' " And in an article about black English, James Baldwin wrote that "[language] is the most vivid and crucial key to identity: It reveals the private identity, and connects one with, or divorces one from, the larger, public, or communal identity." How do both Bowles and Baldwin support Maddocks's point?
12. As Maddocks states, the way a person speaks still indicates

social rank in Britain. What indicates social status in America?

13. Did this article affect your opinion of your own or other people's dialects? Explain.
14. Would you go to an "accent therapist" to lost your dialect? Why? Why not?

Development and Style

1. How does Maddocks get the reader's attention?
2. What is his tone?
3. Point out the concrete/specific words and phrases in Maddocks's article.
4. Point out the various metaphors Mattocks uses. How are they effective? What are the connotations of each?
5. What are the effects of the intentional fragments written alone as paragraphs 5 and 8?
6. In paragraph 6, what is the effect of Maddocks's use of a question and answer?
7. In paragraph 17, why did Maddocks choose to write this statement alone? Would the effect be the same if it were written as the first sentence of the following paragraph?
8. Which words or phrases in the first sentences of paragraphs 9, 10, and 11 make a connection with the preceding paragraphs?
9. How does the comparison Maddocks uses in the last paragraph help emphasize his point?
10. What are the connotations of these words and phrases: "nowhere English," "unispeech," "nightmarish Orwellian fantasy," "Invisible Man"?
11. How does Maddocks's essay support the idea that language is our most valuable possession?

Kim's Two Responses

Reading Journal: "How to Speak without an Accent"
First Response

In reading "How to Speak without an Accent," I decided to read it aloud and became acutely aware of the effects of my voice on my ears. Or rather, my enunciation. Although I no longer have what I would term a true southern drawl, the accent has not been altogether eliminated. It's not something I worked long and hard at, but was something I worked on due to my heritage.

Because of the combination of being brought up in a small southern town and by a mother who was an Italian immigrant, my speech suffered somewhat and was brought to my attention early on. From this and what I could gather from watching television and my firsthand experience in the working world, I realized what a handicap a southern accent could be. A southern drawl was not exactly an enviable trait, and in fact, often led to such connotations by others (not of the southern exposure) as slow, dim-witted, backwards, and so on and so forth. People judge you not only by the way you dress, but perhaps more so by the way you talk.

I don't think definite regional accents are prevalent in larger cities anymore and wonder about the effects on the kids being raised there. I imagine the language will all soon run together into all-American anyway.

Second Response:

In reading this essay a second time, I'm reminded of the trends in accents and even language itself that have been inspired by some of the newer generations—the beatniks, the hippies, the Valley Girls. But once passing that stage in one's life, accents can become so categorizing. Even within themselves.

Here in the South, for instance, a southern accent can determine if you're of the genteel upper class or working middle class and if you're from a large city, small town, or the boonies. And in the business world, accents can make or break you. Who wants to deal with the stupid, lazy southerner, or the pushy, demanding guy from the North?

But the gap between North and South, East and West seems to be lessening as more people become aware of the effects of speech in communication. Particularly in the business world. There seems to be more of a pro-accent language here than anywhere else. And I can see the need for "unispeech" after visiting different parts of the United States. Some places are like entering a foreign country. Particularly New Orleans.

I guess the roots of our accents were buried in the earth along with those first immigrants and the areas in which they settled. It's hard to say whether we'll be able to hold onto those roots or not, especially with the technological advances in the communications field virtually opening everyone's homes to each other.

I think Maddocks is probably fighting a losing battle.

In the following essay, "From the Poets in the Kitchen," Paule Marshall relates the significant influence that the concrete, metaphorical language of her native Barbadian mother and her mother's friends had on her development as a writer. Perhaps on a third reading you might underline some of the metaphors these women used and write down the connotations of each. You might also underline the concrete/specific words and phrases that Marshall herself uses, especially in the section where she describes the library, an important place to her when she was a child.

PAULE MARSHALL

From the Poets in the Kitchen

1 Some years ago, when I was teaching a graduate seminar in fiction at Columbia University, a well-known male novelist visited my class to speak on his development as a writer. In discussing his formative years, he didn't realize it but he seriously endangered his life by remarking that women writers are luckier than those of his sex because they usually spend so much time as children around their mothers and their mothers' friends in the kitchen.

2 What did he say that for? The women students immediately forgot about being in awe of him and began readying their attack for the question and answer period later on. Even I bristled. There again was that awful image of women locked away from the world in the kitchen with only each other to talk to, and their daughters locked in with them.

3 But my guest wasn't really being sexist or trying to be provocative or even spoiling for a fight. What he meant—when he got around to examining himself more fully—was that, given the way children are (or were) raised in our society, with little girls kept closer to home and their mothers, the woman writer stands a better chance of being exposed, while growing up, to the kind of talk that goes on among women, more often than not in the kitchen; and that this experience gives her an edge over her male counterpart by instilling in her an appreciation for ordinary speech.

4 It was clear that my guest lecturer attached great importance to this, which is understandable. Common speech and the plain, workaday words that make it up are, after all, the stock in trade of some of the best fiction writers. They are the principal means by which a character in a novel or story reveals himself and gives voice sometimes to profound feelings and complex ideas about himself and the world. Perhaps the proper measure of a writer's talent is his skill in rendering everyday speech—when it is appropriate to his story—as well as his ability to tap, to exploit, the beauty, poetry and wisdom it often contains.

5 "If you say what's on your mind in the language that comes to you from your parents and your street and friends you'll probably say something beautiful." Grace Paley tells this, she says, to her students at the beginning of every writing course.

6 It's all a matter of exposure and a training of the ear for the

would-be writer in those early years of his or her apprenticeship. And, according to my guest lecturer, this training, the best of it, often takes place in as unglamorous a setting as the kitchen.

7 He didn't know it, but he was essentially describing my experience as a little girl. I grew up among poets. Now they didn't look like poets—whatever that breed is supposed to look like. Nothing about them suggested that poetry was their calling. They were just a group of ordinary housewives and mothers, my mother included, who dressed in a way (shapeless housedresses, dowdy felt hats and long, dark, solemn coats) that made it impossible for me to imagine they had ever been young.

8 Nor did they do what poets were supposed to do—spend their days in an attic room writing verses. They never put pen to paper except to write occasionally to their relatives in Barbados. "I take my pen in hand hoping these few lines will find you in health as they leave me fair for the time being," was the way their letters invariably began. Rather, their day was spent "scrubbing floor," as they described the work they did.

9 Several mornings a week these unknown bards would put an apron and a pair of old house shoes in a shopping bag and take the train or streetcar from our section of Brooklyn out to Flatbush. There, those who didn't have steady jobs would wait on certain designated corners for the white housewives in the neighborhood to come along and bargain with them over pay for a day's work cleaning their houses. This was the ritual even in the winter.

10 Later, armed with the few dollars they had earned, which in their vocabulary became "a few raw-mouth pennies," they made their way back to our neighborhood, where they would sometimes stop off to have a cup of tea or cocoa together before going home to cook dinner for their husbands and children.

11 The basement kitchen of the brownstone house where my family lived was the usual gathering place. Once inside the warm safety of its walls the women threw off the drab coats and hats, seated themselves at the large center table, drank their cups of tea or cocoa, and talked. While my sister and I sat at a smaller table over in a corner doing our homework, they talked—endlessly, passionately, poetically, and with impressive range. No subject was beyond them. True, they would indulge in the usual gossip: whose husband was running with whom, whose daughter looked slightly "in the way" (pregnant) under her bridal gown as she walked down the aisle. That sort of thing. But they also tackled the great issues of the time. They were always, for example, discussing the state of the economy. It was the mid and late 30's then, and the aftershock of the Depression, with its soup lines and suicides on Wall Street, was still being felt.

12 Some people, they declared, didn't know how to deal with ad-

versity. They didn't know that you had to "tie up your belly" (hold in the pain, that is) when things got rough and go on with life. They took their image from the bellyband that is tied around the stomach of a newborn baby to keep the navel pressed in.

13 They talked politics. Roosevelt was their hero. He had come along and rescued the country with relief and jobs, and in gratitude they christened their sons Franklin and Delano and hoped they would live up to the names.

14 If F.D.R. was their hero, Marcus Garvey was their God. The name of the fiery, Jamaican-born black nationalist of the 20's was constantly invoked around the table. For he had been their leader when they first came to the United States from the West Indies shortly after World War I. They had contributed to his organization, the United Negro Improvement Association (UNIA), out of their meager salaries, bought shares in his ill-fated Black Star Shipping Line, and at the height of the movement they had marched as members of his "nurses' brigade" in their white uniforms up Seventh Avenue in Harlem during the great Garvey Day parades. Garvey: He lived on through the power of their memories.

15 And their talk was of war and rumors of wars. They raged against World War II when it broke out in Europe, blaming it on the politicians. "It's these politicians. They're the ones always starting up all this lot of war. But what they care? It's the poor people got to suffer and mothers with their sons." If it was *their* sons, they swore they would keep them out of the Army by giving them soap to eat each day to make their hearts sound defective. Hitler? He was for them "the devil incarnate."

16 Then there was home. They reminisced often and at length about home. The old country. Barbados—or Bimshire, as they affectionately called it. The little Caribbean island in the sun they loved but had to leave. "Poor—poor but sweet" was the way they remembered it.

17 And naturally they discussed their adopted home. America came in for both good and bad marks. They lashed out at it for the racism they encountered. They took to task some of the people they worked for, especially those who gave them only a hard-boiled egg and a few spoonfuls of cottage cheese for lunch. "As if anybody can scrub floor on an egg and some cheese that don't have no taste to it!"

18 Yet although they caught H in "this man country," as they called America, it was nonetheless a place where "you could at least see your way to make a dollar." That much they acknowledged. They might even one day accumulate enough dollars, with both them and their husbands working, to buy the brownstone houses which, like my family, they were only leasing at that period. This was their consuming ambition: to "buy house" and to see children through.

19 There was no way for me to understand it at the time, but the talk that filled the kitchen those afternoons was highly functional. It served as therapy, the cheapest kind available to my mother and her friends. Not only did it help them recover from the long wait on the corner that morning and the bargaining over their labor, it restored them to a sense of themselves and reaffirmed their self-worth. Through language they were able to overcome the humiliations of the work-day.

20 But more than therapy, that freewheeling, wide-ranging, exuberant talk functioned as an outlet for the tremendous creative energy they possessed. They were women in whom the need for self-expression was strong, and since language was the only vehicle readily available to them they made of it an art form that—in keeping with the African tradition in which art and life are one— was an integral part of their lives.

21 And their talk was a refuge. They never really ceased being baffled and overwhelmed by America—its vastness, complexity and power. Its strange customs and laws. At a level beyond words they remained fearful and in awe. Their uneasiness and fear were even reflected in their attitude toward the children they had given birth to in this country. They referred to those like myself, the little Brooklyn-born Bajans (Barbadians), as "these New York children" and complained that they couldn't discipline us properly because of the laws here. "You can't beat these children as you would like, you know, because the authorities in this place will dash you in jail for them. After, all these is New York children." Not only were we different, American, we had, as they saw it, escaped their ultimate authority.

22 Confronted therefore by a world they could not encompass, which even limited their rights as parents, and at the same time finding themselves permanently separated from the world they had known, they took refuge in language. "Language is the only homeland," Czeslaw Milosz, the emigré Polish writer and Nobel Laureate, has said. This is what it became for the women at the kitchen table.

23 It served another purpose also, I suspect. My mother and her friends were after all the female counterpart of Ralph Ellison's invisible man. Indeed, you might say they suffered a triple invisibility, being black, female and foreigners. They really didn't count in American society except as a source of cheap labor. But given the kind of women they were, they couldn't tolerate the fact of their invisibility, their powerlessness. And they fought back, using the only weapon at their command: the spoken word.

24 Those late afternoon conversations on a wide range of topics were a way for them to feel they exercised some measure of control over their lives and the events that shaped them. "Soully-gal, talk yuh talk!" they were always exhorting each other. "In this

man world you got to take yuh mouth and make a gun!'' They were in control, if only verbally and if only for the two hours or so that they remained in our house.

25 For me, sitting over in the corner, being seen but not heard, which was the rule for children in those days, it wasn't only what the women talked about—the content—but the way they put things—their style. The insight, irony, wit and humor they brought to their stories and discussions and their poet's inventiveness and daring with language—which of course I could only sense but not define back then.

26 They had taken the standard English taught them in the primary schools of Barbados and transformed it into an idiom, an instrument that more adequately described them—changing around the syntax and imposing their own rhythm and accent so that the sentences were more pleasing to their ears. They added the few African sounds and words that had survived, such as the derisive suck-teeth sound and the word ''yam,'' meaning to eat. And to make it more vivid, more in keeping with their expressive quality, they brought to bear a raft of metaphors, parables, Biblical quotations, sayings and the like:

27 ''The sea ain' got no back door,'' they would say, meaning that it wasn't like a house where if there was a fire you could run out the back. Meaning that it was not to be trifled with. And meaning perhaps in a larger sense that man should treat all of nature with caution and respect.

28 ''I has read hell by heart and called every generation blessed!'' They sometimes went in for hyperbole.

29 A woman expecting a baby was never said to be pregnant. They never used that word. Rather, she was ''in the way'' or, better yet, ''tumbling big.'' ''Guess who I butt up on in the market the other day tumbling big again!''

30 And a woman with a reputation of being too free with her sexual favors was known in their book as a ''thoroughfare''—the sense of men like a steady stream of cars moving up and down the road of her life. Or she might be dubbed ''a free-bee,'' which was my favorite of the two. I liked the image it conjured up of a woman scandalous perhaps but independent, who flitted from one flower to another in a garden of male beauties, sampling their nectar, taking her pleasure at will, the roles reversed.

31 And nothing, no matter how beautiful, was ever described as simply beautiful. It was always ''beautiful-ugly'': the beautiful-ugly dress, the beautiful-ugly house, the beautiful-ugly car. Why the word ''ugly,'' I used to wonder, when the thing they were referring to was beautiful, and they knew it. Why the antonym, the contradiction, the linking of opposites? It used to puzzle me greatly as a child.

32 There is the theory in linguistics which states that the idiom

of a people, the way they use language, reflects not only the most fundamental views they hold of themselves and the world but their very conception of reality. Perhaps in using the term "beautiful-ugly" to describe nearly everything, my mother and her friends were expressing what they believed to be a fundamental dualism in life: the idea that a thing is at the same time its opposite, and that these opposites, these contradictions make up the whole. But theirs was not a Manichaean brand of dualism that sees matter, flesh, the body, as inherently evil, because they constantly addressed each other as "soully-gal"—soul: spirit; gal: the body, flesh, the visible self. And it was clear from their tone that they gave one as much weight and importance as the other. They had never heard of the mind/body split.

33 As for God, they summed up His essential attitude in a phrase. "God," they would say, "don' love ugly and He ain' stuck on pretty."

34 Using everyday speech, the simple commonplace words—but always with imagination and skill—they gave voice to the most complex ideas. Flannery O'Connor would have approved of how they made ordinary language work, as she put it, "double-time," stretching, shading, deepening its meaning. Like Joseph Conrad they were always trying to infuse new life in the "old old words worn thin . . . by . . . careless usage." And the goals of their oral art were the same as his: "to make you hear, to make you feel . . . to make you *see.*" This was their guiding esthetic.

35 By the time I was 8 or 9, I graduated from the corner of the kitchen to the neighborhood library, and thus from the spoken to the written word. The Macon Street Branch of the Brooklyn Public Library was an imposing half block long edifice of heavy gray masonry, with glass-paneled doors at the front and two tall metal torches symbolizing the light that comes of learning flanking the wide steps outside.

36 The inside was just as impressive. More steps—of pale marble with gleaming brass railings at the center and sides—led up to the circulation desk, and a great pendulum clock gazed down from the balcony stacks that faced the entrance. Usually stationed at the top of the steps like the guards outside Buckingham Palace was the custodian, a stern-faced West Indian type who for years, until I was old enough to obtain an adult card, would immediately shoo me with one hand into the Children's Room and with the other threaten me into silence, a finger to his lips. You would have thought he was the chief librarian and not just someone whose job it was to keep the brass polished and the clock wound. I put him in a story called "Barbados" years later and had terrible things happen to him at the end.

37 I was sheltered from the storm of adolescence in the Macon Street library, reading voraciously, indiscriminately, everything

from Jane Austen to Zane Grey, but with a special passion for the long, full-blown, richly detailed 18th- and 19th-century pica-resque tales: *Tom Jones. Great Expectations. Vanity Fair.*

38 But although I loved nearly everything I read and would enter fully into the lives of the characters—indeed, would cease being myself and become them—I sensed a lack after a time. Something I couldn't quite define was missing. And then one day, browsing in the poetry section, I came across a book by someone called Paul Laurence Dunbar, and opening it I found the photograph of a wistful, sad-eyed poet who to my surprise was black. I turned to a poem at random. "Little brown-baby wif spa'klin'/eyes/Come to yo' pappy an' set on his knee." Although I had a little difficulty at first with the words in dialect, the poem spoke to me as noth-ing I had read before of the closeness, the special relationship I had had with my father, who by then had become an ardent be-liever in Father Divine and gone to live in Father's "kingdom" in Harlem. Reading it helped to ease somewhat the tight knot of sorrow and longing I carried around in my chest that refused to go away. I read another poem. "Lias! Lias! Bles de Lawd!/Don' you know de day's/erbroad?/Ef you don' get up, you scamp/ Dey'll be trouble in dis camp." I laughed. It reminded me of the way my mother sometimes yelled at my sister and me to get out of bed in the mornings.

39 And another: "Seen my lady home las' night/Jump back, honey, jump back./Hel' huh han' an' sque'z it tight . . ." About love be-tween a black man and a black woman. I had never seen that written about before and it roused in me all kinds of delicious feelings and hopes.

40 And I began to search then for books and stories and poems about "The Race" (as it was put back then), about my people. While not abandoning Thackeray, Fielding, Dickens and the oth-ers, I started asking the reference librarian, who was white, for books by Negro writers, although I must admit I did so at first with a feeling of shame—the shame I and many others used to experience in those days whenever the word "Negro" or "col-ored" came up.

41 No grade school literature teacher of mine had ever mentioned Dunbar or James Weldon Johnson or Langston Hughes. I didn't know that Zora Neal Hurston existed and was busy writing and being published during those years. Nor was I made aware of peo-ple like Frederick Douglass and Harriet Tubman—their spirit and example—or the great 19th-century abolitionist and feminist So-journer Truth. There wasn't even Negro History Week when I attended P.S. 35 on Decatur Street!

42 What I needed, what all the kids—West Indian and native black American alike—with whom I grew up needed, was an equivalent of the Jewish shul, someplace where we could go after school—

the schools that were shortchanging us—and read works by those like ourselves and learn about our history.

43 It was around that time also that I began harboring the dangerous thought of someday trying to write myself. Perhaps a poem about an apple tree, although I had never seen one. Or the story of a girl who could magically transplant herself to wherever she wanted to be in the world—such as Father Divine's kingdom in Harlem. Dunbar—his dark, eloquent face, his large volume of poems—permitted me to dream that I might someday write, and with something of the power with words my mother and her friends possessed.

44 When people at readings and writers' conferences ask me who my major influences were, they are sometimes a little disappointed when I don't immediately name the usual literary giants. True, I am indebted to those writers, white and black, whom I read during my formative years and still read for instruction and pleasure. But they were preceded in my life by another set of giants whom I always acknowledge before all others: the group of women around the table long ago. They taught me my first lesson in the narrative art. They trained my ear. They set a standard of excellence. This is why the best of my work must be attributed to them; it stands as testimony to the rich legacy of language and culture they so freely passed on to me in the wordshop of the kitchen.

Ideas and Meaning

1. Why is it that Marshall gives credit to "the poets in the kitchen" for being a major influence on her development as a writer?

2. In paragraph 7, Marshall states that her mother's friends, though poets, did not "look like poets." What is your image of a poet? Give your images of both male and female poets.

3. What were the reasons these Barbadian women gathered in Marshall's home to talk at the end of a day? What purposes did the use of their language serve for these women?

4. Even though these Barbadian women were foreigners as well as victims of racism, why did they come to and remain in America?

5. Why did Marshall feel resentment toward the West Indian guard at the Macon Street Library?

6. Can you give current examples of the "beauty, poetry, and wisdom" of everyday speech?

7. To underscore the power of everyday speech, the poet Robert Frost used this metaphor: "Cut these words and they would bleed." How does this metaphor emphasize the power

of ordinary speech? What are the connotations? Name some of the Barbadian women's words and phrases that would "bleed" if cut.

8. How can you explain the truth of the Polish poet Milosz's statement that "language is the only homeland"? How was it true for Marshall's mother and her friends?

9. Besides the language of her mother's friends, what other influence on her art does Marshall acknowledge?

10. What are some expressions you use that you learned in your family and that differ from the expressions of others? Has one of your parents influenced your speech more than the other? If so, how? What are the reasons this parent has had more influence?

11. Would Marshall agree that language is our most valuable possession? Explain. Do you agree? Explain.

12. Would she agree with Maddocks's position that to lose one's individual speech is to lose a significant part of one's self identity? Explain.

Development and Style

1. How does Marshall's first sentence get your attention?

2. What is her tone? How would you describe her voice?

3. Who is her audience? What is her purpose and what is her point?

4. How does she support her contention that everyday speech can contain "poetry and wisdom"?

5. Discuss the poetry, wisdom, and connotations of the Barbadian women's expressions, beginning with a "few raw-mouth pennies" in paragraph 10.

6. How does the phrase "this man country" differ in denotation and connotation from "this man's country"?

7. How does Marshall attempt to explain the Barbadian's contradictory expression "beautiful-ugly"? From your own experience, can you think of any object or action that you would describe as "beautiful-ugly"?

8. Marshall claims that her mother's friends used language that fulfilled Conrad's aim "to make you see." Which expressions evoke images in your mind? What are these images and what are their connotations?

9. Point out the concrete/specific words Marshall uses in paragraphs 35 and 36. What are their connotations? Which words and phrases in paragraph 36 give a vivid description of the guard and indicate both his attitude toward Marshall and the reason for her resentment towards him?

10. In paragraphs 22 through 26, what are the words and phrases that tie each paragraph to the one before it?

Suzanne's Two Responses

Reading Journal: Nothing Like Grandma Lingua,
First Response

Paule Marshall's essay "From the Poets in the Kitchen" is so true in that "common speech and the plain . . . are the stock and trade of some of the best fiction writers." For example, Huckleberry Finn by Mark Twain captures the black dialect. Although I don't like reading dialects, I also believe that novels like Jane Eyre don't capture the true essence of character. I really loved the part where she mentioned conversations over the kitchen table. These conversations are very important for a prospective writer and a curious child. When I was growing up, they served as therapy for me, as well as for my mother and grandmother. At a simple kitchen table over a hot cup of coffee, I imbibed more wisdom and truth from a little old lady than I did in school or church. Those simple moments were special and so significant. My grandmother also "took refuge in her language," her biblical passages that she relayed across the table to many desperate souls. All those Bible passages and references that passed my ear like an irritating fly, I now appreciate. My grandmother is dead now. She never had the chance to shake out all the wrinkles of college life for me or help mend all my broken hearts. Though I realize she did not have a formal education, I still remember the language and style that made her one of the smartest and wisest people in the world.

Second Response:

After reading Paule Marshall's writing, I realize that if I am to write in the future, I have to be more attentive to how people talk—to their dialects. From being around my grandmother, I learned to pay attention to and to love her old expressions. My grandmother asked me every time I went to her house, "Who's your beau?" or "Who's courtin' you these days?" Hearing these out-of-date expression made me feel as if I had just entered the past. She called liquor "spirits" when she needed to get some rum to make her fantastic rum cake at Christmas. I firmly believe that beautiful language makes a beautiful person. Old words like that don't become funny to hear, they just become more respectable, especially in our society where everything is said so bluntly and crudely now. I prefer writing of the past and how people spoke then as opposed to the language now.

Conclusion

Paule Marshall would probably agree with Suzanne that education may have little to do with wisdom. Perhaps for you there was someone like Suzanne's grandmother who, though uneducated and somewhat old-fashioned in his or her speech, conveyed a great many important concepts to you. Or perhaps, like Paule Marshall, your parents or grandparents were immigrants who have given you the heritage of a second invaluable language.

Finally, even if you should disagree with Maddocks and want to lose an identifiable regional dialect or a foreign accent, surely you agree that language is our most valuable possession. And no doubt you certainly know now that even though a painting may be worth a thousand words, it is not worth even *one* word, if that word is the *right* one—"the proper word in the proper place."

Writing
About Language

Even though language may be our most valuable possession, it is probably equally true that it is the one we take most for granted. Think about it: By this time in your life, you have had many experiences with language, both good and bad. However, chances are you haven't paid much attention to them. Nevertheless, once you concentrate on your experiences with language, perhaps you can remember the difficulty a certain word posed for you when you were learning to read. When I was nine, for example, I began reading my mother's books, and I vividly remember encountering the adjective *innocent* in the first few pages of *A Tree Grows in Brooklyn,* but when I read it, in my mind I pronounced it *iň-nók-sěnt,* with the primary stress on the middle syllable. It took me a long time to realize that the written word *innocent* was a word I already knew both the pronunciation and meaning of. But because I had never seen the word in print before, I did not connect its pronunciation with its spelling.

Besides having trouble of one kind or another with certain words, we may have entirely different experiences with others. We may even "fall in love" with certain words. Maybe, like me, you can remember a favorite word or phrase that you liked to use often. When I was ten or so, I became acquainted with the adjective *gregarious* and fell in love with it, using it at every possible opportunity, and even when I properly shouldn't have. I loved the way it sounded, the way it looked on the page, and, of course, I loved its length, its sophistication. Surely anyone who could pronounce and use the word *gregarious* had truly arrived, was a full-fledged adult, I thought.

On the other hand, there are words that we do not love, that indeed we may have a particular aversion to. Perhaps you have had unpleasant experiences with one or more words or with racist language, or maybe you have a particular aversion to certain sexist words and phrases such as mine for the abbreviation *Mrs.* Or, perhaps there are a few slang terms, the meanings of which intrigue you or the connotations of which you find interesting. I am intrigued, for instance, by the connotations of *smashed* and *lit*, words that were slang for the adjective *drunk* when I was in college. Quite likely, there are some words or phrases people use that you find offensive, for one reason or another. I, for one, have a particular intolerance for the misuse of the word *ill* by some speakers of English when they use it to mean "angry" or "peevish," as in the statements, "I hope you aren't *ill* (angry) with me" or "You surely are *ill* (peevish) today, aren't you?"

Now that you think about it, your experiences with words, their meanings and their connotations, have probably been both as numerous and as varied as mine, so that you should have no trouble finding a subject to write about. The following are some suggestions to help you discover a topic—one that really excites you.

Finding a Topic

In order to explore some of your experiences with language, ones you may not have paid much attention to before, you can begin by brainstorming (listing) under various headings, writing down the experiences and ideas that come to mind. Headings you might begin with are these:

Experiences with Sexist or Racist Language
Particularly Offensive Sexist or Racist Terms
Words or Phrases I Don't Like
Words or Phrases Others Have Used to Define Me
The Language of a Group I Belong To (or Once Belonged To)
Slang Words or Phrases I Like (or Dislike)
Concrete Slang Words or Phrases
The Names of Commercial Products I Like (or Dislike)
Favorite Words or Phrases
Words I'd Like to Delete from Our Language
New Words I'd Like to Add to Our Language
Expressions I Find Interesting
Expressions Peculiar to My Region
Expressions Peculiar to My Family
Outmoded Words or Phrases I Like (or Dislike)
Ridiculous Euphemisms
Ideas in the Essays I Agree or Disagree With

Now that you have read these headings, before you begin listing, don't forget your two most valuable sources of ideas—your responses to the readings (Kim, for instance wrote about Italian expressions she used as a child that people made fun of) and your personal journal. As you look through both of these writings, jot down suitable subjects that interest you. Then, you might list ideas under all the headings just suggested, only a few that appeal to you, or others you think of. In any event, as you list, if something you write down stimulates a related idea, one off the topic of that particular heading, by all means write it down. Also, not listed here as headings are other possibilities for the topic of an essay. For example, you could write about the language of your own family, perhaps about the differences between the language of your mother and your father and about the influence of either one or both on your language, such as Kim did, an idea she got from her response to Maddocks's article.

After you have listed under several headings, these or others, put a checkmark by all the ideas you find particularly interesting. Then, from these, you might choose two or three topics for a focused freewrite. If you have a freewrite draft of more than one idea, you are more likely to discover a really good topic, using your groupmates to help you choose one over the others.

For additional ideas, you might read the following final drafts written by Bonita and Lil.

Bonita's Final Draft

Violence in Slang

1 "That's crusher!"

The first time I heard this expression I was, to say the least, perplexed. My first thought was that it meant bad news, as in "I was crushed." Wrong. After further eavesdropping I realized it meant "very good looking." What bothers me is how violence permeates our language. "Peachy-fine," but "crusher"? No way.

2 For some reason violence seems glamorous or cool. Have you ever noticed that a great number of slang terms have violent connotations? For example, the other day I was sitting in the student union trying to ignore all the babble that surrounded me. There were two male students sitting in the booth behind me rating the girls as they passed by. One girl rated "killer." Here again I said to myself, what in the world does that mean—is she so ugly her looks would kill? No, wrong again. It meant that she was a "knockout" (another violent expression).

3 All this disturbed me, not just that violent terms were used to mean nice things, but that I didn't know what they meant. I am only twenty-two, but I felt like my mother! Where was I when all these cool terms were coming about? What does a

person need to do to keep up with all this coolness? It is really getting annoying because half the time I don't know whether I'm being cutdown (violent) or complimented. If someone had called me "killer," I would have been "crushed" (also violent but with a negative meaning to fit it).

4 That day in the union I was "torn up." This expression used to mean the same thing as "crushed." Now it means "to be under the influence of alcohol or drugs." When I was in high school, almost everyone got "torn up," but could you imagine hearing this expression if you didn't know the slang meaning? Torn up! Oh, my God! What happened? Was it a car accident? "Torn up" is just as violent as "crusher" and "killer." What a gory society we are.

5 Our society is so perverted that we take something as beautiful as lovemaking and call it screwing. Now, who in his or her mind would want to screw? When I hear that word I think of two rough objects being forced together. Face it, it sounds painful. We could say lovemaking all the time, but no, not us. We are a perverted society, remember? We are too tough to make love, so we screw or bang someone to show our affections. Maybe I'm old-fashioned, but "banging" and "screwing" just don't appeal to me.

6 Violence doesn't either, and it bothers me that people today use violent-sounding terms to describe good and beautiful things. I know it sounds like I'm beating a dead horse, but our society is really into violence. Blame it on the media or whatever, but just think about all the violent-sounding terms you hear next time you accidentally eavesdrop.

Ideas and Meaning

1. Why does Bonita object to many of the current slang terms? Can you give other examples of slang expressions that are violent but have a positive meaning?

2. What does Bonita imply about the duration of slang expressions?

3. What is the difference in meaning between the slang term "crushed" and the term "crusher"? Can you think of any other slang words or phrases that have been recycled and in the process changed their meanings from negative to positive or vice versa? Are there any like "torn up" that have changed meanings but retained similar connotations?

4. What are the connotations of the following: *crusher, killer, knockout,* and *torn up?*

5. Bonita suggests that the media may be responsible for the plethora of violent slang. What are the media that she is probably referring to? Do you have any other ideas about the source or cause of the proliferation of violent slang?

6. Does it seem to you more damaging for a word like "crusher" to have a positive meaning or a negative one? Why?

Development and Style

1. How does Bonita get your attention?
2. Who is her audience and what is her purpose?
3. What is her tone? How would you describe her voice? From her voice, how do you picture Bonita?
4. What is her point?
5. How does she support her point?
6. How could Bonita have developed her point further?
7. What words with negative denotations and connotations has Bonita used to convey her attitude toward her subject?
8. Are there any words and phrases that Bonita uses with connotations inconsistent with her attitude?

Lil's Final Draft

Language of the Earth

1   On days when the world is "too much with me," I like to forget it all, sink back in my easy chair, prop up my feet, and reminisce about a tiny shrimping village known as Davis Shore (population 250) where I grew up. I like to remember the way the moon dripped between the trees and splashed puddles on Daddy's face as we sat on our front porch. I like to remember the roar and the crash of the waves as they licked the sides of our backyard dock. I like to remember the way the earth sucked my feet as I ran barefoot through the muddy marsh next to my house. I like to remember the way the shrimp boats shivered as they mowed a path through the misty morning fog of November. But most of all, I like to remember the people of the village. The old ladies who wore floppy straw hats, stooped in their gardens. The old men with snuff-tarnished tongues who rode in old pickup trucks with windshields cracked like spider webs. The muddy children who played in the middle of possum-splotched roads. These are the people who fill the pages of my journal and dance in my dreams at night. These are the people of a distant earth— an earth that pulsates through my veins and clings to my feet. These are the people of my childhood, and they are poetry in its purest sense.

2   Probably one of the most poetic aspects of the people of my hometown is their language, a mixture of British dialect, sprinkled with a coastal southern drawl. This language, known as "hightider language," is probably as foreign to most

speakers of standard American English as an African language. When I moved away from my hometown, I had to change my dialect so that people could understand me. Imagine the stares I received when I walked into a bar and said, "Drime. Walk me back. I matted her on the way, a copperhead bit me, and I ain't even had a chance to cut one in me yet." The translation of this dialectal passage is "I don't believe it. I'm taken aback. I drove my car very fast on the way here, and a policeman pulled me, and I haven't even had anything to drink yet." So, you see, the language is very different indeed. But I managed to slip in and out of it like a comfortable old jacket. When I'm back home, I put it on, but when I leave I have to pack it away with the rest of my memories so that I can communicate with others.

3 This language is poetic, not only because of its unique "foreign" aspect, but also because of its colorful terms that are concrete and very descriptive. These terms and expressions most often involve descriptions of the ocean or the weather because these two elements affect the village most directly. For example, "the clams are in the collards" is an expression which merely means that the tide is extremely high. Now, that's a mighty high tide, but sometimes it doesn't seem to be too far from the truth because of the low elevation of the land. As a matter of fact, my own garden was flooded with salt water quite a few times. I have seen water knee deep on my backporch. We were so close to the sea that our toilets even rose and fell with the tide. I'm not joking.

4 Another example of the descriptive nature of the language is the expression "the wind's rippin' the sheets." This, of course, means that a very strong wind is blowing. Imagine the sound the wind makes as it whips through a bunch of sheets hanging out to dry on a clothesline. This is a very concrete sound.

5 A common simile used in the language is the expression "like a blue crab," which means that someone has a very "ornery" disposition. Anyone who has ever had dealings with a blue crab can attest to the validity of this expression. Blue crabs aren't just ordinary crabs. They're out for blood. And they usually get it.

6 Still other examples of the colorful nature of the language are expressions such as "blow me out" (meaning to cuss me out), "come aroud the bend" (meaning I don't believe you), and "momick" (meaning to mess something up or to harrass someone). I could go on and on because there are many such expressions used in this language that can only be called "poetic."

7 All in all, this language is poetic because of its unique de-

scriptive expressions. It is a language of people. It is a language that bonds together the poor, isolated people of the village where I grew up. It is a language that has survived for ages. It is a language that will last forever. Why? Because it is a language of the earth.

Ideas and Meaning

1. Why does Lil call the dialect of Davis Shore poetic? Do you agree? Why? Why not?
2. What expressions seem to you particularly poetic? What senses do they appeal to? What are their connotations?
3. Can you give examples of the poetry in a dialect that you know?
4. What does Lil mean by "possum-splotched roads" (paragraph 1)?
5. From her translation, what do the following words and phrases mean: *drime*, "walk me back," *matted*, *copperhead*, and "cut me one"?
6. What are the connotations of *copperhead?* What is the attitude conveyed by these connotations?
7. Why does Lil believe that the dialect of Davis Shore will endure? Do you agree or disagree?
8. What reason does she imply for the uniqueness of this dialect?

Development and Style

1. Who is Lil's audience and what is her purpose?
2. What is Lil's attitude toward her subject? What is her tone? How do her attitude and voice differ from Bonita's? From her writer's voice, how do you picture Lil?
3. Despite its length, how does Lil's first sentence get the reader's attention?
4. What is Lil's point?
5. What is her primary means of support for her point?
6. Point out the words, phrases, metaphors, and similes in Lil's own writing that are concrete/specific. What are the connotations of each?
7. In the first paragraph point out the parallel phrases and sentences. What effects do they have?
8. Point out some of the words and phrases Lil uses that have positive connotations.
9. What characteristics of Lil's writing establish her own voice and style? How do these characteristics differ from the characteristics of Bonita's writing? Whose writing do you prefer? Why?

A Further Note on Rhetorical Modes

In Chapter 3 traditional rhetorical modes were defined for you, and in that chapter you were given your first writing assignment. Like the student writers' works you read in Chapter 3, your first essay was very likely a descriptive narrative, although like Dillard, you might have written exposition with description and some narration. It is also possible that you wrote a primarily descriptive essay with some narration.

In the last chapter you probably noticed that the professional writers handled their subjects on language primarily by explaining their ideas; that is, they wrote exposition. However, Paule Marshall's essay also contained some narration, and Maddocks's purpose was persuasive as well as expository.

In this chapter, like the professional writers in the last chapter and the students writers in this one, you might also write an expository essay. Nevertheless, the topic you finally choose to write about will determine the particular mode or combination of modes that you use. For example, if you choose to write about an experience you have had with sexist or racist language, your purpose will be to relate the events of this experience, and, thus, your primary purpose will be to narrate. However, if you decide to explain the meaning of a slang term or phrase, your primary purpose will be expository, although it is possible that, like Maddocks, your purpose might be to persuade as well.

As a writer, your most important consideration always is not to choose a mode or modes, but *first* to choose a topic that interests you because you have something that you truly want to say about it. Your subject and what you want to say about it will determine the mode or combination of modes most appropriate for your audience and purpose.

Audience and Purpose

Because you will be reading and criticizing each other's writing throughout the semester or quarter, it would be easier for you as a writer to continue to picture your audience as the real one you have: your classmates and your instructor. Your purpose each time way vary, as will your tone according to your attitude toward your subject. However, in any particular essay, this one or a later one, if you wish to address a specific audience different from your classmates, you may do so. If you should do this, your classmates and your instructor will no doubt be able to identify your specific audience from what you say and how you say it. For instance, in this essay, suppose you decided to criticize the euphemisms for bodily functions that parents teach their children. Parents would be your audience, but since someday most of your classmates will become parents and some may already be parents, your writing would also be of interest and value to them. In fact, there is probably no specific audience you could name that would negate the value of your essay to your classmates.

Francine's First Draft

Francine, whose various drafts you will be reading, freewrote on three topics: her family's special use of language, the language of the drug culture, and last, her experience with sexist language at work. After she had read all three drafts to her groupmates, they chose the second topic on the language of the drug culture as the one they found most interesting. Francine's first draft of her essay follows.

Second Freewrite

The circle of drug users is wide and varied. It extends from the very poor to the very rich and covers everyone in between. Drug use and abuse stretches back a long way, just as man's search for escape and pleasure goes back a long way. Because most of the "foreign substances" used for such ends are illegal, a varied and unique vocabulary has developed among users, one that reflects the need for secretness and the concentration on physical effects as well.

I remember the first time I was exposed to marijuana. People spoke of taking trips, catching a buzz, getting stoned. The drug itself was called everything from "weed" to the old stand-by "grass" to the currently popular "ganji" to pot. The various types of "bud" even have their own names: "sensi," "red man," "Columbian," "gold," "Peruvian," and on and on. Of course, for those who are economically minded, there's always "home-grown."

Take a look at some of the other words used for equipment associated with pot, hashish, opium and other drugs, and you'll begin to see that they're usually one-syllable, descriptive words, often referring to an action, sound, or even money. You go out and purchase a sack, a bag, an ounce, a dime, a nickel, a quarter, a pound, or a block (depending on how rich you are). Then you choose your equipment for the intake of the drug. If you're doing pot, you might use papers and make a doobie. Once that doobie, or joint, reaches a certain length, you'll need clips to hold it, and eventually you'll put it out and save the roach (what remains of the joint). Once you've accumulated several roaches, you can place them in a bowl (pipe) or smoke them through a bong. But, you don't just smoke this stuff—you take drags (like cigarettes), you take a toke, you take a hit. There are even interesting little wooden block pieces with great designs in which you can place your stash, called one hitters. The list goes on and on.

As time goes on and drugs bounce in and out of popularity, new terms will rise and fall. Cocaine, which has enjoyed a heyday lately in America, goes by coke and snow, and people are drawing lines and tooting them, and they're having drips, frights, and dries. Heroine is on the upswing again in London, and around the big cities here, smack has been seen in the streets a lot lately. People will be getting off on chasing the dragon. Last, lemmons, blotters, and speed will be around, and poppers will probably always exist in some bars. For those throwbacks to the sixties, if the blotters aren't enough, there's always crystal and shroomers.

For most heavy drug users, words become shorter and more to the point. Maybe they're too lethargic, burned out, or spaced out to try to come up with anything else. The group that this doesn't seem to be quite as true for are the hallucinogens. These people come up with some of the longest, most complex, weirdest words . . . or sometimes they come up with them but just can't spit them out.

All of these names for drugs that I've thought of don't even scratch the surface. There are new names for everything now, because they're always changing to avoid the law. Whether you pedal, push, or are just looking to score, you've got to know the lingo or you'll be laughed right out of the neighborhood.

Criticizing First Drafts

When all three members of Francine's group had read their three drafts and chosen one over the others, each writer read the chosen draft a second time, and the other two used the following guide to help the writer further develop and clarify his or her ideas.

The Critic's Guide for First Drafts

1. Could the writer use more concrete/specific words or descriptive detail anywhere in the draft?
2. Does the writer need examples anywhere to support general statements?
3. Is there other information you wish you had on the subject?
4. Is there a puzzling word, phrase, or sentence that the writer needs to clarify?
5. Does everything the writer says pertain to one clear focus?
6. Does the writer have a point yet? If not, discuss the possibilities, and suggest one if you can.

As you respond to these questions, tell the writer specifically where he or she needs examples, what material does not pertain to the focus, and so on. Francine's reviewers pointed out that although she does stick to her focus—the vocabulary of drug users— she is not always clear. For example, they thought that she needed to describe a bong and how it works. Her readers also suggested that Francine explain what lemmons, blotters, poppers, crystal, and shroomers are. In addition, they felt that she needed to explain the meaning of the phrases "having drips, frights, and dries" and that she needed examples of the complex, weird words used for hallucinogens. Finally, Francine's critics thought that she might make a stronger point.

After this first draft Francine wrote a second and then a third, the following one, which she prepared for a second review session in class. In this third draft Francine has developed her topic by adding more examples of the language used by the drug culture. Also, she has revised her beginning in order to get the reader's attention. Furthermore, in this draft she concludes with a more significant point, and she has a clearer organization.

Francine's Revised Draft

1 Float along on the purple haze and catch a glimpse of infinity—it's amazing to consider the doorways of the mind that come flying open when under the influence of drugs. People pass through those doorways for various reasons, including fun, escape, and necessity. Whatever the reason though, they all share a common bond—the bond of language. The drug culture seems to have developed its own vocabulary in order to remain covert to officials, to recognize who's cool and who's not, and, most important, to give easily remembered, simple names to all those complex terms.

2 Marijuana smokers are often quite mellow and seem to range in age from seven to seventy. Their intake of this drug has produced such catch phrases as "getting stoned," "getting high," "taking a trip," and "catching a buzz." All are words that describe the feeling obtained by smoking the drug, and all are fairly well known. Equally public are the terms given to the drug itself. Old standards such as "reefer" and "grass" still apply, as well as "pot," "weed," "bud," and "ganji." Some carry this even further, breaking the various types of marijuana into groups: "sensi," "red man," "Columbian," "Hawaiian," and the list goes on. For the smoker of the leaf, there's a massive amount of lingo to draw from, and the more one knows, the cooler he or she becomes.

3 The language of drugs is sometimes silent. A long time ago, I unexpectedly found myself in a car that ended up at the "tracks" of downtown Roanoke, what used to be a high drug

you need a title!

> good beginning sentence

good use of specific examples

good use of descriptive details

traffic area. The car halted at a certain stop sign, and the driver rolled down his window a tiny bit. From the corner of an old building, a small black boy's head appeared, and he stared intently at the car. The driver reached up and touched his hat once, and then waited. Disappearing, the boy reappeared within a minute's time and handed the driver a small bag. Money and bag exchanged places and we were off. I found out later that rolling down the window and touching the hat was only one of several signals used for making drug purchases. Apparently, it may be cool to use the lingo around friends and at parties, but when making serious purchases, silence is preferred.

AMOUNTS and money.

4 A lot of the words associated with the purchase of marijuana, hashish, opium, and other drugs have to do with ~~numbers.~~ People buy a <u>sack</u>, a <u>bag</u>, an <u>ounce</u>, a <u>dime</u>, a <u>nickel</u>, a <u>quarter</u>, a <u>pound</u>, a <u>block</u>, or a <u>kilo</u>, depending on how rich they are. With all the concentration on money, it's sometimes easy to forget that a lot of people claim to be escaping from the material world and all of its greed-filled charms.

Aren't these amounts not numbers? Maybe put all the measurements together, then the monetary terms

5 If a person is smoking pot, he might use papers and roll a "doobie" or a "joint." After as much of this has been smoked as possible, the remaining portion is often affectionately termed a "roach." Some throw their roaches out, but connoisseurs know better. They keep those roaches and break them up later into bowls (pipes) or bongs. Bongs come in every imaginable size, shape, and color, and most resemble wide-mouthed, upright tubes containing water through which smoke is inhaled. But bowls, bongs, and joints aren't the only instruments for smoking. There are power hitters and battery-operated face masks as well. There is even a little hollow, metal cigarette which comes in a decorative wooden case, referred to as a one-hitter.

good

I think you use a hyphen here.

6 Most words associated with drugs are short, imitations of the effect produced by the drug or its appearance, and usually easy to say. What could be more fitting? Imagine the difficulty a person under the influence or in desperate need of drugs would have saying, "I would like a hypodermic needle so that I might inject heroin into my system." It's much easier and more concrete to say, "I'm going to chase the dragon tonight—can you help me out?"

I don't see how this fits your focus

7 I have a twenty-five-year-old friend who fits in among the coolest of drug users. She counted herself among those who had given up material needs in search of something better. At least, that's how she justified stealing money from her employer to pay for her habit. One night, Linda popped a vein too soon after having done some acid, and freaked out. Her "wonderful" friends who had given up the material world and who

lived in the campground with her didn't want to be involved. The groundskeeper found her the next morning, crying beside the dumpster. During her seven-month detoxification in a hospital, I visited her three times; two times she didn't recognize me, and the third, she screamed that I had come to kill her.

8 Cool is the key, and if you know the words, "you can transfer up, down, in, or out—most anywhere. Any drug, be it dust, lemmons (quaaludes), speed, coke, crystal?, or shroomers? can provide the blast; and it only hurts if reality rears its ugly head.

I really like your Conclusion. This is a good point to make. I also like your first sentence— it really got my attention. Probably most people would think that dust is "angel dust" but I don't know what crystal and shroomers are. Mostly you are concrete and specific. It would be fun to do a paper on the connotations of some of this language, wouldn't it?

Comma fault?

> good concluding statement

I think you need to define these terms. Maybe not dust, but crystal and shroomers

Critical Analysis

Even though Francine does not yet have a title, she definitely has a better beginning sentence. Also, she has developed her topic more extensively, although her reader pointed out a lack of unity in this draft. In paragraph 7 the descriptive narrative of her friend who overdosed does not pertain to Francine's focus here. Last, in her concluding paragraph, Francine's critic asked for definitions of several terms—*dust, crystal,* and *shroomer.*

The following list provides a guide that you may use to criticize your further drafts. In this session, because your essays are more developed, you will probably find it easier and more profitable to read each other's essay and respond in the margins and at the end of the essay, as Francine's reviewer did.

Always read the essay you criticize from beginning to end before you begin writing your queries and comments in the margins and remember to begin your comment at the end with something you liked about the essay.

The Critic's Guide

1. Does the writer have a good title yet? If not, suggest one if you can.
2. How does the first sentence get the reader's attention? If it could be more effective, write this query in the margin: "Could you think of a better beginning sentence?" If you can, suggest one.

3. Is the essay unified? If not, mark any material that is off the focus and write this query in the margin: "Is this on focus?" Or you might abbreviate: "On focus?"

4. What is the writer's attitude toward the subject? What is his or her tone? Are there any words, phrases, or metaphors that have connotations inconsistent with the writer's tone or attitude toward his or her subject? If so, underline these words, phrases, or metaphors and in the margin write this query: "Are your connotations here appropriate?" Or: "Connotations?"

5. Are there any places in the essay where the writer needs more development of his or her ideas? If so, write in the margin: "Could you supply an example or two here?"; "Could you use more descriptive details or a metaphor here?"; "Could you use a more concrete (or specific) word here?" If you can, make suggestions, such as a metaphor that might work or a more concrete or specific word. If more descriptive details are needed, ask for the particular details needed: "Color?"; "How long?"; "What does it look like?"

6. Are there any sentences or phrases that you did not understand? If so, underline them and write in the margin: "? Don't understand" or "? Not clear."

7. What is the writer's point? If it is explicit, underline the thesis sentence and write in the margin: "Is this your point?" If the point is implicit, write at the end of the essay: "Is your point that _____?" If the writer did not have a point, write at the end of the essay: "What is your point? I didn't get it."

When you have finished your review, return the essay to the writer, and take this opportunity to explain further any suggestion you have made or to ask the writer any questions you may have about his or her essay. Also, take this opportunity to answer any questions the writer may have concerning your suggestions for revision.

Coherence: The Tie That Binds

You may have noticed when you read Francine's essay that there appeared to be no connection between some of her sentences and paragraphs. As readers, we need to see how one thought connects with another. We need *coherence,* a word the etymology of which means "to stick together." When writing is coherent, the sentences and paragraphs "stick together" and a reader does not have to struggle for meaning.

A coherent essay is similar to a well-knit sweater. Just as there are no holes in a perfectly knit sweater, there are no "holes" in a coherent essay, no chasms between sentences or paragraphs for a reader to leap and perhaps fall into, losing his or her way altogether. Besides a similarity in the products, there is a similarity in the processes of knitting a sweater and making an essay coherent. As you may know, when knitting, a person puts the needle through a stitch just made in order to make a new one. Thus, knitting is a process of going back before going on. That is exactly what the writer does to achieve coherence. Instead of a needle, however, the writer uses transitions, which always point back to what he or she has just said before going on to the next point. From the Latin words *trans* and *ire,* transition means "to go across." Thus, these are the bridges the writer constructs from thought to thought. If there are bridges "to go across" sentences and paragraphs, there will be no chasms for the reader to leap or fall into.

Focus and Organization: The Indispensable Binders

Because explicit transitional words or phrases merely call attention to the way two or more statements are already either logically, spatially, or chronologically related, they simply make such implicit connections more readily apparent to the reader. As a result, *no* transitional word or phrase can build a bridge between two or more ideas that simply do not relate to each other logically, spatially, or chronologically. That is, if a writer lacks focus, going from one topic to another, his or her essay is doomed to incoherence. And incoherence is fatal to an essay. Consider the following example. The focus of this writer's essay was a car accident. Look at what happens to his focus and, consequently, to his coherence in this one paragraph:

I can never forget that very warm night in June when the headlights, like two enormous cat's eyes, glowed in the dark. It was warm too, the night a year before when I had first visited my grandparents in Illinois. I remember that grandmother burned the blackberry pie she was baking and I can't remember when I've been so disappointed. But now the lights ahead were coming closer and closer.

Maybe these sentences have a connection in the writer's mind, but, unfortunately, that connection has not made it from mind to page, and thus the reader is lost—there is no focus and therefore no way to make this paragraph coherent. When lack of focus occurs in an essay, in addition to sentences, there may be entire paragraphs that veer from the writer's focus. Such deviations are readily apparent to a reader since they partially or completely destroy understanding.

Another *sine qua non* of a coherent essay is the arrangement or organization of ideas. Although organization is given thorough attention later on in Chapters 8 and 10, you need to be aware at this point that without arrangement of ideas, there is little or no coherence in an essay: in short, an unorganized essay will also be an incoherent one. Since writing skills are best learned and mastered one at a time, you should concentrate now on grasping the concept of coherence and practicing the use of explicit transitions. You can leave the important skill of organization for later. For now, you need know only that both focus and organization are essential to a coherent essay and that without both of these indispensable elements, there is no way a writer can use explicit transitional words or phrases to make his or her writing coherent.

If you should have trouble with the organization of the essay you are writing now, chances are your reviewers have either already noticed it or will notice it in your next review session. For example, if in paragraph 9 you have material that repeats, or relates to, the topics of paragraphs 3 and 4, then you have an organizational problem that your readers are sure to notice. Since a lack of either focus or organization almost or entirely destroys the clarity and readability of a text, it is doubtful that your reviewers will fail to alert you to either of these problems. However, after your next review session, if you feel uneasy or uncertain about suggestions readers have made for correction of a lack of either focus or organization (or both, since it is impossible to organize an unfocused essay), by all means, consult your instructor before you begin to revise.

The following is a list of ways you can make the implicit relationships between your ideas explicit to the reader, once you have focused and organized them.

Means of Achieving Coherence

There are various transitions a writer can use as a bridge to connect his or her thoughts, some of them built into the grammar of our language. In the following list examples come, whenever possible, from the professional essays in this chapter. Because transitions are used between two sentences or paragraphs, the examples contain two sentences: the one that illustrates the particular kind of transition and the sentence that precedes it, the one that it points back to. Italics have been added in each example to highlight the type of transition being discussed.

    I. USE TRANSITIONAL WORDS AND PHRASES.
        A. For *narrative/descriptive writing,* use transitional words and phrases that *refer to time or space: then, later, about that time, afterwards, before, before that time, before that, at that time, next, finally,*

after that, during that time, earlier, now, while, there, here, from there, from here, from that point, moving to, going from.

> Example:
> This was the ritual even in the winter.
>   *Later,* armed with the few dollars they had earned, . . . they made their way back to our neighborhood.
>   (Marshall, paragraphs 9 and 10)

B. When *listing points,* use transitional words or phrases that refer to sequence: *first, second, third, first of all, in the first place, above all, another, finally, last.*

> Example:
> I read another poem. "Lias! Lias! Bless de Lawd!" . . .
>   *And another:* "Seen my lady home las' night" . . .
>   (Marshall, paragraphs 38 and 39)

C. When a succeeding sentence or paragraph states *an additional point,* use one of these transitional words or phrases: *in addition, furthermore, also, and, another, too, similarly, likewise, moreover, besides.*

> Example:
> I had never seen that written about before and it aroused in me all kinds of delicious feelings and hopes.
>   *And* I began to search then for books and stories and poems . . . about my people.
>   (Marshall, paragraphs 39 and 40)

D. When a succeeding sentence or paragraph gives *an illustration of a point,* you may use one of these transitional words or phrases: *for example, as an example, to illustrate, as an illustration, for instance.*

> Example:
> There are tall, skinny words and short fat ones, and strong ones and weak ones, and boy words and girl words.
>   *For instance,* title, lattice, latitude, lily, tattle, Illinois and intellect arc all lean and lanky.
>   (Marsteller, Inc., paragraphs 3 and 4)

E. When a succeeding sentence or paragraph states *a contrasting point,* you may use one of the following words or phrases: *in contrast, on the contrary, however, nevertheless, yet, still, on the other hand, by contrast.*

> Example:
> But Dr. Cooper speaks of the "pain" felt by the person who speaks differently, and we are not prepared to sneer "1984!" in the face of that.
> *Still*, a nightmarish Orwellian fantasy does haunt us.
>
> (Maddocks, paragraphs 13 and 14)

F. When a succeeding sentence or paragraph *summarizes, restates,* or *states a result,* you may use one of the following words or phrases: *to sum up, to summarize, in other words, indeed, to put it another way, in fact, therefore, accordingly, as a result, consequently, so, thus.*

> Example:
> According to Melvin Maddocks we are losing our individual accents in favor of "unispeech." *Thus* we are losing part of our selves—our own language.
>
> (student essay)

II. REPEAT KEY WORDS OR PHRASES.

> Example:
> In England accent is the gold stripe on the sleeve. . . .
> A Mayfair *accent* is not without its power of command in the United States either. . . .
>
> (Maddocks, paragraphs 1 and 2)

III. USE A SYNONYM OR A VARIANT FORM OF A KEY WORD TO AVOID BEING UNNECESSARILY REPETITIVE.

> Example with synonyms:
> Perhaps . . . my mother and her friends were expressing . . . the idea that a thing is at the same time its *opposite,* and that . . . these *contradictions* make up the whole. But theirs was not a . . . brand of *dualism.* . . .
>
> (Marshall, paragraph 32)

> Example with a variant form:
> Euphemistic phrases such as "passed away" or "gone to his reward" *conceal* reality. Such *concealment* of the truth allows us to avoid facing our fears—in this case, our fear of death.
>
> (student essay)

IV. USE PERSONAL PRONOUNS, WHICH MUST REFER TO NOUNS PRECEDING THEM.

> Example:
> There was no way for me to understand it at the time, but the *talk* that filled the kitchen those afternoons was highly functional. *It* served as therapy. . . .
> (Marshall, paragraph 19)

V. USE DEMONSTRATIVE PRONOUNS OR ADJECTIVES *(THIS, THAT, THESE, THOSE, SUCH)*. When used as pronouns, these words refer to nouns preceding them. When used as adjectives, they modify a noun after them.

> Example with demonstrative pronoun:
> We have power through art and photography and graphics and typography and all the visual elements that are part of the finished advertisement.
> And *these* are great powers.
> (Marsteller, Inc., paragraphs 27 and 28)

> Example with demonstrative adjective:
> So, you see, the language is very different indeed. . . .
> *This* language is poetic. . . .
> (student essay)

VI. USE PARALLEL STRUCTURE. This is the repetition of the same parts of speech in the same order. (Because of its repetition, parallel structure will also lend emphasis to your writing.)

> Example:
> *They taught me* my first lesson in the narrative art. *They trained my ear. They set a standard* of excellence.
> (Marshall, paragraph 44)

VII. USE A WORD OR PHRASE THAT STATES THE SUBJECT OR THE IMPLIED SUBJECT OF THE PREVIOUS PARAGRAPH.

> Example:
> I could make promises to myself and to other people and there would be all the time in the world to keep them. I could stay up all night and make mistakes, and none of it would count.
> You see, I was in a *curious position* in New York: it never occurred to me that I was living a real life there.
> (Joan Didion, "Goodbye to All That," paragraphs 6 and 7)

These, then, are some of the various transitions available to you, and several of them, such as personal and demonstrative pronouns, are automatically used by speakers of English. For example, we do not write: "Mary is an excellent writer. Mary is also a good engineer." Instead we write: "Mary is an excellent writer. She is also a good engineer." Pronouns must refer to an antecedent noun or pronoun. As a result of this grammatical dictum, they accomplish the aim of all transitions—to point back to what was said before.

Revising for Coherence

To practice using transitions for coherence, you might revise some of your previous writing, such as one of the descriptions you wrote using positive or negative connotation. Chances are you did not pay much attention to coherence in that exercise since you were concentrating more on the denotation and connotation of words.

The following is Lori's revision of her negative description, which she has also revised for concreteness and specificity. Her revisions for both coherence and concreteness were equally successful. In order to make yourself more aware of transitions, like Lori, you might want to underline the transitions you use. Also, like Lori, you might want to revise for concreteness if you were also more or less general in your original description.

Lori's Revised Description of a Place

The sign has two sides—Welcome on one side, Good-bye on the other. Grifton—the family town where your children grow up bored and uncultured. A lovely community full of churches (the only source of entertainment in the town) with friendly congregations. The churches' congregations are delightful and worry about your every move. They are so concerned that they discuss your miserable life at their quilting parties. If they like you (or if you are a relative) they will find a cure for your ill ways. Unfortunately, if they don't like you, you will be killed off like a washed out soap-opera star.

Although these busybodies are alive and kicking, culture—if it ever existed in Grifton—is extinct. For one thing, I hope you never have to stay in Grifton if you are a lover of good wines. Grifton is corkless. If Wild Irish Rose or MD 20-20 is not your type of wine, that's tough because that's it. Not only is the lovely town wineless but cheeseless. The grocers do have Velveeta, Kraft single slices, and Cheez Whiz but hang it up if your palate longs for a Hickory Farm cheese ball. Southern-style food is the Grifton way—fried chicken, country-style steak, green beans, squash, and Mississippi mud cake. Only a heathen would turn their nose up at cuisine like this.

Like this basic fare, music in Grifton is simple—everyone listens to Katy Country. Everyone except the teenagers who listen to top forty. Such songs as "My Baby Is American Made" and "Neon Women" are a couple of the favorites amongst the pool-room dwellers. Bach, Mozart, Beethoven are heard of but that's sissy music. No man ever listens to that stuff; besides that ain't music, that ain't got no steel guitar in it. Also, that classical stuff don't mention heartaches or prison or nothing.

In Grifton, you're definitely out of luck if you like Mozart. But what if you need a new dress? Well, you're not much better off. Pope's dime store has a selection of the finest polyester found in the area. They also have beautiful bright plastic and rhinestone jewelry to give that final touch of elegance. If Pope's is too expensive there is a second-hand store. Of course the people who live in the Country Club area go to Greenville to do their shopping. Only twenty minutes away, Greenville has a lot of dress shops.

Unlike Greenville, Grifton has only the important kinds of stores. It has two grocery stores, a feed store, post office, a bank, dime store, hardware store, and a sewing shop. Who could ask for more? Another nice thing is that all of these fine shops are conveniently located in the space of two blocks. You need only park once and parking is no problem.

Evidently, Grifton is the place to be—only if you're in need of a rest or you want to be bored to death.

Before you revise your essay, you might profit from further analysis of the various transitions used by one of the professional writers you read earlier. Also, after you have read her final draft, which follows, you might analyze the transitions Francine has used to make her essay much more coherent than it was in her previous draft.

Francine's Final Draft

Words from out There

1 Float along on the purple haze and catch glimpses of infinity. It's amazing to consider the doorways of the mind that come flying open when under the influence of drugs. People pass through those doorways for various reasons, including fun, escape, and necessity. Whatever the reason, though, they all share a common bond—the bond of language. The drug culture seems to have developed its own vocabulary to remain covert to officials, to recognize who's cool and who's not, and

most important of all, to give simpler names to all those complex terms.

2   Among the very cool are the marijuana smokers. They're often quite mellow and seem to range in age from seven to seventy. Their intake of this drug has produced such catch phrases as "getting stoned," "getting high," "taking a trip," and "catching a buzz." All these words and phrases describe the feeling obtained when smoking the drug, and all are fairly well known. Equally public are the terms given to the drug itself. Old standards such as "reefer" and "grass" still apply, as well as "pot," "weed," "bud," and "ganji." Some carry this even further, breaking the various kinds of marijuana into groups: "sensi," "red man," "Columbian," "Hawaiian," and the list goes on and on. For the smoker of the "leaf," there's a massive amount of lingo to draw from, and the more one knows, the cooler he becomes.

3   But the language of drugs isn't always verbal. Public purchases are typically made in silence. A long time ago, I unexpectedly found myself in a car that ended up at the "Tracks" of downtown Roanoke, what used to be a high drug traffic area. The car halted at a certain stop sign, and the driver rolled down his window a tiny bit. From the corner of an old building, a small black boy's head appeared, and he stared intently at the car. The driver reached up and touched his hat once, and then waited. Disappearing, the boy reappeared within a minute's time and handed the driver a small bag. Money and bag exchanged places, and we were off. I found out later that rolling down the window and touching the hat was only one of several signals used for making drug purchases. Apparently, it may be cool to use the lingo around friends and at parties, but when making serious purchases, silence is prefered.

4   Because money and drugs go hand in hand, a lot of words associated with the purchase of marijuana, hashish, opium, and other drugs have to do with amount or money. People buy a sack a bag, an ounce, a pound, a block, a kilo, a dime, a nickel, or a quarter, depending on how rich they are. With all the concentration on money, it's sometimes easy to forget that a lot of people claim to be escaping from the material world and all of its greed-filled charm. After all, drugs are supposed to provide an escape from all that. As with everything, though, even escape has its price.

5   Once a purchase has been made, a person need only consider how to partake of his drug. If he's smoking pot, he might use papers and roll a "doobie" or a "joint." After "toking" (smoking) as much of the joint as possible without setting

the lips on fire, the small left-over portion, which looks like a cigarette butt, is often affectionately termed a "roach." Some throw their roaches out, but connoisseurs know better. They keep those roaches and break them up later into bowls (pipes) or bongs. Bongs come in every imaginable size, shape, and color, and most resemble widemouthed, upright tubes containing water through which smoke is inhaled. But bowls, bongs, and joints aren't the only instruments for smoking. There are power hitters and battery-operated face masks as well; there is even a little hollow, metal cigarette which comes in a decorative wooden case, referred to as a one-hitter.

6 At this point, it should begin to be apparent that most words associated with drugs are short, imitative of the effect produced by the drug, and usually easy to pronounce. What could be more fitting? Imagine the difficulty a person under the influence or in desperate need of drugs would have saying, "I would like a hypodermic needle so that I might inject heroin into my system." It's much easier and more concrete to use the metaphorical lingo, "I'm going to chase the dragon tonight, can you help me out?"

7 Such colorful language used to be the norm down at Roanoke's "Tracks." Race never even entered the picture—whites, blacks, Indians, and Puerto Ricans—they all asked for the same things using the same language.

8 Cool is the key, and if you know the language, you can transfer up, down, in, or out—most anywhere. Any drug—the hallucinogens, dust, coke, crystal (mescaline), shroomers (mushrooms); the downer lemmons (Quaaludes), and the uppers, speed—all can provide the blast; and it hurts only if reality rears its ugly head.

Conclusion

Like her classmates Bonita and Lil, Francine improved her transitions in her final draft. As you may have noted, all three students' essays contained a few usage errors of one kind or another. Although none of the three committed the error known as the sentence fragment, both Lil and Bonita used intentional sentence fragments to their advantage. In addition to parallel structure, intentional sentence fragments can be a means of achieving emphasis, and when these fragments are also parallel, as they are in the first paragraph of Lil's essay, they can be particularly effective because they make writing both coherent and emphatic.

Despite the effectiveness of an intentional fragment, an unintentional sentence fragment can be distracting and troublesome for the reader. For this reason, the unintentional sentence fragment is an error you need to be aware of and eliminate from your writing.

Proofreading Tip: The Unintentional Sentence Fragment

Nearly every professional writer uses intentional *sentence fragments* to gain emphasis or to vary rhythm. No professional writer, however, writes unintentional sentence fragments. The reason is that unintentional fragments cause trouble. Because part of the "complete" thought is missing. See what I mean? Writing this dependent clause by itself does not work. It needs to be attached to the sentence before it in order to complete its thought. In English, a sentence expresses a complete thought through the use of a subject and a predicate that states an action, a condition, or a state of being of the subject. A dependent clause, though it has a subject and a finite verb (complete tense form of a verb), does not express a complete thought because it "depends" on an independent clause for its meaning. It merely adds information about the subject or the predicate of the independent clause. As you can see in the following example, Maureen has written a dependent clause separate from the independent clause it modifies.

I like my boss, Mr. Luther. Since he is kind to everyone, no matter who.

To correct this fragment, Maureen need only remove her period in order to join the dependent clause to the sentence before it, the one it "depends" on to complete its meaning.

I like my boss, Mr. Luther, since he is kind to everyone, no matter who.

Besides resulting from dependent clauses written alone, sentence fragments may also result from the omission of a finite verb. For example, look at the following sentence that Jeff wrote.

Seeing, a sense that we take for granted sometimes.

Perhaps Jeff thought that he had a complete sentence because of the subject and finite verb in his dependent clause *that we take for granted sometimes.* However, as you have seen, dependent clauses do not convey a complete thought. *Seeing* is the subject of Jeff's sentence, and *a sense that we take for granted sometimes* consists of the appositive noun *sense* with its modifying adjective clause. Thus, there is no finite verb to state a condition or action of the subject *seeing*. As a result, Jeff has written a sentence fragment stating part of a thought, not a sentence stating a complete thought. By supplying a finite verb for his subject, Jeff corrected his fragment.

Seeing, a sense that we take for granted sometimes, is most important to a writer.

Fragments may also result from using a present or past participle alone, without the auxiliary verbs that make them finite verbs. For example, you might write a sentence like Antonio's:

In the corner, a man gasping and struggling for breath in the darkened room.

Here Antonio has used the verbs *gasping* and *struggling*, two present participles (*-ing* form of a verb), which can be made finite by adding a tense form of the verb *to be*. In this sentence, Antonio needs the past tense form *was* added to the present participles in order to make them finite.

In the corner, a man was gasping and struggling for breath in the darkened room.

Antonio could also have used the simple past tense, although to have done so would have changed the meaning somewhat, as you can see:

In the corner, a man gasped and struggled for breath in the darkened room.

The progressive tenses, composed of the *-ing* form of a verb together with a form of the verb *to be*, convey continuous action at the time indicated, in this case the past.

In contrast, to these examples of the unintentional sentence fragment, the intentional fragment conveys all the information readers need, and thus it is not puzzling. For example, consider this series of dependent clauses written alone:

Why is it a crime if you do not vote? Because it is your right. Because people have died to give you that right. And, finally, because people have continued to die to preserve that right.

Or consider this series of intentional fragments from Loren Eiseley's essay "The Running Man":

Walking home alone in the twilight, I was bitterly ashamed. Ashamed for the violation of my promise to my father. . . . Ashamed for the story that would penetrate the neighborhood. Ashamed for my own weakness. Ashamed. Ashamed.

How do you explain the differences between these intentional fragments that work and those unintentional ones that do not? As you have seen in the previous examples, the answer is that in those fragments that work, the reader has all the information he needs. As a matter of fact, to make the fragments complete in both of these passages results in unnecessary repetition and redundancy.

Why is it a crime if you do not vote? It is a crime because it is your right. It is a crime because people died to give you that right. And, finally, it is a crime because people have continued to die to preserve that right.

Walking home alone in the twilight, I was bitterly ashamed. I was ashamed for the violation of my promise to my father. . . . I was ashamed for the story that would penetrate the neighborhood. I was ashamed for my own weakness. I was ashamed. I was ashamed.

In both passages the repetition of information the reader already has is unnecessary and tiresome. Also, most important, both the vigor and the emphasis of the fragments are lost.

At this point, it may seem to you that there is very little steady ground to stand on when it comes to the grammatical rules of our language. At the same time, however, it is unlikely that you will fail to recognize a sentence fragment that works and one that does not.

Exercise: Recognizing and Correcting the Unintentional Sentence Fragment

To test this assumption, read the following passages and put an SF, standing for sentence fragment, beside those fragments that do not work, that are unintentional.

1. It was clear that Susie had a great talent. Great sensitivity. Great drive. And, most of all, a great heart.
2. Skipping down the road, whistling a tune, his dog following him.
3. Linda decided that nursing was not for her. Because it was too emotionally draining.
4. Jake, having taken the time to review his notes in hopes of a better understanding.
5. People read for many reasons. To be entertained. To escape troubles. And, last, to be informed.
6. Writing, a skill that some find difficult, but that is very rewarding.

7. It is true that I am silly sometimes. Silly and superficial. Or silly and profound.
8. Having come to the end of the story, lying down, sleepily, to rest.
9. When I went to the beach, running to the water as soon as I got there.
10. My father would be coming home because the war was over. It was over. Over forever and ever.

Now correct the unintentional fragments. No doubt you had little difficulty recognizing the distinction between the unintentional and intentional fragments just listed. However, to insure that you do indeed understand both, you might compose both an unintentional and an intentional fragment in the space provided.

When you proofread your final draft, look for both the unintentional sentence fragment and the comma fault. If in doubt whether or not you have a permissible comma fault or an intentional fragment, ask your instructor before turning in your final draft.

Suggestions for Further Writing

1. Choose two advertisements from magazines and newspapers. Underline the words and phrases with positive connotations, and write down the associations you make with each word or phrase. In addition, be sure to write down each product's name and the associations it suggests.
2. Make up your own product and write a copy for it. If you can, draw your own illustration or use clippings from other ads to illustrate your product.
3. Find a newspaper or a magazine that has printed a speech by a local, state, or national politician. Photocopy the speech and determine what the writer's purpose was. Then, under-

line the important words and phrases with connotations that help him or her achieve the desired purpose and that convey the writer's attitude toward the subject.

4. Using the political speech you photocopied for assignment 3, or any other published article or essay, underline the transitional words and phrases between paragraphs. If there are any weak transitions, supply stronger ones. Do the same for sentences within the paragraphs.

5. Think of a controversy on your campus. Write a letter to the editor of your school newspaper supporting your view on the issue. Then, write another letter supporting the opposing point of view. Check each letter for consistency in the connotations of words and phrases and for transitions between sentences and paragraphs.

6. Imagine that you have purchased a watch that you returned to the factory for repair. One month later, it stopped working again. Write the letter you would enclose with the watch asking for a new one. After you have written the letter, check your transitions and underline the words and phrases with connotations that help establish your tone. What attitude do they convey, and what is the tone they establish?

7. Write an essay in which you define the meaning of a slang expression currently used on your campus. Discuss its connotations and give examples of its use.

8. Write an essay in which you defend or attack Melvin Maddocks's position in his essay "How to Speak without an Accent."

9. Write about a personal experience you have had with sexism or racism.

10. Compare the connotations and the effectiveness of a slang expression with its standard equivalent—for example, the expression "laid-back" with the standard "relaxed."

Reading and Writing the Personal Narrative

Reading the
Personal Narrative

7

Thomas Wolfe, the noted American novelist, said this about the material creative writers should use: "It is my conviction that all serious creative work must be at bottom autobiographical, and that a man must use the material and experience of his own life if he is to create anything that has substantial value." Although Wolfe is speaking here of a novelist's creative use of his past experiences, all writing is "creative" in the sense that a writer creates a poem, a story, or an essay that never existed before. In a sense, too, all personal essays are "autobiographical" because the ideas and feelings we have and convey in our writing are a result of our own life experiences. This is true whether we are writing about something that really happened to us or explaining the language of the region we grew up in.

However, many professional writers have chosen to write about actual events in their lives in essays or in autobiographical books. When writers choose to relate a personal experience, they do so because the experience proved to be significant. For example, in the reading selection that follows from his autobiography Nigger, Dick Gregory tells about an experience in his life that hurt him a great deal but that resulted in knowledge he did not have before.

DICK GREGORY

Pain and Growth

1 I never learned hate at home, or shame. I had to go to school for that. I was about seven years old when I got my first big lesson. I was in love with a little girl named Helene Tucker, a light-complected little girl with pigtails and nice manners. She was always clean and she was smart in school. I think I went to school then mostly to look at her. I brushed my hair and even got me a little old handkerchief. It was a lady's handkerchief, but I didn't

want Helene to see me wipe my nose on my hand. The pipes were frozen again, there was no water in the house, but I washed my socks and shirt every night. I'd get a pot, and go over to Mister Ben's grocery store, and stick my pot down into his soda machine. Scoop out some chopped ice. By evening the ice melted to water for washing. I got sick a lot that winter because the fire would go out at night before the clothes were dry. In the morning I'd put them on, wet or dry, because they were the only clothes I had.

2 Everybody's got a Helene Tucker, a symbol of everything you want. I loved her for her goodness, her cleanness, her popularity. She'd walk down my street and my brothers and sisters would yell. "Here comes Helene," and I'd rub my tennis sneakers on the back of my pants and wish my hair wasn't so nappy and the white folks' shirt fit me better. I'd run out on the street. If I knew my place and didn't come too close, she'd wink at me and say hello. That was a good feeling. Sometimes I'd follow her all the way home, and shovel the snow off her walk and try to make friends with her Momma and her aunts. I'd drop money on her stoop late at night on my way back from shining shoes in the taverns. And she had a Daddy, and he had a good job. He was a paper hanger.

3 I guess I would have gotten over Helene by summertime, but something happened in that classroom that made her face hang in front of me for the next twenty-two years. When I played the drums in high school it was for Helene and when I broke track records in college it was for Helene and when I started standing behind microphones and heard applause I wished Helene could hear it, too. It wasn't until I was twenty-nine years old and married and making money that I finally got her out of my system. Helene was sitting in that classroom when I learned to be ashamed of myself.

4 It was a Thursday. I was sitting in the back of the room, in a seat with a chalk circle drawn around it. The idiot's seat, the troublemaker's seat.

5 The teacher thought I was stupid. Couldn't spell, couldn't read, couldn't do arithmetic. Just stupid. Teachers were never interested in finding out that you couldn't concentrate because you were so hungry, because you hadn't had any breakfast. All you could think about was noontime, would it ever come? Maybe you could sneak into the cloakroom and steal a bite of some kid's lunch out of a coat pocket. A bite of something. Paste. You can't really make a meal of paste, or put it on bread for a sandwich, but sometimes I'd scoop a few spoonfuls out of the paste jar in the back of the room. Pregnant people get strange tastes. I was pregnant with poverty. Pregnant with dirt and pregnant with smells that made people turn away, pregnant with cold and pregnant with shoes that were never bought for me, pregnant with five other

people in my bed and no Daddy in the next room, and pregnant with hunger. Paste doesn't taste too bad when you're hungry.

6 The teacher thought I was a troublemaker. All she saw from the front of the room was a little black boy who squirmed in his idiot's seat and made noises and poked the kids around him. I guess she couldn't see a kid who made noises because he wanted someone to know he was there.

7 It was on a Thursday, the day before the Negro payday. The eagle always flew on Friday. The teacher was asking each student how much his father would give to the Community Chest. On Friday night, each kid would get the money from his father, and on Monday he would bring it to the school. I decided I was going to buy me a Daddy right then. I had money in my pocket from shining shoes and selling papers, and whatever Helene Tucker pledged for her Daddy I was going to top it. And I'd hand the money right in. I wasn't going to wait until Monday to buy me a Daddy.

8 I was shaking, scared to death. The teacher opened her book and started calling out names alphabetically.

9 "Helene Tucker?"

10 "My Daddy said he'd give two dollars and fifty cents."

11 "That's very nice, Helene. Very, very nice indeed."

12 That made me feel pretty good. It wouldn't take too much to top that. I had almost three dollars in dimes and quarters in my pocket. I stuck my hand in my pocket and held onto the money, waiting for her to call my name. But the teacher closed her book after she called everybody else in the class.

13 I stood up and raised my hand.

14 "What is it now?"

15 "You forgot me."

16 She turned toward the blackboard. "I don't have time to be playing with you, Richard."

17 "My Daddy said he'd . . ."

18 "Sit down, Richard, you're disturbing the class."

19 "My Daddy said he'd give . . . fifteen dollars."

20 She turned around and looked mad. "We are collecting this money for you and your kind, Richard Gregory. If your Daddy can give fifteen dollars you have no business being on relief."

21 "I got it right now, I got it right now, my Daddy gave it to me to turn in today, my Daddy said . . ."

22 "And furthermore," she said, looking right at me, her nostrils getting big and her lips getting thin and her eyes opening wide, "we know you don't have a Daddy."

23 Helene Tucker turned around, her eyes full of tears. She felt sorry for me. Then I couldn't see her too well because I was crying, too.

24 "Sit down, Richard."

25 And I always thought the teacher kind of liked me. She always picked me to wash the blackboard on Friday, after school. That was a big thrill, it made me feel important. If I didn't wash it, come Monday the school might not function right.

26 "Where are you going, Richard?"

27 I walked out of school that day, and for a long time I didn't go back very often. There was shame there.

28 Now there was shame everywhere. It seemed like the whole world had been inside that classroom, everyone had heard what the teacher had said, everyone had turned around and felt sorry for me. There was shame in going to the Worthy Boys Annual Christmas Dinner for you and your kind, because everybody knew what a worthy boy was. Why couldn't they just call it the Boys Annual Dinner, why'd they have to give it a name? There was shame in wearing the brown and orange and white plaid mackinaw the welfare gave to 3,000 boys. Why'd it have to be the same for everybody so when you walked down the street the people could see you were on relief? It was a nice warm mackinaw and it had a hood, and my Momma beat me and called me a little rat when she found out I stuffed it in the bottom of a pail full of garbage way over on Cottage Street. There was shame in running over to Mister Ben's at the end of the day and asking for his rotten peaches, there was shame in asking Mrs. Simmons for a spoonful of sugar, there was shame in running out to meet the relief truck. I hated that truck, full of food for you and your kind. I ran into the house and hid when it came. And then I started to sneak through alleys, to take the long way home so the people going into White's Eat Shop wouldn't see me. Yeah, the whole world heard the teacher that day, we all know you don't have a daddy.

29 It lasted for a while, this kind of numbness. I spent a lot of time feeling sorry for myself. And then one day I met this wino in a restaurant. I'd been out hustling all day, shining shoes, selling newspapers, and I had goo-gobs of money in my pocket. Bought me a bowl of chili for fifteen cents, and a cheeseburger for fifteen cents, and a Pepsi for five cents, and a piece of chocolate cake for ten cents. That was a good meal. I was eating when this old wino came in. I love winos because they never hurt anyone but themselves.

30 The old wino sat down at the counter and ordered twenty-six cents worth of food. He ate it like he really enjoyed it. When the owner, Mister Williams, asked him to pay the check, the old wino didn't lie or go through his pocket like he suddenly found a hole.

31 He just said: "Don't have no money."

32 The owner yelled: "Why in hell you come in here and eat my food if you don't have no money? That food cost me money."

33 Mister Williams jumped over the counter and knocked the wino off his stool and beat him over the head with a pop bottle. Then

he stepped back and watched the wino bleed. Then he kicked him. And he kicked him again.

34 I looked at the wino with blood all over his face and I went over. "Leave him alone, Mister Williams. I'll pay the twenty-six cents."

35 The wino got up, slowly, pulling himself up to the stool, then up to the counter, holding on for a minute until his legs stopped shaking so bad. He looked at me with pure hate. "Keep your twenty-six cents. You don't have to pay, not now. I just finished paying for it."

36 He started to walk out, and as he passed me, he reached down and touched my shoulder. "Thanks, sonny, but it's too late now. Why didn't you pay it before?"

37 I was pretty sick about that. I waited too long to help another man.

Ideas and Meaning.

1. What did Helene Tucker symbolize for Dick Gregory? Why was it that her face "hung" in front of Gregory until he was twenty-nine?
2. Has any person you have known been a symbol to you? Who was it? What did he or she symbolize?
3. How did Dick Gregory feel about not having a father?
4. Who did the phrase "your kind" refer to? How is it derogatory?
5. Why did Gregory hide when the food truck came?
6. Why did he stuff the mackinaw in the garbage pail?
7. In what sense was Gregory not poor?
8. What was the cruelest thing the teacher said to Gregory?
9. What happened to make Gregory stop feeling sorry for himself?
10. What is the difference in the cause of the two times Gregory felt shame? What is the effect of this difference?
11. What adjectives would you use to describe the young boy, Dick Gregory?
12. What emotions besides shame would you have felt in Gregory's place? What emotions did you have as a reader of the experience?
13. During your career in school, have you ever had a teacher who shamed students? If so, describe the incident.
14. Has anyone ever made you feel ashamed? If so, who? What happened?

Development and Style

1. Even though this is an excerpt from a book, and not an essay, how does Gregory get your attention in the first sentence?

2. What is the tone of this excerpt?
3. Who is Gregory's audience? What is his purpose?
4. What is his point?
5. Point out the concrete/specific details in each paragraph. What images do you get? Identify which senses the concrete data appeal to.
6. What is the effect of Gregory's use of dialogue in paragraphs 9–26? Would the scene have been as effective had Gregory merely reported what was said? Rewrite the scene without dialogue to see the difference.
7. What is the effect of the metaphorical use of *pregnant* in paragraph 5? What are the associations you make with the word? How is it appropriate in each of the statements?
8. What means of transition does Gregory use between paragraphs 5 and 6?
9 Analyze the transitions from paragraphs 28 through 30.
10. What is the difference between the connotations of the words *father* and *daddy*?
11. Point out the intentional fragments and parallel structure that Gregory uses. What are the effects of each?

Jeanette's Two Responses

Reading Journal: "Pain and Growth" First Response

After my first reading of "Pain and Growth," I'm left with the image of that beat-up and bloody wino. Its really awful to know that things like this actually happen.

It makes me wonder, when people talk about how poor they are. I mean when people in school or friends or whoever—obviously they're not incredibly or unbearably poor, they're just poor for that they're used to. I can't imagine what it must be like to be in the utter poverty Dick Gregory speaks of, or even worse, to not have a bed to go home to or any kind of help whatsoever. That must be a terrible feeling. Sometimes it seems like the government, & mission and rescue workers forget that they're dealing with actual people—they don't consider the fact that these people have a sense of pride and personal dignity just as much as they do.

The essay brings to mind some of the people I know living up in Pennsylvania in Wyalusing county. A lot of them have been hit hard by black lung deaths, and there's no one left capable of working for the family. Most of these are older women, and they won't take a cent of help from anyone. They become very snappy and downright mean if anyone tries to help them in any way. One of these women is a pretty good friend of mine, and we often go hiking together. I can ask her about any part of her past that I want to, but anything dealing with the subject of her financial situation is a no-no. When her birthday came around a couple of years ago, I wanted to take her out to eat. She refused my offer outright, said it wasn't the kind of present she needed. I went and got her a hunting knife instead and she loved it! People, I guess, are proud even at their darkest moments.

Second Response

After my second reading of Gregory's essay, I have to wonder how his teacher could have been so cruel. She was apparently teaching in an area that was home for a lot of poor people. Maybe she'd been dealing with things for too long, or maybe she had a bad day, but she still could have gone back and had a little understanding for the kid. When you get bad feelings about teachers at an early age, it can really ruin it for you later.

When I was in the fourth grade, I had to take a test on dinosaurs. Well, I wanted to do my absolute best, and so I took my paper home with me to finish working on it. When I came into the room and proudly turned it in the next day, my teacher, Miss Shell got very angry and began shouting at me. When I tried to run out into the hall she grabbed me and sat me up on a table. She yelled some more and then slapped me across the face. When I look back on it now, I realize that the woman was probably in sad shape mentally. But, I'm sure that that event was probably one of the things at the root of my distrust of teachers through junior high and high school. (It's a whole different scene in college and this is all behind me now!!)

I liked the way Gregory threw in a few lines of thought and speech that read the way people would actually speak. That was really effective. I also liked a lot of his descriptive words—particularly "pregnant" in the fourth paragraph. Pregnancy is normally thought of with hope and new life, but here it becomes the holder of poverty and despair.

I almost don't like the way the essay ends; it's so abrupt. I wanted him to tie it back in with the rest of what he'd been talking about, but I guess in a way he did. Maybe the fact that he says he waited too long to help the man is indicative of the fact that no one had helped him or most of the poor people throughout their lives.

In her second response Jeanette recalls the cruelty of her fourth-grade teacher, an experience that she says caused her to distrust teachers for years. Also, in this last response, Jeanette mentions the effectiveness of Gregory's dialogue. As she notes, it sounds the way people "really speak," certainly the most important requirement of good dialogue.

Using Dialogue in Narration

Often a personal narrative may concern a significant conflict in the writer's life, such as Gregory's conflict with his teacher. When recounting such a confrontation, a writer may choose to use dialogue in order to create vividness and immediacy. That is, the use of dialogue not only creates a clearer image, but it also makes you, the reader, feel as if the scene were happening at the moment you read it, and thus you become a participant in the action as a witness to the scene. In fact, as you read the dialogue between Dick Gregory and his teacher, you probably began to feel very uncomfortable and angry. Some of you may even have thought to yourselves, "Oh don't say that; oh, how cruel!" The dialogue made you a witness to the insensitive cruelty of this woman.

What if Gregory had chosen merely to report what was said? What differences in the effect of the scene would result? Let's see.

> I stood up and raised my hand. She asked me what I wanted, and I told her she had forgotten me. She just turned to the blackboard and said she didn't have time to be playing with me. So I started to say what my Daddy would give, and she told me to sit down and quit disturbing the class. Then I said my Daddy would give fifteen dollars, and she said that the class was collecting money for me and my kind and that if my Daddy could give fifteen dollars, we didn't have any business being on relief.

Do you see the difference? Not only are the vividness and immediacy of the scene lost, but also the repetition of "she said" and "I said" becomes monotonous.

Style and Form in Dialogue

As Jeanette observed, Gregory's dialogue sounds *natural*, the way people really speak. Naturalness is the number one stylistic requirement of good dialogue. Unnatural dialogue is readily apparent, and instead of enhancing a narrative, it can ruin it. Something like this, for example.

> "Now, son, I would really like for you to eat your spinach because of its nutritive value."
> "I can readily comprehend that, Mother, but I regret that I have this recurrent aversion to leafy vegetation."

Let's write this the way people really talk.

"Eat your spinach. It's good for you."
"I know, but I can't stand it."

Besides being natural, there are two other stylistic requirements of good dialogue. First, there should be no unnecessary
speaker tags. Second, modifiers indicating tone of voice and specific verbs denoting tone of voice should not be overused. The
dialogue itself indicates tone of voice, and when the reader knows
who is speaking, constant repetition of "he said" or "she said" is
not only unnecessary but disruptive to the flow of the conversation. Here is Gregory's dialogue with unnecessary speaker tags.

"What is it now?" she asked.
"You forgot me," I said.
She turned to the blackboard. "I don't have time to be playing
with you, Richard," she said.
"My Daddy said he'd . . ." I said.
"Sit down, Richard, you're disturbing the class," she said.

Now here is the dialogue with unnecessary modifiers.

"What is it now?" she asked angrily.
"You forgot me," I stated insistently.
She turned to the blackboard. "I don't have time to be playing
with you, Richard," she said nastily.
"My Daddy said he'd . . ." I said hesitantly.
"Sit down, Richard, you're disturbing the class," she said im-
patiently.

And here it is with specific verbs indicating tone of voice.

"What is it now?" she hissed.
"You forgot me," I blurted.
She turned to the blackboard. "I don't have time to be playing
with you, Richard," she growled.
"My Daddy said he'd . . ." I declared.
"Sit down, Richard, you're disturbing the class," she spat.

To recapitulate, these are the stylistic requirements of good
dialogue:

1. naturalness
2. no unnecessary speaker tags
3. no unnecessary modifiers or verbs indicating tone of voice

The form of dialogue writing is also easy to learn. There are
basically three conventions to remember:

1. Indent when speakers change.
2. Put one pair of marks at the beginning of a speech and another pair at the end. Do not enclose each sentence of a speech
   in quotation marks.

3. If the quoted speech of a person continues for more than one paragraph, put quotations marks at the beginning of each paragraph, but not at the end until the quoted speech ends.

Look at paragraphs 13 through 19 in Gregory's narrative for examples of the first two formal conventions. Note that in paragraph 20, the teacher makes two statements but that there are quotation marks only at the beginning and end of her speech.

Not this:	"We are collecting this money for you and your kind, Richard Gregory." "If your Daddy can give fifteen dollars, you have no business being on relief."
But this:	"We are collecting this money for you and your kind, Richard Gregory. If your Daddy can give fifteen dollars, you have no business being on relief."
Not this:	"What is it now?" "You forgot me." . . . "I don't have time to be playing with you, Richard."
But this:	"What is it now?"
	"You forgot me."
	. . . "I don't have time to be playing with you, Richard."

The following excerpt from Sherwood Anderson's essay "Discovery of a Father" is an example of the third formal convention of dialogue writing. However, it is unlikely that you will have an occasion to use it since it is unlikely that you will quote someone telling a story as Anderson does here.

"Huh," said father. "He was in the woods with me.

"I was there looking for Grant. He had got off his horse and come into the woods. He found me. He was covered with mud.

"I had the bottle in my hand. What'd I care? The war was over. I knew we had them licked."

These are the only three formal conventions of dialogue writing, although there are several rules of punctuation that you should note.

Rules of Punctuation with Quotation Marks

1. Periods and commas always go inside the final pair of quotation marks.

"You forgot me."
"You forgot me," I said.
"And furthermore," she said, looking right at me . . .
"we know you don't have a Daddy."

2. Question marks and exclamation marks go *inside* the final pair of quotation marks if the speech is a question or an exclamation.

> "What is it now?"
> "My goodness!" Sue exclaimed.

3. Question marks and exclamation marks go *outside* the final pair of quotation marks when the quotation is neither a question nor an exclamation.

> Do you know the maxim "It is better to give than to receive"?
> I can't believe you never heard Pope's famous line "To err is human"!

4. For a quotation within a quotation, use single quotation marks.

> "Have you ever heard Pope's famous line 'To err is human'?" the teacher asked.

5. Never use more than one punctuation mark at a time.

> *Not this:* "Can you believe it?," Tom asked.
> *But this:* "Can you believe it?" Tom asked.

Keeping these formal conventions and stylistic precepts in mind, you should have no trouble writing formally correct and natural-sounding dialogue. So that you can see the vividness and immediacy that dialogue can lend your own writing, you might think of a conflict you had in the past with someone—a parent, boss, teacher, or friend—and write a narrative describing what happened and reporting what was said. Afterwards, rewrite the narrative using dialogue. Writing these two versions of your conflict will demonstrate the positive effects that dialogue can have on narration, as well as making you confident that you can write good, natural dialogue. One way to ensure the naturalness of your speech is to remember what you and the other person really said. Juan's two narratives that follow will give you an idea of what you can do.

Juan's Narrative without Dialogue

A Misunderstanding

Last summer I got a full-time job at the Hardee's near the university. When I took the job, I told Sylvia the manager that when school started, I would have to reduce my hours to part-time and that since I was planning to enroll at the university as a full-time student, we would have to work my schedule around my class hours. At the time, she said that was fine.

I registered last Friday morning and went to work at three that afternoon. At ten o'clock, Sylvia asked me to stop by her office when I got off to pick up my schedule for the next week.

When I went in, she was in her chair behind her desk, tapping a pencil on the top. She told me to have a seat and then handed me my schedule. I looked at it and told her that classes began Monday, and that I had four classes on Monday, Wednesday, and Friday, but only one on Tuesday and Thursday so that I could work the three till eleven shift on those days and four hours on Saturday or Sunday.

Well, she blew her top. She said that it was her understanding that I would continue working full-time and that my class schedule could be arranged around my schedule at Hardee's. Since I had three o'clock classes on Mondays, Wednesdays, and Fridays, I obviously couldn't work the three till eleven shift those days. Besides, I had a class from six to seven-fifteen on Monday and Wednesday nights.

I reminded Sylvia that when I took the job, she had assured me that my schedule at Hardee's could be arranged according to my class schedule.

Then she said that she did not remember anything of the kind.

I also told her that I'd mentioned to her when I took the job that I would work only part-time after school began.

Sylvia replied that she certainly didn't remember that either and that if I couldn't work the hours she had given me the next week, then I was fired.

My heart sank because I needed a part-time job. So, I pleaded with her to give me a break.

She said that she was sorry but that she had to have a full-time person.

I said that I supposed I was fired then and left. But I'd learned something important: never trust a verbal agreement. Get it in writing.

Juan's Narrative with Dialogue

A Misunderstanding

Last summer I got a job at the Hardee's near the university. When I took the job, I explained to Sylvia the manager that when school started I would have to reduce my hours to part-time and that since I was planning to take fifteen hours, a full-time load at school, we'd have to arrange a work schedule around my class time.

Registration was last Friday morning, and I went to work

at three that afternoon. At ten o'clock I was sweeping up the kitchen when Sylvia walked over.

"When you get off, Juan, stop by my office for a minute and pick up your schedule for next week."

"Sure." I nodded my head and kept on sweeping. At eleven I knocked on her door.

"Come on in, Juan," she called.

I went in and stood by the doorway. She was tapping a red pencil on the desktop.

"Sit down. Here's your schedule."

I took the paper she handed me across the desk. After glancing at it, I felt shocked. I was down for Monday, Tuesday, and Wednesday three till eleven and Saturday and Sunday three till eleven.

"Sylvia, I can't work these hours!" My voice all but shrieked. "Didn't you know I registered today at the university? Classes start Monday. Here, look at my schedule." I handed her my green class card.

"I don't need to see that! It doesn't matter to me when you have classes. I thought you agreed when I hired you that you'd work full-time. I thought you said that you'd work a class schedule around your time here."

I was stunned. I just sat there for a minute in disbelief. "Well, what I remember is a lot different from your memory of our agreement. I thought we'd agreed that when school started, I'd be part-time. I was planning on working Tuesdays and Thursdays from three till eleven and four hours on Saturday and Sunday. That'd be twenty hours a week, and that's all I can handle, taking five courses at the university." I held my breath and said a silent prayer, but she didn't hesitate a second.

Jumping up from her chair, Sylvia glared at me across the desk. "I don't care what you remember. If you can't work full-time, you're fired! I need a full-time person and you know it. Furthermore, I'm really disappointed in you. I thought you were someone I could count on."

Since I had to have a part-time job, I thought I'd plead with her once more. "Don't you think you could hire someone else part-time and then you'd have the hours covered? There are plenty of students who'd love to have the job. Couldn't you consider that?" I thought this was a reasonable suggestion, but Sylvia didn't.

"Do you really think that between now and Monday someone is going to walk in here who just happens to want to work from three till eleven on Mondays and Wednesdays? I mean, really, Juan, use your brain. I'm responsible for this place running smoothly—all the time. I just can't take chances like that."

Obviously there was nothing I could do. "I guess I'm fired," I muttered. I felt angry and overwhelmed because I didn't know how I was going to find another job in two days. "And I'm disappointed, too," I said as I walked out the door.

On the way home, I decided that that was the last time I'd make a verbal agreement with anyone. The next time it'd be in writing.

Juan's narrative is so much more interesting with dialogue that it doesn't even seem like the same event, does it? One of the differences in the impact of the two versions is that when he uses dialogue, you feel so much sorrier for Juan. There are several reasons for this difference in the effect of the two versions: Because of the dialogue in the second version, you are a witness to the scene; you experience the conflict between Juan and Sylvia; also, speech helps to characterize a person. Thus, in the second version, what Sylvia says makes her a very unsympathetic character. She's not a very considerate or understanding person.

All in all, Juan was very successful in his first attempt to write dialogue: his speech sounds natural, and he has followed the formal conventions of dialogue writing.

Although some personal narratives may not contain dialogue, all personal narratives contain concrete, specific details. The professional writers of the personal narratives that follow wanted their readers to experience what they did—to see what they saw, hear what they heard, and so on. For this reason, you will find these writers using metaphors also. In fact, when you write your own narrative, you will use all the writing skills that you have acquired thus far.

In the following essays, Loren Eiseley, a noted anthropologist, Sherwood Anderson, author of the novel *Winesburg, Ohio*, and Maya Angelou, a renowned black writer, have written about significant personal experiences. In his essay, Eiseley writes about a special cat that taught him something, but he does not use dialogue since his experience does not involve either a conflict or a confrontation with another person. In the next essay, Anderson uses a great deal of quotation, but no real dialogue, to help him recount an event that changed his feelings about his father. Last, in a selection from her autobiographical book *I Know Why the Caged Bird Sings*, Maya Angelou does quote her characters' speech at times, although there is no true dialogue in this narrative account of her wise grandmother's triumph over several crude and impudent young white girls. As you will see, like Dick Gregory, these three writers learned a great deal from their vastly different experiences.

LOREN EISELEY

Madeline

1 Maddy was what we called her familiarly. Madeline was her real name and she was a prima donna and a cat—in that order. Maddy was a cat that bowed, the only one I have ever encountered. She is part of my story, what one might call the elocution or stage part. We patronized each other. Maddy performed her act, and I assumed the role of her most ardent admirer. In discharging this duty I learned a great deal from Maddy, my patroness, whom I here acknowledge.

2 I have known a good many cats in my time—some that scratched, some that bit, some who purred, and even one who, by my standards at least, talked. I liked Maddy, I suppose, because we had so much in common. Maddy was an isolate. Maddy lived with three other more aggressive and talented animals who took the major attention of my host. Maddy, by contrast, was not so much antisocial as shy, when you came to know her. She wandered a little forlornly in back rooms and concealed herself under furniture, or in a recess above the fireplace.

3 Maddy, in short, wanted a small place in the sun which the world refused to grant her. She was at heart simply a good-natured ginger cat in a world so full of cats with purrs less hoarse that Maddy, like many of us, had learned to slink obscurely along the wall and hope that she might occasionally receive a condescending pat. Nothing was ever going to go quite right for Maddy. In this we reckoned without poor Maddy's desperation. She discovered a talent, and, I at least, among her human friends, was appalled at how easily this talent might have gone unguessed, except for a chance episode and an equally uncanny tenacity on Maddy's part. Maddy learned to bow.

4 Perhaps you may think, as a human being, that this is a very small accomplishment indeed. Let me assure you that it is not. On four feet it is a hard thing to do and, in addition, the cat mind is rarely reconciled to such postures. No one among us in that house, I think now, realized the depths of Maddy's need or her perception.

5 It happened, as most things happen, by accident, but the accident was destined to entrap both Maddy and ourselves. She was ensconced in her favorite recess upon the mantel of the fireplace, watching us, as usual, but being unwatched because of the clever gyrations of one of her kindred down on the floor. At this point, Mr. Fleet, our host, happened to stoop over to adjust a burning log in the fireplace.

6 Easing his back a moment later, he stood up by the mantel and poked a friendly finger at Maddy, who came out to peer down at

the sparks. She also received an unexpected pat from Mr. Fleet. Whether by design or not, the combination of sparks and the hand impinging upon her head at the same time caused Maddy to execute a curious little head movement like a bow. It resembled, I can only say, a curtsey, an Old World gesture out of another time at the Sun King's court.

7 Maddy both hunched her forefeet and dropped her head. All she needed to complete the bow was a bonnet or a ribbon. Everyone who saw applauded in astonishment and for a few moments Maddy, for once, was the center of attention. In due course that would have been the end of the matter, but a severe snowstorm descended over our part of the state. We were thus all housebound and bored for several days. This is where Maddy's persistence and physical memory paid off; on the next night upon the mantle she came out of her own volition, and bowed once more with precisely similar steps. Again everyone applauded. Never had Madeline received such a burst of affectionate encouragement. If there were any catcalls they could only have come from her kin beneath the davenport. Her audience was with her. Maddy seized her opportunity. She bowed three times to uproarious applause. She had become the leading character in the house. The event had become memorable. Maddy, no more than a dancer, would forget the steps and the graceful little nod of the head. It became an evening routine.

8 I have said that in the end both Maddy and her audience were entrapped. It happened in this way: finally the snow went away and we, all except Maddy, tried to resume our usual nocturnal habits—the corner bar, the club, the book. But the bow had become Maddy's life. She lived for it; one could not let her down, humiliate her, relegate her unfeelingly to her former existence. Maddy's fame, her ego, had to be sustained at any cost, even if, at times, her audience was reduced to one. That one carried, at such times, the honor of the house. Maddy's bow must be applauded. Maddy would be stricken if her act began to pall.

9 To me the act never did pall. More than once I gave up other things to serve as a substitute audience. For, you see, I had come to realize even then that Maddy and myself were precisely alike; we had learned to bow in order to be loved for our graceless selves. The only difference was that as a human being living in a more complex world it had taken me longer to develop the steps and the routine. I talked for a living. But to talk for a living, one must, like Maddy, receive more applause than opprobrium. One must learn certain steps.

10 I was born and grew up with no burning desire to teach. Sea captain, explorer, jungle adventurer—all these, in my childhood books, had been extolled to me. Unfortunately my reading had not included the great educators. Thus upon completing my doc-

torate I had no real hope in those still depressed times of 1937 of finding a university post. While I was casting about for a job among newspaper folk of my acquaintance, word came that I had been proffered a position at the University of Kansas.

11 Most of the midwestern universities of that period had joint departments of sociology and anthropology, or at best one tame anthropologist who was expected to teach in both fields. When I appeared that fall before my first class in introductory sociology I realized two things as I walked through the door. I did not dare sit down. I did not dare use my notes for anything but a security blanket to toss confidently on the table like a true professor. The class was very large. A sizable portion of the football squad was scattered in the back row. I was, I repeat, an isolate like Maddy. If I ever lost that audience there would be chaos. The class met every day in the week.

12 Each night I studied beyond midnight and wrote outlines that I rarely followed. I paced restlessly before the class, in which even the campus dogs were welcome so long as they nodded their heads sagely in approval. In a few weeks I began to feel like the proverbial Russian fleeing in a sleigh across the steppes before a wolf pack. I am sure that Carroll Clark, my good-natured chairman, realized that a highly unorthodox brand of sociology was being dispensed in his domain, but he held his peace. By then everything from anecdotes of fossil hunting to observations upon Victorian Darwinism were being hurled headlong from the rear of the sleigh. The last object to go would be myself. Fortunately for me, the end of the semester came just in time.

13 At the close of the first year I had acquired, like Madeline the ginger cat, some followers. I had learned figuratively to bow and I was destined to keep right on bowing through the next thirty years. There was no escape. Maddy had taught me how necessary it was that one's psyche be sustained. An actor, and this means no reflection upon teaching, has to have at least a few adoring followers. Otherwise he will begin to doubt himself and shrink inward, or take to muttering over outworn notes. This is particularly true in the case of a cat who has literally come out of nowhere to bow under everyone's gaze on a fireplace. Similarly I had emerged as a rather shy, introverted lad, to exhort others from a platform. Dear Maddy, I know all you suffered and I wish I could think you are still bowing to applause. You triumphed over your past in one great appreciative flash. For me it has been a lifelong battle with anxiety. . . .

Ideas and Meaning

1. How were Loren Eiseley and Maddy alike? What difference between them does he point out at the end of the excerpt?
2. How does Eiseley use Maddy's bow figuratively?

3. In what sense do we all learn to "bow"? How have you learned to bow?
4. What are some adjectives you would use to describe Eiseley as he presents himself in this excerpt?
5. What is your image of Eiseley as a teacher?
6. How are teaching and acting similar?
7. Have you ever learned anything about yourself from an animal? Explain.

Development and Style

1. How does Eiseley get the reader's attention in his first sentence?
2. What is his tone? What is his purpose and who is his audience?
3. What is his point?
4. Where do you find humor in the excerpt?
5. What concrete/specific details does Eiseley give that create images? Which of the senses does each appeal to?
6. Eiseley describes both himself and Maddy as "shy," and at one point he calls them both "isolates." At the end of the excerpt he calls himself "introverted." What are the connotations of each of these words? Which has the most negative connotations?
7. Analyze the transitions from paragraphs 6 through 11.
8. How would you compare Eiseley's voice to Dick Gregory's? Which writer was easier for you to read? Why?

Gretta's Two Responses

Reading Journal: "Madeline" First Response

Loren Eiseley's essay "Madeline" was a superb narrative. It seems to be a narrative much more about himself than merely the antics of a cat. Like Madeline, Eiseley longs for approval and attention because he considers himself "graceless" like the cat. Eiseley's learning to teach is much like Madeline's learning to bow. Eiseley's description of the anxiety which he felt before a class caused me to be very sympathetic. I have never been in the position of a teacher, but I imagine that it could be an extremely trying profession.

I have been in classes in which teachers had a very rough time because of the immaturity of the students. One particular class was awful, not because of the teacher, but because of the attitude of the majority of the students. They were not concerned in the least about learning. They merely wanted to be handed an easy A. They were restless, talked amongst themselves about parties past and present, and they constantly complained about classwork, homework, and tests. The poor teacher tried his best and did an excellent job, considering what he had to face.

The paragraph in Eiseley's essay about how much he prepared for classes reminded me of this man. He was very well prepared, and he always brought a stack of notes which he only glanced at. The only difference is that this teacher didn't (or rarely) received the approval that Eiseley "bowed" for. At least, he didn't receive it in this particular class. Luckily, I had him for another class, and it was a much better class. I guess this is just part of teaching. He had to take the good ones along with the bad ones.

Second Response

"Madeline" was just as enjoyable to read the second time as it was the first. I like the light tone which Eiseley uses in order to prove a serious point. I can really relate to his point of view, also. Being a "graceless" creature like Madeline and Eiseley, I, too, have often learned to "bow" in order to receive approval. I did this a lot when I was a teenager in high school. It's a typical story.

I was not beautiful or graceful like the cheerleaders and so many of the other girls. Like Madeline the cat, I often sulked along deserted corridors in the shadows by myself. But I compensated for my outward ugliness by trying to make myself more beautiful inwardly. I always smiled and was cheerful even to people I didn't particularly like. I made it a point to be good to people and never gossip or hurt anyone. This had its disadvantages, though, because some people took advantage of my good-natured ways. But all in all, I received my pats of approval by making friends and being well liked. I also became very well liked by teachers and parents. I think that my humbleness caused me to receive approval in high school.

Now that I have grown out of the childish desire to "belong," I enjoy being different, but I still try to be a good person "inwardly." But I think that what Eiseley says is true when he states that we are like actors and we have to have at least some followers in order to sustain a type of dignity. I think that humbleness is a good thing for everyone to learn. Through humbleness, we can often achieve approval, and everyone needs this.

Reading: A Dialogue between Reader and Writer

Although responding to a text through association is very good since you might write about past experiences that could become subjects of future essays, to associate entirely is not as profitable as a response to meaning in addition to association. That is, there should be an interaction between the reader and the writer's text. To put it another way, to read a text is to engage in a dialogue between yourself and the writer, via his or her text. For example, in her second response, Gretta says that she thinks humbleness is a good thing for people to learn because they can receive approval for it. This statement is a true indication of Gretta's participation in a dialogue with Eiseley, for nowhere in his essay does Eiseley explicitly say that we can receive approval by being humble.

To give an example of how you participate in a dialogue all the time, imagine that your roommate comes home from a date with someone that he or she has not dated before. The dialogue between the two of you might go something like this:

> You: Well, how was it?
>
> Roommate: Fine. The dinner was good and so was the movie. She's (He's) a little quiet, but nice.
>
> You: So, you weren't real impressed, huh?

Your roommate has not said that she or he was not impressed. You listened and inferred this meaning from what your roommate said. This is precisely what Gretta has done in her dialogue with Eiseley. We interpret meaning by reading beneath the superficial utterance, by adding the meaning of statement A to statement B, and deriving an implied meaning, statement C, such as your last response in the preceding dialogue. That is what dialogue is all about. The important thing is to listen to the writer as you read and to engage in a dialogue in which you interpret not only what is said, but also what is implied.

SHERWOOD ANDERSON

Discovery of a Father

1 You hear it said that fathers want their sons to be what they feel they cannot themselves be, but I tell you it also works the other way. A boy wants something very special from his father. I know that as a small boy I wanted my father to be a certain thing he was not. I wanted him to be a proud, silent, dignified father. When I was with other boys and he passed along the street, I wanted to feel a flow of pride. "There he is. That is my father."

2 But he wasn't such a one. He couldn't be. It seemed to me then that he was always showing off. Let's say someone in our town had got up a show. They were always doing it. The druggist would

be in it, the shoe-store clerk, the horse doctor, and a lot of women and girls. My father would manage to get the chief comedy part. It was, let's say, a Civil War play and he was a comic Irish soldier. He had to do the most absurd things. They thought he was funny, but I didn't.

3 I thought he was terrible. I didn't see how mother could stand it. She even laughed with the others. Maybe I would have laughed if it hadn't been my father.

4 Or there was a parade, the Fourth of July or Decoration Day. He'd be in that, too, right at the front of it, as Grand Marshal or something, on a white horse hired from a livery stable.

5 He couldn't ride for shucks. He fell off the horse and everyone hooted with laughter, but he didn't care. He even seemed to like it. I remember once when he had done something ridiculous, and right out on Main Street, too. I was with some other boys and they were laughing and shouting at him and he was shouting back and having as good a time as they were. I ran down an alley back of some stores and there in the Presbyterian Church sheds I had a good long cry.

6 Or I would be in bed at night and father would come home a little lit up and bring some men with him. He was a man who was never alone. Before he went broke, running a harness shop, there were always a lot of men loafing in the shop. He went broke, of course, because he gave too much credit. He couldn't refuse it and I thought he was a fool. I had got to hating him.

7 There'd be men I didn't think would want to be fooling around with him. There might even be the superintendent of our schools and a quiet man who ran the hardware store. Once I remember there was a white-haired man who was a cashier of the bank. It was a wonder to me they'd want to be seen with such a windbag. That's what I thought he was. I know now what it was that attracted them. It was because life in our town, as in all small towns, was at times pretty dull and he livened it up. He made them laugh. He could tell stories. He'd even get them to singing.

8 If they didn't come to our house they'd go off, say at night, to where there was a grassy place by a creek. They'd cook food there and drink beer and sit about listening to his stories.

9 He was always telling stories about himself. He'd say this or that wonderful thing had happened to him. It might be something that made him look like a fool. He didn't care.

10 If an Irishman came to our house, right away father would say he was Irish. He'd tell what county in Ireland he was born in. He'd tell things that happened there when he was a boy. He'd make it seem so real that, if I hadn't known he was born in southern Ohio, I'd have believed him myself.

11 If it was a Scotchman the same thing happened. He'd get a burr into his speech. Or he was a German or a Swede. He'd be any-

thing the other man was. I think they all knew he was lying, but they seemed to like him just the same. As a boy that was what I couldn't understand.

12 And there was mother. How could she stand it? I wanted to ask but never did. She was not the kind you asked such questions.

13 I'd be upstairs in my bed, in my room above the porch, and father would be telling some of his tales. A lot of father's stories were about the Civil War. To hear him tell it he'd been in about every battle. He'd known Grant, Sherman, Sheridan and I don't know how many others. He'd been particularly intimate with General Grant so that when Grant went East to take charge of all the armies, he took father along.

14 "I was an orderly at headquarters and Sim Grant said to me, 'Irve,' he said, 'I'm going to take you along with me.' "

15 It seems he and Grant used to slip off sometimes and have a quiet drink together. That's what my father said. He'd tell about the day Lee surrendered and how, when the great moment came, they couldn't find Grant.

16 "You know," my father said, "about General Grant's book, his memoirs. You've read of how he said he had a headache and how, when he got word that Lee was ready to call it quits, he was suddenly and miraculously cured.

17 "Huh," said father. "He was in the woods with me.

18 "I was in there with my back against a tree. I was pretty well corned. I had got hold of a bottle of pretty good stuff.

19 "They were looking for Grant. He had got off his horse and come into the woods. He found me. He was covered with mud.

20 "I had the bottle in my hand. What'd I care? The war was over. I knew we had them licked."

21 My father said that he was the one who told Grant about Lee. An orderly riding by had told him, because the orderly knew how thick he was with Grant. Grant was embarrassed.

22 "But, Irve, look at me. I'm all covered with mud," he said to father.

23 And then, my father said, he and Grant decided to have a drink together. They took a couple of shots and then, because he didn't want Grant to show up potted before the immaculate Lee, he smashed the bottle against the tree.

24 "Sim Grant's dead now and I wouldn't want it to get out on him," my father said.

25 That's just one of the kind of things he'd tell. Of course the men knew he was lying, but they seemed to like it just the same.

26 When we got broke, down and out, do you think he ever brought anything home? Not he. If there wasn't anything to eat in the house, he'd go off visiting around at farmhouses. They all wanted him. Sometimes he'd stay away for weeks, mother working to keep us fed and then home he'd come bringing, let's say, a ham.

He'd got it from some farmer friend. He'd slap it on the table in the kitchen. "You bet I'm going to see that my kids have something to eat," he'd say, and mother would just stand smiling at him. She'd never say a word about all the weeks and months he'd been away, not leaving us a cent for food. Once I heard her speaking to a woman in our street. Maybe the woman had dared to sympathize with her. "Oh," she said, "it's all right. He isn't ever dull like most of the men in this street. Life is never dull when my man is about."

27 But often I was filled with bitterness, and sometimes I wished he wasn't my father. I'd even invent another man as my father. To protect my mother I'd make up stories of a secret marriage that for some strange reason never got known. As though some man, say the president of a railroad company or maybe a Congressman, had married my mother, thinking his wife was dead and then it turned out she wasn't.

28 So they had to hush it up but I got born just the same. I wasn't really the son of my father. Somewhere in the world there was a very dignified, quite wonderful man who was really my father. I even made myself half believe these fancies.

29 And then there came a certain night. He'd been off somewhere for two or three weeks. He found me alone in the house, reading by the kitchen table.

30 It had been raining and he was very wet. He sat and looked at me for a long time, not saying a word. I was startled, for there was on his face the saddest look I had ever seen. He sat for a time, his clothes dripping. Then he got up.

31 "Come on with me," he said.

32 I got up and went with him out of the house. I was filled with wonder but I wasn't afraid. We went along a dirt road that led down into a valley, about a mile out of town, where there was a pond. We walked in silence. The man who was always talking had stopped his talking.

33 I didn't know what was up and had the queer feeling that I was with a stranger. I don't know whether my father intended it so. I don't think he did.

34 The pond was quite large. It was still raining hard and there were flashes of lightning followed by thunder. We were on a grassy bank at the pond's edge when my father spoke, and in the darkness and rain his voice sounded strange.

35 "Take off your clothes," he said. Still filled with wonder, I began to undress. There was a flash of lightning and I saw that he was already naked.

36 Naked, we went into the pond. Taking my hand he pulled me in. It may be that I was too frightened, too full of a feeling of strangeness, to speak. Before that night my father had never seemed to pay any attention to me.

37 "And what is he up to now?" I kept asking myself. I did not swim very well, but he put my hand on his shoulder and struck out into the darkness.

38 He was a man with big shoulders, a powerful swimmer. In the darkness I could feel the movement of his muscles. We swam to the far edge of the pond and then back to where we had left our clothes. The rain continued and the wind blew. Sometimes my father swam on his back and when he did he took my hand in his large powerful one and moved it over so that it rested always on his shoulder. Sometimes there would be a flash of lightning and I could see his face clearly.

39 It was as it was earlier, in the kitchen, a face filled with sadness. There would be the momentary glimpse of his face and then again the darkness, the wind, and the rain. In me there was a feeling I had never known before.

40 It was a feeling of closeness. It was something strange. It was as though there were only we two in the world. It was as though I had been jerked suddenly out of myself, out of my world of the schoolboy, out of a world in which I was ashamed of my father.

41 He had become blood of my blood; he the strong swimmer and I the boy clinging to him in the darkness. We swam in silence and in silence we dressed in our wet clothes, and went home.

42 There was a lamp lighted in the kitchen and when we came in, the water dripping from us, there was my mother. She smiled at us. I remember that she called us "boys."

43 "What have you boys been up to," she asked, but my father did not answer. As he had begun the evening's experience with me in silence, so he ended it. He turned and looked at me. Then he went, I thought, with a new and strange dignity out of the room.

44 I climbed the stairs to my own room, undressed in the darkness and got into bed. I couldn't sleep and did not want to sleep. For the first time I knew that I was the son of my father. He was a story teller as I was to be. It may be that I even laughed a little softly there in the darkness. If I did, I laughed knowing that I would never again be wanting another father.

Ideas and Meaning

1. What kind of man was Anderson's father? What did Anderson not like about him?
2. What kind of father did Anderson want? Why did he want this kind of father?
3. If you had been Anderson, would you have been embarrassed to be this man's son? Explain.
4. What physical image of Anderson's father do you have? What details in the narrative helped to shape that image?

5. What is the one physical characteristic of his father that Anderson tells us about at the end of the story? Why is this characteristic important in the context?

6. Why doesn't Anderson give a more detailed physical description of his father? Would the narrative have been better if he had done so? Why? Why not?

7. Why did men like the superintendent of schools and the bank clerk like Anderson's father? Why was Anderson surprised that men like these would "fool around" with his father?

8. Anderson writes that his father would "be anything the other man was." What effect did this have on other people? What effect would it have on you?

9. How did Anderson's mother feel about her husband?

10. When and why did Anderson's father begin staying away from home for periods of time? Did his periodic abandonment of his family change your feelings about him? Explain.

11. What was the reason that Anderson's father lost his business? What does this reveal about the father's character?

12. Why did Anderson change his mind about his father? How was his father different that night? What do you imagine caused this difference? Why was the father's face sad?

13. In the last scene what is significant about Anderson's mother calling Anderson and his father "boys"? Is there any irony implied?

14. Have you ever wished that either of your parents were a different kind of person? Explain.

15. Have you ever had an experience similar to Anderson's when you changed your mind about someone? Who was it and what happened to make you chance your opinion of this person?

Development and Style

1. How does Anderson get the reader's attention?
2. What is his point?
3. What is his tone?
4. What is his purpose, and who is his audience?
5. From his writer's voice what picture do you have of Anderson?
6. What is the effect of Anderson's use of colloquialisms such as "couldn't ride for shucks" and "fooling around"?
7. What are some of the words and phrases Anderson uses to refer to his father before he changes his mind? What are their connotations?

8. Discuss the various concrete/specific words and phrases that Anderson uses. Are there any places where you wish that he had been more concrete or specific? Explain.

9. Why does Anderson relate the story his father told about himself and Grant? What other details does Anderson give to support his statement that his father was "always showing off"?

10. What images do you retain of the night swim? Which concrete words and phrases helped to give you these images?

11. What physical characteristic of his father does Anderson repeat from paragraphs 30 through 43? What is the effect of these repetitions?

12. Analyze the transitions Anderson uses from paragraphs 27 through 36. What is his means of transition between paragraphs 10 and 11?

13. Point out the transitions that begin with coordinate conjunctions. How are these effective?

14. Why does narration require the use of transitions related to time? What transitional words or phrases has Anderson used to avoid being overly repetitious of *then* or *and then?*

15. What is the effect of Anderson's use of a question and answer in paragraph 26? What is the effect of the intentional fragment "Not he."?

16. Of the three writers, Gregory, Eiseley, and Anderson, which do you prefer? Explain. In your estimation, which essay has the most significant subject? Explain.

Barry's Two Responses

Reading Journal: "Discovery of a Father" First Response

My primary reaction to this piece is one of empathy with the writer, since I've had to come to terms with my relationship with my own father, which sometimes has involved the sort of painful emotions Anderson is writing about. I find myself envying the writer, because he at least had a scene of reconciliation which my life lacked, at least in the same fulfilling sense that Anderson speaks of.

Since I'm able to relate to Anderson's essay in a fairly basic way, I have to wonder if the things which underlie his story are somewhat universal. I write that with the suspicion that they are, at least to the degree that every son must somehow come to terms with his father, in order to come to terms with himself. The effectiveness of Anderson's essay, I think, is that it allows such "universal" meaning to be derived from a limited set of details: the story told here is set in a specific small town, and involves a specific set of characters, but at the same

time a sensitive reader can understand that what is really
going on within the father-son relationship is of broader
meaning than the surface narrative might lead one to believe.

On a technical level, it seems to me that Anderson uses two
devices to good effect. First, the integration of dialogue within
the narrative is well placed and, because it's used sparingly,
helps to give a sense of "realism" to the essay. This in turn
gave me, as a reader, the feeling of empathy which I've mentioned, as well as removing any suspicion that Anderson
might have manufactured material for his essay. It seems to
me that Anderson has drawn upon his memories of childhood
emotions and experiences to give a portrayal of an aspect of
life in a meaningful and truthful sense.

Second Response

As I read Anderson's essay once more, a vague notion that
somehow what he is writing about is "mythic" came to mind.
In particular, I'm thinking about the two paragraphs near the
end which begin "It was a feeling of closeness" and "He had
become blood of my blood," respectively. In these passages
Anderson succeeds in communicating some emotional sense
which can only be partially explained, I think. But it has a
real power.

Another aspect of this piece is the author's use of language.
The whole tone of "Discovery of a Father" is simple and direct,
with short sentences and informal speech. One question I had
while reading the essay, however, is: who is Anderson's intended reader? His style and "voice" seem to indicate that he
meant this for a general audience; it's interesting to me that
he could write about himself and his past so bluntly. I've
heard more than once that a real author always exposes himself, but it's always a bit of a surprise to actually see that happening.

Being an adult male, it's impossible to avoid seeing Anderson's essay in connection with my own past. It's also ironic,
since in my case I wanted my father to be more normal than
he was (or could be), whereas Anderson writes that he
wanted something almost opposite from that: "I wanted him
to be a proud, silent, dignified father." I wanted my father to
teach me the things that a middle-class, suburban kid needed
to know, like how to play football or how to work with cars. I
don't want to get too personal in this response, but this essay
naturally elicits such a reaction.

Finally, as I was reading the essay I wondered whether Anderson ever questioned the veracity of his writing. By this I
mean whether he felt any mistrust about the clarity of his

memory, and if so how he came to terms with that. Of course, that's an impossible question to answer, but the inner process of the writer's mind intrigues me. Along with this, I have to wonder how much time had passed between the author's childhood and his attempt to write about it. It seems to me that the distance required to write about such experiences is gained for the most part by allowing years to go by. That poses another quandary: if one relies too much upon memory, how truthful can the writing be? No matter what the exact length of time, Anderson seems to have resolved this (probably unconsciously) creatively indeed.

MAYA ANGELOU

Grandmother's Encounter

1 "Thou shall not be dirty" and "Thou shall not be impudent" were the two commandments of Grandmother Henderson upon which hung our total salvation.

2. Each night in the bitterest winter we were forced to wash faces, arms, necks, legs and feet before going to bed. She used to add, with a smirk that unprofane people can't control when venturing into profanity, "and wash as far as possible, then wash possible."

3 We would go to the well and wash in the ice-cold, clear water, grease our legs with the equally cold stiff Vaseline, then tiptoe into the house. We wiped the dust from our toes and settled down for schoolwork, cornbread, clabbered milk, prayers and bed, always in that order. Momma was famous for pulling the quilts off after we had fallen asleep to examine our feet. If they weren't clean enough for her, she took the switch (she kept one behind the bedroom door for emergencies) and woke up the offender with a few aptly placed burning reminders.

4 The area around the well at night was dark and slick, and boys told about how snakes love water, so that anyone who had to draw water at night and then stand there alone and wash knew that moccasins and rattlers, puff adders and boa constrictors were winding their way to the well and would arrive just as the person washing got soap in her eyes. But Momma convinced us that not only was cleanliness next to Godliness, dirtiness was the inventor of misery.

5 The impudent child was detested by God and a shame to its parents and could bring destruction to its house and line. All adults had to be addressed as Mister, Missus, Miss, Auntie, Cousin, Unk, Uncle, Buhbah, Sister, Brother and a thousand other appellations indicating familial relationship and the lowliness of the addressor.

6 Everyone I knew respected these customary laws, except for the powhitetrash children.

7 Some families of powhitetrash lived on Momma's farm land behind the school. Sometimes a gaggle of them came to the Store, filling the whole room, chasing out the air and even changing the well-known scents. The children crawled over the shelves and into the potato and onion bins, twanging all the time in their sharp voices like cigarbox guitars. They took liberties in my Store that I would never dare. Since Momma told us that the less you say to whitefolks (or even powhitetrash) the better, Bailey and I would stand, solemn, quiet, in the displaced air. But if one of the playful apparitions got close to us, I pinched it. Partly out of angry frustration and partly because I didn't believe in its flesh reality.

8 They called my uncle by his first name and ordered him around the Store. He, to my crying shame, obeyed them in his limping dip-straight-dip fashion.

9 My grandmother, too, followed their orders, except that she didn't seem to be servile because she anticipated their needs.

10 "Here's sugar, Miz Potter, and here's baking powder. You didn't buy soda last month, you'll probably be needing some."

11 Momma always directed her statements to the adults, but sometimes, Oh painful sometimes, the grimy, snotty-nosed girls would answer her.

12 "Naw, Annie . . ."—to Momma? Who owned the land they lived on? Who forgot more than they would ever learn? If there was any justice in the world, God should strike them dumb at once!—"Just give us some extra sody crackers, and some more mackerel."

13 At least they never looked in her face, or I never caught them doing so. Nobody with a smidgen of training, not even the worst roustabout, would look right in a grown person's face. It meant the person was trying to take the words out before they were formed. The dirty little children didn't do that, but they threw their orders around the Store like lashes from a cat-o'-nine-tails.

14 When I was around ten years old, those scruffy children caused me the most painful and confusing experience I had ever had with my grandmother.

15 One summer morning, after I had swept the dirt yard of leaves, spearmint-gum wrappers and Vienna-sausage labels, I raked the yellow-red dirt, and made half-moons carefully, so that the design stood out clearly and masklike. I put the rake behind the Store and came through the back of the house to find Grandmother on the front porch in her big, wide white apron. The apron was so stiff by virtue of the starch that it could have stood alone. Momma was admiring the yard, so I joined her. It truly looked like a flat redhead that had been raked with a big-toothed comb. Momma

didn't say anything but I knew she liked it. She looked over toward the school principal's house and to the right at Mr. McElroy's. She was hoping one of those community pillars would see the design before the day's business wiped it out. Then she looked upward to thc school. My head had swung with hers, so at just about the same time we saw a troop of the powhitetrash kids marching over the hill and down by the side of the school.

16 I looked to Momma for direction. She did an excellent job of sagging from her waist down, but from the waist up she seemed to be pulling for the top of the oak tree across the road. Then she began to moan a hymn. Maybe not to moan, but the tune was so slow and the meter so strange that she could have been moaning. She didn't look at me again. When the children reached halfway down the hill, halfway to the Store, she said without turning, "Sister, go on inside."

17 I wanted to beg her, "Momma, don't wait for them. Come on inside with me. If they come in the Store, you go to the bedroom and let me wait on them. They only frighten me if you're around. Alone I know how to handle them." But of course I couldn't say anything, so I went in and stood behind the screen door.

18 Before the girls got to the porch I heard their laughter crackling and popping like pine logs in a cooking stove. I suppose my life-long paranoia was born in those cold, molasses-slow minutes. They came finally to stand on the ground in front of Momma. At first they pretended seriousness. Then one of them wrapped her right arm in the crook of her left, pushed out her mouth and started to hum. I realized that she was aping my grandmother. Another said, "Naw, Helen, you ain't standing like her. This here's it." Then she lifted her chest, folded her arms and mocked that strange carriage that was Annie Henderson. Another laughed, "Naw, you can't do it. Your mouth ain't pooched out enough. It's like this."

19 I thought about the rifle behind the door, but I knew I'd never be able to hold it straight, and the .410, our sawed-off shotgun, which stayed loaded and was fired every New Year's night, was locked in the trunk and Uncle Willie had the key on his chain. Through the fly-specked screen-door, I could see that the arms of Momma's apron jiggled from the vibrations of her humming. But her knees seemed to have locked as if they would never bend again.

20 She sang on. No louder than before, but no softer either. No slower or faster.

21 The dirt of the girls' cotton dresses continued·on their legs, feet, arms and faces to make them all of a piece. Their greasy uncolored hair hung down, uncombed, with a grim finality. I knelt to see them better, to remember them for all time. The tears that had slipped down my dress left unsurprising dark spots, and made

the front yard blurry and even more unreal. The world had taken a deep breath and was having doubts about continuing to revolve.

22 The girls had tired of mocking Momma and turned to other means of agitation. One crossed her eyes, stuck her thumbs in both sides of her mouth and said, "Look here, Annie." Grandmother hummed on and the apron strings trembled. I wanted to throw a handful of black pepper in their faces, to throw lye on them, to scream that they were dirty, scummy peckerwoods, but I knew I was as clearly imprisoned behind the scene as the actors outside were confined to their roles.

23 One of the smaller girls did a kind of puppet dance while her fellow clowns laughed at her. But the tall one, who was almost a woman, said something very quietly, which I couldn't hear. They all moved backward from the porch, still watching Momma. For an awful second I thought they were going to throw a rock at Momma, who seemed (except for the apron strings) to have turned into stone herself. But the big girl turned her back, bent down and put her hands flat on the ground—she didn't pick up anything. She simply shifted her weight and did a hand stand.

24 Her dirty bare feet and long legs went straight for the sky. Her dress fell down around her shoulders, and she had on no drawers. The slick pubic hair made a brown triangle where her legs came together. She hung in the vacuum of that lifeless morning for only a few seconds, then wavered and tumbled. The other girls clapped her on the back and slapped their hands.

25 Momma changed her song to "Bread of Heaven, bread of Heaven, feed me till I want no more."

26 I found that I was praying too. How long could Momma hold out? What new indignity would they think of to subject her to? Would I be able to stay out of it? What would Momma really like me to do?

27 Then they were moving out of the yard, on their way to town. They bobbed their heads and shook their slack behinds and turned, one at a time:

28 " 'Bye, Annie."

29 " 'Bye, Annie."

30 " 'Bye, Annie."

31 Momma never turned her head or unfolded her arms, but she stopped singing and said, " 'Bye, Miz Helen, 'bye, Miz Ruth, 'bye, Miz Eloise."

32 I burst. A firecracker July-the-Fourth burst. How could Momma call them Miz? The mean nasty things. Why couldn't she have come inside the sweet, cool store when we saw them breasting the hill? What did she prove? And then if they were dirty, mean and impudent, why did Momma have to call them Miz?

33 She stood another whole song through and then opened the

screen door to look down on me crying in rage. She looked until I looked up. Her face was a brown moon that shone on me. She was beautiful. Something had happened out there, which I couldn't completely understand, but I could see that she was happy. Then she bent down and touched me as mothers of the church "lay hands on the sick and afflicted" and I quieted.

34 "Go wash your face, Sister." And she went behind the candy counter and hummed, "Glory, glory, hallelujah, when I lay my burden down."

35 I threw the well water on my face and used the weekday handkerchief to blow my nose. Whatever the contest had been out front, I knew Momma had won.

36 I took the rake back to the front yard. The smudged footprints were easy to erase. I worked for a long time on my new design and laid the rake behind the wash pot. When I came back in the Store, I took Momma's hand and we both walked outside to look at the pattern.

37 It was a large heart with lots of hearts growing smaller inside, and piercing from the outside rim to the smallest heart was an arrow. Momma said, "Sister, that's right pretty." Then she turned back to the Store and resumed, "Glory, glory, hallelujah, when I lay my burden down."

Ideas and Meaning

1. How did Angelou's grandmother win her confrontation with the "powhitetrash" girls?
2. How are the girls and their behavior a contrast to the two precepts that Maya's grandmother had taught her?
3. What adjectives would you use to describe Angelou's grandmother?
4. What adjectives would you use to describe Maya Angelou?
5. Is Maya still confused at the end of the narrative? If so, why? How would you feel in her place?
6. Why was this a painful and confusing experience for Angelou?
7. Why did Maya's grandmother order her to go inside before the girls got there?
8. Why did Maya rake the new design in the dirt? How is it symbolic?
9. How is the hymn that Maya's grandmother sings appropriate to the occasion? What is the grandmother's "burden"? (There may be more than one.)
10. What does Angelou mean in paragraph 18 when she says that her "lifelong paranoia" was born as she waited for the girls?
11. Have you ever witnessed the humiliation of someone close

to you? How did you react? How did you feel? Was the incident racist?

Development and Style

1. How does Angelou get the reader's attention?
2. What is her tone? Who is her audience and what is her purpose?
3. What is Angelou's point?
4. Point out some of the concrete/specific words and phrases in the narrative. Which ones are particularly effective in giving you images? Which of your senses does each appeal to?
5. Point out the metaphors and similes Angelou uses. How are they appropriate? What are their connotations? (Don't overlook "gaggle of them" in paragraph 7.)
6. Although there really is no dialogue, because there is no exchange between two speakers, there is use of quotation. How do these quotations indicate the character of Maya's grandmother? Of the girls? How do the quotations help create a more vivid image of the grandmother and the "powhitetrash" girls?
7. Analyze the transitions from paragraphs 5 to 12.

Marcia's Two Responses

Reading Journal: "Grandmother's Encounter" First Response

A lesson in austerity. "Do not go gentle into that good night—rage, rage against the dying of the light." Rather than succumb to the malicious antics of the "powhitetrash" girls, Momma raged in her own quiet, holy, good way against their efforts to extinguish her light. She shone. She taught her granddaughter to shine.

Like the designs in the red clay dirt that Maya made with a rake, Momma designed her behavior to govern against the belittling actions of the "powhitetrash" girls. Her hymns and prayers were her only response. Her faith and trust in the time when she would "lay down her burdens" is all that matters.

Yet the injustice is so very hard to swallow, especially for the young ones who are so confused and feel the worst hurt.

Yet before Maya let go into the rage, she clung to the rock of her grandmother—this saved her from sinking. The dirty white girls tried to get them to swim into their scummy pool. But it didn't work because the rock of faith is stronger than any swift currents.

There is dignity in simplicity. The simplicity of a clean-raked yard is dignified. The simplicity of a starched apron and a hymn is the dignity of design. The "powhitetrash" girls will never see the design because they don't know what dignity entails. Daughter to daughter to daughter, designs are shared, and the strength of faith and simplicity overcomes all the rising, muddy waters.

Second Response

The caged bird sings. He sings of times when no cage will hold him in; he sings of winging across open fields where no color lines are drawn except the colors of wildflowers and dragonflies. His song, like Momma's, is of undying hope. Caged, one's wings are clipped. Yet, in a cage, dreams can fly in and out and around the bars free and unfettered.

Caged by ignorance and these harsh times of prejudice and injustice, we can still sing full-throated of freedom that's bound to come as a result of our songs. Though we grow hoarse at times and our voices tremble with weakness or are drowned out by noises from our captors, our song remains the same in spirit. Hope and dreams cannot be caged, but the sound of strength and determination in the music is heard. It may not always be listened to, but it is heard. Songs of such strength cannot be ignored.

Caged birds sing of freedom of flight. They sing of breezes, of berries, of nests and children. Though their freedom of movement is restricted, their freedom of voice and song is uncageable. Momma sang loud and clear from her cage in the white man's world. And she sang louder and stronger than the squawks and shrill shrieks of her trying captors. The beauty and purity of her song prevailed. Even in a cage, there is some freedom.

Conclusion

There is no doubt that in both of her responses, Marcia has participated in a meaningful dialogue with Angelou by means of the text.

Last, it is interesting to note that although all four reading selections differ from each other in subject matter and in style, emotional pain of one kind or another is at the heart of all four writers' experiences. Whether or not you write about an experience that caused you emotional pain, in the next chapter you will be given the opportunity to write about a significant experience in your life.

Writing the Personal Narrative

8

Like Maya Angelou, Loren Eiseley, Sherwood Anderson, and Dick Gregory, you will want to use concrete/specific words and metaphors to help you describe the people and places in the narrative you write. Like them also, you will find that paying attention to connotation will help you choose just the right word to convey your attitudes towards the people and places in your narrative. In addition, like Dick Gregory, if your narrative contains a verbal conflict between two people, you might use dialogue to give vividness and immediacy to the scene. In fact, with the exception, perhaps, of dialogue writing, all the skills you have learned thus far will be important to you as you draft an essay that concerns a significant event in your life.

Finding a Topic

All vastly different from each other, the four reading selections in the last chapter may have already given you several ideas for your own personal narrative. Perhaps in one or more of your responses to these essays or even to those in previous chapters, you have written about experiences of your own through association with the various writers' experiences. Also, if you have continued to keep a journal, you may have written about several experiences that would make good subjects for a narrative. In fact, your journal and reading responses can be invaluable sources of ideas not only for this essay but for all the others you will write throughout the course. Because these sources of ideas also give you a "head start," so to speak, it would be a good idea for you to get in the habit of looking through both your reading responses and your journal before you try any other method of getting ideas for an essay.

After you have looked through your journal and responses, you can begin to list under some or all of the following headings to help you discover even more possibilities. It is likely that any ideas you may have garnered from your journal or responses will fit under one of these headings, but if not, create a heading of your own to fit your experience. (And, by all means, share your additional headings with your classmates!)

Confusing or Painful Experiences

    Shame—second-grade teacher
    Grandmother—"powhitetrash" girls

Times I Understood Something I Hadn't Before

    My swim with father
    Grandmother—dignity in face of humiliation

Animals or People I Learned From

    Maddy—taught me how to "bow"
    Wino—help others

Roles I've Learned to Play

    Teacher/performer

Times I Changed My Mind about Someone

    My swim with father

Discovery of (Fill in the blank with any word or phrase that names a discovery you made as a result of a certain experience.)
    A father
    Dignity in the face of humiliation
    How to get approval

My Encounter with (Fill in the blank with any word or phrase that names a person, thing, or idea you have encountered.)
    Racism
    Fear
    The need for approval

Experiences with Racism or Other Prejudices
Grandmother and the girls
Second-grade teacher

These headings are by no means all the possibilities. For example, you could list times that you were wrong, things you regret doing, or decisions you regret making, to name just a few other ideas that could result in your listing a number of significant personal experiences. In any event, list under several headings—those just suggested or those you think of yourself. As you list, don't discard anything that comes to mind, even if it doesn't happen to fit under the particular heading you are working on at the time. After you have listed under several headings, read your list and check those subjects that interest you most. Then, about each of these subjects, ask this question: Was this a significant experience? That is, did the experience change you in some way, perhaps giving you a new insight into yourself or another person, perhaps changing an attitude you had had, or changing your perception of yourself or another person? Also, if you have listed the death of someone close to you or a topic such as religious conversion, you might want to exclude these for a number of reasons. For one thing, these are significant experiences for everyone. Also, most of us are affected much the same by the death of a close relative. Furthermore, religious conversion is very difficult to make concrete, as well as being a very private matter and one that is difficult to write about without sounding "preachy." Do not let these cautionary remarks prevent you from choosing either one of these topics, however, if you feel that your experiences were unique and describable in concrete terms.

To give you more ideas, you can read Cheryl's and Maria's final drafts, which follow.

Cheryl's Final Draft

Daddy

1 Daddy: a man I happened to visit twice a year for two weeks of fun-filled adventure—until I got old enough to say "No, I can't this year. I'm busy" (the excuse he used to use on us at Christmas).

2 My childhood images of Daddy are very romanticized. (All childhood images are, I suppose.) Daddy: a six-foot-two handsome doctor; one-eighth American Indian; a pipe smoker. "My Daddy this, my daddy that," I used to say. I was easily impressed.

3 We were picked up in his Vista Cruiser station wagon with the sunroof twice a year for the visit. (Or we were flown out to him if Stepmother was in an especially vile mood.) Then we set out on a trip as far away from Stepmother (Sue, that is, Melba Sue) as possible. I was never sure if Daddy was embarrassed about Her and her fits, or if he was trying to hide his OLD family from his NEW town or if, pure and simply, she couldn't stand us; loathed us; hated us with every ounce of her country blood. (She used to slam doors, scream, cry, then leave when he brought us home.)

4 Nevertheless, we enjoyed being on the road with Daddy— treated to luxuries my mother couldn't dream of providing for us: an endless flow of Coca-Cola, barbecue potato chips on de-

mand, cameras bought just for the trip, and the trips themselves—camping in style in a rented Winnebago high in the Virginia mountains. The pool in his backyard wasn't so bad, either, but we never got to use it much. Needless to say, my mother tired easily of our stories about the trips to Daddy's.

5   Mom had stories of her own. The stories of Daddy I had to live with the remaining fifty weeks of the year. Daddy: the man my mother slaved for, to put through medical school only to be left high and dry with 5 and 1/4 children. Daddy: the man who deserted his five "beautiful" children and wife for the cheap floozy (Sue, Melba Sue). Daddy: the man who reluctantly conceded to pay my mother $500 a month so that she could raise HER children and so that he could wipe his hands of child-raising. Daddy: the man who raised his children's hopes and expectations only to shatter them with a phone call and an apology for another no-show. Daddy: the man of empty promises.

6   I don't think my mother meant to hurt us with the Daddy stories. I think she wanted to make us wiser, not to let us be fooled by him as she had been. She was a tired, lonely, poor mother desperately trying to raise five girls on her own meagre salary and his even more meagre child support. I guess she was doing her best with the resources available.

7   Gradually, as the Daddy stories developed and grew worse, and I developed enough sense to really understand their meaning, my romantic images began to be replaced by reality. One story (it's not a story, it's steadfast reality that can never be washed away) has been neatly imprinted on my brain; it shattered all hopes of my hanging on to Daddy as the idolized father. I read the divorce transcripts. I found them and I read them. My mother had hidden the real horror from us because she still loved him. She loved him after he came home with lipstick on his collar—a patient had died; he comforted the widow. She loved him after she crawled out from under the car, having escaped shots from his rifle. She loved him after he kept her bedridden, doping her up on drugs which led to her miscarriage of my only brother. She loved him so much she gave him a divorce. She may love him still. I don't.

8   Now the memories of Daddy are hard to remember, some harder to forget. Only Caroline, the youngest, has not broken ties with him. She perhaps still has a little of the romantic vision intact. Once as the Trailways pulled away, little Caroline cried. Bawled. "He looks so sad!" She was young and naive enough to feel sorry for him. He didn't have the home she had with her four sisters and mother. All he had was his bank account to go home to. Maybe this insane sympathy has kept her calling him. And she's now in college. She depends on his

financial support. I hypocritically did the same for a time, sweetly calling him up to talk . . . ending with a mention of the tuition bill in the mail. I used to wish so hard that I could do it somehow without his help, to stuff all of my anger and resentment back in his face, and my phone calls to him got fewer and fewer. Then stopped.

9 My mother raised me and I am my mother's child. Her best advice she gave me from her own life experience—"Never trust a man. Make a life of your own before you make a life with him." I like to think that I am this independent and I like to think I never missed not having a daddy. But I know I missed something, something my stepsister knows. I regret not ever having had time to really know him (if I could ever forgive him). I wish he had taken time to know me. Daddy now?: a man I never really knew.

Ideas and Meaning

1. Why does Cheryl resent her father?
2. How had she felt about him as a young child? What caused her to change her feelings?
3. What picture do you have of Cheryl's father? How do you feel about him?
4. What picture do you have of Cheryl's mother? How do you feel about her?
5. If you had been Cheryl's mother, would you have told your children anything about their father? Explain.
6. Is the advice her mother has given Cheryl wise? Explain.
7. Who does Cheryl blame more for her not knowing her father? Her mother, her father, or herself?
8. Why did she wish that she did not have to ask her father for financial help when she was in college? Would you feel the same? Explain.
9. Is the picture of the stepmother a stereotypical one? Explain.
10. If you had been Cheryl, would you have written about this experience? Explain.
11. What has Cheryl learned as a result of her parents' divorce? Are all the effects of the divorce negative? Explain.

Development and Style

1. How does Cheryl get the reader's attention?
2. What is her tone? Who is her audience?
3. What is her point?
4. What details in Cheryl's narrative support her point?
5. Point out the concrete/specific words and phrases in paragraphs 2, 3, 4, 7, and 8.

6. Are there any places in her narrative where Cheryl needs more concrete/specific details? If so, what would you suggest?

7. In paragraph 3, which words or phrases associated with the stepmother have negative connotations? What are the connotations of each?

8. In paragraph 6, what are the connotations of the adjectives Cheryl uses to describe her mother?

9. Point out the transitions from paragraphs 3 through 7. Are there any weak transitions in the essay? If so, how would you strengthen them? Which transitions are particularly strong?

10. In paragraph 3, why does Cheryl capitalize these words that ordinarily would not be capitalized? *Stepmother, Her, She, OLD,* and *NEW?*

11. In paragraph 1, what is the effect of Cheryl's use of a dash between the noun *adventure* and the conjunction *until?* Ordinarily, what would the punctuation be? Which do you prefer? Why?

12. In paragraph 2, why does Cheryl use semicolons instead of commas between the series of noun phrases in apposition to the noun *Daddy?* What mark do you prefer? Why?

13. Discuss the effects of Cheryl's use of parenthetical phrases and clauses in paragraphs 1, 2, 3, 5, 7, and 9. Are there any parentheses you would not use? In each instance, what punctuation would you substitute?

14. Point out the parallelism in paragraphs 5 and 7. What are the effects?

15. What are the effects of the intentional fragments in paragraph 5?

16. What is the effect of Cheryl's beginning and ending her essay with the same construction?

Maria's Final Draft

Primrose Perfect

1 Mother loved us and always called us her flowers, the fastest growing she had ever raised. There were six of us in her garden, which sometimes became so crowded that the more fragile blossoms were shaded from warmth by the bolder, brighter blooms.

2 In that plot of ample chrysanthemums and brilliant dahlias, I saw myself as a primrose, if not a weed, who wanted more than anything to be sublime.

3 And so I became the perfect flower. The more perfect I became, the more nourishing attention was lavished upon me. If

I made a B in school, I was good; but if I made an A, I was
perfect. Never did I sway or bend to temptations to adolescent
storms as did my siblings. Never did I show anger. Never did I
lie. Never did I live. But I was perfect—perfect in every way.

4 So perfect was I, that, when mother had to take a job, I was
picked to tend the garden—picked and held tight in my father's hand at the age of twelve.

5 Then I became the paragon of domestic efficiency—the perfect cook, the perfect housekeeper, the perfect peacemaker.

6 Peace among my brothers and sisters, but never within myself, for the best was no longer sufficient. I could not be perfect enough. No matter how perfectly I performed, I could always find fault. A neurotic choking vine had taken root in the
garden and would constrict and stunt my growth for years to
come.

7 That same vine was transplanted along with me in the virgin, but not so perfect, soil of marriage in which the attention
and praise that fed the flower was withheld and I began to
shrivel. In this new garden I received no praise. My husband
did not know how to give it; and my parents, angry at having
their flower snatched from their hands, withheld all nourish-
ment.

8 For want of approval, I thought I would surely starve, and
so I tried harder. I was such a good little wife. So efficient. So
patient. So perfect.

9 Still there was no praise for the perfect little wife soon to
become perfect mother. The Virgin Mary was no match for
me—and still—no praise; not even when I gave birth to a
flawless baby boy.

10 As my baby grew, so too, did I. Eating seemed my only sol-
ace, my only reward—eating and my baby boy. No longer was
I perfect. I was fat.

11 This flaw nagged me and disgusted me, but at least then, I
could see why my husband didn't love me. He had a reason.

12 Furthermore, I hated myself. I had failed at perfection,
failed at marriage, failed at my own expectations.

13 The flower seemed bigger and brighter than ever before, but
poisonous self-hatred ran through its veins and stems, finally
reaching the petals, where it began to manifest itself out-
wardly. Then the blossom shriveled due to excessive dieting
and freakish fasting.

14 Healthy became thin. Thin became gaunt. And gaunt became emaciated as I plummeted from 140 pounds to 90 in six
months. I was determined to be perfectly thin, and to regain
the praise and love that I had lost. But even my parents, who
were reconciled by now to my marriage, did not approve.
Their faces were anxious and full of disgust for the body that I

still deemed less than perfectly thin. That body, too weak and small to resist, was falling prey to the neurotic killing weed, anorexia nervosa. The bloom was dying, fading slowly, senselessly away.

15 That weed began to take control of my life. I made excuses for missing meals, turned down party invitations, and pretended to eat to appease my family. Becoming a master of deceit, I left candy wrappers in my purse and car so that my husband would think I was not dieting. Hour after hour, I weighed myself. When I lost, I was high. When I didn't, I was suicidal.

16 Like diseased petals dropping from a withered flower, my hair began to fall. Joints swelled from malnutrition, and bulging veins, raised green and ridged, encircled and twined around my cadaverous arms. No longer was I a functioning adult female. Stamen-starved, I was biologically a child—an unhealthy little girl. And still no praise.

17 Those manifestations that shocked and horrified others, I looked upon as marks of achievement on my way to perfection—or death.

18 I really didn't want to live. I see that now, not without praise which to me was equivalent to love. My soul was parched for want of approval. This drought lasted for months and months, until my family convinced me to seek help. I found the help I needed under the guidance of a patient and sensitive therapist. Showering myself day after day with approval, I learned to listen to my own applause. Unconditionally I began to accept myself, realizing that each flower in the universe is unique, and that this individuality is more precious than the most perfect bloom.

19 In a garden where rain doesn't always fall, I have learned to make my own rain—I have learned to love myself.

Ideas and Meaning

1. What does Maria suggest were the causes of her anorexia? What was the primary cause?
2. What were the symptoms of the disease?
3. How did Maria differ from most women who develop anorexia?
4. How was she cured?
5. Were Maria's parents at fault in any way? Why? Why not?
6. Was Maria's husband in any way to blame for her anorexia? Why? Why not?
7. How did Maria learn to live without the praise of others? Can people live comfortably without any approval from others? Why? Why not?

8. What are the dangers of this disease? What were some of the effects on Maria?

9. If you have known someone who had anorexia, what happened to this person? If she recovered, what were the permanent damages she suffered?

10. If you had had anorexia, would you have written about it? Why? Why not? Do you admire Maria for writing about her experience with the disease? Why? Why not? Why do you think she wrote about it?

Development and Style

1. How does Maria get the reader's attention?

2. What is her tone? Who is her audience? What is her point?

3. How does Maria use the garden/flower metaphor? Is it effective? Why? Why not? Is it appropriate? Why? Why not? Does it seem overused to you? Why? Why not?

4. What adjectives does Maria use to describe herself as the disease progressed? What are the denotations and connotations of each?

5. What concrete/specific details has Maria used in her essay? Are there any places where she could have been more concrete or specific?

6. Analyze the transitions Maria has used. Has she varied the means of transition?

7. Point out Maria's use of parallel structure and intentional fragments. What are the effects of each?

8. Which student's writing did you prefer—Maria's or Cheryl's? Why? Which student wrote about the more significant experience, or would you say that their subjects were equally significant? Explain. From her writer's voice, which student would you prefer to meet? Explain.

Talking through Ideas

Once you have several subjects that are significant experiences, it might be useful at this point to talk through them with several classmates in a small group. Your groupmates can respond by telling you which subjects they think would make the best essays. After you get this feedback, it would be best, perhaps, to choose two or three subjects that your groupmates liked. Then, if you write a short draft of each topic, getting down only what happened, you will have something to fall back on if the one you prefer and decide to develop doesn't work out as well for you as you thought it would. Also, if you write short drafts of two or three subjects, you could have another meeting with groupmates and read all drafts aloud to them, asking which one they prefer. If it should happen that your groupmates prefer a subject that does not interest you as much as another one does, by all means write about the experience that interests you most.

Following is Angie's first draft of the subject both she and her group preferred. You will notice that the subject of this draft is a fire that resulted in the death of a playmate. However, the essay is not about grief, but about a realization that Angie had as a result of the fire that caused her playmate's death.

Angie's First Draft

Event that Caused a Painful Emotion

An event which stands out vividly in my memory occurred when I was a very small child. This experience happened on a Sunday afternoon. Sunday afternoons at my house when I was a child were always so nice.

I was sitting on the floor in the kitchen, and my brother and I were looking at the Sunday comics. We had just come home from church, and it was a beautiful, sunny day. Mama was standing in the kitchen in her pink checkered apron frying chicken for dinner. I remember staring at her and thinking that she was very beautiful.

Suddenly, the phone rang, and Mama picked it up. I noticed that Mama's happy expression suddenly changed into a look of anxiety. She turned the stove off and took my two brothers and me next door. Then she left in a hurry.

While we were playing outside, we noticed smoke in the distance and decided to go see what was going on, even though we weren't supposed to leave the yard.

Well, to make a long story short, it was my best friend's house that was on fire, and she died inside the house before anyone could get her out. I remember watching the firemen drag a crumpled little body out and cover it up.

That was my first experience with death, and as a very young child I first realized that life is not permanent. I also realized how cruel life can be. Even the very young are not promised tomorrow.

This is a good start. Angie has gotten down what happened, and now she needs to make her reader experience what she did by using the sensory data that she remembers. Before Angie wrote another draft of her essay, she "cubed" her subject.

Cubing: An Invention Technique

An invention technique called cubing, developed by Elizabeth and Gregory Cowan, is useful because it makes you look at your subject from six points of view, hence the name of the technique. Since cubing forces you to look at your subject from several perspectives, it is a useful method of invention for all kinds of subjects, those suitable for exposition and persuasion, as well as for narration. Furthermore, you will find that cubing will be a useful technique in your other college courses and beyond—in "real-world" writing itself.

To cube a subject, you freewrite for three to five minutes as you respond to each point of view of your subject prescribed by the cube. Therefore cubing will take you eighteen to thirty minutes to complete, depending on how long you write on each side of the cube. A description of cubing follows, as well as the results of Angie's cubing of her subject, so that you can see how the process works.

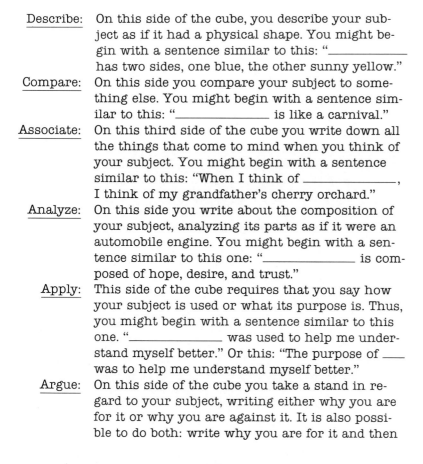

Describe: On this side of the cube, you describe your subject as if it had a physical shape. You might begin with a sentence similar to this: "_____ has two sides, one blue, the other sunny yellow."

Compare: On this side you compare your subject to something else. You might begin with a sentence similar to this: "_____ is like a carnival."

Associate: On this third side of the cube you write down all the things that come to mind when you think of your subject. You might begin with a sentence similar to this: "When I think of _____, I think of my grandfather's cherry orchard."

Analyze: On this side you write about the composition of your subject, analyzing its parts as if it were an automobile engine. You might begin with a sentence similar to this one: "_____ is composed of hope, desire, and trust."

Apply: This side of the cube requires that you say how your subject is used or what its purpose is. Thus, you might begin with a sentence similar to this one. "_____ was used to help me understand myself better." Or this: "The purpose of ___ was to help me understand myself better."

Argue: On this side of the cube you take a stand in regard to your subject, writing either why you are for it or why you are against it. It is also possible to do both: write why you are for it and then why you are against it. If you do so, of course, you'll have a seven-sided cube, but in the interest of more ideas, surely adherence to mathematical verities is unimportant. You might begin this side of the cube with a sentence similar to one of these (or both): "I am for _____ because it taught me something about myself that I didn't know before." Or: "I am against _____ because it was very painful, not only to me but to someone I care for deeply."

Angie's Cubing

Describe: Rather than to give my subject a physical description, I'd prefer to describe the way the day began. It began as a rather typical summer Sunday. This is the pleasant side of the story. I was a six-year-old child sitting on the kitchen floor. The smell of the chicken frying warmed my nose and caused my mouth to begin watering. Gospel music drifted in from the television, and the comics were spread out before me on the floor like a huge fan. I could hear the rambunctious laughter of my brothers in another room. This pleasant scene contrasts with the horrible scene at the end. I hope this will come across.

Compare: This experience was like dark clouds on a sunny day or like shadows in the sunshine. I was thinking of this for a title. It was a very painful experience. It starts out pleasant but ends tragically. This is typical of life.

Associate: When I think of the fire that killed my best friend, I think of a huge, terrible beast. I have been terribly frightened of fires ever since, especially when I was a child. I seemed to think of the fire as if it were a real living, breathing creature that was angry. I also think of my friend, of course, and I remember many afternoons we spent playing house with our dolls.

Analyze: My subject is composed of two parts. The first part is very pleasant and I need to use a pleasant tone. Things included in this section are sunshine, laughter, pleasant music, Mama's smile, good smells, and nice images. I wrote down a sensory list before each section and these are some of the things I remembered for this one. The first section ends with the piercing ring of

the telephone. This section is where my "troubles begin." The last section is the unpleasant
one and it consists of painful emotions and imagery.

Apply: The purpose of my subject is to prove the harsh
impermanence of life. Nothing is constant, and
this is a sad fact of life. Unfortunately, I had to
learn it at an early age. I suppose that all the
sad facts we learn about life are used to help us
better meet those calamities that befall us as we
live our lives. I have used this experience to help
me accept the fact that we are not guaranteed
life beyond the moment.

Argue: If I had to write why I'm for this experience, I'd
say that it taught me an important truth of life
early. And, I'm against it because my friend died
cruelly at an early age. There's not much argument here. I think the point is pretty obvious.
I'm not questioning this fact or trying to come
up with a deep, philosophical "Annie Dillard" answer. I am saying that it was terrible, but I accept it. That's the way life is.

Although Angie has generated some good details here, she might
have been more specific and concrete in some of her statements.
For example, perhaps she could have put in the various odors she
smelled as she sat on the kitchen floor. Then, instead of "gospel
music," which is general, she might have put in the title of a
hymn that she remembered hearing. However, there are two particularly useful consequences of Angie's cubing. One is that she
began to think of her organization when she analyzed her subject,
and when she associated, she came up with a metaphor that she
used in her conclusion.

Because your narrative has many parts to it, it might be profitable to cube one or more of these parts in addition to cubing the
subject as a whole. For example, you could cube an important
person or persons in your narrative, or you could cube the climax,
which was Angie's choice.

Cubing: The Climax

Describe: The climax of this narrative was extremely painful. I remember the shock and the hurt I felt
when I saw my best friend being taken away
from the fire. I remember feeling dizzy from the
shock and the heat of the fire. The fire was a
huge orange monster that crunched everything

in its sight, including my friend. She was burned black and her once fair skin was charred black.

Compare: The shock of seeing my friend's death was like being slapped in the face. It was like actually seeing someone from a German concentration camp or something terrible like that. Her face was almost unrecognizable. She looked like she had actually melted and her skin was sagging from her bones. The house looked a lot like she did. It was black and caved in.

Associate: When I think of the fire that killed my friend, I think of ugliness and death. I think of all the terrible disasters that are unexplainable, like the one in the essay "Scorpions in Amber." I think of "Dame Fortune," who spins her wheel and decides who will live and who will die (and who will suffer).

Analyze: My subject is made up of a lot of emotions—sadness, fear, frustration, and despair. These were the emotions I simultaneously felt when I witnessed the event. I think I was too young to be angry. I don't remember feeling any anger.

Apply: The climax of this essay was "helpful" in only one respect. It helped me to realize, at a very early age, that nothing in life is permanent. Up until that time, everything in my life was permanent. I was so very young. I then realized that no matter how sweet and pretty the flowers are, they are going to wilt. No matter how beautiful a day is, a bad day will come. No matter how good things seem, something bad will definitely come along to mess everything up. This is only a part of life.

Argue: I can't really argue for or against this climax. I wish it hadn't happened. That's my only real argument. But it did, and there's nothing I can do about it except come to terms with it. Unlike Annie Dillard, I'm not going to question whether or not God has absconded from the universe. I don't understand why it happened. All I know is that it happened, and it was terrible. I don't think there's any reason or explanation for it, though.

Angie's cubing of her climax has resulted in several descriptive details that did not occur in the first cubing of her narrative. Most of these details are the consequence of the first two sides of the cube—description and comparison. On these two sides she has described the fire as a "huge monster" that "crunched" (an effective, specific verb here since the sound a fire makes is rather like a crunch) everything in its sight. Then, there is the rather ghastly description of her friend's charred black skin that sagged from her bones as if it had melted. Last, on the fifth side of the cube, there is a series of very effective parallel sentences.

Selecting and Organizing Descriptive Details

Angie has plenty of concrete, specific details to use in a further draft. Like her, you will need to select and organize your descriptive details. The first task, selecting the details you need to use, is relatively easy. As a beginning writer, your tendency will probably be to use too many details, but overdoing it, especially at first, is definitely better than underdoing it. Let's use Angie's cubing of her climax as an example. In this cubing, Angie centers only on a description of the fire, her friend, and the house. As a consequence, she really has no details here that may be extraneous to her focus in the climax of her essay. But, in the last paragraph of her essay what if she veered from her focus and began describing *all* her surroundings—the people standing next to her, the fire engines, or the firemen? Let's see how these details would be superfluous and actually detract from the narrative.

Long, harsh tongues of fire licked the sides of the house, swallowing all life inside without mercy. People were milling about like frightened insects. One little man next to me had on a blue and green plaid shirt and dirty blue overalls. His oily brown hair fell over his forehead and his bloodshot eyes watered as he looked at the burning house. . . .

What does this man have to do with Angie's focus at this point in her narrative? Clearly, she does not need these details about the man beside her because he is not the focus of the climax. One more example here should suffice. Suppose that a description of a person is important to your narrative. Suppose you wrote about a night in high school when you were caught coming home several hours late, and your mother came flying down the stairs the moment you closed the front door. Which details would you put in? *Only* the ones you remember. For example, you might write something like this:

I closed the door softly, taking off my shoes at the same time. "Mike!" my mother screamed.
I looked up, and there she was, racing down the stairs, her blue robe flying out behind her and her face full of fear and anger.

You would not write the following description because it contains details that are unnecessary. In this particular scene, you, the narrator, simply would not have noticed the following details.

> I closed the dark mahogany door softly, removing my brown suede oxfords at the same time.
> "Mike!" my mother screamed.
> I looked up, and there she was, racing down the red-carpeted stairs in her blue satin bedroom slippers, her blue velour, wraparound robe flying out behind her, her frosted brown hair a furious cloud, and her pale oval face with its crimson lips and pale green eyes contorted with fear and rage.

Would you really have noticed your mother's shoes? Are they important to the narrative? Would you have noticed her frosted hair, her crimson lips? Would you have noticed that her robe was a velour wrap-around? Do these details matter? You *might* have noticed your mother's eyes if they looked angry or fearful and her mouth, too, if it were in an angry straight line.

Keep this question in mind when you select details for your narrative: what do I remember seeing, hearing, smelling, touching, tasting? After you answer this question, you will know which details are important and which ones are not. The point is that you do not use details for the sake of using details. You use them for the sake of your reader, so that the images he or she has of a scene are similar to the ones that remain in your mind.

Your second task, organizing the descriptive details you choose, is easily accomplished since people, places, and objects exist in space. Therefore, you decide whether to describe a person from top to bottom or bottom to top; or whether to describe the setting from right to left, left to right, bottom to top, far to near, or near to far, and so on. For example, suppose you were describing a person's face. Afterwards, you described what he or she was wearing. You would not then return to a facial feature that you had omitted earlier:

> *Not this:*   With a face round as a moon, Joan stood in the doorway wearing an old trench coat with holes in it. She had a rather short, pug nose.

> *But this:*   With a face round as a moon, punctuated by a rather short, pug nose, Joan stood in the doorway, wearing an old trench coat with holes in it.

Or suppose that you were describing a room. After you chose the details you needed, you would decide upon some order. As a result, you would not write a description like this:

> The living room of the old house was quite large, a square, about twenty feet by twenty feet. The ceiling was perhaps twenty feet high also. In the middle of the wall to the left of the entrance was

an old, coal-burning fireplace. A chandelier hung from the middle
of the ceiling, and painted around it was a mural of pink and blue
cherubim.

The problem here is that the descriptive details of the ceiling are
separated from each other. After you select the important details
that you need to describe a person, a place, or an object, decide
where you should begin and what order you will follow. Whatever
sequence of details you decide upon, you cannot disrupt that sequence by returning to a point that you have already passed.

Now, following are some suggestions for ways that you can
organize the events in your narrative.

Organizing Narrative Essays

The organization of a narrative is just as easy as the organization of descriptive details. Instead of existing in space, however,
a series of events takes place in time: first the phone rang; then
my mother took us to the sitter's; afterwards I had a fight with
my brother; after that, I ran away, and so on.

If you relate your story like this, following the order of events
as they happened, you are using a *chronological order*. However,
there is another option a narrative writer may choose. Instead of
telling the story as it happened, you might begin with the climax
or the end, or any point well into the story, and then relate the
events that led to that particular point. This method is called the
flashback.

Either the chronological or flashback method of relating the
events in a narrative will work. The advantage of the flashback
technique is that you could choose to begin with a dramatic moment in your narrative, and thus you would hook your readers
easily. Something like this, for example:

> My palms were wet, my eyes were wet, and I felt numb and dazed
> as I stared at the bronze casket holding my friend Brad. Three days
> before seemed like three thousand years ago, and it had all begun
> with so much excitement and fun.

Do you want to know more? Of course you do. Choose either
method, the flashback or the chronological, whichever appeals to
you more.

One last note: Whichever organizational method you choose,
you will need to be careful of your transitions. The tendency is to
use one or two transitions repeatedly, such as *then* or *and then.*
You might read again the various temporal transitions listed in
Chapter 6.

The following is Angie's further draft, criticized by one of her
classmates who used the guide that follows Angie's essay.

Angie's Revised Draft

What about a title?

Could you supply the names of one or two hymns?

1 The day it happened I was six years old. It was a typical summer Sunday at my house, or at least, it began that way. Still clad in my Sunday best, I sat on the kitchen floor staring at the colorful newspaper cartoons spread before me like a fan. Gospel music from the television and the smell of chicken frying wafted through the air, and long tongues of sun lapped through the venetian blinds. Mama's face smiled down at me as she adjusted her pink checkered apron and clicked across the kitchen floor in her high heels. The refrigerator opened and shut with a swoosh and a gasp, dishes rattled in the drain, and the sink gurgled and gulped as it swallowed dishwater. As I said before, it was a typical summer Sunday. At least it was until we found out what had happened.

good image

Good concreteness and alliteration

2 Mama had just plucked the last piece of chicken from the huge, black frying pan when the telephone sang out with its piercing soprano voice, shattering the serenity of the kitchen. Mama's smile dropped from her face like a plate crashing on the floor as she received the news on the other end of the line. Even though I was very young, I knew that something was wrong.

good alliteration

good metaphor

good transition

3 Yes, something was wrong, and it was the worst something I had ever encountered in my young years. As I stood in front of the huge brick home where my best friend, Gina Rivers lived, I realized how impermanent life really is.

How did you get there? What happened between this paragraph and the one before?

good metaphor

4 Long, harsh tongues of fire licked the sides of the house swallowing all life inside without mercy. People were milling about like frightened insects. Screams, cries, and the blare of sirens pierced through the black smoke as I watched them carry little Gina's lifeless body from the house. Little Gina, a sweet girl with pink cheeks and pigtails that bounced when she ran. Little Gina, who smelled of jasmine and spring showers. Little Gina, who ran with me through dew-damp backyards with sticky ice-cream fingers, lay crumpled and black on the ground beside the skeleton house that shivered as vulture winds picked at its bones.

good use of repetition and intentional parallel fragments

This is a good essay with some good concrete description. The only problem is that there is a gap between paragraphs 2 and 3.

The Critic's Guide

1. Does the writer have a good title? If not, suggest one if you can.
2. How does the writer get the reader's attention? If he or she needs a better beginning sentence, suggest one if you can.
3. Are there any paragraphs that need development with concrete/specific details or metaphors? If so, ask for the details you wish you had or suggest where a metaphor would help.
4. Could the writer use dialogue anywhere in the essay to make his or her writing more vivid and immediate? If so, write in the margin, "Could you use dialogue here?"
5. If the writer has used dialogue, is the form correct and is the style good? Correct any errors in form, and if there are any problems with the style, write the appropriate question in the margin, such as "Do you need all these speaker tags here?"
6. Does the writer need stronger transitions between any two sentences or paragraphs? If so, mark the places, and if you can, suggest better transitions.
7. What is the writer's tone? Are there any words, phrases, or metaphors with connotations that are inconsistent with the writer's tone? If so, underline these words or phrases and write in the margin, "Are these (or is this) consistent with your tone?"
8. Does the writer have a point? If not, at the end of the essay tell him or her that you did not get the point.
9. Does the writer stray from his or her focus anywhere in the essay? If so, mark the place and write in the margin, "Is this on focus?" Or simply, "On focus?"

Critical Analysis

Angie has used some very concrete language in this further draft of her essay, and she has also attempted to use metaphors and similes to make her writing more concrete. However, her last metaphor, a personification of the house, may be a little too much. In any event, she does not need the word *skeleton* before *house* because the metaphor "picked at its bones" would certainly suggest the skeletal image. Furthermore, using the noun *skeleton* as an adjective is awkward. The adjective is *skeletal*. Nevertheless, in this last paragraph Angie has used three intentional fragments that are also parallel, thus lending both emphasis and coherence to her writing. Also, as her critic pointed out, she has a good beginning sentence and good transitions between her paragraphs.

However, it is between paragraphs 2 and 3 that there is a big gap in Angie's narrative. What happened between these two paragraphs? How did Angie come to encounter the "worst something" in her life? Suddenly she's standing at her best friend's house. How did she get there? The last we knew Angie was sitting on the kitchen floor when the phone rang. In her next draft, Angie needs to fill in this gap for the reader.

Sentence Structure: Varying Beginnings

Although Angie's sentence beginnings are varied and she does not have any short, choppy sentences, many young writers have a tendency to start all their sentences with the subject. If beginning most of your sentences with the subject is characteristic of your writing, you may want to revise your sentence structure before you prepare your final draft. Also, you may need to combine some of your sentences if you have a series of short sentences that result in a choppy rhythm.

A monotonous rhythm is a result of beginning several consecutive sentences with the subject. In the following list are various constructions you can use in order to avoid beginning sentences with the subject. The examples from professional and student essays have italics added to emphasize the variations used.

Ways to Vary Sentence Beginnings

1. Use one or more prepositional phrases.

> *At the close of the first year* I had acquired, like Madeline the ginger cat, some followers.
>
> (Eiseley, paragraph 13)

2. Use the present or past participle of a verb or use a participial phrase. The participial phrase is composed of the present or past participle of a verb together with one or more words that are grammatically attached to it. A participial phrase may also consist of two or more participles joined by a coordinate conjunction.

> *Tired,* we trudged back up the hill.
>
> (student essay)

> *Easing his back a moment later*, he stood up by the mantle and poked a friendly finger at Maddy. . . .
>
> (Eiseley, paragraph 6)

> *Troubled and exhausted*, I finally fell asleep just before dawn.
>
> (student essay)

3. Use an infinitive or an infinitive phrase. An infinitive is composed of the preposition *to* followed by the base form of a verb—*to play, to write.* An infinitive phrase consists of two or more infinitives or an infinitive together with one or more words grammatically attached to it.

> *To win*, I knew that I would have to train at least three hours a day.
> (student essay)

> *But to talk for a living*, one must, like Maddy, receive more applause than opprobrium.
> (Eiseley, paragraph 9)

> *To get approval and to be accepted*, I found myself doing all sorts of things I didn't really want to do.
> (student essay)

4. Use an absolute phrase. An absolute phrase consists of a noun and its modifiers. The phrase seems to modify either the entire sentence it is attached to or one or more words in the sentence.

> *My ankle obviously broken*, I hobbled off the floor with the help of one of my teammates.
> (student essay)

5. Use an adverbial clause. Adverbial clauses modify a verb, an adjective, or another adverb in the main clause. They answer such questions as where, when, how, in what manner, and to what degree, and they begin with subordinate conjunctions such as *after, before, since, because, if, when, whenever,* and *although,* to name a few. When an adverbial clause begins a sentence, a comma comes after it unless the clause is very short.

> *If there were any catcalls* they could only have come from her kin beneath the davenport.
> (Eiseley, paragraph 7)

Note: Although Eiseley does not do so, many writers would use a comma after this introductory clause.

6. Use an adverb alone or an adverbial phrase. An adverbial phrase consists of an adverb with other adverbial modifiers, or it may be composed of two or more adverbs joined by a coordinate conjunction.

> *Then* she turned back to the Store and resumed, "Glory, glory hallelujah. . . ."
> (Angelou, paragraph 37)

Slowly, so slowly, the crippled old lady made her way up the courthouse steps.

(student essay)

Carefully and quietly, I crept out of bed so as not to wake Sue.

(student essay)

7. Use the expletives *there* and *here.* An expletive is a word that stands in place of another word, such as *there* and *here* when they are used at the beginning of a sentence in place of the subject.

There was shame there.

(Gregory, paragraph 26)

Here was where I wanted to stay forever.

(student essay)

8. Use inversion, the result of writing the elements of a sentence out of their normal order. For example, the normal order of English sentences is as follows:

subject	verb	direct object
subject	verb	predicate adjective
subject	verb	predicate noun

When you use inversion, you will avoid beginning with the subject, but you will also gain emphasis as well since inversion is not what the reader expects.

A career in engineering Barbara wanted above all else.

(direct object)

Calm and confident my mother looked as she leaned against the doorframe.

(predicate adjectives)

To be a teacher and a writer—these were my sister's ambitions.

(predicate nouns)

Depending upon the sentence, you may have several options when you rearrange it. Also, when combining two or more sentences, you may be able to create several different beginning constructions—the participial phrase, the absolute phrase, or the adverbial clause, for example. It can be a great deal of fun to play with sentences—to arrange and rearrange them until you discover the best arrangement in your particular context. Both the context and your purpose, however, are the final determinants of the most effective arrangement of a particular sentence.

(If you write a great many short sentences, you might want to consult the section on sentence combining in Appendix A at the end of the text.)

Exercise I: Varying Sentence Beginnings

You might like to practice varying the beginning of a sentence by rewriting the sentence that follows. Try to begin it with each of the constructions previously listed. In order to use some of these constructions, especially inversion, you will need to add to the sentence. Use your imagination and add whatever you like to this sentence:

> Several lively squirrels scampered through the fallen leaves, searching for acorns to store for the winter months ahead.

When you have written this sentence beginning it with all the options outlined earlier, you might share your sentences in small groups. Even though you lack a particular context and purpose, you might choose the sentences you consider most effective. Afterwards, with the whole class, you could discuss the sentences that each group chose, giving the reasons for your choices.

Sentence Structure and Emphasis

You may have noticed when you read a sentence that you remember the words at the end most readily. Next, you remember those at the beginning, whereas you may not remember the words in the middle at all. Therefore, when you construct sentences, you should put the most important words last or first, not in the middle. Consider this sentence, for example.

> The pine trees' feathery limbs waved in the wind against the dusky sky.

Now let's rearrange the sentence.

> Against the dusky sky the pine trees' feathery limbs waved in the wind.

There are several other arrangements that work, but all of the following statements except the first one sound strange, especially the last two.

> In the wind the pine trees' feathery limbs waved against the dusky sky.

> In the wind against the dusky sky, waved the pine trees' feathery limbs.

In the wind against the dusky sky, the pine trees' feathery limbs waved.

Against the dusky sky in the wind waved the pine trees' feathery limbs.

For the purpose of analysis, let's consider the first three sentences only. In each of these sentences which words are emphasized? Since the end of a sentence is the most emphatic position, in the first sentence the phrase *against the dusky sky* receives primary emphasis, whereas the phrase *the pine trees' feathery limbs* receives secondary emphasis. In the second arrangement the phrase *waved in the wind* receives primary emphasis, whereas the phrase *against the dusky sky* receives secondary emphasis. Both of these arrangements are effective because the positions of emphasis in both are filled by concrete phrases. In the third sentence, however, the concrete phrase *the pine trees' feathery limbs* loses emphasis, whereas the rather abstract phrase *in the wind* receives secondary emphasis and the concrete phrase *against the dusky sky* receives the most emphasis. We would need to know both the context and the writer's purpose to know whether or not one of these arrangements was superior to the other two.

For example, if the time of day, dusk, was more important than the fact that it was windy, the first sentence would be better. If the reverse were true, the second would be better. If neither fact was particularly important in the context, then the writer might consider the sentences that come before and after this one. Which arrangement results in the better transition or rhythm? Or the writer might consider the beginnings of his or her sentences. Are there several consecutive sentences that begin with the subject? If so, he or she might choose the second or third arrangement for the sake of rhythm since the first sentence begins with the subject *limbs.* If a sentence begins with an article *(a, an,* or *the)* followed by adjectives, possessive nouns, or pronouns, it still begins with the subject, no matter how many adjectives or possessives precede the subject noun or pronoun.

Exercise II: Rearranging Sentences for Emphasis

Although you will be practicing what you have learned about rearranging sentences out of the context of a particular piece of writing, use the sentences that you wrote in Exercise I in this chapter, and put stars by those sentences that you consider the most emphatic with the most pleasing rhythms. If you like, you may compose several additional sentences. When everyone has made his or her choices, you might form groups and choose several sentences that everyone in the group agrees are the most effective. Afterwards, each group might share its choices with the others. Be sure that you and your groupmates can defend your choices by explaining why each sentence you have chosen is effective.

Having completed this exercise and the previous one, you should be better prepared now to tackle revision of your own writing, especially in regard to your sentence structure. Now you can look at "old" writing again, seeing it in a new light, especially in the light of your newly acquired knowledge about sentences. You will be amazed at how much you will improve the sound, flow, and effectiveness of your writing by revising your sentences with beginnings, length, emphasis, and coherence in mind.

Further Practice Varying Sentence Structure

In Chapter 4, when you wrote objective and subjective descriptions of a person or a place, chances are that you wrote short sentences, often beginning with the subject. Since you have already been asked to revise one of these descriptions to improve coherence, you might choose one of the other two and revise it by trying to vary sentence beginnings and combining sentences to avoid choppiness.

You will find it easier to revise writing that is "cold" to you. If you prefer, you could revise any other past writing, such as your first or second essay. However, if you choose to revise the sentence structure in either of these essays, you might want to revise several paragraphs only, rather than the entire essay. Whatever writing you choose, you will find it much easier to revise the sentence structure in your present writing once you have practiced rearrangement on other writing.

As you will see in the following example, Juanita did a fine job when she revised her negative description of someone she knows.

Juanita's Original Description of a Person

1 Barbara is pushing fifty. Her frame is bulky and she is fat. She has skin like an old fisherman, swarthy and crepy, with a greasy, shiny, sallow complexion. She has a bulbous pug nose.
2 Neanderthal brows slash across her face like large caterpillars. Her sooty hair hangs in uneven shingles cropped short at the second roll of flesh on her neck. It used to be black, but now it is streaked with grey. Her shoulders slump forward like a caveman's. Her eyes are bulgy and dark. She is a lush, and as prime as a rabbit, having four unwanted children. Her husband is a sot too and frequently beats her. Barbara is so gullible and spineless, she doesn't defend herself or leave.
3 If an organ is not utterly necessary to her existence, she has it yanked out, so that she can lie around in a hospital bed and do nothing. Welfare foots the bill for her hypochondria. She wouldn't even get welfare if her income was known to so-

cial services, but she's so sleazy and stingy, she takes every-thing she can get. Her language is filthy.

4 She uses no makeup to hide her deformities and dresses in a frumpy dress or tight knit pants that encase her legs like sausages.

5 Barbara, being the hypocrite that she is, makes her appear-ance in church every Sunday. She is always sticking her nose into my life and condemning me for wearing makeup.

Juanita's Revised Description of a Person

1 Fat and pushing fifty, Barbara has a bulky frame with shoulders that slump forward like a caveman's.

2 In fact, her Neanderthal brows slash across her face like large hairy caterpillars, and her skin is like an old fisher-man's—swarthy and crepy with a greasy sheen. In uneven shingles, cropped short at the second roll of flesh on her neck, her sooty hair, streaked with gray, frames a face punctuated by a bulbous pug nose.

3 Because she is a lush, her dark, bulging eyes are usually bloodshot. As prime as a rabbit, Barbara has had four un-wanted children. A sot, too, her husband frequently beats her, but she is so gullible and spineless she doesn't defend herself or leave.

4 If a bodily organ is not utterly necessary for her existence, she has it yanked out so that she can lie around in a hospital bed and do nothing. Her hypochondria supported by welfare, she's so sleazy and stingy that her actual income is unknown to social services, and she takes everything she can get.

5 Barbara wears no makeup to hide her deformities. But some of her deformities she can't hide. With no taste, she wears frumpy dresses or tight knit pants that make her legs look like sausages.

6 Despite her filthy tongue, Barbara has the hypocritical nerve to appear in church every Sunday and criticize me for wearing makeup.

Besides combining some of her short sentences, Juanita has varied the beginnings of sentences, and she has also improved her organization. Even so, the next to last paragraph of her descrip-tion would be better placed after the second paragraph in which she describes Barbara's appearance. Nevertheless, Juanita has suc-cessfully eliminated the choppiness of her original draft. Are there any sentences that you would write another way? Can you label the constructions she has used to begin each sentence?

Angie's Handwritten Draft in the Process of Revision

The following is Angie's handwritten draft of the material she needed to fill the gap in the previous draft of her essay.

The ~~soothing sound of~~

Gospel music drifted from the television in the living room, and the warm scent of chicken frying ~~around me~~ wafted through the air ~~as~~ I could hear ~~myth~~ the rambunctious laughter of my two older brothers as they wrestled playfully in the adjoining room. →Long tongues of sun lapped through the venetian blinds, and

Mama's face ——→
Mama's smile slipped

dishes tinkled
swallowed pink bubbly dishwater

~~Yes, something was wrong~~

~~I knew that something was wrong as Mama hurriedly turned off the oven, grabbed me by the hand, and ordered my two older brothers to follow in a tone the of voice that meant business.~~

Grabbing me firmly by the hand, she quickly turned off the oven and ordered my two older brothers to follow in a tone that meant business. We weren't too thrilled when we realized she was taking us next door so Sherry, the sixteen-year-old neighbor could babysit us.

"Now, you kids do as Sherry says, and do not leave this yard. I'll be back in a little while," Mama said as she ~~darted~~ hurried off. I watched her shrink smaller + smaller as she rounded the curve on our road ~~until she~~ and finally disappeared.

Sherry, the babysitter, ~~as~~ sat staring ~~hungrily~~ w/ big admiring eyes as she watched her pimply

I'm going over to the river for a little while

faced boyfriend blow smoke rings in the air.

"Why don't you kids go outside & play?" Sherry hissed through braced teeth as she gently but insistently nudged us out the front door.

"I bet they're in there kissin'," remarked David, my eldest brother.

"~~Shut up~~"

"Yuck," I smirked

"Shut up. You're just a baby, anyway", David sneered as he scratched his crew-cut head. David, who was twelve, was extremely proud of the fact that he was going to junior high school in the fall.

"Pull me in the wagon! Pull me in the wagon!" I began to chime over and over like the irritating little sister that I was.

"Shut up!" roared David as he tossed a rock that ~~bounced~~ ^bounced^ firmly against my head with a ~~harsh~~ ^harsh^ thud.

"I'm tellin ~~you too~~ Mama! I'm tellin' tellin' tellin' right now," I began to cry in a high pitched voice.

"I said shut up you brat!" David shouted as he gave me a shove that sent me tumbling on the gravel driveway.

"I'm tellin'," ~~I cried~~ "~~I know~~ I'm goin' to the Rivers right now and I'm tellin'," I cried as I stomped off down the road in search of Mama.

I marched indignantly down the road expecting David to run after me & apologize. When he didn't, I decided to walk to the Rivers anyway & find Mama. I thought that she would surely be on my side when she found out what David had done, even though I wasn't supposed to leave the yard.

The walk to the Rivers seemed endless. My shiny black leather shoes became scuffed & dusty, and my pigtails wilted in the sweltering heat, but still I walked on. I knew the way by heart, because that's where my best friend, Gina Rivers lived, and Mama had often taken me there to play.

As I rounded a sharp curve on the road, though, I ~~sensed~~ sensed that something was wrong.

Yes, ⟶

⟶ That's when I first realized how impermeable life really is

~~I knew something was wrong~~

In the distance, I could see Gina's house engulfed in a thick cloud of smoke. Long, harsh tongues of fire licked the sides of the house. The huge orange beast ~~chomed~~ chomped through the roof, spitting out unwanted debris. People were ⟶

Angie's Final Draft

Shadows in the Sunshine

1 The day it happened I was six years old. It was a typical summer Sunday at my house, or at least, it began that way. Still clad in my Sunday best, I sat on the kitchen floor staring at the colorful newspaper cartoons spread before me like a fan. "Rock of Ages" drifted in from the television in the living room, and the warm scent of chicken frying wafted through the air around me. Long tongues of sunshine lapped through the venetian blinds, and I could hear the rambunctious laughter of my two older brothers as they wrestled playfully in the adjoining room. Mama's face smiled down at me as she adjusted her pink checkered apron and clicked across the kitchen floor in her shiny, black patent heels. The refrigerator opened and shut with a swoosh and a gasp, dishes tinkled in the drain, and the sink gurgled and gulped as it swallowed pink, bubbly dishwater. As I said before, it was a typical summer Sunday. At least it was until I saw what happened.

2 Mama had just plucked the last piece of chicken from the huge, black frying pan when the telephone sang out with its piercing soprano voice, shattering the serenity of the kitchen. Mama's smile slipped from her face like a plate crashing on the floor as she received the news on the other end of the line.

3 Grabbing me firmly by the hand, she quickly turned off the oven and ordered my two older brothers to follow in a tone that meant business. We weren't too thrilled when we realized she was taking us next door so Sherry, the sixteen-year-old neighbor, could babysit us.

4 "Now you kids do as Sherry says, and do not leave this yard. I'm going to the Rivers's. I'll be back in a little while," Mama said as she hurried off. I watched her shrink smaller and smaller as she rounded the curve in our road and finally disappeared.

5 Sherry, our sitter, sat staring with big admiring eyes as she watched her pimply-faced boyfriend blow smoke rings in the air.

6 "Why don't you kids go outside and play?" Sherry hissed through braced teeth as she gently but insistently nudged us out the front door.

7 "I bet they're in there kissin'," remarked David, my oldest brother.

8 "Yuck!" I said.

9 "Shut up. You're just a baby, anyway," David sneered as he scratched his crew-cut head. David, who was twelve, was extremely proud that he was going to junior high in the fall.

10 "Pull me in the wagon! Pull me in the wagon!" I began to chime over and over like the irritating little sister that I was.

11 "Shut up!" roared David as he tossed a rock that bounced firmly against my head with a harsh thud.

12 "I'm tellin' Mama! I'm tellin', and I'm tellin' right now!" I began to cry in a high-pitched voice.

13 "I said shut up you brat!" David shouted as he gave me a shove that sent me tumbling in the gravel driveway.

14 "I'm tellin'! I'm goin' to the Rivers's right now and I'm tellin'!" I cried as I stomped off down the road in search of Mama.

15 I marched indignantly down the road expecting David to run after me and apologize. When he didn't, I decided to walk to the Rivers's anyway and find Mama. I thought that she would surely be on my side when she found out what David had done, even though I wasn't supposed to leave the yard.

16 I knew the way by heart because that's where my best friend, Gina Rivers lived, and Mama had often taken me there to play. The walk to the Rivers's seemed endless. My shiny black leather shoes became scuffed and dusty, and my pigtails wilted in the sweltering heat. As I rounded a sharp curve in the road, though, I sensed that something was wrong.

17 Yes, something was wrong, and it was the worst something I had ever encountered in my young years. Standing in front of the huge brick home where Gina lived, I realized for the first time how uncertain life really is.

18 Gina's house was engulfed in a thick cloud of smoke. Long, harsh tongues of fire licked the sides of the house. The huge orange beast squeezed the house unmercifully and chomped through the roof as it spat out unwanted debris. People were screaming and crying and milling about. The blare of sirens pierced through the black smoke as I watched firemen carry little Gina's lifeless body from the house. Little Gina, a sweet girl with pink cheeks and pigtails that bounced when she ran. Little Gina, who smelled of jasmine and spring showers. Little Gina, who ran with me through dew-damp backyards with sticky ice-cream fingers, lay crumpled and black on the ground beside the house that shivered as vulture winds picked at its bones.

Conclusion

Even though the personification of the house in the adjective clause "that shivered" may be overdone, this is a decidedly better draft than the previous one, and the material added to fill the gap contains some very good dialogue between Angie and her brother.

All three students—Cheryl, Maria, and Angie—wrote interesting, concrete, and coherent narratives of significant experiences in their lives. Successfully using parallel structure and intentional fragments for coherence or emphasis, all three students also attempted to vary the beginning and length of their sentences. If you were asked to pick the best of the three essays, using the skills that you have learned thus far as your bases of evaluation, which one would you choose? If you were asked to choose the essay about the most significant experience, would your choice be the same?

No mater which of these student essays you prefer, no doubt you found that reading and writing narrative essays can be a great deal of fun. Although writing "to tell a story" can certainly be a pleasurable and satisfying experience, writing to explore and explain your ideas can be equally fascinating and rewarding, as you will discover when you read the professional essays in the next chapter. In these essays, four writers explore and explain their ideas on a variety of subjects: how and why to keep a notebook, what being a journalist entails, the various kinds of friendships women have, and, last, why men's friendships are not as rewarding as women's. Sound interesting? After you have read them, I am sure you will agree that they are both interesting and thought-provoking.

Proofreading Tip: The Dangling Modifier

Both the participial and infinitive phrase, two constructions that you may use to begin sentences, must be followed by the noun or pronoun that they modify. If the word that the phrase modifies does not come immediately after it, you will have written a dangling modifier such as this one George has written.

> Carefully explaining why I did not get the position, the truth was that the board decided that I was best qualified for the position, but that my being black might interfere with customer relations.

The noun that follows this participial phrase is the word *truth*. But obviously the word *truth* did not explain why George did not get the position. His friend Mr. James did. Thus, the noun *Mr. James* must come immediately after the participial phrase.

> Carefully explaining why I did not get the position, Mr. James told me that the board decided that I was best qualified for the position, but that my being black might interfere with customer relations.

Now consider this sentence:

> To compete in track, daily practice was essential.

The noun that follows this infinitive phrase is the word practice. But the noun practice cannot compete in track. The word that the phrase truly modifies is either a pronoun that stands for a person or people—*I, you, he, she, we, they*—or a noun that names a person or people who compete in track.

> To compete in track, I had to practice daily.

> To compete in track, Sheila had to practice daily.

> To compete in track, the team had to practice daily.

> To compete in track, Tonya and Maria had to practice daily.

Now here is an example you may have noticed in Andrea's essay in Chapter 3:

> Reaching the end of the lane, his home loomed before us, large, warm, and intriguing.

Can you correct Andrea's dangling modifier?

> Reaching the end of the lane, we saw his home looming before us, large, warm, and intriguing.

There is also another option here. To retain the independent clause as it is, you can change the participial phrase to a dependent clause.

> When we reached the end of the lane, his home loomed before us, large, warm, and intriguing.

A dangling modifier can also result from a prepositional phrase with a gerund as its object. A gerund is the present participle of a verb *(running, playing, writing, sitting,)* used as a noun. For example, read this sentence:

> While jogging, my watch stopped.

As it stands now, the sense of this sentence is that a watch went jogging!

> While jogging, I noticed that my watch had stopped.

> or

> While I was jogging, my watch stopped.

EXERCISE: *Recognizing and Correcting the Dangling Modifier*

Read the following statements, and if there is a dangling modifier, correct it in the space beneath the sentence. If the sentence is correct, write "correct" in the space provided.

1. To get a good tan, the middle of the day is the best time to sunbathe.

2. While reading a good book, the doorbell rang and startled me.

3. Running down the sidewalk, the small boy whistled for his dog.

4. After eating a huge piece of chocolate cake, my diet was shot.

5. Rowing for hours, the oars rubbed blisters on both my hands.

6. After having worked on my essay all afternoon, a movie sounded great.

7. To become a good typist, concentration is most important.

8. After waiting an hour and a half, the waitress finally brought our food.

9. To cook good spaghetti, proper seasoning is important.

10. Before taking a nap, Jennifer revised several sentences in her essay.

Some dangling modifiers may sound correct to you at first. Thus, remember when you use these constructions to check the first noun or pronoun after them. Then ask yourself if the beginning phrase modifies that word. If it does not, you can now correct the error.

When you proofread the final draft of your narrative, be on the alert for dangling modifiers and do not forget the errors discussed in previous chapters—the comma fault and the unintentional sentence fragment. If you feel that you need to refresh your memory, you might review these two tips before you proofread.

Suggestions for Further Writing

1. Imagine that a famous person from a past century—Henry VIII, Madame Curie, or Charlotte Brontë, for example—visited America and you were invited to meet him or her. In the form of an interview, write the dialogue that might occur between the two of you. What questions would each of you have for the other? What might be this person's reactions to our modern world?

2. If you did not use dialogue in your previous narrative, choose a subject from your listing that would allow you to do so, and write another narrative.

3. If you used dialogue in your previous narrative, choose a subject from your listing that would not allow its use and write another narrative.

4. Choose another topic from your listing and write your narrative from another person's point of view. Instead of using the pronoun *I* to refer to yourself, you would use your name and the appropriate pronoun *(he* or *she)* to refer to yourself.

Instead of this:	It was early Sunday morning when I awoke to a strange noise.
This:	It was early Sunday morning when Sherry awoke to a strange noise.

5. Choose a classmate of the opposite sex if possible. Each of you tell the other about one of the experiences you listed but did not write about. Afterwards, make careful notes of the details. Then, each of you write the other person's narrative as if it had happened to you. That is, you will use the pronoun *I.*

6. Think of a conflict you had with someone in the past. Write about it from the other person's point of view and use dialogue.

Instead of this: Then I shouted, "Get out of here!"
This: Then Jesse shouted, "Get out of here!"

7. Imagine that you are applying for a job that you would like very much. On the application you are asked to write a narrative account of the jobs you have had and what your duties were for each one. Begin with your first job and end with your last one. You are also asked to conclude by telling what personal characteristics make you particularly suitable for this position.

8. You have bought a watch from Mr. Diamondback, a local jeweler, and it has quit running twice. The jeweler fixed it free of charge, but it has stopped running again. Although it is still under warranty, you have decided that you want your money back. However, Mr. Diamondback does not want to return your money but offers instead to fix the watch again. Write the dialogue that might occur between the two of you, and be as persuasive as you can.

9. Write a narrative, true or fictional, beginning with this sentence: "Just when I thought I had things straightened out, I found out differently."

Reading and
Writing
Exposition

C H A P T E R

The Act of Saying "I": Writers Exploring and Explaining Their Ideas

9

In the last chapter you wrote about yourself, but as you know, in one sense all the personal essays are autobiographical: they are all centered in the writer himself or herself, in the writer's *ego*, the writer's *I*: "This is what *I* think, this is what *I* feel." As a matter of fact, many writers of the personal essay have noted that their profession is indeed a very egocentric business.

For example, Joan Didion has said the following about the writer in her essay "Why I Write," which appears in Chapter 11:

> In many ways writing is the act of saying *I*, of imposing oneself upon other people, of saying *listen to me, see it my way, change your mind*. It's an aggressive, even a hostile act. . . . Setting words on paper is the tactic of a secret bully, an invasion, an imposition of the writer's sensibility on the reader's most private space.

These are strong words indeed; nevertheless, the truth that the writer of the personal essay is saying "Listen to me, this is what *I* think" cannot be disputed. If this were not true, why bother to write? Writers have something to say—a point to make—and if they did not care whether anyone else listened to what they thought, they would not put pen to paper.

In agreement with Didion concerning the essayist's essential egocentricity, E. B. White, one of the greatest practitioners of the art of the personal essay, had this to say:

> The essayist is . . . sustained by the childish belief that everything he thinks about, everything that happens to him, is of general interest. . . . Only a person who is congenitally self-centered has the effrontery and stamina to write essays.
>
> (E. B. White, *The Essays of E. B. White*)

To this statement White added his notion that the essay is an "excursion," a "rambling" in the writer's mind. He put it this way to one young person who had inquired about his writing:

"My essays . . . are a ramble in the woods, or a ramble in the basement of my mind" *(The Letters of E. B. White).* White suggests here what you read earlier in this text: that writing is a way of discovering; it is a voyage, an excursion, or a "rambling" if you like, an exploration of what's really in one's mind.

Probably more than any other, the titles used by Didion and Ellen Goodman in their essays "On Keeping a Notebook" and "On Being a Journalist" hint at the exploratory, undefined form that White is talking about. The preposition *on* does not promise the reader a final definition of a subject, a final word, but this: Let me explore this subject; let me explore why and how I keep a notebook, or let me explore what being a journalist entails.

In the essay that follows, Joan Didion, an accomplished essayist and novelist, tells us when she began her habit of writing things down in a notebook. In addition, she explores why and how she keeps a journal and what kinds of things she writes in it. In the next essay, "On Being a Journalist," Ellen Goodman, a syndicated columnist with *The Boston Globe,* explores what being a journalist involves. Next, in her exploration of women's friendships, Judith Viorst, poet and journalist, discovers that there are really several different kinds of friendships formed by women. Last, in a chapter from his book *The Male Machine,* Marc Fasteau, an attorney, explains why the more satisfying and intimate friendships that women enjoy have been denied to men.

JOAN DIDION

On Keeping a Notebook

1 " 'That woman Estelle,' " the note reads, " 'is partly the reason why George Sharp and I are separated today.' *Dirty crepe-de-Chine wrapper, hotel bar, Wilmington RR, 9:45 a.m. August Monday morning.*"

2 Since the note is in my notebook, it presumably has some meaning to me. I study it for a long while. At first I have only the most general notion of what I was doing on an August Monday morning in the bar of the hotel across from the Pennsylvania Railroad station in Wilmington, Delaware (waiting for a train? missing one? 1960? 1961? why Wilmington?), but I do remember being there. The woman in the dirty crepe-de-Chine wrapper had come down from her room for a beer, and the bartender had heard before the reason why George Sharp and she were separated today, "Sure," he said, and went on mopping the floor. "You told me." At the other end of the bar is a girl. She is talking, pointedly, not to the man beside her but to a cat lying in the triangle of sunlight cast through the open door. She is wearing a plaid silk dress from Peck & Peck, and the hem is coming down.

3 Here is what it is: the girl has been on the Eastern Shore, and now she is going back to the city, leaving the man beside her, and all she can see ahead are the viscous summer sidewalks and the 3 A.M. long-distance calls that will make her lie awake and then sleep drugged through all the steaming mornings left in August (1960? 1961?). Because she must go directly from the train to lunch in New York, she wishes that she had a safety pin for the hem of the plaid silk dress, and she also wishes that she could forget about the hem and the lunch and stay in the cool bar that smells of disinfectant and malt and make friends with the woman in the crepe-de-Chine wrapper. She is afflicted by a little self-pity, and she wants to compare Estelles. That is what that was all about.

4 Why did I write it down? In order to remember, of course, but exactly what was it I wanted to remember? How much of it actually happened? Did any of it? Why do I keep a notebook at all? It is easy to deceive oneself on all those scores. The impulse to write things down is a peculiarly compulsive one, inexplicable to those who do not share it, useful only accidentally, only secondarily, in the way that any compulsion tries to justify itself. I suppose that it begins or does not begin in the cradle. Although I have felt compelled to write things down since I was five years old, I doubt that my daughter ever will, for she is a singularly blessed and accepting child, delighted with life exactly as life presents itself to her, unafraid to go to sleep and unafraid to wake up. Keepers of private notebooks are a different breed altogether, lonely and resistant rearrangers of things, anxious malcontents, children afflicted apparently at birth with some presentiment of loss.

5 My first notebook was a Big Five tablet, given to me by my mother with the sensible suggestion that I stop whining and learn to amuse myself by writing down my thoughts. She returned the tablet to me a few years ago; the first entry is an account of a woman who believed herself to be freezing to death in the Arctic night, only to find, when day broke, that she had stumbled onto the Sahara Desert, where she would die of the heat before lunch. I have no idea what turn of a five-year-old's mind could have prompted so insistently "ironic" and exotic a story, but it does reveal a certain predilection for the extreme which has dogged me into adult life; perhaps if I were analytically inclined I would find it a truer story than any I might have told about Donald Johnson's birthday party or the day my cousin Brenda put Kitty Litter in the aquarium.

6 So the point of my keeping a notebook has never been, nor is it now, to have an accurate factual record of what I have been doing or thinking. That would be a different impulse entirely, an instinct for reality which I sometimes envy but do not possess. At no point have I ever been able successfully to keep a diary; my

approach to daily life ranges from the grossly negligent to the merely absent, and on those few occasions when I have tried dutifully to record a day's events, boredom has so overcome me that the results are mysterious at best. What is this business about "shopping, typing piece, dinner with E, depressed"? Shopping for what? Typing what piece? Who is E? Was this "E" depressed, or was I depressed? Who cares?

7 In fact I have abandoned altogether that kind of pointless entry; instead I tell what some would call lies. "That's simply not true," the members of my family frequently tell me when they come up against my memory of a shared event. "The party was *not* for you, the spider was *not* a black widow, *it wasn't that way at all.*" Very likely they are right, for not only have I always had trouble distinguishing between what happened and what merely might have happened, but I remain unconvinced that the distinction, for my purposes, matters. The cracked crab that I recall having for lunch the day my father came home from Detroit in 1945 must certainly be embroidery, worked into the day's pattern to lend verisimilitude; I was ten years old and would not now remember the cracked crab. The day's events did not turn on cracked crab. And yet it is precisely that fictitious crab that makes me see the afternoon all over again, a home movie run all too often, the father bearing gifts, the child weeping, an exercise in family love and guilt. Or that is what it was to me. Similarly, perhaps it never did snow that August in Vermont; perhaps there never were flurries in the night wind, and maybe no one else felt the ground hardening and summer already dead even as we pretended to bask in it, but that was how it felt to me, and it might as well have snowed, could have snowed, did snow.

8 *How it felt to me:* that is getting closer to the truth about a notebook. I sometimes delude myself about why I keep a notebook, imagine that some thrifty virtue derives from preserving everything observed. See enough and write it down, I tell myself, and then some morning when the world seems drained of wonder, some day when I am only going through the motions of doing what I am supposed to do, which is write—on that bankrupt morning I will simply open my notebook and there it will be, a forgotten account with accumulated interest, paid passage back to the world out there: dialogue overheard in hotels and elevators and at the hat-check counter in Pavillon (one middle-aged man shows his hat check to another and says, "That's my old football number"); impressions of Bettina Aptheker and Benjamin Sonnenberg and Teddy ("Mr. Acapulco") Stauffer; careful *aperçus* about tennis bums and failed fashion models and Greek shipping heiresses, one of whom taught me a significant lesson (a lesson I could have learned from F. Scott Fitzgerald, but perhaps we must meet the very rich for ourselves) by asking, when I arrived to interview

her in her orchid-filled sitting room on the second day of a paralyzing New York blizzard, whether it was snowing outside.

9   I imagine, in other words, that the notebook is about other people. But of course it is not. I have no real business with what one stranger said to another at the hat-check counter in Pavillon; in fact I suspect that the line "That's my old football number" touched not my own imagination at all, but merely some memory of something once read, probably "The Eighty-Yard Run." Nor is my concern with a woman in a dirty crepe-de-Chine wrapper in a Wilmington bar. My stake is always, of course, in the unmentioned girl in the plaid silk dress. *Remember what it was to be me:* that is always the point.

10   It is a difficult point to admit. We are brought up in the ethic that others, any others, all others, are by definition more interesting than ourselves; taught to be diffident, just this side of self-effacing. ("You're the least important person in the room and don't forget it," Jessica Mitford's governess would hiss in her ear on the advent of any social occasion; I copied that into my notebook because it is only recently that I have been able to enter a room without hearing some such phrase in my inner ear.) Only the very young and the very old may recount their dreams at breakfast, dwell upon self, interrupt with memories of beach picnics and favorite Liberty lawn dresses and the rainbow trout in a creek near Colorado Springs. The rest of us are expected, rightly, to affect absorption in other people's favorite dresses, other people's trout.

11   And so we do. But our notebooks give us away, for however dutifully we record what we see around us, the common denominator of all we see is always, transparently, shamelessly, the implacable "I." We are not talking here about the kind of notebook that is patently for public consumption, a structural conceit for binding together a series of graceful *pensées:* we are talking about something private, about bits of the mind's string too short to use, an indiscriminate and erratic assemblage with meaning only for its maker.

12   And sometimes even the maker has difficulty with the meaning. There does not seem to be, for example, any point in my knowing for the rest of my life that, during 1964, 720 tons of soot fell on every square mile of New York City, yet there it is in my notebook, labeled "FACT." Nor do I really need to remember that Ambrose Bierce liked to spell Leland Stanford's[1] name "£eland $tanford" or that "smart women almost always wear black in Cuba," a fashion hint without much potential for practical application. And does not the relevance of these notes seem marginal at best?:

1. Railroad magnate (1834–1893) who founded the university.—ED.

In the basement museum of the Inyo County Courthouse in Independence, California, sign pinned to a mandarin coat: "This
MANDARIN COAT was often worn by Mrs. Minnie S. Brooks when
giving lectures on her TEAPOT COLLECTION."

Redhead getting out of car in front of Beverly Wilshire Hotel,
chinchilla stole, Vuitton bags with tags reading:

        MRS LOU FOX

        HOTEL SAHARA

        VEGAS

13 Well perhaps not entirely marginal. As a matter of fact, Mrs.
Minnie S. Brooks and her MANDARIN COAT pull me back into my
own childhood, for although I never knew Mrs. Brooks and did
not visit Inyo County until I was thirty, I grew up in just such a
world, in houses cluttered with Indian relics and bits of gold ore
and ambergris and the souvenirs my Aunt Mercy Farnsworth
brought back from the Orient. It is a long way from that world to
Mrs. Lou Fox's world, where we all live now, and is it not just as
well to remember that? Might not Mrs. Minnie S. Brooks help me
to remember what I am? Might not Mrs. Lou Fox help me to remember what I am not?

14 But sometimes the point is harder to discern. What exactly did
I have in mind when I noted down that it cost the father of someone I know $650 a month to light the place on the Hudson in
which he lived before the Crash? What use was I planning to make
of this line by Jimmy Hoffa: "I may have my faults, but being
wrong ain't one of them"? And although I think it interesting to
know where the girls who travel with the Syndicate have their
hair done when they find themselves on the West Coast, will I
ever make suitable use of it? Might I not be better off just passing
it on to John O'Hara? What is a recipe for sauerkraut doing in my
notebook? What kind of magpie keeps this notebook? *He was
born the night the Titanic went down.*" That seems a nice enough
line, and I even recall who said it, but is it not really a better line
in life than it could ever be in fiction?

15 But of course that is exactly it: not that I should ever use the
line, but that I should remember the woman who said it and the
afternoon I heard it. We were on her terrace by the sea, and we
were finishing the wine left from lunch, trying to get what sun
there was, a California winter sun. The woman whose husband
was born the night the *Titanic* went down wanted to rent her
house, wanted to go back to her children in Paris. I remember
wishing that I could afford the house, which cost $1,000 a month.
"Someday you will," she said lazily. "Someday it all comes." There
in the sun on her terrace it seemed easy to believe in someday,
but later I had a low-grade afternoon hangover and ran over a black
snake on the way to the supermarket and was flooded with inex-

plicable fear when I heard the checkout clerk explaining to the man ahead of me why she was finally divorcing her husband. "He left me no choice," she said over and over as she punched the register. "He has a little seven-month-old baby by her, he left me no choice." I would like to believe that my dread then was for the human condition, but of course it was for me, because I wanted a baby and did not then have one and because I wanted to own the house that cost $1,000 a month to rent and because I had a hangover.

16 It all comes back. Perhaps it is difficult to see the value in having one's self back in that kind of mood, but I do see it; I think we are well advised to keep on nodding terms with the people we used to be, whether we find them attractive company or not. Otherwise they turn up unannounced and surprise us, come hammering on the mind's door at 4 a.m. of a bad night and demand to know who deserted them, who betrayed them, who is going to make amends. We forget all too soon the things we thought we could never forget. We forget the loves and the betrayals alike, forget what we whispered and what we screamed, forget who we were. I have already lost touch with a couple of people I used to be; one of them, a seventeen-year-old, presents little threat, although it would be of some interest to me to know again what it feels like to sit on a river levee drinking vodka-and-orange-juice and listening to Les Paul and Mary Ford and their echoes sing "How High the Moon" on the car radio. (You see I still have the scenes, but I no longer perceive myself among those present, no longer could even improvise the dialogue.) The other one, a twenty-three-year-old, bothers me more. She was always a good deal of trouble, and I suspect she will reappear when I least want to see her, skirts too long, shy to the point of aggravation, always the injured party, full of recriminations and little hurts and stories I do not want to hear again, at once saddening me and angering me with her vulnerability and ignorance, an apparition all the more insistent for being so long banished.

17 It is a good idea, then, to keep in touch, and I suppose that keeping in touch is what notebooks are all about. And we are all on our own when it comes to keeping those lines open to ourselves: your notebook will never help me, nor mine you. *"So what's new in the whiskey business?"* What could that possibly mean to you? To me it means a blonde in a Pucci bathing suit sitting with a couple of fat men by the pool at the Beverly Hills Hotel. Another man approaches, and they all regard one another in silence for a while. "So what's new in the whiskey business?" one of the fat men finally says by way of welcome, and the blonde stands up, arches one foot and dips it in the pool, looking all the while at the cabaña where Baby Pignatari is talking on the telephone. That is all there is to that, except that several years later I saw

the blonde coming out of Saks Fifth Avenue in New York with her California complexion and a voluminous mink coat. In the harsh wind that day she looked old and irrevocably tired to me, and even the skins in the mink coat were not worked the way they were doing them that year, not the way she would have wanted them done, and there is the point of the story. For a while after that I did not like to look in the mirror, and my eyes would skim the newspapers and pick out only the deaths, the cancer victims, the premature coronaries, the suicides, and I stopped riding the Lexington Avenue IRT because I noticed for the first time that all the strangers I had seen for years—the man with the seeing-eye dog, the spinster who read the classified pages every day, the fat girl who always got off with me at Grand Central—looked older than they once had.

18 It all comes back. Even that recipe for sauerkraut: even that brings it back. I was on Fire Island when I first made that sauerkraut, and it was raining, and we drank a lot of bourbon and ate the sauerkraut and went to bed at ten, and I listened to the rain and the Atlantic and felt safe. I made the sauerkraut again last night and it did not make me feel any safer, but that is, as they say, another story.

Ideas and Meaning

1. Why did Joan Didion record what the woman in the dirty crepe de Chine said?
2. Who is the girl in the plaid silk dress? Why isn't she talking to the man next to her?
3. According to Didion, what kind of people "write things down"? When did she begin to write things down? Why did she begin at such an early age?
4. Why is Didion's notebook *not* a record of events?
5. How is her first writing at the age of five similar to what Didion still records in her notebook? How do you picture Didion as a child?
6. Why does Didion say that what she writes others might call lies? Why doesn't it matter whether or not others would say that her writing is lies?
7. Even though Didion records things about other people, what is her true purpose in keeping a journal?
8. Why are notebooks always about the writer?
9. In paragraph 8, what did Joan Didion learn about the wealthy from the Greek shipping heiress?
10. What is the significance of Didion's entry about Minnie Brooks and Lou Fox?
11. What does Didion recall about herself as a result of the statement "He was born the night the *Titanic* went down"?

12. Why does Didion think that it is valuable to keep in touch with yourself? With what two selves has she lost touch?
13. What memories did the question "So what's new in the whiskey business?" evoke in Didion? What does she reveal about herself in this anecdote?
14. What was the significance of the recipe for sauerkraut?
15. What adjectives would you use to describe the Didion that emerges from these pages? What fears does she have? Are there any examples of her "predilection for the extreme"?
16. Why doesn't Didion call her essay "On Keeping a Journal" or "On Keeping a Diary"? (Look up the meanings and etymologies of the words *journal* and *diary*.)
17. If you have continued to keep a personal journal in addition to your reading journal, do you write in it daily? What kinds of things do you record? If you were to read your journal at the age of thirty, would it help you remember the self you are now? Explain. Like Didion, do you imagine that at thirty, you would not be able to write dialogue saying the things you say now? Explain.
18. Is there a self you used to be that you do not feel in touch with or remember? Explain.
19. Is there a self you used to be that you don't really like, don't really care to remember? Explain.
20. If you do not keep a personal journal now, did reading this essay make you want to keep one? Why? Why not?

Development and Style

1. How does the first sentence get the reader's attention?
2. What is Didion's point? Who is her audience? What is her purpose?
3. What examples does Didion give to support her statement that regardless of what writers record, it is always a record of themselves?
4. What example follows Didion's statement that her notebook would not help you, nor would yours help her?
5. Point out the concrete/specific details in several or all of the following paragraphs: 1, 2, 3, 5, 7, 8, 9, 10, 12, 13, 14, 15, 16, 17, and 18.
6. How is the metaphor Didion uses in paragraph 11 particularly appropriate to her point that a notebook is private? How does it fit the examples she gives from her own notebook? What are the connotations of the metaphor?
7. What examples does Didion give of her statement that sometimes even she has difficulty finding meaning in some of her recordings.
8. What is the effect of Didion's repetition of the statement

"It all comes back" in paragraphs 16 and 18? Does the statement have anything to do with her thesis?

9. What is the effect of Didion's use of repetition in the first two sentences of paragraph 18?

10. In the very long last sentence of paragraph 17, Didion uses dashes to set off a series of appositives to the noun *strangers.* She could have used commas instead. What is the difference between the two? Why would commas not work as well in this sentence?

11. In this last sentence of paragraph 17, Didion has written several consecutive clauses joined by *and,* a practice you may have been warned against. Why does she do this? Rewrite the sentence a number of ways, breaking it up into two or more statements. Which is more effective—your revision or Didion's original construction? Why?

12. In the second sentence of paragraph 18, Didion could have used a comma or a dash in place of the colon. What is the effect of each of these marks? Which of the three marks works best here? Why?

13. What makes the last paragraph particularly effective? In which paragraph had Didion first mentioned the sauerkraut? In that paragraph, what generalization did the sauerkraut support as an example? What generalization does it support in her concluding paragraph?

14. Analyze the transitions between paragraphs, beginning with paragraph 11 and ending with paragraph 18.

15. In paragraph 7, Didion uses semicolons twice to separate two pairs of sentences. In each instance, she could have used a period. Why did she choose the semicolon instead? In each instance, what is the relationship between the two sentences that are separated by the semicolon?

16. Analyze the beginning and length of Didion's sentences in paragraphs 7 and 16.

Josie's Two Responses

Reading Journal: "On Keeping a Notebook" First Response

After reading Joan Didion's essay, I'm reminded of a notebook that I used to write my thoughts in when I was nine or ten. It was during the height of my forced march into Catholicism, and I felt like a very guilty person. I used to spend hours recounting all my sins and trying to decide what I should do to atone for them. I also made extra copies to take into the confessional with me in case I forgot anything. (I was usually too busy crying in there, though, to even see what I had written on the paper.) About a year or two later, I knew this practice had to come to an end, or I would be in a mental hospital before I turned 13. I burned all those notes and threw the ashes into the woods behind our house. I'm sure the soil gained more from them than I ever did.

In a way its scary to think that what Didion says is true—that a lot of the memories she has recorded aren't exactly factual. They're more representative of what events meant for her. It's scary to think that what actually happened wasn't the real thing; its what that meant and represented that's real. It makes me wonder just how much of what we perceive through our senses is actually there—often its not important at all. I guess Didion feels that by writing down what things meant for her—rather than an actual account of what she did—those events become more real and significant for her.

Second Response

After reading "On Keeping a Notebook" the second time, I find that the first thing that sticks out in my mind is what Didion said about having scraps of dialogue or just sentences written down that she didn't know the meaning of. I've been involved in writing a play for a while now, and the notebook I've been putting it together in is probably unintelligible to anyone but me. Sometimes even I don't know where my mind was when I wrote those things down. I went around for a long time just listening to people talk and writing down what I thought were interesting or funny sketches of conversation. When I look at these, like Didion, I don't necessarily remember exactly what the people were talking about, but I do remember them, and what the feeling was. In a lot of ways, a play represents a good picture of what Didion talks about. You get a lot of outward action and dialogue, but its the feeling and emotional response as a whole that the play leaves with you that really counts.

I also liked what Didion had to say about the fact that most of us write pretty selfishly—and that's good. I think that's why I find it so much harder to write about things that have nothing to do with me or what I'm interested in. Besides, it can't really be an interesting or important piece of writing unless it means something to the person who writes it. (I guess that's what these personal essays are all about anyway!)

In one of her responses Josie writes that she thinks it is "scary" that there may be no objective reality; that is, that what our senses tell us may not be "reality." Does it really matter? If what we perceive is "real" to us, isn't that all that matters? Isn't this the point Didion makes about her own perception of reality that others might call lies?

If Didion's essay inspired you to continue keeping a journal, the following essay, which introduces Ellen Goodman's collection of essays entitled *Close to Home,* may inspire you to take up both Didion's and Goodman's profession—journalism.

ELLEN GOODMAN

On Being a Journalist

1 When my daughter Katie was seven years old, I overheard her telling a friend, "My mommy is a columinst." "What's that?" asked the other little girl, reasonably enough. Katie thought about it awhile and finally said, "Well, my mother gets paid for telling people what she thinks."

2 All in all, that's not such a bad job description. The pieces collected in this book represent several years of "telling people what I think." They also represent two of the main qualifications for this business: nerve and endurance.

3 To write a column you need the egocentric confidence that your view of the world is important enough to be read. Then you need the pacing of a long-distance runner to write day after day, week after week, year after year. One journalist who dropped out of this endurance contest with a sigh of relief said that writing a column was like being married to a nymphomaniac: every time you think you're through, you have to start all over again. This was an unenlightened, but fairly accurate, analogy.

4 To meet my "quota," I need two opinions a week, although I assure you that some weeks I overflow with ideas, percolate opinions, while other weeks I can't decide what I think about the weather. Moreover, I have to fit these thoughts into a carefully reserved piece of newspaper property. I am allotted approximately the same number of words whether I am writing about life, love or the world-shattering problem of a zucchini that is sterile.

5 Despite these constraints, I tend to go through life like a vacuum cleaner, inhaling all the interesting tidbits in my path, using almost everything I observe, read or report. For me at least, this makes life more interesting and more integrated. I don't "go" to work or "return" to home life. The lines between the personal and professional sides of my life are far less rigidly drawn in this job than in virtually any other.

6 I suppose that is because I do write close to home.

7 I never wanted to be a package tour sort of columnist who covered thirteen countries in twenty-seven days. Nor do I want to write at arm's length about the Major Issues of Our Times. I think

it's more important for all of us to be able to make links between our personal lives and public issues.

8 The most vital concerns can't be divided into internal and external affairs. What is more private a concern than the public policy decisions made about the family? What is more public a concern than the impact of divorce, or the new isolation, or the two-worker family? The ups and downs of presidential polls are no more crucial to our society than the way we raise our children.

9 As a writer, I've wanted to be seen as a person, not a pontificator. Why should people believe what I have to say if they know nothing about me? I don't want to present myself as a disembodied voice of authority but as a thirty-eight-year-old woman, mother and vegetable gardener, failed jogger and expert on only one subject: the ambivalence of life.

10 I see myself in these pieces, and in fact, as a fellow struggler. In that sense too I write close to home.

11 What else can I say about the collection? The pieces show that I am more comfortable observing—people, change, events—than judging. I am more concerned with the struggles between conflicting values than the struggles between conflicting political parties. I don't think there is anything undignified about being silly when all about me are grave.

12 And maybe these columns also show how much I like my work.

Ideas and Meaning

1. What are the various meanings that Goodman gives to the phrase "close to home"?
2. As Goodman perceives it, what is paradoxically both the most difficult and easiest aspect of her job?
3. Why did she not want to become a "package tour" columnist or one who wrote about the "Major Issues of Our Times"?
4. According to Goodman, what are the two requisites for a journalist?
5. Do you agree with her that the "most vital concerns can't be divided into internal and external"? Explain.
6. In paragraph 3 why does Goodman call the analogy used by her former colleague "unenlightened"?
7. Even though Goodman "tells people what she thinks," how does she define her relationship to her audience? What is a "pontificator"? As a newspaper columnist, why would she not want to pontificate?
8. From this essay, what activities do you imagine that Goodman engages in?
9. What does Goodman mean when she calls herself an expert on "the ambivalence of life"?

10. Why does Goodman compare herself to a vacuum cleaner?
11. From this short introduction to her book, do you believe Goodman's statement that she likes her work? Why? Why not?

Development and Style

1. How does Goodman get the reader's attention?
2. What is her point? What is her tone and who is her audience?
3. What are some of the concrete/specific words and phrases Goodman uses to clarify her statements?
4. In paragraph 3, what are the connotations of the comparison Goodman's colleague used?
5. What are the connotations of the comparison Goodman uses in paragraph 5? Is this a trite comparison? Explain. How is it appropriate?
6. In paragraph 4 how is the metaphorical phrase "percolate opinions" particularly appropriate? What are the connotations?
7. What are the connotations of *pontificator?*
8. Analyze the transitions from paragraphs 4 through 9. Are there any weak transitions in the essay? If so, how would you strengthen them?
9. Analyze the sentence structure in paragraphs 3 through 5. What are the beginning constructions? How does the length of sentences vary? Is the most important information at the end of sentences? Begin the last sentence of paragraph 4 with the dependent clause "whether I am . . ." Which construction is better? Why?
10. What are the effects of the one-sentence paragraphs 6 and 12?
11. In paragraph 11 what is the effect of Goodman's use of a question and answer?
12. In this same paragraph, why does Goodman use dashes to separate the noun objects *people, change,* and *events* from the participle *observing?* Do you think that Goodman's sentence or the following one is more effective? Why?

> The pieces show that I am more comfortable observing people, change, and events than I am judging them.

13. How do Joan Didion's and Ellen Goodman's styles differ? Who is Goodman's audience? Who is Didion's audience? (Remember that Didion is an essayist who writes for magazines such as the *Saturday Evening Post,* whereas Goodman, a columnist, writes for *The Boston Globe.*) You might read one or more additional columns from Goodman's col-

lection *Close to Home.* Would you describe her as a "fellow struggler" who writes "close to home"?

John's Two Responses

Reading Journal: "On Being a Journalist" First Response

I like this woman's style! She's easy to read, zippy, and she makes a lot of sense. The only thing that bothers me a little is that I don't understand why her colleague's analogy that being a columnist is like being married to a nymphomaniac is "unenlightened." If it "illuminates" the similarity, then it's enlightening, isn't it?

Actually, despite the never-ending business of it, writing a newspaper column sounds like a lot of fun to me. I'd love to be paid to write what I think. But then, I suppose, I'd have to stay awfully busy reading things and doing things—out observing people to come up with 104 different topics a year that I had opinions on. I wonder how many columns in all that she's written? How many years has she been at it? Say ten. That means 1,040 different topics?! Terrifying. And I even have trouble sometimes coming up with a topic for my essays in this class.

Second Response

In this reading I noticed that Ellen Goodman says some things about writing that our text has said: that writing is an egocentric business and that good writers pay attention to the world around them. They're "observers," they're "vacuum cleaners," as Goodman put it. Well, frankly, that's how I felt at the beginning of this semester when I had to walk around those days paying attention to everything I heard, or smelled, or tasted. . . . Frankly, I felt OD-ed on the whole thing. It was too much. And now I'm thinking that maybe being a columnist isn't such a good idea after all. But one thing she said that I really liked was that in her columns she is a "fellow struggler." I suppose she means by that that she's struggling with life, too, like her readers.

I agree that life's a struggle, but I'm not sure what she means by being an expert on "life's ambivalence." I looked up "ambivalence" in the dictionary just to make sure that I knew what it meant. Sure enough, I had the right idea about the word, but I still don't get it: life doesn't seem to me to be ambivalent, not just made up of conflicting things like love and hate, but more complex than that, more prismatic. Maybe that's not the right word either. I learned a new word the other day for puzzle: conundrum. That's it—Life's a conundrum. Maybe that's what Goodman was getting at. I don't know, but I know one thing: This woman's a whole lot easier to understand than Joan Didion.

And now, the following is Judith Viorst's essay on another subject altogether—friendship.

JUDITH VIORST

Friends, Good Friends—And Such Good Friends

1 Women are friends, I once would have said, when they totally love and support and trust each other, and bare to each other the secrets of their souls, and run—no questions asked—to help each other, and tell harsh truths to each other (no, you can't wear that dress unless you lose ten pounds first) when harsh truths must be told.

2 Women are friends, I once would have said, when they share the same affection for Ingmar Bergman, plus train rides, cats, warm rain, charades, Camus, and hate with equal ardor Newark and Brussel sprouts and Lawrence Welk and camping.

3 In other words, I once would have said that a friend is a friend all the way, but now I believe that's a narrow point of view. For the friendships I have and the friendships I see are conducted at many levels of intensity, serve many different functions, meet different needs and range from those as all-the-way as the friendship of the soul sisters mentioned above to that of the most nonchalant and casual playmates.

4 Consider these varieties of friendship:

5 1. Convenience friends. These are the women with whom, if our paths weren't crossing all the time, we'd have no particular reason to be friends: a next-door neighbor, a woman in our car pool, the mother of one of our children's closest friends or maybe some mommy with whom we serve juice and cookies each week at the Glenwood Co-op Nursery.

6 Convenience friends are convenient indeed. They'll lend us their cups and silverware for a party. They'll drive our kids to soccer when we're sick. They'll take us to pick up our car when we need a lift to the garage. They'll even take our cats when we go on vacation. As we will for them.

7 But we don't, with convenience friends, ever come too close or tell too much; we maintain our public face and emotional distance. "Which means," says Elaine, "that I'll talk about being overweight but not about being depressed. Which means I'll admit being mad but not blind with rage. Which means I might say

that we're pinched this month but never that I'm worried sick over money."

8 But which doesn't mean that there isn't sufficient value to be found in these friendships of mutual aid, in convenience friends.

9 2. Special-interest friends. These friendships aren't intimate, and they needn't involve kids or silverware or cats. Their value lies in some interest jointly shared. And so we may have an office friend or a yoga friend or a tennis friend or a friend from the Women's Democratic Club.

10 "I've got one woman friend," says Joyce, "who likes, as I do, to take psychology courses. Which makes it nice for me—and nice for her. It's fun to go with someone you know and it's fun to discuss what you've learned, driving back from the classes." And for the most part, she says, that's all they discuss.

11 "I'd say that what we're doing is *doing* together, not being together," Suzanne says of her Tuesday-doubles friends. "It's mainly a tennis relationship, but we play together well. And I guess we all need to have a couple of playmates."

12 I agree.

13 *My* playmate is a shopping friend, a woman of marvelous taste, a woman who knows exactly *where* to buy *what*, and furthermore is a woman who always knows beyond a doubt what one ought to be buying. I don't have the time to keep up with what's new in eyeshadow, hemlines and shoes and whether the smock look is in or finished already. But since (oh, shame!) I care a lot about eyeshadow, hemlines and shoes, and since I don't *want* to wear smocks if the smock look is finished, I'm very glad to have a shopping friend.

14 3. Historical friends. We all have a friend who knew us when . . . maybe way back in Miss Meltzer's second grade, when our family lived in that three-room flat in Brooklyn, when our dad was out of work for seven months, when our brother Allie got in that fight where they had to call the police, when our sister married the endodontist from Yonkers, and when, the morning after we lost our virginity, she was the first, the only, friend we told.

15 The years have gone by and we've gone separate ways and we've little in common now, but we're still an intimate part of each other's past. And so whenever we go to Detroit we always go to visit this friend of our girlhood. Who knows how we looked before our teeth were straightened. Who knows how we talked before our voice got un-Brooklyned. Who knows what we ate before we learned about artichokes. And who, by her presence, puts us in touch with an earlier part of ourself, a part of ourself it's important never to lose.

16 "What this friend means to me and what I mean to her," says Grace, "is having a sister without sibling rivalry. We know the

texture of each other's lives. She remembers my grandmother's cabbage soup. I remember the way her uncle played the piano. There's simply no other friend who remembers those things."

17 4. Crossroads friends. Like historical friends, our crossroads friends are important for *what was*—for the friendship we shared at a crucial, now past, time of life. A time, perhaps, when we roomed in college together; or worked as eager young singles in the Big City together; or went together, as my friend Elizabeth and I did through pregnancy, birth and that scary first year of new motherhood.

18 Crossroads friends forge powerful links, links strong enough to endure with not much more contact than once-a-year letters at Christmas. And out of respect for those crossroads years, for those dramas and dreams we once shared, we will always be friends.

19 5. Cross-generational friends. Historical friends and crossroads friends seem to maintain a special kind of intimacy—dormant but always ready to be revived—and though we may rarely meet, whenever we do connect, it's personal and intense. Another kind of intimacy exists in the friendships that form across generations in what one woman calls her daughter-mother and her mother-daughter relationships.

20 Evelyn's friend is her mother's age—"but I share so much more than I ever could with my mother"—a woman she talks to of music, of books and of life. "What I get from her is the benefit of her experience. What she gets—and enjoys—from me is a youthful perspective. It's a pleasure for both of us."

21 I have in my own life a precious friend, a woman of 65 who has lived very hard, who is wise, who listens well; who has been where I am and can help me understand it; and who represents not only an ultimate ideal mother to me but also the person I'd like to be when I grow up.

22 In our daughter role we tend to do more than our share of self-revelation; in our mother role we tend to receive what's revealed. It's another kind of pleasure—playing wise mother to a questing younger person. It's another very lovely kind of friendship.

23 6. Part-of-a-couple friends. Some of the women we call our friends we never see alone—we see them as part of a couple at couples' parties. And though we share interests in many things and respect each other's views, we aren't moved to deepen the relationship. Whatever the reason, a lack of time or—and this is more likely—a lack of chemistry, our friendship remains in the context of a group. But the fact that our feeling on seeing each other is always, "I'm *so* glad she's here" and the fact that we spend half the evening talking together says that this too, in its own way, counts as a friendship.

24 (Other part-of-a-couple friends are the friends that came with

the marriage, and some of these are friends we could live without. But sometimes, alas, she married our husband's best friend; and sometimes, alas, she *is* our husband's best friend. And so we find ourself dealing with her, somewhat against our will, in a spirit of what I'll call *reluctant* friendship.)

25 7. Men who are friends. I wanted to write just of women friends, but the women I've talked to won't let me—they say I must mention man-woman friendships too. For these friendships can be just as close and as dear as those that we form with women. Listen to Lucy's description of one such friendship.

26 "We've found we have things to talk about that are different from what he talks about with my husband and different from what I talk about with his wife. So sometimes we call on the phone or meet for lunch. There are similar intellectual interests— we always pass on to each other the books that we love—but there's also something tender and caring too."

27 In a couple of crises, Lucy says, "he offered himself, for talking and for helping. And when someone died in his family he wanted me there. The sexual, flirty part of our friendship is very small, but *some*—just enough to make it fun and different." She thinks— and I agree—that the sexual part, though small is always *some*, is always there when a man and a woman are friends.

28 It's only in the past few years that I've made friends with men, in the sense of a friendship that's *mine*, not just part of two couples. And achieving with them the ease and the trust I've found with women friends has value indeed. Under the dryer at home last week, putting on mascara and rouge, I comfortably sat and talked with a fellow named Peter. Peter, I finally decided, could handle the shock of me minus mascara under the dryer. Because we care for each other. Because we're friends.

29 8. There are medium friends, and pretty good friends, and very good friends indeed, and these friendships are defined by their level of intimacy. And what we'll reveal at each of these levels of intimacy is calibrated with care. We might tell a medium friend, for example, that yesterday we had a fight with our husband. And we might tell a pretty good friend that this fight with our husband made us so mad that we slept on the couch. And we might tell a very good friend that the reason we got so mad in that fight that we slept on the couch had something to do with that girl who works in his office. But it's only to our very best friends that we're willing to tell all, to tell what's going on with that girl in his office.

30 The best of friends, I still believe, totally love and support and trust each other, and bare to each other the secrets of their souls, and run—no questions asked—to help each other, and tell harsh truths to each other when they must be told.

31 But we needn't agree about everything (only 12-year-old girl friends agree about *everything*) to tolerate each other's point of view. To accept without judgment. To give and to take without ever keeping score. And to *be* there, as I am for them and as they are for me, to comfort our sorrows, to celebrate our joys.

Ideas and Meaning

1. What was Viorst's original idea of friendships between women?

2. Why did she change her mind? What is her idea of female friendships now?

3. How does she define the six kinds of relationships among women? Do these seem valid classifications to you? Why? Why not? If you are an unmarried woman, do you have friends who fit into the first five categories Viorst mentions? If you are married, do you have friends who fit into the first six types? Explain.

4. If you are a man, do any of Viorst's types of women friends apply to the kinds of friendships you have with other men? If so, explain and give examples. If you have several types of friendships with other men that do not coincide with Viorst's types, define them and give examples.

5. How does Viorst define her friendships with the opposite sex? Does her definition include any of the characteristics of her friendships with women? What characteristic of her male friendships is excluded from her friendships with women?

6. Viorst's eighth category classifies friendships with women on the basis of intimacy. What are the four levels of intimacy that she mentions? If you are a woman, how do these levels of intimacy coincide with or differ from your own experience? Explain and give examples. Would you add to or delete any of the levels she mentions? Explain. If you are a man, how do these levels of intimacy coincide with or differ from your experience with male friends? Explain and give examples.

7. If you have friendships with the opposite sex, how are they similar to and different from your friendships with the same sex?

8. In your experience, is it more difficult or less difficult to maintain friendships with the opposite sex than with the same sex? Why? Is it easier for you to form friendships with the same sex or with the opposite sex? Explain.

9. How have the number of friendships and the kinds of friends you have had fluctuated during the course of your life? Ex-

plain. Do you have more friends and a greater variety of friends now than you have ever had, or do you have fewer friends and a lesser variety than you have ever had? Explain.

10. If you are a woman, do you agree or disagree with Viorst's statement that only twelve-year-old girlfriends agree on everything. Why? If you agree, can you theorize about the probable cause of this phenomenon?

11. Ellen Goodman once wrote a column in which she said that men who are friends "do" things together, whereas women who are friends, simply "were" together. If you are male, is it true that you and your friends are generally involved in an activity of some kind when you are together? Explain. If you are a man, have you ever spent time just talking about yourself, "baring your soul," to a best friend? If you are a woman, why do you agree or disagree with Goodman's statement?

12. According to Viorst, is there a type of female friendship that would contradict Goodman's statement?

13. Like Goodman, do you find a difference between male friendships and female friendships? If so, what are the differences? How do you account for them?

Development and Style

1. How does Viorst get the reader's attention in the first sentence?

2. Who is her audience and what is her purpose?

3. What is her tone? From her writer's voice, how do you picture Viorst?

4. What is her point? How has she supported it?

5. How has Viorst organized the classes of women's friendships? Why does she put couple-friends sixth? How is the eighth classification different from the others?

6. What are the connotations of the noun *convenience?* What are the connotations of the phrase "convenience friends"? Does Viorst's use of the noun *convenience* where ordinarily the adjective *convenient* would be used save the phrase from negative connotations? Why? Why not? Can you think of a label for this type of friend that is less negative than the one Viorst uses?

7. By what means does Viorst support each of her generalizations defining each of the classes of friends? In paragraph 29 how has she supported her generalization that there are medium friends, pretty good friends, very good friends, and best friends?

8. In order to illustrate types of professors, can you think of an example you could use the way that Viorst uses hers in paragraph 29?

9. Point out the specific nouns Viorst has used in several of the following paragraphs: 2, 5, 7, 9, 10, 11, 14, 15, 16, 17, 20, 27, and 28.

10. In paragraphs 13 and 21, Viorst uses her own friends as examples. Unlike the other examples, she does not use specific names for these friends. Would it have helped her writing had she used pseudonyms for each—Anna and Violet, for example? Why? Why not? Why do you think Viorst did not use names in these examples?

11. Point out the intentional fragments and parallel structure that Viorst has used. What are the effects of each? (Hint: most of the fragments are also parallel.)

12. In paragraph 21, Viorst uses a semicolon before the last two dependent clauses in a series of five. Ordinarily, a comma would be used here. Another alternative for Viorst would have been to create two intentional fragments by using periods before the last two clauses in place of the two semicolons. Substitute first the comma, then the period for the two semicolons. Which of the three marks works best? Why?

13. Ordinarily, the semicolon is used between two sentences when there is no coordinate conjunction. A period may also be used to separate two sentences. In paragraph 7, Viorst uses a semicolon to separate the first two sentences. Rewrite the sentences using a period. Why is the semicolon a better choice?

14. Frequently Viorst uses dashes to set off parenthetical or appositive phrases. Point out examples throughout the essay, and determine why the dashes are more effective than her other options: commas or parentheses for parenthetical expressions and the comma or the colon for appositives.

15. In the second sentence of paragraph 10, Viorst uses a dash in an intentional fragment where she could have no punctuation at all or where she could have used parentheses instead of the dash. Which is most effective—no punctuation at all, the dash, or parentheses? Why?

16. More than any other writer you have read thus far, Viorst uses parallelism, intentional fragments, and dashes. What are the effects of these stylistic features?

17. Locate examples of Viorst's uses of these two means of transition: (1) the repetition of key words or phrases, and (2) parallel structure. (*Note:* Sometimes the repetition of key words and phrases is also parallel.)

18. Rearrange the sentence structure in paragraph 13 until you

have a version that you think is as effective, or more effective than Viorst's.

Trudy's Two Responses

Reading Journal. "Friends, Good Friends" First Response

After reading Judith Viorst's essay, I think it's interesting to realize how few good, good friends I really have right now. After reading all these categories, I realize that most of the people I call my friends would probably fit into any category but the best, true friend.

I found what she said about the historical and crossroads friends especially interesting. They really are people who, when you see them, make you think of yourself, or some event, and not the person. There is a girl that I refer to as my friend who I run into from time to time in R. She is a reminder of a very dark time in my past, and everytime I see her, I cringe. And yet, somehow I feel compelled to keep that very tense friendship alive. It's as if I need this person there to always remind me of that time.

I wonder what makes people need friends. Some don't seem to—hermits, mystics, etc. But for most people there seems to be something deep inside that needs someone to talk to and be with in a way that's often different from the relationship of man-wife or mother-daughter and so on. I think it's because ultimately the intellectual, emotional, mental needs surpass physical needs, and maybe since most people connect physical needs with husbands or mothers, they seek out other people. That seems pretty bizarre—but who knows?

Second Response

After my second reading of Viorst's essay, I think she needs another category—friends who were best friends but are now not friends at all. Friends aren't always permanent. Someone told me once that no matter what happens, if you were once really good friends, you'll always be friends. That same person said that if you lose a friend, it means that you weren't really ever good friends at all. Well, I've come to the conclusion that that just isn't true. I recently split with someone who I believed to be a good friend for about eight years—I didn't just believe it, we were good friends. I can still think happily on good times we had, but this person isn't someone I like anymore.

Friendships with men are interesting as well. I have one very good friend who happens to be male, and who I would tell just about anything to. These friendships can be socially awkward (people assume things that just aren't true), but they're so rewarding that they make up for it. I've received the inside scoops as far as what goes on in male-only bars, stag parties, and locker rooms. Most of it I could have guessed, some of it I didn't really want to know, but a lot of it was interesting and informative. It's funny to realize the way the sexes perceive one another, and often it's pretty sad as well.

Do you have a "historical" friend similar to Trudy's in "R." who makes you "cringe," but who serves a function similar to Didion's notebook—to keep you in touch with your past? Although Trudy reveals that not all female friendships are rewarding, men do not have *any* satisfying friendships with each other, according to Marc Fasteau in the following excerpt from his book *The Male Machine*.

MARC FASTEAU

On Male Friendships

1 There is a long-standing myth in our society that the great friendships are between men. Forged through shared experience, male friendship is portrayed as the most unselfish, if not the highest form, of human relationship. The more traditionally masculine the shared experience from which it springs, the stronger and more profound the friendship is supposed to be. Going to war, weathering crises together at school or work, playing on the same athletic team, are some of the classic experiences out of which friendships between men are believed to grow.

2 By and large, men do prefer the company of other men, not only in their structured time but in the time they fill with optional, nonobligatory activity. They prefer to play games, drink, and talk, as well as work and fight together. Yet something is missing. Despite the time men spend together, their contact rarely goes beyond the external, a limitation which tends to make their friendships shallow and unsatisfying.

3 My own childhood memories are of doing things with my friends—playing games or sports, building walkie-talkies, going camping. Other people and my relationships to them were never legitimate subjects for attention. If someone liked me, it was an opaque, mysterious occurrence that bore no analysis. When I was slighted, I felt hurt. But relationships with people just happened. I certainly had feelings about my friends, but I can't remember a single instance of trying consciously to sort them out until I was well into college.

4 For most men this kind of shying away from the personal continues into adult life. In conversations with each other, we hardly

ever use ourselves as reference points. We talk about almost everything except how we ourselves are affected by people and events. Everything is discussed as though it were taking place out there somewhere, as though we had no more felt response to it than to the weather. Topics that can be treated in this detached, objective way become conversational mainstays. The few subjects which are fundamentally personal are shaped into discussions of abstract general questions. Even in an exchange about their reactions to liberated women—a topic of intensely personal interest—the tendency will be to talk in general, theoretical terms. Work, at least its objective aspects, is always a safe subject. Men also spend an incredible amount of time rehashing the great public issues of the day. Until early 1973, Vietnam was the work-horse topic. Then came Watergate. It doesn't seem to matter that we've all had a hundred similar conversations. We plunge in for another round, trying to come up with a new angle as much to impress the others with what we know as to keep from being bored stiff.

5 Games play a central role in situations organized by men. I remember a weekend some years ago at the country house of a law-school classmate as a blur of softball, football, croquet, poker, and a dice-and-board game called Combat, with swimming thrown in on the side. As soon as one game ended, another began. Taken one at a time, these "activities" were fun, but the impression was inescapable that the host, and most of his guests, would do anything to stave off a lull in which they would be together without some impersonal focus for their attention. A snapshot of almost any men's club would show the same thing, ninety percent of the men engaged in some activity—ranging from backgammon to watching the tube—other than, or at least as an aid to, conversation.[1]

6 My composite memory of evenings spent with a friend at college and later when we shared an apartment in Washington is of conversations punctuated by silences during which we would internally pass over any personal or emotional thoughts which had arisen and come back to the permitted track. When I couldn't get my mind off personal matters, I said very little. Talks with my father have always had the same tone. Respect for privacy was the rationale for our diffidence. His questions to me about how things were going at school or at work were asked as discreetly as he would have asked a friend about someone's commitment to a hospital for the criminally insane. Our conversations, when they touched these matters at all, to say nothing of more sensitive

---

1. Women may use games as a reason for getting together—bridge clubs, for example. But the show is more for the rest of the world—to indicate that they are doing *something*—and the games themselves are not the only means of communication.

matters, would veer quickly back to safe topics of general interest.

7   In our popular literature, the archetypal male hero embodying this personal muteness is the cowboy. The classic mold for the character was set in 1902 by Owen Wister's novel *The Virginian* where the author spelled out, with an explicitness that was never again necessary, the characteristics of his protagonist. Here's how it goes when two close friends the Virginian hasn't seen in some time take him out for a drink:

> All of them had seen rough days together, and they felt guilty with emotion.
> "It's hot weather," said Wiggin.
> "Hotter in Box Elder," said McLean. "My kid has started teething."
> Words ran dry again. They shifted their positions, looked in their glasses, read the labels on the bottles. They dropped a word now and then to the proprietor about his trade, and his ornaments.[2]

One of the Virginian's duties is to assist at the hanging of an old friend as a horse thief. Afterward, for the first time in the book, he is visibly upset. The narrator puts his arm around the hero's shoulders and describes the Virginian's reaction:

> I had the sense to keep silent, and presently he shook my hand, not looking at me as he did so. He was always very shy of demonstration.[3]

And, for explanation of such reticence, "As all men know, he also knew that many things should be done in this world in silence, and that talking about them is a mistake."[4]

8   There are exceptions, but they only prove the rule.

9   One is the drunken confidence: "Bob, ole boy, I gotta tell ya—being divorced isn't so hot. . . . [and see, I'm too drunk to be held responsible for blurting it out]." Here, drink becomes an excuse for exchanging confidences and a device for periodically loosening the restraint against expressing a need for sympathy and support from other men—which may explain its importance as a male ritual.[5] Marijuana fills a similar need.

10   Another exception is talking to a stranger—who may be either someone the speaker doesn't know or someone who isn't in the same social or business world. (Several black friends told me that

---

2. Owen Wister, *The Virginian* ([Macmillan: 1902] Grosset & Dunlap ed.: 1929), pp. 397–98.

3. *Ibid.*, p. 343.

4. *Ibid.*, p. 373.

5. Lionel Tiger, *Men in Groups* (Random House: 1969), p. 185.

they have been on the receiving end of personal confidences from white acquaintances that they were sure had not been shared with white friends.) In either case, men are willing to talk about themselves only to other men with whom they do not have to compete or whom they will not have to confront socially later.

11 Finally, there is the way men depend on women to facilitate certain conversations. The women in a mixed group are usually the ones who make the first personal reference, about themselves or others present. The men can then join in without having the onus for initiating a discussion of "personalities." Collectively, the men can "blame" the conversation on the women. They can also feel in these conversations that since they are talking "to" the women instead of "to" the men, they can be excused for deviating from the masculine norm. When the women leave, the tone and subject invariably shift away from the personal.

12 The effect of these constraints is to make it extraordinarily difficult for men to really get to know each other. A psychotherapist who has conducted a lengthy series of encounter groups for men summed it up:

> With saddening regularity [the members of these groups] described how much they wanted to have closer, more satisfying relationships with other men: "I'd settle for having one really close man friend. I supposedly have some close men friends now. We play golf or go for a drink. We complain about our jobs and our wives. I care about them and they care about me. We even have some physical contact—I mean we may even give a hug on a big occasion. But it's not enough."[6]

13 The sources of this stifling ban on self-disclosure, the reasons why men hide from each other, lie in the taboos and imperatives of the masculine stereotype.

14 To begin with, men are supposed to be functional, to spend their time working or otherwise solving or thinking about how to solve problems. Personal reaction, how one feels about something, is considered dysfunctional, at best an irrelevant distraction from the expected objectivity. Only weak men, and women, talk about—i.e, "give in," to their feelings. "I group my friends in two ways," said a business executive:

> those who have made it and don't complain and those who haven't made it. And only the latter spend time talking to their wives about their problems and how bad their boss is and all that. The

6. Don Clark, "Homosexual Encounter in All-Male Groups," in L. Solomon and B. Berzon (eds.), *New Perspectives on Encounter Groups* (Jossey-Bass: 1972), pp. 376–77. See also Alan Booth, "Sex and Social Participation," *American Sociological Review*, Vol. 37 (April 1972), p. 183, an empirical study showing that, contrary to Lionel Tiger's much publicized assertion *(Men in Groups)* women form stronger and closer friendship bonds with each other than men do.

ones who concentrate more on communicating . . . are those who have realized that they aren't going to make it and therefore they have changed the focus of attention.[7]

In a world which tells men they have to choose between expressiveness and manly strength, this characterization may be accurate. Most of the men who talk personally to other men *are* those whose problems have gotten the best of them, who simply can't help it. Men not driven to despair don't talk about themselves, so the idea that self-disclosure and expressiveness are associated with problems and weakness becomes a self-fulfilling prophecy.

15 Obsessive competitiveness also limits the range of communication in male friendships. Competition is the principal mode by which men relate to each other—at one level because they don't know how else to make contact, but more basically because it is the way to demonstrate, to themselves and others, the key masculine qualities of unwavering toughness and the ability to dominate and control. The result is that they inject competition into situations which don't call for it.

16 In conversations, you must show that you know more about the subject than the other man, or at least as much as he does. For example, I have often engaged in a contest that could be called My Theory Tops Yours, disguised as a serious exchange of ideas. The proof that it wasn't serious was that I was willing to participate even when I was sure that the participants, including myself, had nothing fresh to say. Convincing the other person—victory— is the main objective, with control of the floor an important tactic. Men tend to lecture at each other, insist that the discussion follow their train of thought, and are often unwilling to listen.[8] As one member of a men's rap group said,

> When I was talking I used to feel that I had to be driving to a point, that it had to be rational and organized, that I had to persuade at all times, rather than exchange thoughts and ideas.[9]

Even in casual conversations some men hold back unless they are absolutely sure of what they are saying. They don't want to have to change a position once they have taken it. It's "just like a woman" to change your mind, and, more important, it is inconsistent with the approved masculine posture of total independence.

7. Fernando Bartolomé, "Executives as Human Beings," *Harvard Business Review*, Vol 50 (November-December 1972), p. 64.

8. The contrast with women on this point is striking. Casual observation will confirm that women's conversations move more quickly, with fewer long speeches and more frequent changes of speaker.

9. *Boston Globe*, March 12, 1972, p. B-1.

17 Competition was at the heart of one of my closest friendships, now defunct. There was a good deal of mutual liking and respect. We went out of our way to spend time with each other and wanted to work together. We both had "prospects" as "bright young men" and the same "liberal but tough" point of view. We recognized this about each other, and this recognition was the basis of our respect and of our sense of equality. That we saw each other as equals was important—our friendship was confirmed by the reflection of one in the other. But our constant and all-encompassing competition made this equality precarious and fragile. One way or another, everything counted in the measuring process. We fought out our tennis matches as though our lives depended on it. At poker, the two of us would often play on for hours after the others had left. These *mano a mano*[0] poker marathons seem in retrospect especially revealing of the competitiveness of the relationship: playing for small stakes, the essence of the game is in outwitting, psychologically beating down the other player—the other skills involved are negligible. Winning is the only pleasure, one that evaporates quickly, a truth that struck me in inchoate form every time our game broke up at four a.m. and I walked out the door with my five-dollar winnings, a headache, and a sense of time wasted. Still, I did the same thing the next time. It was what we did together, and somehow it counted. Losing at tennis could be balanced by winning at poker; at another level, his moving up in the federal government by my getting on the *Harvard Law Review*.

18 This competitiveness feeds the most basic obstacle to openness between men, the inability to admit to being vulnerable. Real men, we learn early, are not supposed to have doubts, hopes and ambitions which may not be realized, things they don't (or even especially do) like about themselves, fears and disappointments. Such feelings and concerns, of course, are part of everyone's inner life, but a man must keep quiet about them. If others know how you really feel you can be hurt, and that in itself is incompatible with manhood. The inhibiting effect of this imperative is not limited to disclosures of major personal problems. Often men do not share even ordinary uncertainties and half-formulated plans of daily life with their friends. And when they do, they are careful to suggest that they already know how to proceed—that they are not really asking for help or understanding but simply for particular bits of information. Either way, any doubts they have are presented as external, carefully characterized as having to do with the issue as distinct from the speaker. They are especially guarded about expressing concern or asking a question that would invite personal comment. It is almost impossible for men to simply exchange

0. *Mano a mano* hand-to-hand, competitive (Spanish).

thoughts about matters involving them personally in a comfortable, non-crisis atmosphere. If a friend tells you of his concern that he and a colleague are always disagreeing, for example, he is likely to quickly supply his own explanation—something like "different professional backgrounds." The effect is to rule out observations or suggestions that do not fit within this already reconnoitered protective structure. You don't suggest, even if you believe it is true, that in fact the disagreements arise because he presents his ideas in a way which tends to provoke a hostile reaction. It would catch him off guard; it would be something he hadn't already thought of and accepted about himself and, for that reason, no matter how constructive and well-intentioned you might be, it would put you in control for the moment. He doesn't want that; he is afraid of losing your respect. So, sensing he feels that way, because you would yourself, you say something else. There is no real give-and-take.

19 It is hard for men to get angry at each other honestly. Anger between friends often means that one has hurt the other. Since the straightforward expression of anger in these situations involves an admission of vulnerability, it is safer to stew silently or find an "objective" excuse for retaliation. Either way, trust is not fully restored.

20 Men even try not to let it show when they feel good. We may report the reasons for our happiness, if they have to do with concrete accomplishments, but we try to do it with a straight face, as if to say, "Here's what happened, but it hasn't affected my grown-up unemotional equilibrium, and I am not asking for any kind of response." Happiness is a precarious, "childish" feeling, easy to shoot down. Others may find the event that triggers it trivial or incomprehensible, or even threatening to their own self-esteem—in the sense that if one man is up, another man is down. So we tend not to take the risk of expressing it.

21 What is particularly difficult for men is seeking or accepting help from friends. I, for one, learned early that dependence was unacceptable. When I was eight, I went to a summer camp I disliked. My parents visited me in the middle of the summer and, when it was time for them to leave, I wanted to go with them. They refused, and I yelled and screamed and was miserably unhappy for the rest of the day. That evening an older camper comforted me, sitting by my bed as I cried, patting me on the back soothingly and saying whatever it is that one says at times like that. He was in some way clumsy or funny-looking, and a few days later I joined a group of kids in cruelly making fun of him, an act which upset me, when I thought about it, for years. I can only explain it in terms of my feeling, as early as the age of eight, that by needing and accepting his help and comfort I had compromised myself, and took it out on him.

22 "You can't express dependence when you feel it," a corporate executive said, "because it's a kind of absolute. If you are loyal 90% of the time and disloyal 10%, would you be considered loyal? Well, the same happens with independence: you are either dependent or independent; you can't be both."[10] Feelings of dependence," another explained, "are identified with weakness or 'untoughness' and our culture doesn't accept those things in men."[11] The result is that we either go it alone or "act out certain games or rituals to provoke the desired reaction in the other and have our needs satisfied without having to ask for anything."[12]

23 Somewhat less obviously, the expression of affection also runs into emotional barriers growing out of the masculine stereotype. When I was in college, I was suddenly quite moved while attending a friend's wedding. The surge of feeling made me uncomfortable and self-conscious. There was nothing inherently difficult or, apart from the fact of being moved by a moment of tenderness, "unmasculine" about my reaction. I just did not know how to deal with or communicate what I felt. "I consider myself a sentimentalist," one man said, "and I think I am quite able to express my feelings. But the other day my wife described a friend of mine to some people as my best friend and I felt embarrassed when I heard her say it."[13]

24 A major source of these inhibitions is the fear of being, or being thought, homosexual. Nothing is more frightening to a heterosexual man in our society. It threatens, at one stroke, to take away every vestige of his claim to a masculine identity—something like knocking out the foundations of a building—and to expose him to the ostracism, ranging from polite tolerance to violent revulsion, of his friends and colleagues. A man can be labeled as homosexual not just because of overt sexual acts but because of almost any sign of behavior which does not fit the masculine stereotype. The touching of another man, other than shaking hands or, under emotional stress, an arm around the shoulder, is taboo. Women may kiss each other when they meet; men are uncomfortable when hugged even by close friends.[14] Onlookers might misinterpret what they saw, and more important, what would we think of ourselves if we felt a twinge of sensual pleasure from the embrace.

25 Direct verbal expressions of affection or tenderness are also

10. Bartolomé, *op. cit.*, p. 65.

11. *Ibid.*, p. 64.

12. *Ibid.*, p. 66.

13. *Ibid.*, p. 64.

14. *Ibid.*, p. 65.

something that only homosexuals and women engage in. Between "real" men affection has to be disguised in gruff, "you old son-of-a-bitch" style. Paradoxically, in some instances, terms of endearment between men can be used as a ritual badge of manhood, dangerous medicine safe only for the strong. The flirting with homosexuality that characterizes the initiation rites of many fraternities and men's clubs serves this purpose. Claude Brown wrote about black life in New York City in the 1950s:

> The term ["baby"] had a hip ring to it. . . . It was like saying, "Man, look at me. I've got masculinity to spare. . . . I can say 'baby' to another cat and he can say 'baby' to me, and we can say it with strength in our voices." If you could say it, this meant that you really had to be sure of yourself, sure of your masculinity.[15]

Fear of homosexuality does more than inhibit the physical display of affection. One of the major recurring themes in the men's groups led by psychotherapist Don Clark was:

> "A large segment of my feelings about other men are unknown or distorted because I am afraid they might have something to do with homosexuality. Now I'm lonely for other men and don't know how to find what I want with them."

As Clark observes, "The spectre of homosexuality seems to be the dragon at the gateway to self-awareness, understanding, and acceptance of male-male needs. If a man tries to pretend the dragon is not there by turning a blind eye to erotic feelings for all other males, he also blinds himself to the rich variety of feelings that are related."[16]

26 The few situations in which men do acknowledge strong feelings of affection and dependence toward other men are exceptions which prove the rule. With "cop couples," for example, or combat soldier "buddies," intimacy and dependence are forced on the men by their work—they have to ride in the patrol car or be in the same foxhole with somebody—and the jobs themselves have such highly masculine images that the men can get away with behavior that would be suspect under any other conditions.

27 Furthermore, even these combat-buddy relations when looked at closely, turn out not to be particularly intimate or personal. Margaret Mead has written:

> During the last war English observers were confused by the apparent contradiction between American soldiers' emphasis on the buddy, so grievously exemplified in the break-downs that fol-

---

15. Claude Brown, *Manchild in the Promised Land* ([Macmillan: 1965] Signet ed.: 1965), p. 171.

16. Clark, *op. cit.*, p. 378.

lowed a buddy's death, and the results of detailed inquiry which showed how transitory these buddy relationships were. It was found that men actually accepted their buddies as derivatives from their outfit, and from accidents of association, rather than because of any special personality characteristics capable of ripening into friendship.[17]

One effect of the fear of appearing to be homosexual is to reinforce the practice that two men rarely get together alone without a reason. I once called a friend to suggest that we have dinner together. "O.K.," he said. "What's up?" I felt uncomfortable telling him that I just wanted to talk, that there was no other reason for the invitation.

28 Men get together to conduct business, to drink, to play games and sports, to re-establish contact after long absences, to participate in heterosexual social occasions—circumstances in which neither person is responsible for actually wanting to see the other. Men are particularly comfortable seeing each other in groups. The group situation defuses any possible assumptions about the intensity of feeling between particular men and provides the safety of numbers—"All the guys are here." It makes personal communication, which requires a level of trust and mutual understanding not generally shared by all members of a group, more difficult and offers an excuse for avoiding this dangerous territory. And it provides what is most sought after in men's friendships: mutual reassurance of masculinity.

29 Needless to say, the observations in this chapter did not spring full-blown from my head. The process started when I began to understand that, at least with Brenda, a more open, less self-protective relation was possible. At first, I perceived my situation as completely personal. The changes I was trying to effect in myself had to do, I thought, only with Brenda and me, and could be generalized, if at all, only to other close relationships between men and women. But, as Brenda came to be deeply involved in the women's movement, I began to see, usually at one remove but sometimes directly, the level of intimacy that women, especially women active in the movement, shared with each other. The contrast between this and the friendships I had with men was striking. I started listening to men's conversations, including my own, and gradually the basic outlines of the pattern described here began to emerge. I heard from women that the men they knew had very few really close male friends; since then I have heard the same thing from men themselves. It was, I realized, my own experience as well. It wasn't that I didn't know a lot of men, or that

17. Margaret Mead, *Male and Female* ([William Morrow: 1949] Mentor ed.: 1949), p. 214.

I was not on friendly terms with them. Rather, I gradually became dissatisfied with the impersonality of these friendships.

30 Of course, some constraints on self-disclosure do make sense. Privacy is something you give up selectively and gradually to people you like and trust, and who are capable of understanding— instant, indiscriminate intimacy is nearly always formularized, without real content and impact. Nor does self-disclosure as a kind of compartmentalized rest-and-recreation period work: "Well, John, let me tell you about myself. . . ."

31 Having said all this, it is nonetheless true that men have carried the practices of emotional restraint to the point of paralysis. For me, at least, the ritual affirmations of membership in the fraternity of men that one gets from participation in "masculine" activities do nothing to assuage the feeling of being essentially alone; they have become a poor substitute for being known by and knowing other people. But the positive content of what will replace the old-style friendship is only beginning to take shape. I am learning, though, that when I am able to articulate my feelings as they arise in the context of my friendships, I often find that they are shared by others. Bringing them out into the open clears the air; avoiding them, even unconsciously, is stultifying. I have found also that I am not as fragile as I once thought. The imagined hazards of showing oneself to be human, and thus vulnerable, to one's friends tend not to materialize when actually put to the test. But being oneself is an art, an art sensitive to variations in the receptivity of others as well as to one's own inner life. It is still, for me, something to be mastered, to be tried out and practiced.

Ideas and Meaning

1. According to Fasteau, what are the various reasons that men's friendships are "shallow and unsatisfying"?
2. As outlined by Fasteau, what are some of the taboos and imperatives of the masculine stereotype that prevent men from disclosing themselves to other men?
3. How is this male stereotype presented in the novel *The Virginian*, which Fasteau quotes?
4. What are the usual subjects of male conversations?
5. In what context are men most comfortable being together?
6. What was the basis of one of Fasteau's closest friendships? Can you imagine why this friendship is now "defunct"?
7. What is the reason men fear showing affection for each other? In which two professions has it been acceptable for men to show emotion for one another, and why has it been acceptable in these two professions?
8. Why is it permissible for men to show emotion if they are drunk or stoned?

9. What caused Fasteau to question the traditional male friendship?

10. If you are male and have a friendship with at least one female, how does this friendship differ from your friendship with men? Which is more satisfying on a personal level? Why?

11. If you are a man, would you feel reluctant to invite a friend to have dinner with you or to go to a movie? Why? Why not?

12. If you are a man, would you feel embarrassed about greeting a friend with a hug? Why? Why not? If you were completely sober, would you feel embarrassed about crying in front of a friend? Why? Why not?

13. If you are a woman, do you consider crying an unmasculine trait? Explain. If you should have a son of your own, would you teach him that "boys don't cry"? Why? Why not? If you already have a son, have you taught him that boys and men don't cry? Explain.

14. Do you consider Fasteau's opinions out of date (his book was published in 1974)? That is, has women's liberation "liberated" men from some of the taboos and masculine stereotypes that Fasteau lists here? Explain.

15. Fasteau states that competition is at the heart of all male interactions. If you are male, do you agree or disagree? Why? If you are female, is there a corollary component at the heart of all female interactions? Explain.

16. According to Viorst, there are female friendships based on shared activities, some of which, like tennis, for example, certainly have competition at the heart. She also points out that there are "convenience," "medium," and "pretty good" friends, with whom one shares little or no intimacy. Thus, is Fasteau overgeneralizing about the contrast in the "level of intimacy" he observes between female and male friendships? Why? Why not?

17. Is it possible that Fasteau may be overgeneralizing in regard to male friendships? In other words, are there various types of male friendships such as those that Viorst delineates for women? Explain.

18. After reading this excerpt from Fasteau's book, do you believe that traditional male friendships, if not in the present, at least in the past, were "shallow and unsatisfying"? Explain.

Development and Style

1. How does Fasteau get the reader's attention?
2. Who is his audience and what is his purpose?
3. What is his tone of voice?

4. What is his point? If it is explicit, where does he state it? What is Fasteau's primary means of supporting his point?

5. In paragraph 4, how does Fasteau support his generalization that men shy away from the personal?

6. In paragraph 5, how does Fasteau support his generalization that games play a central part in men's gatherings?

7. In paragraph 7, Fasteau makes reference to *The Virginian*, a novel by Owen Wister, to support his generalization in that paragraph. What is his generalization? In which other paragraphs has Fasteau used references to other sources in order to support his generalizations? In each of these paragraphs what is the generalization?

8. In each of the paragraphs in which Fasteau lists a characteristic of the male stereotype, how does he illustrate the particular characteristic?

9. Does Fasteau make any generalizations that need further support? If so, what are the generalizations, and what kind of support does he need?

10. Paragraphs 8 and 13 are each only one sentence. Why does Fasteau write them alone when each could be written as the first sentence of the following paragraph?

11. Identify the transitions between paragraphs, beginning with paragraph 8 and ending with 17.

12. In paragraph 23, analyze the constructions Fasteau uses to begin each sentence.

13. What are some of the stylistic differences between Viorst's writing and Fasteau's? Consider punctuation, sentence structure, parallelism, intentional fragments, and word choice. Which writer's style do you prefer? Why?

Marty's Two Responses

Reading Journal: "On Male Friendships" First Response

"On Male Friendships" was very interesting. That might seem a little strange after my next statement, because if this is a really accurate portrayal of male friendships, men must have a lot of problems! They must also be pretty bored.

It seems like a few years ago the "in" thing was the emotional man. Men were crying in movies, and there was a big to do with the idea that men really should allow their emotions to escape more often. Now though, it seems like things are drifting back to the older ways—more traditional clothes, styles, and values. All the magazine ads and TV shows portray tough guys who seem to be incapable of showing their emotions.

It really tickles me to see the way some guys act around one another. If I go to a movie with a girlfriend, we'll always sit right beside each other, and lean into each other's face to say something quietly. Watch any two guys come in, and they'll sit one or two seats apart, and if they have something to say, it's yelled to one another. Another thing that seems strange to me is the way guys on campus greet their friends. They don't walk up and say hi, they walk up and shake hands. They always keep their distance and are very formal. I think that both of these things probably have to do with what Fasteau mentions as a fear of being labeled homosexual. But I wonder why it's so apparently different for women?

Second Response

After my second reading of this essay, I realize that Dad seems to fall into a lot of these patterns. He and Mom have a very close relationship and discuss everything, and he discusses his feelings with me, but I can never recall seeing him have even a halfway intimate conversation with a man. They always discuss football, work, or politics. I guess that according to Fasteau Dad would fall into the category of those who haven't made it. He isn't what he really wants to be career-wise, but I think he's just accepted that. He'll turn forty-five this weekend, and as long as I've known him, I don't think I've seen him with this strange kind of silly-happy attitude. He's become really playful, and he's so much more open.

Fasteau mentions a close friendship that seems to exist through competition, and I think that probably exists with both males and females. I've had a couple of good friends whom I always felt in competition with. First it was with grades, then occupations, and unfortunately it just never ends until the friendship ends. Of course, these friendships weren't based solely on competition. They involved intellectual and emotional things as well.

This idea about dependence is interesting as well. I guess there's a big possibility that even in this age of the liberated woman, many women still have no problem depending on others. I don't think it's a completely male characteristic though—I for one can't stand to be dependent on anyone but myself.

In her last response Marty writes about independence and women's liberation. Do you believe parents today are rearing their female children to be independent, in contrast to the way girls were reared in the past? If you are a woman, how did your parents rear you? Were you taught the idea that you should get a college degree, have a career, and become independent, or that marriage was your ultimate goal, the college degree merely a kind of insurance in case you should ever need it?

Conclusion

In this chapter four professional writers have taken you on "excursions" as they explored various topics and explained their ideas to you. In the next chapter you will have the chance to explore your own mind and explain your ideas to others.

C H A P T E R

The Act of Saying "I": Writing to Explore and Explain Your Ideas

10

The purpose of each of the professional writers in the last chapter was quite different from the purpose of each writer whose work you read in Chapter 7. In Chapter 7 each writer attempted to relate a personally experienced series of events that resulted in a significant insight of one kind or another. Thus, these writers were writing *narration.* And in Chapter 8 you also wrote a narrative. On the other hand, the writers whose works you read in Chapter 9 attempted *to explain* their ideas about the particular topics of their essays. Because all four writers' purpose was to explain their ideas, they were writing *exposition.*

However, as you learned in Chapters 3 and 6, writing exposition does not mean that you cannot use description or narration to help you explain your ideas. A case in point is Annie Dillard's essay "Scorpions in Amber," in which Dillard uses both narration and description to help her explain her views on the entanglement of beauty and cruelty in nature. And, as you saw in the last chapter, Joan Didion also uses both description and narration to help her explain how and why she keeps a journal. Nevertheless, despite their inclusion of description and narration, Dillard's and Didion's primary purpose in each of their essays is *to explain* their ideas.

Exposition, Persuasion, and College Writing

No doubt you remember what you read in Chapters 3 and 6, something on this order: writers do not choose a mode or modes first; first of all, they have something to say and that something determines their mode or modes. And now, you are being told to write exposition, and you will be told to do so again in Chapter 12. Furthermore, you will be asked to write persuasion in Chapter 14. Sounds like a contradiction, doesn't it? In a way it is; from another point of view, perhaps, it is not such a contradiction, given the artificiality of any "course" in composition. For one thing, your reason for putting pen to paper is quite different from the reason a professional writer has for doing so.

Professional writers write because they have something to say. You do not really. Not initially, at any rate. You write, instead, because your instructor tells you that you must, and both your instructor and your text help you to *find something to say*. So, professional writers begin with something to say, and their choice of a mode or modes depends upon their subjects and what they want to say, not upon someone telling them, "You will write an expository essay now" or, "You will write a persuasive essay this time."

So far there are two differences between you and professional writers. But why this second difference? Why *must* you write exposition or persuasion? The answer is simply this: You are in college, and expository and persuasive writing are the kinds of writing that you will be asked to do throughout your college career in nearly every college course you take. Furthermore, nearly every professional writer in this text writes primarily exposition or persuasion. And I can go even further: Exposition, persuasion, or a combination of both is the world's writing—the writing of politics, medicine, engineering, commerce, business, science, law, academe, and technology.

But before you enter the world, let's get back to expository and persuasive writing in college. Just how will you use expository writing in college? Here's a list: On a history exam you might be asked to *explain* the causes of the Civil War or to *explain* the effects of Reagan's decision to bomb Libya in the spring of 1986. And on a chemistry exam you might be asked to *explain* osmosis, or on a biology exam to *explain* the process of cell division, or on a sociology exam to *explain* the causes of the changes in the demographic patterns in the United States during the 1970s, or on a political science exam to *explain* the differences among oligarchy, monarchy, autocracy, aristocracy, and plutocracy. Explain, explain, explain.

And, furthermore, not just on essay exams will you be asked to write exposition. Most of the research papers you are assigned will be expository, and many will be persuasive. For example, you might be asked to research the chemical aspartame and to *explain* its advantages or disadvantages, or to *explain* how it is similar to or different from other artificial sweeteners such as saccharin. Or you might be asked to research the issue of mandatory seat-belt laws and to write a persuasive essay, taking a stand either for or against such laws.

Thus, you need practice writing to *explain* what you've learned or what you think. You also need practice to persuade others that what you think is not just the better idea, but the best. In your second-semester composition course you will gain more experience in writing persuasive essays, probably using secondary sources to help you be more persuasive.

At this point in the course you may have already written one or two expository essays, depending on your choice of subjects in Chapters 3 and 6. If you did not write exposition in Chapter 3, you probably did in Chapter 6 because the three student essays in that chapter were all expository. Whether or not you have written exposition before, you will have the chance to do so now, and like Didion in her essay "On Keeping a Notebook," you might use a great deal of description or narration to help you explain your views. Regardless of what you explain and how you go about explaining it, you almost certainly will find that writing exposition is as much fun as reading it.

Finding a Topic

Your task now is to find a topic to write about. Like some of the students whose responses you read in the last chapter, you may have mentioned one or more ideas in your own responses that could be developed into one or more essays. Also, don't forget your personal journal, an excellent source of ideas. Thus, you might begin by rereading your responses and scanning your journal entries. As you look through both of these sources, jot down the ideas that appeal to you. You could make a list under the heading "Ideas in Responses and Journal." Like this, for example:

Ideas in Responses and Journal

What it means to be an independent woman
Why I don't want to be dependent on anyone
Why I like friendships with the opposite sex

Other headings suggested by the readings are these:

On _____ (Fill in the blank with any topic you'd like to explore.)

Skipping Class
Klutzes
Wasting Time
Living Together
Marriage
Failing a Course
Enemies
Breakups

On Being ⎯⎯⎯⎯⎯⎯   (Fill in the blank with any noun or adjective that defines yourself or others you have observed and know well.)

Short
a Wimp
Lazy
a Basketball Star
a Woman
a Man
a Husband
a Wife
a Worrier
Antivegetarian
a Slob
a Feminist
Macho

If you have other ideas beyond your responses or the ones just listed, by all means consider them also. Furthermore, in addition to listing, or instead of listing, you might freewrite to find a topic, as Cynthia did.

But first, you might want to read Cecil's and Beth's final drafts to help stimulate your thinking.

Cecil's Final Draft

On Being Short

1 "Help! Help! Help!" Sweet Polly Purebread, a maiden in distress, shouted as she jumped upward, hopelessly, unable to reach the contents of her top-row mailbox. Though no phone booth was near, I rushed toward the call of desperation to the rescue! But alas, standing at a mere five feet five inches, I too was unable to perform the heroic feat.

2 I was too short—again.

3 When my parents planned a second child, certainly they must have expressed a desire to keep things "short and sweet." I was born to fulfill those very expectations. At twenty-two years of age, people, virtually everyone it seems, continue to look down on me.

4 Though no medical proof is available, enough evidence suggests an ongoing illness robbed potential inches, stunting my growth. Perhaps a more realistic accusation may be placed on genes. I suppose I should consider myself lucky, as I did manage to grow above either of my parents.

5 My first date provided the first realization that I was destined to face a life plagued by "stiff-neck." (A symptom of watching the world pass above the field of vision.) I was four-

teen when I escorted the lovely Mona Lisa Burns to my first
school dance. Graciously, to salvage my pride, she removed
her heels so at least I could look into her mouth as we ventured onto the floor. I have never grown even as much as an
inch since that night, and the number of available dance partners dwindled as prospects towered. I discovered that few
girls are "turned on" by the romantic compliment: "What a
gorgeous tongue you have!" (I make this observation on tiptoe.)

6 Two years after my disastrous date, I continued to enter
theaters for child admission prices. As the number of dates increased, however, I put a stop to the use of a child's ticket for
protection of self-esteem.

7 Still, my size continues to lead others to make mistakes
when judging my age. Recently, while fulfilling observation requirements for a psychology course at a local high school, I
was nearly escorted to the principal's office when I failed to
produce the necessary hall pass essential to students.

8 Like Rodney, I get no respect.

9 I associate the lack of respect with my size. Many people
assume that I am vulnerable and take advantage. However, I
earned my nicknames "Feisty" and "Mad-Dog," though they
still are accompanied by several other epithets: Small Portions, Little Man, Short-stuff, and Munchkin.

10 My occasionally embarrassing size frequently limits and re-
stricts. From day one, many sports were inconceivable, and
unrealistic. Always I was the last on the street to be chosen
for the neighborhood basketball tournaments. From the library to the grocery, I must climb, raise myself, hide a blush-
ing face, or belittle my pride and ask for top-shelf assistance
from a passing Jolly Green.

11 Shopping for my clothes provides continuous, degrading experiences. Many of my clothes I've worn since the seventh
grade. New items are either hand-me-ups from a still-growing
"big" little brother, or they are acquired from the dreaded
boy's department. There is a void between boy's and men's
sizes, and unfortunately, I'm lost there in no-man's land.
Styles differ for the ages, making clothes selection even more
difficult. When girls began wearing guy's clothing, I was faced
with the new complication of a diminished supply.

12 It's not easy to face clerks when purchasing shoes in a children's shoe store. I have no choice. My little piggies forgot to
grow up.

13 I long ago tired of the expression "cute" and am embarrassed by always being first in a height lineup, or being in the
front row in choir. I hate watching backs while missing the
passing parade. At times I fall into Scott Hamilton's big-guy

fantasies, which every less-than-average-size male in the world must experience.

14 "Wouldn't it be nice to be big just once, really huge, like a football lineman for example—and just kick the hell out of a few bad guys."

15 I suppose there are advantages to my being short-changed. I've saved a bundle on movie passes and children's clothes, which are both cheaper than adult's. Like the clothes in my suitcase, I seldom have need of much space. I don't bump my head on low clearances. Comfortably I drive an economical compact. Never am I mistaken for a basketball star, nor do my feet hang off the end of the bed. In case of fire, I'll stand below smoke level, and I may brag of muscular toes, developed out of necessity.

16 I haven't grown for eight years. Who cares how tall I am? I've got no serious hang-ups about my size and am happy with myself and my leprechaun status, which I honestly inherited from Irish ancestry. I refrain from self-pity as a result of my shortcomings and smile as I live to prove the adage that indeed good things do come in small packages.

Ideas and Meaning

1. What advantages has Cecil enjoyed by being short? What have been the disadvantages?
2. If you are taller than average, what have been the advantages? The disadvantages? Give examples.
3. How does Cecil feel about being "short-changed"? If you are shorter than average, how do you feel about your stature? Explain.
4. Would you say that Cecil has a healthy self-image? Why? Why not?
5. Have you known anyone who was adversely affected by his or her height or weight, or have you yourself been adversely affected by your height or weight? Explain.
6. Do people in our society place importance on a person's height and weight? Explain. Does the sex of a person matter in regard to his or her height and weight? Explain. Do you attach any importance to a person's size? Explain.
7. If you were a five-foot-five-inch male, would you find it difficult to have the attitude about it that Cecil does? Why? Why not?

Development and Style

1. How does Cecil get the reader's attention?
2. Who is his audience? What is his purpose?

3. What is his tone? From his writer's voice (and description of himself), how do you picture Cecil?

4. When do you know the point of his first paragraph?

5. What is the point of Cecil's essay? If it is explicit, where is it? How does Cecil support his point?

6. Give examples of the humor in Cecil's essay. At whom is his laughter directed in each instance?

7. Point out the concrete and specific words and phrases. Are there any general words and phrases that you would replace with more specific ones?

8. What are the connotations of "Small Portions," "Little Man," "Short-stuff," and "Munchkin"?

9. Where has Cecil used one-sentence paragraphs for emphasis?

10. Are there any weak transitions between sentences or paragraphs? If so, how would you improve them? Point out examples of particularly strong transitions.

11. Analyze the beginnings of Cecil's sentences in paragraphs 10 and 11. Are there any sentences that you would revise? If so, why? How would you rewrite them?

12. What is the effect of Cecil's use of the pseudonyms "Polly Purebred" and "Mona Lisa Burns"?

13. In paragraph 5, Cecil has used parentheses to enclose an appositive phrase. To connect the phrase to the preceding sentence, he could have used a dash in place of the first parenthesis and a period in place of the second. Which pair of marks do you prefer? Why?

Beth's Final Draft

Klutzes, Weird Klutzes—And Such Weird Klutzes

1 There are many different types of people that I have met in my lifetime, but there is one kind of person who has my unending compassion: the klutz. For some reason, an inordinate number of people that are close to me happen to be klutzes. I have become familiar with the troubled paths they tread. Years of close association have taught me much about the variety of forms that klutziness may take and the penalties klutzes are subject to as a normal part of their lives.

2 Some klutzes fall off chairs, hit their thumbs with hammers, or walk into large immobile objects, such as walls, fire hydrants, or the corners of bedframes. Others perennially spill drinks, lock their keys in the car, or lose gloves (only one of any pair), wallets, or handbags. Still others burn meals or forget to turn on the dishwater before dashing off to work. Anyone can be a klutz.

3   It is a malady, like alcoholism, that cuts across the human strata of race, socioeconomics, and shoe size. Based on close observations, my theory is that it is a genetic affliction. Without exception, klutzes I have questioned have agreed that they were born, not made. Despite the suspected commonality of origin, klutziness is expressed idiosyncratically. A case in point is that of a girl that I grew up with named Betty Jo Chronister. She was not an obvious candidate for klutzhood. She was petite, pretty, and athletically inclined. Betty Jo was even a cheerleader in high school. But Betty Jo was always breaking her bones. Her mother told me once that it began while she was an infant; she rolled off her bassinette and broke her thigh bone. Later, in the first grade, Betty Jo stepped into a gopher hole and sprained her ankle so severely that she had to hobble around for two weeks on miniature, crutches. The next year, she fell off the "monkey bars" on the playground at school and broke her arm. Things were kind of quiet for her for a few years, until the sixth grade when she was in a car accident. Nobody else was scratched, but Betty Jo's arm was broken. Two years later, she fell off her horse and broke her leg. The week after her cast came off, she fell off the horse again and rebroke the same bone! In high school, she dropped a bowling ball on her instep and had to wear a cast to the prom!

4   Of course not all klutziness is as dramatic as Betty Jo's; but the beleaguering daily battle against it seems to be far more debilitating over all. This is the root of a great conflict: will klutzes triumph over it, or will klutziness rule their lives? Every sufferer must work it out for himself.

5   Ned Fullerton was in my math class in high school. Every day, before class, I noticed that he took a drink from the hall water fountain located by the classroom door. Without fail, he would get water up his nose and emerge gasping and choking. That never stopped him.

6   Then there was my mother's best friend who was a terrible baker. Whatever Mrs. Wexler baked tasted horrid. She remained the eternal optimist, though, and continues to bake cakes that taste like sawdust and bake bread that is only suitable to be shellacked and used as a doorstop. At her daughter's baby shower, she furnished the tea table with an array of palate-gagging morsels that only the tastebuds of a camel would appreciate. I drank a lot of tea that day to disguise the fact that on those trips to the goody table, I left those belly-breaking piles of mistakes alone. One spring, she sent over two beautiful, golden-crusted strawberry rhubarb pies. Mother served us each a slice after dinner. With great trepidation, I took a bite. I wished immediately that I had not; it was bit-

ter—and slimy. She had forgotten to put sugar in the fruit filling! Everyone spat it out. Even Mother.

7   Next, there is my Aunt Terry, a bit of a klutz when it comes
to clothes. If there is a nail sticking out, some part of her
clothing will catch on it. She lives in St. Louis and only visits
infrequently, but on one of those visits, she just happened to
catch her expensive silk blouse on an invisible nail that pro-
truded ever so slightly from the end of the windowsill. Even
though I practically lived at my grandmother's house, I had
never touched it, seen it, or noted its existence ever before. It
had probably been there since 1950. My aunt, who has never
reconciled herself to her klutziness, became incensed. She was
not content until she hunted through the "hardware drawer"
for a hammer and revenged herself on that nail by thoroughly
pounding it in.

8   There is indeed a varying array of klutzes. My friend Kathleen Flanagan is one of the group of klutzes that keep insurance adjusters and analysts busy and prosperous. For her, a
short errand to K-Mart to pick up a few cans of motor oil can
result in a rumpled fender, a quart of tears, and an emergency
hour of therapy. She hasn't accepted it either and insists on
asking, "Why me?" This keeps her a faithful psychiatric patient. Kathleen is also one of those unfortunates who collects
insurance cancellation notices the way a philatelist collects
stamps.

9   Feet are frequently a special klutz affliction. A prime example is my former college roommate, Alice Bergdoll. She would
constantly trip over things: curbs, chairs, carpet, doorsteps,
flights of stairs, you name it. Her body bears many scars from
her frequent tumbles, and her toes hurt most of the time. She
is remarkable: I have seen her trip while walking across the
deserted, smooth, lobby floor of the main hall at college. She
just tripped and fell down, just like that. There was nothing
there to trip over, so we decided that it was a freak pocket of
low-level air turbulence.

10 Some klutziness can masquerade as habit. My husband's
klutziness is that he loses his keys. He can have them in his
hand one moment, do something, and then be completely unable to find them the next. This is not because they are a
small item. Quite the contrary: his keys are a substantial
lump of brass-and-nickle-alloy pieces of technology, attached
on three rings which are looped together with sturdy nylon
twine. This collection must weigh more than half a pound.
That is precisely why he lays them down so much. It remains
a mystery to me and a frustration to him HOW he can lay
them down somewhere, (anywhere!) completely unconsciously, and never remember where it was that he left

them—until he finds them again. Then he can remember clearly. I remember a particularly long hunt one time, when we eventually found them in his toolbox. We had combed the house . . . and finally checking every weird place we could think of, we looked in the toolbox. As soon as he saw his keys nestled between the wrenches and screwdrivers, he remembered distinctly that he had put them there. "When I was leaning over the fender, the keys were uncomfortably pressed against my leg" he said, "so I threw them into the toolbox for safekeeping." That's reasonable; I would probably have done the same thing myself. But the difference is that I would remember; he forgets.

11 It is real that klutzes cannot help themselves. It is tragic to think of all of them, out there in the world, without hope for relief or recourse against it. They are a noble group, condemned, yet persevering until the end when they will climb up Jacob's ladder, trip that final time to stumble into the Pearly Gates, only to arrive to wait in line while all of Heaven searches for St. Peter's mislaid keys.

Ideas and Meaning

1. What kinds of people has Beth labeled "klutzes"? Do you agree that the types of people she lists are klutzes? Why? Why not? Can you think of any other types of people you would label klutzes? Explain.

2. To what does Beth attribute klutziness?

3. Where does Beth imply that some klutzes could change their behavior? Do you agree or disagree? Explain.

4. Which of the types of klutzes Beth lists are you familiar with? Give examples of one of more of these types from your own experience.

5. Why shouldn't it be possible to divide the klutzes Beth lists into two groups: those that were annoying to others and those that were annoying only to themselves? Give at least one example from Beth's essay of a type of klutz who could fall into both categories and thus invalidate such a division.

6. Why does Beth state that Betty Jo Chronister was an unlikely candidate for "klutzhood"? What is the stereotypical image of a klutz?

7. How does Betty Jo's last name fit her particular kind of klutziness? (If you do not know what the Latin prefix *chron* or *chrono* means, look it up in the dictionary.)

8. How do the names Fullerton and Wexler suggest the kind of klutziness attributed to them?

9. What attitude toward klutzes does Beth express in her last paragraph? If you were one of the types of klutzes Beth de-

scribes, how would you feel about her and her essay after reading this paragraph?

Development and Style

1. How does Beth get the reader's attention?
2. Who is her audience? What is her purpose?
3. What is her tone? What is her attitude toward klutzes?
4. What is her point? By what means primarily does she support this point?
5. What examples of humor do you find in Beth's essay?
6. List the specific details that you find in paragraphs 2, 3, 6, 7, 8, 9, and 10.
7. In paragraph 6, Beth uses the general phrase "belly-breaking piles of mistakes." Would she have been better off to substitute specific items of food for the general word *mistakes*? Why? Why not?
8. Which paragraph in Beth's essay is used as a transition?
9. Analyze the transitions between paragraphs, beginning with paragraph 6 and ending with paragraph 10. Between which paragraphs does Beth need a stronger transition? Suggest transitions that you would use.
10. Are there any sentences that you would revise in order to vary beginnings or length? If so, which ones? Why would you revise them? How would you rewrite them?
11. Are there any statements you would rewrite as one-sentence paragraphs for emphasis?

Both Beth and Cecil have successfully used humor in their essays, and although Cynthia's final draft blends humor with seriousness, her first drafts were quite serious, as you will see. The following is Cynthia's original freewrite to find a topic.

Cynthia's Freewrite for a Topic

I become so furious every time I think of the gender roles that our society prescribes for us, especially as children. I think that these roles restrict the growth of the individual as well as society as a whole. If a person feels that he or she must conform to fit a certain mold which has been established in society, then that person cannot become an individual, and if the individual cannot grow, society as a whole becomes stagnant and moss covered.

It also frustrates me that in today's so-called advanced modern-day society, many people still hold narrow backwards views concerning the roles people are supposed to play. In our advanced space age, many, many people still feel that women should be fragile, feminine, and dumb, whereas men should be strong, level-headed, and abstain from showing any emotion whatsoever.

This reminds me of the words to a Sunday school song that I had to learn as a child—"wringing mops and scrubbing floors, in the house and out of doors. Washing, ironing, mending too. These are things that girls should do." This song always put me on a guilt trip because I <u>hated</u> doing things that "girls should do" because I was a tomboy.

Cynthia's Revised Draft

After this freewrite, Cynthia wrote the following draft.

Untitled

"Women are emotional. They are also unaware of the exigencies of life, and they lack objectivity."—Joseph B. Della Polla, Philadelphia. "Having a woman for Vice President sounds great. We would not have to pay her as much as a man."—Herbert F. Whyte, Worden, Illinois. "Stop encouraging women to seek the presidency or vice presidency or any position that will take them outside their homes."—Charles C. Carr, Cleveland.

These three quotes, taken from the letters to the editor in the June 25, 1984 issue of <u>Time</u> magazine, are prime examples of the narrow views which many people still hold even in modern-day society. Views such as these are products of the roles which society has placed upon men and women, thereby restricting the growth of the individual and society as a whole.

As children, we are often taught "gender" roles that we are expected to follow, and if we don't, we must face the "consequences." I remember being told in the first grade that little girls are "sugar and spice and everything nice," and little boys are "sticks and snails and puppy dog tails." Even the words to a Sunday school song follow me hideously to this day: "Wringing mops and scrubbing floors, in the house and out of doors. Washing, ironing, mending too. These are things that girls should do." The song goes on to tell us that we should do this for Jesus. I don't think so. I personally don't think Jesus expects this out of me; society does.

Even the toys that children are given to play with are "role defining." Boys get guns, girls get dolls.

So how does this restrict the growth of the individual child? Well, for one thing, these roles restrict the creative growth of a child. He or she is not allowed to choose a certain role because society has already defined it for them at birth, and if a child does not want to be something he or she is "supposed to be," they are labeled as misfits. This can cause much emotional trauma for a child. I was labeled as a "tomboy" by the old cronies in my neighborhood merely because I liked to climb trees, play ball, and get dirty. "She'll grow out of it," they'd "comfort" my worried parents. I thought I was weird. I tried hard to be "good" and "dainty," but it just wasn't part of my nature. Because of this, I often had inferior feelings of being a "bad little girl."

On the other hand, I knew a little boy who liked to play with dolls and play "house," and he was labeled as a "Mama's boy." His parents actually made him join a junior football team because of their fears that he might become a "wimp" or even (heaven forbid) a homosexual. Naturally, he was terribly harrassed by the other little boys because he couldn't catch or throw a ball, run, tackle or do any of the things that little boys are supposed to do. The point is, though, he didn't <u>want</u> to do these things, and he felt weird because he didn't. The little boy wasn't weird, but he was made to feel guilty because of the narrow roles society placed upon him.

The problems which we often experience because of the roles society shoves down our throats often follow us into adulthood. The little girls that play with baby dolls are supposed to grow up, get married, and produce little baby dolls of their own. Phrases such as "catching a man" or "landing a man" are often applied to women in their quest for a man. Women are not supposed to have any initiative other than this. An unmarried woman often feels as if she is an unattractive failure.

These views aren't as prevalent as they used to be, but as evidenced by the three quotations at the beginning of this essay, they still abound. One of these quotations, "women are emotional" is a typical view which many people hold even in today's modern society. What is wrong with being emotional? Obviously, men aren't "supposed" to be emotional. This would make them appear too much like women, a thought which horrifies the heterosexual male. The little boys that played with guns, trucks, and G.I. Joes are supposed to grow up and be successful workers in the business world. These tough workers are not supposed to show any emotion whatsoever. Heaven forbid if the president of the United States broke down sobbing at the sight of a starving child. That would be unmanly! Such a wimp couldn't possibly have enough strength to rule our great country.

These roles that society expects us to display are harmful. We are not allowed to grow as individuals with different interests. Little boys are programmed to be rough-and-tumble creatures that grow into tough, unfeeling robots that go to work, come home, prop their feet up, drink beer and burp while the "little woman" cooks supper. True, these attitudes aren't as prevalent as they used to be, but until they are abolished completely, our society will never have the chance to grow and advance.

As you see, Cynthia has written an essay with a point that she has supported well by listing the roles prescribed to children in our society and then by giving the deleterious effects of these prescriptions. Despite this good beginning, at this point in the writing process, Cynthia decided to start again. In the freewrite that follows, Cynthia thinks on paper, writing first why she didn't like her previous approach, and next what she thinks she would like to do, recording her thoughts as they come.

Cynthia's Freewrite to Find Another Topic

I was not satisfied with the paper I began with, so I decided to do another one. For one thing, the subject was much too broad. I wanted to write a paper which puts down the roles that society has shoved down our throats, but I think I was doing too much.

Another problem I had was with the subject matter. I felt my subject was "old," and it has already been discussed so many times I felt discouraged. I felt that it was like "beating a dead horse." I wanted to make my paper "fresh" and unique.

So I decided to narrow my subject down to one specific point to start out with, then think of a unique way to write it. I think I am going to narrow my topic down to the definition of womanhood—or "what is a woman?" This would be a much better topic to work with, and I think I would be much more satisfied as an end result.

Well, what is a woman? What does womanhood mean? This is a bit more difficult than I thought because a woman can be so many different things. Maybe that's the key—my point—a woman can be many different things! Who has the right to say what a woman should and shouldn't be? But the problem is, though, that so many people try to do just that. The generalizations that so many people make about women are oppressive and very offensive to me. I would like to write an essay that pokes fun at the generalizations made about women. Satire can be very interesting because of its light, humorous tone. I need to organize my thoughts, though, possibly in outline form.

What are some of the generalizations made about women that burn me up? The woman's place is in the home. There are only two places a woman is good—the kitchen and the bedroom. Grrr! Women are emotional. Hysterical, sobbing,

shrieking, can't handle emergencies. Women are feminine.
Women have babies (barefoot and pregnant). Women gossip.
When will society ever learn?

I think a woman should be whatever she wants to be. I
should be careful not to belittle those women who like to be
"traditional" women, even though I'm not.

After doing this freewrite, Cynthia decided to cube her new
subject—What Is a Woman.

Cynthia's Cubing: What Is a Woman?

1. Describe—My subject gets me excited and often makes me
   angry because of the generalizations that often accompany
   womanhood. Womankind is an abstraction, not a concrete
   term because I think it should mean different things to different people like love, hate, peace, or happiness. Womanhood, like women, comes in all shapes and sizes. It can be
   big, little, tough, feminine, angry, mellow, etc. Womanhood
   is as individual as each separate woman. It may be traditional, or it may be different. It may be a 300-pound weight-
   lifter, a 90-pound hysterical waitress, or a 36–24–36 model
   in New York City. The list goes on and on.
2. Compare—Womanhood is like clothing. It can come in all
   shapes, sizes, styles, and colors, according to individual
   preference. It may be electric purple size 5, light pink size
   50, black size 13, etc. No two sizes are exactly the same.
   Women are as individual as fingerprints, and I don't know
   why society can't get this fact through its thick skull. Trying
   to pinpoint one definition for womanhood is as narrow as
   trying to pinpoint one definition for happiness. What makes
   me happy may not work for the next person.
3. Associate—When I think of womanhood, I think of all the
   narrow generalizations that have been said throughout the
   ages about women. I would like to disprove these ignorant
   ideas. When I think of womanhood, I think of a huge oak
   tree with many fall leaves. They are all beautiful, and no
   two are exactly the same. This is a lot like snowflakes.
4. Analyze—Womanhood is made up of individual experiences,
   ideas, dreams, disappointments, and frustrations. Not all
   women are feminine. Some may be. Not all women are emotional, and some women can't have children. It burns me
   up to hear a woman belittle herself because she can't have
   children or because she has had a breast removed. Does this
   make her less of a woman? No! I don't know why they should
   think that.
5. Apply—The generalizations applied to womanhood are used
   to oppress women and "keep them in their place." I want

to prove them wrong! I can't do this by making general statements. Two wrongs certainly don't make a right. My essay should be an intelligent, well organized "comeback" which defends the individuality of women. Womanhood is often used as a category, and I want to prove this category wrong.

6. Argue—I am obviously very strongly for my subject. "Womanhood" is an abstract term. I cannot tell you in all fairness what a woman is any more than you can tell me. Many people feel it is their right to say what women are and what they aren't, but this is not right.

As you can see in the following draft, which one of her classmates criticized, Cynthia has used a number of ideas from her freewrite and from her cubing.

Cynthia's Revised Draft

On Womanhood: What Is a Woman?

1 I began my menstruation cycle one month before my twelfth birthday. On that day I thought, "Surely I must be a woman now because I'm doing something that my mama's doing." but when my stomach began to cramp, and I cried from stiffness and frustration, I thought, "If this is what it is to be a woman, then it's not as great as I thought it would be: I must not have reached womanhood yet."

2 My body began to change rapidly when I was sixteen. During that time I thought, "Surely I must be a woman now because my body looks like a woman's body." But when the men began to grab me and stare at my crotch when I was trying to hold an intelligent conversation or make a point, I thought, "If this is what it is to be a woman, then it's not as great as I thought it would be: I must not have reached womanhood yet."

3 I became pregnant when I was nineteen. At first, I thought, "Surely I must be a woman now because I'm doing the most wonderful thing a woman could ever do by harboring this life in my womb." But as my curses echoed in the toilet while I was throwing up, I thought, "If this is what it is to be woman, then it's not as great as I thought it would be. I must not have reached womanhood yet." So when do I become a woman, and what exactly is womanhood? I don't think I'll ever be capable of pinpointing womanhood because it is an abstraction like "love" and "hate," and the definition should be left up to each individual person.

4 Although this may sound absurd, before you laugh and toss this essay aside along with yesterday's congealed soup, let me prove why there is no defineable thing such as womanhood. I

This is a good title

I think the adjective is menstrual isn't it?

Good beginning

Transition could be stronger. How about "Then when I was sixteen"? How about while here to avoid rep. of when?

5 f

will do so by disproving some of the generalizations we have all heard about women. By doing this, I will be able to disprove the concreteness of the term "womanhood."

5 Generalization 1—Women are emotional.—This is a statement which I have heard time and time again. "The hysterical woman," "the sobbing woman," and "the easily exciteable woman" are all pictures of women that have been drawn for us throughout life. We've all read it in books, seen it in movies and plays and heard it in conversations.

SP ?

Could you give some examples?

6 Well, if women are emotional, and men don't cry, scream, or do anything as silly as this, then why is it that I remember seeing my father break down and sob. Is my father a woman? My father is often easily exciteable, and he's a very sensitive person. Is my father a woman? No, of course he's not. So, the statement "women are emotional' is obviously a false generalization. This is fun. Let's try another one.

good example

SP ?

7 Generalization 2—Women are feminine.—Oh, the feminine "mystique". This is something I have been told all my life. Be dainty! Don't sit like a man. Women are fragile and pretty creatures. I'm certainly not feminine. What am I? A man? A chair? A figment of the imagination? Certainly not, I hope. I know a person of the male gender who is dainty and fragile and pretty. He's not a woman. Therefore, our second generalization must also be false.

good

doesn't the period go inside?

Could you describe your characteristics that aren't feminine?

Could you describe him more concretely?

8 Generalization 3—To be a woman, one must have a baby.— This is a typical generalization that has been with us for ages. "Get married! Settle down! Have babies like a normal woman," I remember an elderly woman once told me. Nothing stirs our hearts so much as to witness mother and child at a quiet moment of intimacy. But, must one must have a baby in order to be a woman? Who are all these female people walking around that have never had children? They certainly look like women. What are they? Martians? Does a person become a woman the moment her child enters the world? Of course not. Therefore, this generalization must also be false.

9 Generalization 4—Women are talkative.—This is one of my favorites. How many times have we seen women pictured as cackling hens who sit around the barn laying eggs and blabbing or gossiping about nothing of any importance whatsoever. This is very prevalent in cartoons and satires. (Naturally, men are "level-headed' dogs or something of the sort.) Think about all of the roles females play on television or in books. The truth is that there are many talkative men. (They just won't admit it.) President Reagan sure knows how to talk. Is President Reagan a woman? Hitler was a great orator who charmed crowds into submission with his smooth tongue. Was Hitler a woman? (I hope not.) I cannot say for sure about Reagan and Hitler, but I know many talkative men who are

Could you give an example or two from TV or a book?

nice touch

Why don't you address the reader and use you?

Shouldn't this be lie?

Don't you mean "one definition for"?

certainly <u>not</u> women. Therefore, this generalization has got to be untrue.

10 These are merely a few examples but I feel that these are the major generalizations made about women. I could go on and on (and have a lot of fun doing it) at the risk of losing the <u>reader's</u> interest, but I think that <u>he or she</u> should get the idea by now. If being a woman is being an emotional feminine, talkative person who does nothing but have babies, then I think I'd rather be a dog. That way, I could <u>lay</u> around on the porch all day and get scratched because that's what dogs are "supposed" to do.

11 What I am merely striving to say is that there can be no <u>definite term</u> for "womanhood" because no definite set of <u>rules</u> should define <u>anything</u>. A woman <u>could</u> be an emotional, feminine, talkative person who does nothing but have babies if she <u>wanted</u> to, and that would be fine. Or, a woman could be an emotionless 300-pound wrestler who dips snuff. Or, a woman could be a hysterical 90-pound waitress who works at Barney's Bar and Grill, Or, a woman could be a 36—24—36 model who loves guacamole. Or, a woman could be a 150-year-old invalid who drinks a pint of whiskey and smokes three packs of cigarettes a day. The list is endless.

This is a good essay. I really liked what you said, and though you're serious, it's funny, too.

One of Cynthia's classmates used the following guide to criticize her essay.

The Critic's Guide

1. Does the writer have a good title? If not, suggest one if you can.
2. How does the first sentence get the reader's attention? If the writer needs a better beginning sentence, suggest one if you can.
3. What is the writer's tone? Are there any words, phrases, or meaphors with connotations that are inconsistent with the writer's tone?
4. What is the writer's point?
5. Does the writer need to be more concrete or specific anywhere in his or her essay?
6. Does the writer make any statements that need examples to support them?
7. Does the writer need stronger transitions between any two sentences or paragraphs?
8. Are sentence beginnings varied? Are sentence lengths varied?

When you review an essay following a guide, you will probably need to read the composition several times. After the first reading, you may know whether or not there is a thesis, and the first two questions in the preceding guide are easily checked because they concern the beginning of an essay. However, questions 3, 5, 6, 7, and 8 may each require separate readings so that you can focus on just the skill specified in the question.

Critical Analysis

Although Cynthia has a good thesis with a number of supportive paragraphs, some of these paragraphs need examples or further descriptive details to support their central ideas.

In paragraph 5, for example, Cynthia needs further examples to support her statement that we see women portrayed as extremely emotional. And in paragraph 7 she needs to describe what she considers her "unfeminine" characteristics. In this paragraph she could also be more concrete and specific when describing the male she knows who is "dainty, fragile, and pretty." Then, in paragraph 9, Cynthia needs at least one example of a talkative woman from a television show or a book.

Thus, Cynthia's primary problem in this draft of her essay is an occasional lack of paragraph development. That is, she needs more support for some of the generalizations she makes in her paragraphs. Even though some of her paragraphs lack development, her point does not—she has a number of supportive statements for it.

Sometimes beginning writers have trouble developing their ideas. Occasionally, they may lack support for a point or for the central idea of one or more paragraphs. The following are some suggestions to help you develop the points of your essays and the central ideas of your paragraphs.

Developing Theses and Paragraphs

Thesis Development

In expository and persuasive essays the main point that the writer makes is often called a *thesis*. A thesis is developed when there are an adequate number of statements to support it. For example, Cynthia's thesis is that womanhood cannot be defined. To support this thesis, she refutes a number of statements that people have commonly used to define women.

Thesis: Womanhood cannot be defined according to commonly held notions of women.

1. That women are emotional is untrue.
2. That women are "feminine" is untrue.
3. That to be a woman, one must have a baby is untrue.
4. That women are talkative is untrue.

In refuting these generalizations that people have used to define women, Cynthia has supported her thesis primarily by *listing the reasons (causes)* that these statements are untrue. In addition, she has used another means of development by giving *examples* to illustrate the falsity of each statement.

Similarly, Marc Fasteau supported his thesis that male friendships were shallow and unsatisfying by *giving the reasons (causes)* that this was so. In her article on women's friendships, however, Judith Viorst supported her thesis that women have many kinds of friends by *classifying* the various types of friends women have and by giving *examples* of each type. And in her essay "On Keeping a Notebook," Joan Didion supported her thesis that keeping a notebook helps her keep in touch with herself by giving *examples* of these private communications and by *explaining how* these communications have kept her in touch with herself.

Ways to Develop a Thesis

Scientists who want to explain the phenomena they observe ask certain questions that lead them to discover knowledge of the particular subjects in question. Also, classical rhetoricians such as Aristotle used similar questions when seeking to understand, or to discover knowledge of, the phenomena they observed. Even though you are not a scientist seeking to discover scientific knowledge of a subject, you can use the questions scientists use in order to discover ideas about your particular subject. As a result, you will discover knowledge that will help you support a thesis.

The questions you can ask about the subject of an expository or persuasive essay are illustrated by Cecil's responses using the subject of his essay—being short. You can see from Cecil's writing that as you respond to each question, you may list ideas or write in paragraphs.

1. What are the *effects* (the *results*) of being short?

I can't help maidens in distress if it means reaching heights.
I have "stiff-neck" syndrome.
I got into movies with a child's ticket for a long time.
People misjudge my age.
I get no respect like Rodney. [Dangerfield]
I learned to be feisty and got a lot of nicknames, some having to do with my feistiness, others to do with my small size.

Basketball and other sports are out.

I have trouble reaching the top shelf in grocery stores and libraries.

It's degrading having to buy clothes in the boy's department and since girls started wearing boy's clothing the supply is sometimes short.

It's embarrassing sometimes to have to buy my shoes in the children's department.

I get tired of being in the front row in choir and of always being first in a line-up according to height.

I also get tired of being called "cute."

Like Scott Hamilton I fantasize about being big and tall.

I've saved a bundle on movie passes and clothes.

I don't need much space.

I'm comfortable in a compact car.

My feet never hang off a bed.

I have muscular toes.

I have a healthy self-esteem because I believe that good things come in small packages.

2. What are the *causes (reasons)* of being short?

Maybe my parents wanted to keep things short and sweet.
Genes. My parents are short and I'm of Irish ancestry.
A prolonged illness, perhaps.
Could be a hormone deficiency in the pituitary gland, but that might be heredity, too.

3. Can being short be broken into *classes* or types?

Well, types or short people might be very short, medium short, and not very short, or you could classify short types as short and thin, short and fat, and short and muscular. Or, you could classify them as those who are happy being short, those who aren't happy, and those who don't really care or think about it, which would be really hard in our society.

4. How is being short like being average or tall *(comparison)*?

Like average or tall people, I want to be respected and I fantasize like everyone does. I want to develop my potential, I want to succeed, I want to be liked. Just because a person is short does not mean that he differs from average or tall people in all respects.

5. How does being short differ from being average or tall *(contrast)*?

Well, contrasted to other people, short people are more comfortable in compact cars, in regular-sized beds, and they don't have to pay as much for clothes and shoes. A short person in contrast to a tall one may not be able to reach heights or to be a professional basketball player. There are lots of ways being short contrasts with being tall.

6. What is the *process* involved in being short?

I don't know. That seems more like a scientific problem, but I could discuss the process of my coming to accept my height. First of all, it wasn't really bad until the end of junior high and high school when other boys shot up and I didn't. Since I couldn't make myself grow, I just decided to develop other aspects of myself—I decided to develop my sense of humor—especially about being short—and I asked out the girls I wanted to date, regardless of their height. First there was a girl whose mouth was the only part of her face I could see. I also took wrestling and did weight lifting for a while to develop the musculature I had. Not that I wanted to prove anything, I just wanted to develop the potential I was born with. I also found that I enjoyed writing so I began to write a lot and became editor of my high school newspaper and yearbook. All in all, I did things to develop my talents and as a result I developed a healthy self-esteem. That's the key to it I think.

7. Who are some *examples* of short people?

I know a lot of short people, but I suppose that well-known ones are the ones I should list. Well, there's Choo-choo Justice, a football player my dad talked about all the time. There's the comedian George Gobel, and the famous Napoleon. Who else? I can't think.

Most writers, as you have seen, use a combination of means to develop their theses. Like them, Cecil used several means of development in his essay. Primarily, he used his responses to the *effects* of being short and to the *causes* of being short, but he has also used some of the ideas he mentioned when he *compared* himself to others and when he discussed the *process* of his acceptance of his height. Although answering these questions will lead you to discover ideas that will help you explain your views, you can still use freewriting and cubing as additional techniques of discovery.

For your reference, here again are the questions you can ask yourself in order to discover knowledge of a subject for the purpose of developing either an expository or persuasive thesis.

1. What are the *causes* (the *reasons why*) of this subject?
2. What are the *effects* (the *results*) of this subject?
3. What are the *types* or *classes* of this subject?

4. How does this subject *compare* with others in its class? (Here you point out similarities.)
5. How does this subject *contrast* with others in its class? (Here you point out differences.)
6. What is the *process* involved in producing this subject?
7. What are some examples of this subject?

As you may have noted in Cecil's essay, each of the generalizations that supports his thesis is itself supported in a paragraph within the body of his essay. (The body of an essay consists of all the paragraphs in it with the exception of the introduction and conclusion.)

To clarify the process of development even further, you should keep in mind that the thesis is the most general idea in an essay. Less general are the ideas that support it, which become the central ideas of paragraphs.

Exercise: Practice Developing a Thesis Statement

At this point, before you look at your own thesis for possible further development, you might practice development of a thesis by choosing one of the following generalizations. Use the list of seven questions to help you discover ideas, and then write a number of supportive statements beneath the thesis you choose. Hint: You have probably noticed that a general statement almost invariably prompts one or more questions. For example, read the first of the following generalizations. What is the first question that comes to mind? Was it Why? *If so, then you know that one means you can use to support this statement is to give the* reasons why *it is true, or its* causes.

1. Sometimes being a student is difficult.
2. Men's friendships differ from women's.
3. Much can be gained from friendships with the opposite sex.
4. A writer's journal is useful in many ways.
5. Unfortunately, friendships may not always last.

The following is Jessica's development of the fourth thesis to give you an example.

Thesis: A writer's journal is useful in many ways.

1. A journal helps to put you in touch with your feelings.
2. A journal is someone you can talk to always because it is readily accessible.
3. Journals prod your memory and let you have bits of your life.
4. Journals let you change your mind, whereas spoken words can't be taken back.
5. Journal entries may result in an essay, a story, or a poem.

Exercise: Practice Developing Your Own Thesis Statement

After you have practiced development with one of these theses, write the thesis of the essay you are composing now and list as many supportive statements as you can beneath it. If you have any trouble, write your responses to the seven questions you have learned to use. Chances are that you will discover additional support for your thesis, just as Jessica did.

The following example shows Jessica's development of her own thesis.

Thesis: The perfect husband has many virtues.

1. The perfect husband is sensitive to my needs.
2. He is able to express his feelings.
3. He is skilled in the tasks demanded by child-raising.
4. He takes my interests seriously.
5. He shares household tasks.
6. He gives me time alone.
7. He keeps romance alive.

Organizing Supportive Statements

After you have listed supportive statements for a thesis, you may want to rearrange them and put last the ideas you consider most important. Begin, however, by listing supportive ideas as they come to you. You can organize them afterwards. When you organize, put similar ideas together and put the important ones near the end because readers remember the end of an essay, like the end of a sentence, more readily than either the beginning or the middle. In the preceding list of Jessica's supporting points, for example, what would *you* put last? (Your classmates' answers will vary, of course, depending upon what each of you considers the most important attribute of an ideal husband.) Not so arbitrary, however, is the arrangement of Jessica's statements so that like ideas come together. How would you arrange her ideas? If Jessica considered the final statement most important, she might have an arrangement like this:

The perfect husband shares household tasks.
He is skilled in the tasks demanded by child-rearing.
He is sensitive to my needs.
He gives me time alone.
He takes my interests seriously.
He is able to express his feelings.
He keeps romance alive.

Do you see the logic behind this arrangement? What is the logic behind ours?

There is one other point to be made here. Jessica's arrangement of her supportive points would not be affected, no matter where she stated her thesis—near the beginning of her essay, in the middle of it, or at the end.

More will be said later in this chapter about the placement of a thesis, if you state one explicitly. Of importance now is that you understand how to organize the statements that support an expository thesis. To recapitulate: The statements that support a thesis become the central ideas of paragraphs. They should have a logical and discernible order with similar ideas together, and the most important ones should come near the end of your essay.

You have become acquainted with the various ways that you can develop a thesis and organize supportive ideas. Now you need to learn the many ways that you can develop these ideas.

Paragraph Development

The ideas that support a thesis become the *topic sentences,* or central ideas of paragraphs. Frequently writers do not have an explicit topic sentence, so that it is perhaps simpler to use the phrase "central idea." Because these ideas are also generalizations, they too need support. There are many ways that writers can support the central ideas of paragraphs, and, generally speaking, most writers find that as they develop a given paragraph, they will use a combination of the means of development available to them.

Here, then, is a list of ways that you can develop your paragraphs, most often using various combinations. You will note that you can develop a paragraph using all the ways you have learned to develop a thesis. In addition, there are several means of developing a paragraph that you could not use alone to develop a thesis.

Ways to Develop Paragraphs

1. Give *examples.*
2. Use *description.*
3. Use *analogies* or *metaphors.*
4. Use an *anecdote* (a short tale that has a point).
5. Give *facts.*
6. Use *statistics.*
7. Quote the *opinion of authorities.*
8. Use a *pertinent quotation.*
9. Give *reasons* or *causes.*
10. Give the *effects.*
11. Analyze the subject by *classifying.*
12. Analyze the subject by *contrasting.*
13. Analyze the subject by *comparing.*
14. Analyze the subject by giving the *process* involved.

Professional Examples of Developed Paragraphs

If you analyze several of the paragraphs from the professional essays you read earlier, you can see how these writers have supported the central ideas of their paragraphs.

Let's consider first this paragraph form "On Keeping a Notebook":

17 It is a good idea, then, to keep in touch, and I suppose that keeping in touch is what notebooks are all about. And we are all on our own when it comes to keeping those lines open to ourselves: your notebook will never help me, nor mine you. *So what's new in the whiskey business?* What could that possibly mean to you? To me it means a blonde in a Pucci bathing suit sitting with a couple of fat men by the pool at the Beverly Hills Hotel. Another man approaches, and they all regard one another in silence for a while. "So what's new in the whiskey business?" one of the fat men finally says by way of welcome, and the blonde stands up, arches one foot and dips it in the pool, looking all the while at the cabaña where Baby Pignatari is talking on the telephone. That is all there is to that, except that several years later I saw the blonde coming out of Saks Fifth Avenue in New York with her California complexion and a voluminous mink coat. In the harsh wind that day she looked old and irrevocably tired to me, and even the skins in the mink coat were not worked the way they were doing them that year, not the way she would have wanted them done, and there is the point of the story. For a while after that I did not like to look in the mirror, and my eyes would skim the newspapers and pick out only the deaths, the cancer victims, the premature coronaries, the suicides, and I stopped riding the Lexington Avenue IRT because I noticed for the first time that all the strangers I had seen for years—the man with the seeing-eye dog, the spinster who read the classified pages every day, the fat girl who always got off with me at Grand Central—looked older than they once had.

Here Didion has begun with the central idea that notebooks are for keeping in touch with oneself and that they are therefore a very private matter. Then she *gives an example,* a question from her own notebook: "So what's new in the whiskey business?" This question is followed by an *anecdote* that explains how the question got in Joan's notebook. But the point of the question ends years later when Didion saw the blonde again in New York. Then, Didion gives the *effects* of her seeing the woman again. And as she does this, she gives *examples* with concrete, specific details: the deaths of the cancer victims, the premature coronaries, the suicides she skims the papers for; the man with the seeing-eye dog, the spinster who reads the classifieds, and the fat girl, all of whom led Didion to the point of the question—that time changes everything and that no one is exempt from it: neither the blonde, nor the people on the IRT, nor Didion herself. Last, of course, this paragraph is developed throughout with *descriptive details* using specific words and phrases.

Now analyze the means of development Fasteau uses in paragraphs 7 and 12 from "On Male Friendships."

7   In our popular literature, the archetypal male hero embodying this personal muteness is the cowboy. The classic mold for the character was set in 1902 by Owen Wister's novel *The Virginian* where the author spelled out, with an explicitness that was never again necessary, the characteristics of his protagonist. Here's how it goes when two close friends the Virginian hasn't seen in some time take him out for a drink:

> All of them had seen rough days together, and they felt guilty with emotion.
>   "It's hot weather," said Wiggin.
>   "Hotter in Box Elder," said McLean. "My kid has started teething."
>   Words ran dry again. They shifted their positions, looked in their glasses, read the labels on the bottles. they dropped a word now and then to the proprietor about his trade, and his ornaments.[2]

One of the Virginian's duties is to assist at the hanging of an old friend as a horse thief. Afterward, for the first time in the book, he is visibly upset. The narrator puts his arm around the hero's shoulders and describes the Virginian's reaction:

> I had the sense to keep silent, and presently he shook my hand, not looking at me as he did so. He was always very shy of demonstration.[3]

And, for explanation of such reticence, "As all men know, he also knew that many things should be done in this world in silence, and that talking about them is a mistake."[4]

12 The effect of these constraints is to make it extraordinarily difficult for men to really get to know each other. A psychotherapist who has conducted a lengthy series of encounter groups for men summed it up:

> With saddening regularity [the members of these groups] described how much they wanted to have closer, more satisfying relationships with other men: "I'd settle for having one really close man friend. I supposedly have some close men friends now. We play golf or go for a drink. We complain about our jobs and our wives. I care about them and they care about me. We even have some physical contact—I mean we may even give a hug on a big occasion. But it's not enough."[6]

In paragraph 7, Fasteau's means of development are several *quotations* from the novel *The Virginian,* and in paragraph 12 he uses the *quotation of* an *authority* Don Clark, a psychotherapist, to support his central idea that it is hard for men to really get to know each other.

Now consider the means of development in paragraphs 5 through 7 from Judith Viorst's essay on women's friendships.

5 1. Convenience friends. These are the women with whom, if our paths weren't crossing all the time, we'd have no particular reason to be friends: a next-door neighbor, a woman in our car pool, the mother of one or our children's closest friends or maybe some mommy with whom we serve juice and cookies each week at the Glenwood Co-op Nursery.

6 Convenience friends are convenient indeed. They'll lend us their cups and silverware for a party. They'll drive our kids to soccer when we're sick. They'll take us to pick up our car when we need a lift to the garage. They'll even take our cats when we go on vacation. As we will for them.

7 But we don't, with convenience friends, ever come too close or tell too much; we maintain our public face and emotional distance. "Which means," says Elaine, "that I'll talk about being overweight but not about being depressed. Which means I'll admit being mad but not blind with rage. Which means I might say that we're pinched this month but never that I'm worried sick over money."

In paragraph 5, Viorst has supported her generalization by giving *examples* of convenience friends. In paragraph 6, she also gives several specific *examples* that show *why* "convenience friends are convenient." Last, in paragraph 7, Viorst's support of her central idea is a *quotation* from a particular person "Elaine," who gives *examples* as further support.

Last, here is the third paragraph of an essay in the next chapter.

3 One implication is the importance of just plain receptivity. When I write, I like to have an interval before me when I'm not likely to be interrupted. For me, this means usually the early morning, before others are awake. I get pen and paper, take a glance out the window (often it is dark out there), and wait. It is like fishing. But I do not wait very long, for there is always a nibble—and this is where receptivity comes in. To get started I will accept anything that occurs to me. Something always occurs, of course, to any of us. We can't keep from thinking. Maybe I have to settle for an immediate impression: it's cold, or hot, or dark, or bright, or in between! Or—well, the possibilities are endless. If I put down something, that thing will help the next thing come, and I'm off.

If I let the process go on, things will occur to me that were not at all in my mind when I started. These things, odd or trivial as they may be, are somehow connected. And if I let them string out, surprising things will happen.

> (William Stafford, "A Way of Writing")

In this paragraph Stafford's primary means of development is analysis of the *process* of his writing, beginning with the first step. As a secondary means of support, he uses a *comparison* of his waiting for ideas to waiting for fish. And he also uses *examples* to support his statement that he may have to settle for writing about immediate impressions.

As you have seen in these paragraphs, writers most often use various means of development in combination with each other, and giving examples is one of the most frequently used means of support, either alone or with other means of development. As noted earlier in this chapter, a particular generalization will suggest the various means that can be used to support it. For example, consider this statement as the central idea of a paragraph:

> Racquetball is my favorite recreational activity.

With this particular generalization, could you use examples as the primary means of support? No. You would need to *give reasons* why it is your favorite recreational activity. Could these reasons involve the *effects* the sport has on you? Certainly. And you could also *give examples* of these effects. For instance, suppose you said that after playing racquetball you felt energetic. You could give some examples of what you were able to accomplish as a result of your renewed energy.

Exercise: Developing the Central Ideas of Paragraphs

Choose one of the following central ideas and write a developed paragraph. You need not begin with the statement you choose, nor does it have to appear anywhere in your paragraph. It may be implicit.

1. Keeping a journal can be helpful to a writer.
2. College students must learn to budget their time.
3. Men find it difficult to display emotion.
4. Female friends often go to each other for emotional support.

To give you an idea, here is Jessica's developed paragraph in which the generalization she chose is implied.

Imagine yourself a young mother in a strange city where you know no one. It is a full two days before your husband's paycheck arrives, and there is nothing in the apartment to eat. You have beaten the pavement and shrubs for soft-drink bottles to return for deposit, averting your eyes from the stares of commiseration on the faces of strangers. The forty cents return deposit sweats in your hand as you clench your fist, and looking to our infant's hungry eyes for courage, you beg the clerk for credit. He refuses. He sneers. And you swallow tears that hit your empty stomach with the force of the overripe apples that the clerk throws into the empty garbage can outside. But your two-month-old baby can't eat apples. He needs milk, milk that you cannot buy—milk that you must take.

What are Jessica's means of development in this paragraph? What is the implied central idea?

Revising Paragraphs for Development

After you also have developed one of these generalizations, you might choose one of the paragraphs from the essay you are writing now and develop it more. As you can tell from the following original and revised paragraphs by Jessica, she is a married student who enjoys creative writing.

Jessica's Original Paragraph

Let's look at an example: Take any man. Take my husband. Sometimes I think he is special, different from the others—more sensitive and fair. But other times—and I find this happens frequently—it seems that his happiness and aspirations are our ultimate goal in life and that I am allowed to have my dreams as long as they do not conflict with his.

Jessica's Revised Paragraph

Let's look at an example: Take a man. Take any man. Take my husband. Sometimes I think he is special, different from others—more sensitive and fair. But other times (and I find this happens frequently) it seems that his happiness and aspirations are our ultimate goal in life and that I am allowed to have my dreams as long as they do not conflict with or take priority over his. For instance, it doesn't matter that I am in the midst of writing a story, that the mood is right, that if I stop I will lose all intimacy with my characters. He has a film that must go to the lab before Friday, or he will lose face for not having reached a deadline. So I am expected to stop, put my "little" story away and rise to the call of duty—editing, cutting, and splicing. Slicing myself from my story, splicing his film together.

Jessica's revision is much more developed because she has added an example to support her statement that her husband's work takes priority over her activities, such as writing a story. The following paragraph by Cynthia is one that needed development, and like Jessica, she has made it much better by adding a concrete example.

Cynthia's Original Paragraph

Generalization 4—Women are talkative.—This is one of my favorites. How many times have we seen women pictured as cackling hens who sit around the barn laying eggs and blabbing or gossiping about nothing of any importance whatsoever. This is very prevalent in cartoons and satires. (Naturally, men are "level-headed" dogs or something of the sort.) Think about all of the roles females play on television or in books. The truth is that there are <u>many</u> talkative men. (They just won't admit it.) President Reagan sure knows how to talk. Is President Reagan a woman? Hitler was a great orator who charmed crowds into submission with his smooth tongue. Was Hitler a woman? (I hope not.) I cannot say for sure about Reagan and Hitler, but I know many talkative men who are <u>certainly not</u> women. Therefore, this generalization has got to be untrue.

Cynthia's Revised Paragraph

Generalization 4: Women are talkative. This is one of my favorites. How many times have we seen women pictured as cackling hens who sit around the barn laying eggs and babbling or gossiping about nothing of any importance whatsoever. This is very prevalent in cartoons and satires. (Naturally, men are "level-headed" dogs or something of the sort.) Think about all the roles females play on television or in books. One example among many is good old Mrs. Crabbits on the television show "Bewitched." Of course her husband is an easy-going, level-headed good guy who is constantly being punished by the screeching tone of Mrs. Crabbits's voice as she shrieks, "Abner! Abner! Guess what Mrs. Stevens has done <u>now!</u>" Despite what we see on television, the truth is that there are <u>many</u> talkative men. (They just won't admit it.) President Reagan sure knows how to talk. Is President Reagan a woman? Hitler was a great orator who charmed crowds into submission with his devious tongue. Was Hitler a woman? (I hope not.) I cannot say for sure about Reagan and Hitler, but I know many talkative men who are certainly <u>not</u> women. Therefore, this generalization has also got to be untrue.

Theses and Topic Sentences: Where to Put Them

The Thesis

Although a thesis may be implied, most beginning writers find that it helps them to have a focus if they can state their point in a sentence. And even though many professional writers may have an implied thesis, many others state a thesis somewhere in their essays—near the beginning, somewhere in the middle, or near the end.

Consider Joan Didion's essay "On Keeping a Notebook," for example. There are two sentences that partially state her thesis and then a third that states it almost completely:

> *How it felt to be me:* that is getting closer to the truth about a notebook. (first sentence, paragraph 8)
> *Remember what it was to be me:* that is always the point. (last sentence, paragraph 9)
> It is a good idea then, to keep in touch, and I suppose that keeping in touch is what notebooks are all about. (first sentence, paragraph 17)

If you consider the last statement to be Didion's thesis, you must supply what she said earlier concerning what her notebook keeps her in touch with: "How it felt to be me and what it was to be me." Still, with her main point near the end of her essay, Didion has what is called an *inductive organization*, which means that more specific statements precede the generalization that encompasses them all. For example, the following statements are arranged inductively.

> The alarm did not go off this morning.
> I was late for work.
> My refrigerator went on the blink.
> It rained and I had forgotten my umbrella.
> I had a bad day.

In an essay, an inductive arrangement may have the advantage of maintaining the reader's interest since he or she must continue reading to discover the point.

In contrast to Didion's inductive organization is Judith Viorst's *deductive organization*. You may remember that her thesis is the second sentence of the third paragraph.

> For the friendships I have and the friendships I see are conducted at many levels of intensity, serve many different functions, meet different needs and range from those as all-the-way as the friendship of the soul sisters mentioned above to that of the most nonchalant and casual playmates.

Thus, in deductive organization, the generalization that encompasses all the more specific statements comes first. If you reversed the order of the statements in the preceding example of inductive order, you would have a deductive arrangement.

> I had a bad day.
> The alarm did not go off this morning.
> I was late for work.
> My refrigerator went on the blink.
> It rained and I had forgotten my umbrella.

The advantage of a deductive order is that the reader knows what to expect; he knows what point it is that you are attempting to support.

Last, a writer may use a mixture of inductive and deductive arrangement. An example illustrating this mixture of inductive and deductive order would be the following:

> The alarm did not go off this morning.
> I was late for work.
> *I had a bad day.*
> The refrigerator went on the blink.
> It rained and I had forgotten my umbrella.
> *I had one of the worst days I've ever had.*

This particular mixture of inductive and deductive organization has this advantage: It allows a writer to emphasize the point through repetition. You might consider Didion's essay an example of this mixed arrangement because she does state parts of her thesis near the beginning, in the middle, and at the end of her essay. If a writer's subject is particularly difficult, or if the essay is long, the repetition afforded by a mixed arrangement would be a good idea.

The most important point that you should derive from these illustrations is not only that you *need not*, but that you *should not*, mechanically write a thesis statement at the end of your first paragraph. In fact, in short or moderately long essays, you might want to use an inductive arrangement, saving your main point until the end or near the end. Furthermore, even if you use a deductive arrangement, you still do not need to write your thesis statement at the end of the first paragraph, a fact that you have seen illustrated in both Viorst's and Fasteau's essays. The important thing to remember is that a good essay cannot be written according to formula. There is no such thing as a formula for an organic process that not only differs with each trial, but that also results in a different product each time. To realize the truth of this statement, you need only observe the differences in the products of the four professional writers in the last chapter. How could one formula produce these four essays? The answer is obvious— there is no such thing as a formula for good writing.

The Topic Sentence

Like the thesis of an essay, the topic sentence, or central idea of a paragraph, may be implied, or if it is stated, it may come first, last, or somewhere in the middle of a paragraph.

First, here is an example of a paragraph in which the central idea is implied.

> 6   That is the tone stories take out here, and there are quite a few of them. And it is more than the stories alone. Across the road at the Faith Community Church a couple of dozen old people, come here to live in trailers and die in the sun, are holding a prayer sing. I cannot hear them and do not want to. What I can hear are occasional coyotes and a constant chorus of "Baby the Rain Must Fall" from the jukebox in the Snake Room next door, and if I were also to hear those dying voices, those Midwestern voices drawn to this lunar country for some unimaginable atavistic rites, *rock of ages cleft for me*, I think I would lose my own reason. Every now and then I imagine I hear a rattlesnake, but my husband says that it is a faucet, a paper rustling, the wind. Then he stands by a window, and plays a flashlight over the dry wash outside.
>
> (Joan Didion, "On Morality")

Can you compose a sentence that states the central idea of this paragraph? You might come up with something on this order: Not only the stories out here are bizarre and sinister, but even now I hear the songs of a church group juxtaposed against the songs from a jukebox in the Snake Room next door. But this statement does not provide an umbrella to cover every specific statement here. For one thing, it leaves out the references to an ominous and sinister nature (the coyotes, the rattlesnake, and the wind).

Even though there is no explicit topic sentence, readers of Didion's entire essay have no difficulty knowing what this paragraph is about, nor do they have any difficulty discerning either its purpose or its relationship to Didion's thesis.

Now, consider these two paragraphs from Judith Viorst's essay "Friends, Good Friends—And Such Good Friends." Where is the central idea stated in each one?

> 28 It's only in the past few years that I've made friends with men, in the sense of a friendship that's *mine*, not just part of two couples. And achieving with them the ease and the trust I've found with women friends has value indeed. Under the dryer at home last week putting on mascara and rouge, I comfortably sat and talked with a fellow named Peter. Peter, I finally decided, could

handle the shock of me minus mascara under the dryer. Because we care for each other. Because we're friends.

29 8.   There are medium friends, and pretty good friends, and very good friends indeed, and these friendships are defined by their level of intimacy. And what we'll reveal at each of these levels of intimacy is calibrated with care. We might tell a medium friend, for example, that yesterday we had a fight with out husband. And we might tell a pretty good friend that this fight with our husband made us so mad that we slept on the couch. And we might tell a very good friend that the reason we got so mad in that fight that we slept on the couch had something to do with that girl who works in his office. But it's only to our very best friends that we're willing to tell all, to tell what's going on with that girl in his office.

Although most of Viorst's paragraphs begin with a topic sentence, the central idea of paragraph 28 is stated in the second sentence.

In contrast to Viorst's deductive arrangement is the following inductive paragraph by Lisa. In this paragraph Lisa states her central idea last.

I still have sudden lapses of memory and stand around in front of Teller II trying to remember my bank number. And I still lose my car in parking lots. During Christmas holidays I got lost at the mall and cried for an hour before my mother found me. But I carry my little notes and maps. I am coping.

Like the arrangement of an essay, the arrangement of a paragraph may be deductive, inductive, or both. In the following paragraph, Jeff has a mixed arrangement—inductive and deductive. Where has he twice stated his central idea?

My grade on the first exam was 50. Then the second exam grade came—a 45. I was doing even worse; I was failing my mathematics course. At midsemester, we had a third exam; I made a 65. When I saw my professor about my homework grades, he told me what I already knew—failing there, too. It looked as if I were doomed in Math 101.

One last comment here about paragraphs: Although a paragraph is generally defined as a series of related sentences on a particular topic, you will find over and over again that "real" writers may not adhere to this or to many other dicta you may have heard about the "right way" to compose a paragraph. Look at this last paragraph of Joan Didion's essay "On Morality," for example.

You see I want to be quite obstinate about insisting that we have no way of knowing—beyond that fundamental loyalty to the social code—what is "right" and what is "wrong," what is "good" and what is "evil." I dwell so upon this because the most disturbing aspect of "morality" seems to me to be the frequency with which the word now appears; in the press, on television, in the most perfunctory kinds of conversation. Questions of straightforward power (or survival) politics, questions of quite indifferent public policy, questions of almost anything: they are all assigned these factitious moral burdens. There is something facile going on, some self-indulgence at work. Of course we would all like to "believe" in something, like to assuage our private guilts in public causes, like to lose our tiresome selves; like, perhaps, to transform the white flag of defeat at home into the brave white banner of battle away from home. And of course it is all right to do that; that is how, immemorially, things have gotten done. But I think it is all right only so long as we do not delude ourselves about what we are doing, and why. It is all right only so long as we remember that all the *ad hoc* committees, all the picket lines, all the brave signatures in *The New York Times*, all the tools of agit-prop straight across the spectrum, do not confer upon anyone any *ipso facto* virtue. It is all right only so long as we recognize that the end may or may not be expedient, may or may not be a good idea, but in any case has nothing to do with "morality." Because when we start deceiving ourselves into thinking not that we want something or need something, not that it is a pragmatic necessity for us to have it, but that it is a *moral imperative* that we have it, then is when we join the fashionable madmen, and then is when the thin whine of hysteria is heard in the land, and then is when we are in bad trouble. And I suspect we are already there.

How could anyone say that this paragraph concerns *one* topic? Where could you break this paragraph so that there were two paragraphs, each more nearly concerning one topic? Why do you suppose that Didion chose not to do so? Which do you prefer— one paragraph or two? Why? What would Didion lose by breaking her paragraph into two shorter ones?

Sometimes the break in a paragraph is completely arbitrary. For example, a writer may break a paragraph only because readers tire of extremely long ones. In other words, one reason to break a paragraph is to give the reader a rest and a chance to absorb a moderate amount of information, rather than too much. As a matter of fact, one might justify breaking Didion's concluding paragraph into two for just this reason—its length. However, the deciding factor in this instance and all others is whether or not the reader's rest is more important than the effect the writer wants to achieve. Almost without exception, this question will be (and properly should be) answered in favor of the writer's purpose and intentions.

Like a thesis, whether the central idea of a paragraph is implicit or explicit and whether it comes at the beginning, middle, or end of a paragraph are entirely up to the writer.

Again, there is no magic formula. Nor should there be. In formula lies deadness. Think of it: what if there were a "formula" that every writer followed to write paragraphs and essays? Imagine, for example, that "On Being a Journalist," "On Keeping a Notebook," and "On Male Friendships" were *all* written following Judith Viorst's pattern exactly. Then imagine that every essay you wrote, every essay your classmates wrote, and every essay written by everyone else followed this pattern exactly. Could you endure reading more than one or two essays? I doubt it.

Other Uses of Paragraphs

Besides supporting a thesis, paragraphs can function in other ways. As you know, essays have introductory and concluding paragraphs that perform specific functions different from the function of supporting a thesis. In addition, paragraphs may be a means of achieving either emphasis or transition. And, as you will see, sometimes both simultaneously.

Paragraphs that Emphasize

In Judith Viorst's essay there are two emphatic paragraphs; in fact, the first is an intentional fragment written alone as a paragraph. In addition, it is parallel to several intentional fragments in the preceding paragraph. Thus, it gains emphasis not only because it is written alone as a paragraph, but also because it is the last in a series of parallel fragments.

7 . . . "Which means I'll admit being mad but not blind with rage. Which means I might say that we're pinched this month but never that I'm worried sick over money."
8 But which doesn't mean that there isn't sufficient value to be found in these friendships of mutual aid, in convenience friends.

And the second example is a two-word sentence written alone as a paragraph.

11 . . . "It's mainly a tennis relationship, but we play together well. And I guess we all need to have a couple of playmates."
12 I agree.

You can readily see the emphasis gained by writing a sentence or a fragment alone as a paragraph.

Transitional Paragraphs

Now, here are two paragraphs from the excerpt by Fasteau. In both of these one-sentence, emphatic paragraphs (8 and 13), reference to the preceding paragraph occurs in the first part of the sentence, whereas the last part states the topic of the succeeding paragraph. Thus, these paragraphs are transitional as well as emphatic.

7 . . . "As all men know, he also knew that many things should be done in this world in silence, and that talking about them is a mistake."
8 There are exceptions, but they only prove the rule.
9 One is the drunken confidence: "Bob, ole boy, I gotta tell ya—being divorced isn't so hot. . . ."
12 ". . . We even have some physical contact—I mean we may even give a hug on a big occasion. But it's not enough."[6]
13 The sources of this stifling ban on self-disclosure, the reasons why men hide from each other, lie in the taboos and imperatives of the masculine stereotype.
14 To begin with, men are supposed to be functional, to spend their time working or otherwise solving or thinking about how to solve problems. . . .

At this point, you have learned a great deal about the development of both theses and the central ideas of paragraphs. In addition, you know now that besides supporting a thesis, paragraphs may be used to provide emphasis or transition. Before writing your final draft, you may want to have another peer review session. If so, you may use the following guide.

The Critic's Guide

1. Does the writer have a good title? If not, suggest one if you can.
2. How does the first sentence get the reader's attention? If the writer needs a better beginning sentence, suggest one if you can.
3. What is the writer's tone? Are there any words, phrases, or metaphors with connotations that are inconsistent with the writer's tone?
4. What is the writer's thesis?
5. Is the support for the thesis adequate? If more supportive statements are needed, say so in your note at the end of the essay.

6. Are supportive statements ordered logically, with the more important ones near the end of the essay?

7. Are supportive statements adequately developed? If not, write an appropriate query in the margin, asking for the means of development needed, i.e., examples, description, statistics, comparisons, and so on. Also, could the support be better—better examples, better descriptive detail? If so, write the appropriate question: "Better example here?"*

8. Do any words or phrases need to be more concrete or specific?

9. Are transitions weak between any two sentences or paragraphs?

10. Are sentence beginnings and lengths varied?

The following is Cynthia's final draft in which she has added descriptive details or examples to several paragraphs in order to develop them more.

Cynthia's Final Draft

On Womanhood: What Is a Woman?

1 I began my menstrual cycle exactly one month before my twelfth birthday. On that day I thought, "Surely I must be a woman now because I'm doing something that my Mama's doing." But when my stomach began to cramp, and I cried from stiffness and frustration, I thought, "If this is what it is to be a woman, then it's not as great as I thought it would be. I must not have reached womanhood yet."

2 Then, when I was sixteen, my body began to change rapidly. During that time I thought, "Surely I must be a woman now because my body looks like a woman's body." But when the men began to grab me and stare at my crotch while I was trying to hold an intelligent conversation or make a point, I thought, "If this is what it is to be a woman, then it's not as great as I thought it would be. I must not have reached womanhood yet."

3 At nineteen, I became pregnant. At first, I thought, "Surely I must be a woman now because I'm doing the most wonderful thing a woman could ever do by harboring this life in my womb." But as my curses echoed in the toilet while I was throwing up, I thought, "If this is what it is to be a woman, then it's not as great as I thought it would be. I must not have reached womanhood yet."

---

* To reinforce your learning, you might note the means of development in each of the paragraphs of the essay you review. If you cannot identify a particular means of support that your writer has used, refer to the list on page 291.

4 So, when <u>do</u> I become a woman, and what exactly <u>is</u> womanhood? I don't think I'll ever be capable of pinpointing <u>womanhood</u> in absolute terms because it is an abstraction like "love" or "hate," and the definition should be left up to each individual person.

5 Although this may sound absurd, before you laugh and toss this essay aside along with yesterday's congealed soup, let me prove why there is no one definition or certain set of rules for the term "womanhood." I will do so by disproving some of the generalizations we have all heard about women. By doing this, I will be able to disprove the concreteness of the term "womanhood."

6 Generalization 1: Women are emotional. This is a statement which I have heard time and time again. "The hysterical woman," the "sobbing woman," and the "easily excitable woman" are all pictures of women that have been drawn for us throughout life. We've all read it in books, seen it in movies and plays, and heard it in conversations. Who is the first to scream at a disaster in a movie? A woman, of course. What kind of spine-chilling screams do we hear in horror movies? A woman's. And, last, but not least, who does the big, brave fireman have to comfort at the scene of a disaster? You guessed it—a woman. Her husband is usually standing nearby trying to calm her down, to no avail, of course.

7 Well, if women are emotional, and men don't cry, scream, or do anything as silly as that, then why is it that I remember seeing my father break down and sob. My father is often easily excitable, and he's a very sensitive person. Is my father a woman? No, of course he's not. So, the statement "women are emotional" is obviously a false generalization. This is fun. Let's try another one.

8 Generalization 2: Women are feminine. Oh, the feminine mystique! This is something I have been told all my life. Be dainty! Don't sit like a man! Women are fragile and pretty creatures. Well, for starters, let me describe myself. I am 5'11" tall and I have broad shoulders and a bulky frame with large bones. I'm certainly not "feminine." What am I? A man? A chair? A figment of the imagination? Certainly not, I hope. On the other hand, I know a person of the male gender who is dainty and fragile and pretty. He has long, curly black hair with dark brown eyes like Judy Garland's and a pale, pale complexion. He's not a woman. Therefore, our second generalization must also be false.

9 Generalization 3: To be a woman, one must have a baby. This is a typical generalization that has been with us for ages. "Get married! Settle down! Have babies like a woman should!" I remember an elderly woman once told me. Nothing stirs our

hearts so much as to witness mother and child at a quiet moment of intimacy. But, must one have a baby in order to be a woman? Who are all these female people walking around who have never had children? They certainly look like women. What are they? Martians? Does a person become a woman the moment her child enters the world? Of course not. Therefore, this generalization must also be false.

10 Generalization 4: Women are talkative. This is one of my favorites. How many times have we seen women pictured as cackling hens who sit around the barn laying eggs and blabbing or gossiping about nothing of any importance whatsoever. This is very prevalent in cartoons and satires. (Naturally, men are "level-headed" dogs or something of the sort.) Think about all of the roles females play on television or in books. One example among many is good old Mrs. Crabbits on the television show "Bewitched." Of course her husband is an easy-going, level-headed good guy who is constantly being punished by the screeching tone of Mrs. Crabbit's voice as she shrieks, "Abner! Abner! Guess what Mrs. Stevens has done now!" Despite what we see on television, the truth is that there are many talkative men. (They just won't admit it.) President Reagan sure knows how to talk. Is President Reagan a woman? And then there was Hitler, a great orator who charmed crowds into submission with his evil tongue. Was Hitler a woman? (I hope not.) I cannot say for sure about Reagan and Hitler, but I know many talkative men who are certainly not women. Therefore this generalization has also got to be untrue.

11 These are merely a few examples, but I feel that these are the major generalizations made about women. I could go on and on (and have a lot of fun doing it) at the risk of losing your interest, but I think that you should get the idea by now. If being a woman is being an emotional, feminine, talkative person who does nothing but have babies, then I think I'd rather be a dog. That way, I could lie around on the porch all day and get scratched because that's what dogs are "supposed" to do.

12 What I am merely striving to say is that there can be no definite meanings for "womanhood" because no definite set of meanings should define anything about an individual. A woman could be an emotional, feminine, talkative person who does nothing but have babies if she wanted to be, and that would be fine. Or, a woman could be an emotionless 300-pound wrestler who dips snuff. Or a woman could be a hysterical 90-pound waitress who works at Barney's Bar and Grill. Or a woman could be a 36–24–36 model who loves guacamole. Or, a woman could be a 150-year-old invalid who drinks a pint

of whiskey and smokes three packs of cigarettes a day. The list goes on and on, just like womanhood—endless, various, indefinable.

Wonderful. And, like any good satire, successfully humorous and serious at the same time, just as Cynthia had intended. In this draft she has a concrete essay with adequate support for all her generalizations.

Conclusion

Since you have become more or less expert now at thesis and paragraph development, which of the three students—Cecil, Beth, or Cynthia—has the least developed thesis? Which one has the least developed paragraphs? Which student has the most developed thesis? The most developed paragraphs? Or is it a toss-up between two or all three of them? Considering the professional essays in the last chapter and the student essays in this one, which was your favorite? Why? Which one had the most significant thesis?

Even though you and your classmates may disagree on your answers to one or more of these questions, I think you will agree that writing and reading exposition can be a great deal of fun. In the next chapter you will read expository essays again, this time by four professional writers whose purposes are to explain the habits or beliefs they have that differ from others'. Because there is nothing so fascinating as the ways we differ from each other, you should have a good time reading these essays and later explaining a way that you, too, differ from other people.

Proofreading Tip: The Use and Misuse of the Semicolon

If you sometimes use semicolons where you should not, you are most assuredly not alone. Perhaps in an overly zealous attempt to avoid the comma fault, many uncertain students put semicolons not only where they do not belong, but where a comma or some other mark is the appropriate punctuation. For example, look at this sentence:

In addition to liking science fiction movies; I love exciting crime dramas as well.

To correct her sentence, Julie needs a comma, the correct mark of punctuation after introductory phrases or clauses.

In addition to liking science fiction movies, I like exciting crime dramas as well.

Next, you might make this error that Felix made:

I definitely will not eat three foods; eggplant, turnips, and squash.

Felix corrected his sentence three ways because words in apposition to another word at the end of sentence may be separated from it by a comma, a dash, or a colon, but never by a semicolon.

I definitely will not eat three foods, eggplant, turnips, and squash.
I definitely will not eat three foods—eggplant, turnips, and squash.
I definitely will not eat three foods: eggplant, turnips, and squash.

Last, do not use a semicolon where Jake has used it in this sentence:

I like to play tennis; racquetball; and soccer.

Here is another example of this particular misuse of the semicolon:

The old horse galloped around the barn; down the grassy lane; and onto the field with the other animals.

In both of these sentences a semicolon has been used to separate items in a series. In the first sentence, the series of items consists of one word. In the second, the series consists of three prepositional phrases. Both sentences may be corrected by replacing the semicolon with a comma, the correct mark to use when separating items in a series.

I like to play tennis, racquetball, and soccer.

The old horse galloped around the barn, down the grassy lane, and onto the field with the other animals.

Generally this rule applies also to a series of dependent clauses, but as you may remember, Judith Viorst *intentionally* broke this particular rule in a series of dependent adjective clauses. This is Viorst's sentence:

I have in my own life a precious friend, a woman of 65 who has lived very hard, who is wise, who listens well; who has been where I am and can help me understand it; and who represents not only an ultimate ideal mother to me but also the person I'd like to be when I grow up.

This is a very long sentence, but that is not the only reason that Viorst chose to break it up by using semicolons before the last two adjective clauses. Because of the longer pause, the semicolon tends to emphasize these last two clauses that convey more important information than the previous three clauses and that are also much longer than the first three.

The point is that almost any grammatical rule can be broken by the knowledgeable who deviate from standard usage deliberately for *conscious* reasons.

These, then are the most frequent misuses of the semicolon. There are only a few constructions in which the use of a semicolon is correct; thus, it is fairly easy to remember them.

1. The semicolon is properly used between two independent clauses when there is *no coordinate conjunction.*

> But we don't, with convenience friends, ever come too close or tell too much; we maintain our public face and emotional distance.
>
> (Viorst, paragraph 7)

2. It is also used between two independent clauses when the second clause begins with an adverbial conjunction (*however, nevertheless, moreover, furthermore, consequently, as a result,* and *in fact,* among others).

> I have no real business with what one stranger said to another at the hat-check counter in Pavillon; in fact I suggest that the line "That's my old football number" touched not my imagination at all.
>
> ("On Keeping a Notebook," paragraph 9)

Note: Generally, a comma comes after an adverbial conjunctive that begins an independent clause. Most writers would have used a semicolon before the phrase *in fact* and a comma after it.

3. The semicolon is used to separate items in a series when these items contain internal commas or when they are extremely long phrases or clauses.

> Last spring, the basketball team traveled to Alexandria, Virginia; Waco, Texas; Little Rock, Arkansas; and Wheeling, West Virginia.

. . . on that bankrupt morning I will simply open my notebook and there it will all be, a forgotten account with accumulated interest, paid passage back to the world out there:
dialogue overheard in hotels and elevators and at the hat-
check counter in Pavillon (one middle-aged man shows his
hat check to another and says, "That's my old football
number"); impressions of Bettina Apthecker and Benjamin
Sonnenberg and Teddy ("Mr. Acapulco") Stauffer; careful
apercus about tennis bums and failed fashion models and
Greek shipping heiresses, one of whom taught me a significant lesson. . . .

("On Keeping a Notebook,"
paragraph 8)

4. Last, the semicolon may be used before a coordinate conjunction that joins two independent clauses if one or both of
the clauses contain internal commas.

Over and over, the small boy bounced the ball, its once grainy
brown skin now worn smooth; and the hoop high above
him, he spiraled the ball through the air from his out-
stretched fingertips.

Sometimes, writers may use a semicolon before a coordinate
conjunction even though neither clause contains internal commas. You may recall Beth's sentence, for example:

Of course not all klutziness is as dramatic as Betty Jo's; but
the beleaguering daily battle against it seems to be far more
debilitating over all.

By using the semicolon here, Beth emphasizes her second clause
because of the longer pause provided by the semicolon.

To summarize: use the semicolon in these four constructions:

1. Between two independent clauses when there is no coordinate conjunction.
2. Before a coordinate conjunction that joins two independent
   clauses containing internal commas.
3. Between two independent clauses when an adverbial conjunction begins the second clause.
4. Between items in a series that contain internal commas or
   that consist of long phrases or clauses.

Exercise: Recognizing and Correcting the Misuse of the Semicolon

*Before you proofread your essay, checking your use of the
semicolon, read the following sentences and correct any punc-*

tuation errors that you see. If a sentence contains an error, rewrite it in the space provided beneath.

1. After we had showered and dressed; Dave and I went to hear a lecture on nuclear arms control.

2. Joann had finished her essay; but Sylvia and I were still working hard at midnight.

3. When Jake had finished reviewing his math, he turned out the light, in a minute he was sound asleep.

4. There are three spectator sports that Jenny finds boring; tennis; golf; and basketball.

5. Last summer several members of the French Club traveled to Paris, France, London, England, Dublin, Ireland, and Frankfurt, Germany.

6. When Jane opened her grade report, she had A's in three subjects—math, English, and geology.

7. Some people would like to see less violence on television and in films, however, no one does anything about it.

8. A dictionary comes in handy many times; when you need to check a pronunciation; when you are uncertain of the spelling of a word (especially those that have doubled consonants); and above all, when you are uncertain of the meaning of the word.

9. After Gloria read the poem; she said that it was shocking; obscene; and almost unintelligible.

10. The sun was shining brightly; but it was too windy to play tennis.

Now you should be able to proofread your essay, confident that you will spot any misuse of the semicolon. Also keep in mind the previous three errors you have studied—the comma fault, the unintentional sentence fragment, and the dangling modifier.

Suggestions for Further Writing

1. Write an essay entitled "On _____" and fill in the blank with an activity you enjoy. Like Didion, you might tell when you began this activity, why you do it, and how.
2. List some terms or phrases we apply to groups of people, for example, *bookworm, loser, go-getter, jock, workaholic.* Choose one and write an essay defining this group either by giving examples, as Beth does when she defines klutzes, or by classifying them, as Judith Viorst does women's friendships.
3. Choose any two paragraphs from past writing and develop them more.
4. Choose any paragraph from one of the professional essays in this chapter and rewrite it, changing sentence structure and punctuation until you have a revision that you like as well as, or better than, the original.
5. Choose any paragraph from one of the student essays in this chapter and rewrite it, changing sentence structure and punctuation until you have a revision that you like as well as, or better than, the original.
6. Choose a paragraph from either Viorst's or Fasteau's writing and rewrite it, changing the tone by substituting words with more negative or positive connotations and denotations.
7. Write a letter to Cynthia, Cecil, or Beth in response to his or her essay. You may say anything you like, perhaps recalling questions or reactions you had after your initial reading of the essay.
8. Write a letter to Joan Didion, Judith Viorst, Ellen Goodman, or Marc Fasteau about her or his essay.
9. Make a list of all the negative characteristics you have—

anything you consider a liability, such as being too tall, being lazy, being hot-tempered, and so on. Choose one of these characteristics and write an essay entitled "On Being _____." (Like Cecil, you may choose to be humorous.)

10. Write a response, exploring first what Didion means and then either agreeing or disagreeing with the following quotation from her essay "On Morality":

Of course you will say that I do not have the right, even if I had the power, to inflict [my] unreasonable conscience upon you; nor do I want you to inflict your conscience, however enlightened, upon me.

11. In his essay "Civil Disobedience," Henry Thoreau wrote the following statement:

Is there not a sort of blood shed when the conscience is wounded? Through this wound a man's real manhood and immortality flow out, and he bleeds to an everlasting death.

Write a response, exploring what Thoreau means and giving examples of what you think he means. Then write why you do or do not believe that in every situation a person has the right to act according to his or her conscience.

12. To test Ellen Goodman's assertion that one needs endurance to be a newspaper columnist, like her, write two columns this week and two next week of approximately 400 to 500 words each. In addition, like Ellen Goodman, try to make the subjects of these columns "close to home," using the voice of a "fellow struggler." Suggestion: You might read several of her columns from either her collection *Close to Home* or *At Large,* another collection.

13. Read the columns "It's Failure, Not Success" and "Time is for Savoring" in Ellen Goodman's book *Close to Home.* Then write a column of approximately 400 to 500 words on one of these subjects that *agrees* or *disagrees* with Goodman's position.

Through the Looking-Glass: Writers Explaining Their Differences From Others

11

"I don't know what you mean by 'glory,' " Alice said.

Humpty Dumpty smiled contemptuously. "Of course you don't—till I tell you. I meant 'there's a nice knock-down argument for you!' "

"But 'glory' doesn't mean a 'nice knock-down argument,' " Alice objected.

"When *I* use a word," Humpty Dumpty said, in rather a scornful tone, "it means just what I choose it to mean—neither more or less."

Like Alice in her encounter with Humpty Dumpty in Lewis Carroll's wonderful fantasy *Through the Looking-Glass,* you have no doubt met many people who are different from you in their beliefs, actions, or attitudes. You may not have met anyone quite as eccentric as Humpty Dumpty, however.

As you know, Humpty Dumpty would have a great deal of trouble communicating in writing with an audience to whom he could not explain his idiosyncratic semantics, but Alice's encounter with him provides an example of the kind of experiences we have quite often as we go through life. We have all been Humpty Dumpty and we have all been Alice. That is, we have all had to explain to someone else why we do what we do, why we believe what we believe, or perhaps, how we do what we do or how we came to believe what we believe. On the other hand, we have also had the experience of meeting other Humpty Dumpties, of meeting other people whose beliefs, attitudes, or actions differ from our own or others' and, thus, like Alice, we want to know more. We want to know why this person enjoys rock climbing or how he goes about it or why this person uses the world *glory* to mean a "nice, knock-down argument."

Even though none of us may be as eccentric as Humpty Dumpty, whenever our habits, beliefs, or actions differ from those of others, we have a good subject for an expository essay, one that an audience would find interesting, just as Alice finds Humpty Dumpty's linguistic manipulations interesting (if not appalling).

The professional writers in this chapter are all concerned with their habits, beliefs, or actions that differ from those of most people. Certainly writing for a living is an activity that most people do not choose. As a consequence, many professional writers have explained why they write or how they write. Why she writes is the subject of the following essay by Joan Didion. After her essay, the poet William Stafford describes the process of his writing. Then, in a personal letter, E. B. White explains to his wife why he is taking a year off work in order to write a book. Last, the British novelist D. H. Lawrence explains why he believes the novel is an important art.

JOAN DIDION

Why I Write

1 Of course I stole the title for this talk, from George Orwell. One reason I stole it was that I like the sound of the words: *Why I Write.* There you have three short unambiguous words that share a sound, and the sound they share is this:

I

I

I

2 In many ways writing is the act of saying I, of imposing oneself upon other people, of saying *listen to me, see it my way, change your mind.* It's an aggressive, even a hostile act. You can disguise its aggressiveness all you want with veils of subordinate clauses and qualifiers and tentative subjunctives, with ellipses and evasions—with the whole manner of intimating rather than claiming, of alluding rather than stating—but there's no getting around the fact that setting words on paper is the tactic of a secret bully, an invasion, an imposition of the writer's sensibility on the reader's most private space.

3 I stole the title not only because the words sounded right but because they seemed to sum up, in a no-nonsense way, all I have to tell you. Like many writers I have only this one "subject," this one "area": the act of writing. I can bring you no reports from any other front. I may have other interests: I am "interested," for example; in marine biology, but I don't flatter myself that you would come out to hear me talk about it. I am not a scholar. I am not in the least an intellectual, which is not to say that when I hear the word "intellectual" I reach for my gun, but only to say that I do not think in abstracts. During the years when I was an undergraduate at Berkeley I tried, with a kind of hopeless late-adolescent

energy, to buy some temporary visa into the world of ideas, to forge for myself a mind that could deal with the abstract.

4 In short I tried to think. I failed. My attention veered inexorably back to the specific, to the tangible, to what was generally considered, by everyone I knew then and for that matter have known since, the peripheral. I would try to contemplate the Hegelian dialectic and would find myself concentrating instead on a flowering pear tree outside my window and the particular way the petals fell on my floor. I would try to read linguistic theory and would find myself wondering instead if the lights were on in the bevatron up the hill. When I say that I was wondering if the lights were on in the bevatron you might immediately suspect, if you deal in ideas at all, that I was registering the bevatron as a political symbol, thinking in shorthand about the military-industrial complex and its role in the university community, but you would be wrong. I was only wondering if the lights were on in the bevatron, and how they looked. A physical fact.

5 I had trouble graduating from Berkeley, not because of this inability to deal with ideas—I was majoring in English, and I could locate the house-and-garden imagery in "The Portrait of a Lady" as well as the next person, "imagery" being by definition the kind of specific that got my attention—but simply because I had neglected to take a course in Milton. For reasons which now sound baroque I needed a degree by the end of that summer, and the English department finally agreed, if I would come down from Sacramento every Friday and talk about the cosmology of "Paradise Lost," to certify me proficient in Milton. I did this. Some Fridays I took the Greyhound bus, other Fridays I caught the South Pacific's City of San Francisco on the last leg of its transcontinental trip. I can no longer tell you whether Milton put the sun or the earth at the center of his universe in "Paradise Lost," the central question of at least one century and a topic about which I wrote 10,000 words that summer, but I can still recall the exact rancidity of the butter in the City of San Francisco's dining car, and the way the tinted windows on the Greyhound bus cast the oil refineries around Carquinez Straits into a grayed and obscurely sinister light. In short my attention was always on the periphery, on what I could see and taste and touch, on the butter, and the Greyhound bus. During those years I was traveling on what I knew to be a very shaky passport, forged papers: I knew that I was no legitimate resident in any world of ideas. I knew I couldn't think. All I knew then was what I couldn't do. All I knew then was what I wasn't, and it took me some years to discover what I was.

6 Which was a writer.

7 By which I mean not a "good" writer or a "bad" writer but simply a writer, a person whose most absorbed and passionate hours are spent arranging words on pieces of paper. Had my cre-

dentials been in order I would never had become a writer. Had I been blessed with even limited access to my own mind there would have been no reason to write. I write entirely to find out what I'm thinking, what I'm looking at, what I see and what it means. What I want and what I fear. Why did the oil refineries around Carquinez Straits seem sinister to me in the summer of 1956? Why have the night lights in the bevatron burned in my mind for twenty years? *What is going on in these pictures in my mind?*

8 When I talk about pictures in my mind I am talking, quite specifically, about images that shimmer around the edges. There used to be an illustration in every elementary psychology book showing a cat drawn by a patient in varying stages of schizophrenia. This cat had a shimmer around it. You could see the molecular structure breaking down at the very edges of the cat: the cat became the background and the background the cat, everything interacting, exchanging ions. People on hallucinogens describe the same perception of objects. I'm not a schizophrenic, nor do I take hallucinogens, but certain images do shimmer for me. Look hard enough, and you can't miss the shimmer. It's there. You can't think too much about these pictures that shimmer. You just lie low and let them develop. You stay quiet. You don't talk to many people and you keep your nervous system from shorting out and you try to locate the cat in the shimmer, the grammar in the picture.

9 Just as I meant "shimmer" literally I mean "grammar" literally. Grammar is a piano I play by ear, since I seem to have been out of school the year the rules were mentioned. All I know about grammar is its infinite power. To shift the structure of a sentence alters the meaning of that sentence, as definitely and inflexibly as the position of a camera alters the meaning of the object photographed. Many people know about camera angles now, but not so many know about sentences. The arrangement of the words matters, and the arrangement you want can be found in the picture in your mind. The picture dictates the arrangement. The picture dictates whether this will be a sentence with or without clauses, a sentence that ends hard or a dying-fall sentence, long or short, active or passive. The picture tells you how to arrange the words and the arrangement of the words tells you, or tells me, what's going on in the picture. *Nota bene:*

10 It tells you.

11 You don't tell it.

12 Let me show you what I mean by pictures in the mind. I began "Play It As It Lays" just as I have begun each of my novels, with no notion of "character" or "plot" or even "incident." I had only two pictures in my mind, more about which later, and a technical intention, which was to write a novel so elliptical and fast that it would be over before you noticed it, a novel so fast that it would

scarcely exist on the page at all. About the pictures: the first was of white space. Empty space. This was clearly the picture that dictated the narrative intention of the book—a book in which anything that happened would happen off the page, a "white" book to which the reader would have to bring his or her own bad dreams—and yet this picture told me no "story," suggested no situation. The second picture did. This second picture was of something actually witnessed. A young woman with long hair and a short white halter dress walks through the casino at the Riviera in Las Vegas at one in the morning. She crosses the casino alone and picks up a house telephone. I watch her because I have heard her paged, and recognize her name: she is a minor actress I see around Los Angeles from time to time, in places like Jax and once in a gynecologist's office in the Beverly Hills Clinic, but have never met. I know nothing about her. Who is paging her? Why is she here to be paged? How exactly did she come to this? It was precisely this moment in Las Vegas that made "Play It As It Lays" begin to tell itself to me, but the moment appears in the novel only obliquely, in a chapter which begins:

13 "Marie made a list of things she would never do. She would never: walk through the Sands or Caesar's alone after midnight. She would never: ball at a party, do S-M unless she wanted to, borrow furs from Abe Lipsey, deal. She would never: carry a Yorkshire in Beverly Hills."

14 That is the beginning of the chapter and that is also the end of the chapter, which may suggest what I meant by "white space."

15 I recall having a number of pictures in my mind when I began the novel I just finished, "A Book of Common Prayer." As a matter of fact one of these pictures was of that bevatron I mentioned, although I would be hard put to tell you a story in which nuclear energy figured. Another was a newspaper photograph of a hijacked 707 burning on the desert in the Middle East. Another was the night view from a room in which I once spent a week with paratyphoid, a hotel room on the Colombian coast. My husband and I seemed to be on the Colombian coast representing the United States of America at a film festival (I recall invoking the name "Jack Valenti" a lot, as if its reiteration could make me well), and it was a bad place to have fever, not only because my indisposition offended our hosts but because every night in this hotel the generator failed. The lights went out. The elevator stopped. My husband would go to the event of the evening and make excuses for me and I would stay alone in this hotel room, in the dark. I remember standing at the window trying to call Bogotá (the telephone seemed to work on the same principle as the generator) and watching the night wind come up and wondering what I was doing eleven degrees off the equator with a fever of 103. The view from that window definitely figures in "A Book of Common Prayer,"

as does the burning 707, and yet none of these pictures told me the story I needed.

16 The picture that did, the picture that shimmered and made these other images coalesce, was the Panama airport at 6 A.M. I was in this airport only once, on a plane to Bogotá that stopped for an hour to refuel, but the way it looked that morning remained superimposed on everything I saw until the day I finished "A Book of Common Prayer." I lived in that airport for several years. I can still feel the hot air when I step off the plane, can see the heat already rising off the tarmac at 6 A.M. I can feel my skirt damp and wrinkled on my legs. I can feel the asphalt stick to my sandals. I remember the big tail of a Pan American plane floating motionless down at the end of the tarmac. I remember the sound of a slot machine in the waiting room. I could tell you that I remember a particular woman in the airport, an American woman, a *norteamericana*, a thin *norteamericana* about 40 who wore a big square emerald in lieu of a wedding ring, but there was no such woman there.

17 I put this woman in the airport later. I made this woman up, just as I later made up a country to put the airport in, and a family to run the country. This woman in the airport is neither catching a plane nor meeting one. She is ordering tea in the airport coffee shop. In fact she is not simply "ordering" tea but insisting that the water be boiled, in front of her, for twenty minutes. Why is this woman in this airport? Why is she going nowhere, where has she been? Where did she get that big emerald? What derangement, or disassociation, makes her believe that her will to see the water boiled can possibly prevail?

18 "She had been going to one airport or another for four months, one could see it, looking at the visas on her passport. All those airports where Charlotte Douglas's passport had been stamped would have looked alike. Sometimes the sign on the tower would say 'Bienvenidos' and sometimes the sign on the tower would say 'Bienvenue,' some places were wet and hot and others were dry and hot, but at each of these airports the pastel concrete walls would rust and stain and the swamp off the runway would be littered with the fuselages of cannibalized Fairchild F-227's and the water would need boiling.

19 "I knew why Charlotte went to the airport even if Victor did not.

20 "I knew about airports."

21 These lines appear about halfway through "A Book of Common Prayer," but I wrote them during the second week I worked on the book, long before I had any idea where Charlotte Douglas had been or why she went to airports. Until I wrote these lines I had no character called "Victor" in mind: the necessity for mentioning a name, and the name "Victor," occurred to me as I wrote the

sentence. *I knew why Charlotte went to the airport* sounded incomplete. *I knew why Charlotte went to the airport even if Victor did not* carried a little more narrative drive. Most important of all, until I wrote these lines I did not know who "I" was, who was telling the story. I had intended until that moment that the "I" be no more than the voice of the author, a 19th-century omniscient narrator. But there it was:

22 "I knew why Charlotte went to the airport even if Victor did not.

23 "I knew about airports."

24 This "I" was the voice of no author in my house. This "I" was someone who not only knew why Charlotte went to the airport but also knew someone called "Victor." Who was Victor? Who was this narrator? Why was this narrator telling me this story? Let me tell you one thing about why writers write: had I known the answer to any of these questions I would never had needed to write a novel.

Ideas and Meaning

1. Why does Didion write, and how does she define a writer?
2. How long did it take Didion to discover that she was a writer?
3. Do you agree or disagree with her statement that the writer is a "secret bully"? Why?
4. How does she define the intellectual? Do you agree or disagree with her definition? Why? If you disagree, how would you define the intellectual? Why does she claim that she is not an intellectual? Do you agree or disagree with her claim? Why?
5. What does Didion mean when she says that her attention was always on the periphery?
6. What does she mean by "images that shimmer around the edges"?
7. How does she define "grammar"? Why does she say that grammar is a piano she plays by ear?
8. Do you agree that shifting the structure of a sentence alters its meaning? Why? Why not? Can you give an example to support your position?
9. Why do the "pictures" in her mind dictate Didion's sentence structure?
10. What was the image that resulted in Didion's novel *Play It as It Lays*? What is the central image of *A Book of Common Prayer*?
11. What idea in paragraph 7 is reiterated in the concluding paragraph? Why is this idea repeated?
12. Describe one or more images from your past that remain

clear in your mind. Explain their significance. Are there any images whose importance you do not understand? Explain.

13. Didion implies that writers pay attention to sensory data. What evidence in this essay supports her implication?
14. Why is the title of this essay particularly appropriate?

Development and Style

1. How does Didion get the reader's attention? What is her tone?
2. Who is her audience, and what is her purpose?
3. What is Didion's thesis? How does she develop it?
4. What is the central idea of paragraph 5, and how does Didion develop it? What are the concrete/specific details she gives?
5. What are the central ideas of paragraphs 8 and 12? How does Didion develop them?
6. To illustrate Didion's statement that altering sentence structure alters meaning, reconstruct the first two sentences of paragraph 17. How does the meaning conveyed by your two sentences differ from the meaning of hers?
7. Point out examples of parallelism and intentional fragments in Didion's essay. What are the effects of each?
8. Point out the one-sentence paragraphs (including the intentional fragment indented by itself) in Didion's essay. What is the effect of each?
9. Analyze the transitions between paragraphs, beginning with paragraph 2 and ending with paragraph 12.
10. Are there any sentences in the essay that you would reconstruct? If so, rewrite them and analyze the difference in the effects of Didion's original and your revision.
11. According to standard English grammar, colons should not be used between any two parts of a sentence, that is, between a subject and the verb; between a preposition and its object; between a verb and its indirect or direct object; or between a verb and a predicate noun, pronoun, or adjective. In the second, third, and fourth sentences of paragraph 13, between what two parts of each sentence does Didion use a colon? What is the effect in each sentence? Would you call this an example of Didion's playing grammar by ear? Why? Why not?
12. Consider these sentences:
    1. Jeff always gave: his teachers, his coaches, and his parents a hard time.
    2. Melissa was a member of: the choir, the student government, and the debating team.

Are these effective violations of the standard use of the colon? Why? Why not? What is the difference between these sentences and Didion's three sentences in paragraph 13? Would it make any difference if the sentences above were one of a series of three parallel constructions such as Didion's? Why? Why not? Try to write your own series of three parallel constructions, using Didion's as your guide. Are your constructions effective violations of the standard use of the colon? Why? Why not?

Glenda's Two Responses

Reading Journal: "Why I Write" First Response

Joan Didion's essay, "Why I Write," is my favorite of the two we've read by her. I especially like her introduction. Now that was an attention grabber! The "I—I—I" sound in why I write was a good point. Writing is a self-centered activity, and like Didion says, no matter how hard we try to cover this up, we are always the "subject" of everything we write. If I write something it is always my point of view and my voice that comes through.

I never thought of writing as a "hostile act," as Didion points out, but this is a good point. Writing is a way of "forcing" one's own viewpoint on other people.

Didion's first sentence is also a good attention-grabber. She states that she stole the title of her essay. Now that's a brave way to start an essay. Many writers "steal" certain ideas from other sources, but leave it to Didion to admit it.

I also liked the way Didion uses one-sentence paragraphs in paragraphs 10 and 11. "It tells you. You don't tell it" was also an interesting statement. That's part of being a good writer, I think—knowing when to use abrupt statements and also knowing what to say. This is so characteristic of Didion's writing.

Second Response

I thought Didion's discussion of her interest in the "specific" was excellent. She had a lot of trouble with deep, often abstract interpretations of writing. The one passage that stands out most vividly in my mind was the one in which she states that she can't remember whether Milton put the sun or the earth at the center of the universe in her study of Milton at Berkeley, but she can remember the rancidity of the butter on the San Francisco dining car on her way to school. She remembers images instead of "prescribed" abstractions found in textbooks. I have often found this to be true in my own life.

I have so many memories of school tossing and turning in my head, but most of them are images. I could not tell you a thing about the algebra I took my freshman year. I probably couldn't even solve a simple equation for x, but I have memories of images about this class. I remember certain sights, sounds, and smells on the way to this class. These are the things that are most important for a writer.

I also thought that Didion's discussion of her own writing was interesting. She is such an excellent writer.

Now consider William Stafford's essay in which he explains not *why* he writes, but *how* he writes. Since every writer's process differs somewhat or a great deal from the process of other writers, you might find it interesting to compare your own writing process with Stafford's.

WILLIAM STAFFORD

A Way of Writing

1   A writer is not so much someone who has something to say as he is someone who has found a process that will bring about new things he would not have thought of if he had not started to say them. That is, he does not draw on a reservoir; instead, he engages in an activity that brings to him a whole succession of unforeseen stories, poems, essays, plays, laws, philosophies, religions, or—but wait!

2   Back in school, from the first when I began to try to write things, I felt this richness. One thing would lead to another; the world would give and give. Now, after twenty years or so of trying, I live by that certain richness, an idea hard to pin, difficult to say, and perhaps offensive to some. For there are strange implications in it.

3   One implication is the importance of just plain receptivity. When I write, I like to have an interval before me when I am not likely to be interrupted. For me, this means usually the early morning, before others are awake. I get pen and paper, take a glance out the window (often it is dark out there), and wait. It is like fishing. But I do not wait very long, for there is always a nibble—and this is where receptivity comes in. To get started I will accept anything that occurs to me. Something always occurs, of course, to any of us. We can't keep from thinking. Maybe I have to settle for an immediate impression: it's cold, or hot, or dark, or bright, or in between! Or—well, the possibilities are endless. If I put down something, that thing will help the next thing come, and I'm off. If I let the process go on, things will occur to me that were not at

all in my mind when I started. These things, odd or trivial as they may be, are somehow connected. And if I let them string out, surprising things will happen.

4 If I let them string out. . . . Along with initial receptivity, then, there is another readiness: I must be willing to fail. If I am to keep on writing, I cannot bother to insist on high standards. I must get into action and not let anything stop me, or even slow me much. By "standards" I do not mean "correctness"—spelling, punctuation, and so on. These details become mechanical for anyone who writes for a while. I am thinking about what many people would consider "important" standards, such matters as social significance, positive values, consistency, etc. I resolutely disregard these. Something better, greater, is happening! I am following a process that leads so wildly and originally into new territory that no judgment can at the moment be made about values, significance, and so on. I am making something new, something that has not been judged before. Later others—and maybe I myself—will make judgments. Now, I am headlong to discover. Any distraction may harm the creating.

5 So, receptive, careless of failure, I spin out things on the page. And a wonderful freedom comes. If something occurs to me, it is all right to accept it. It has one justification: it occurs to me. No one else can guide me. I must follow my own weak, wandering, diffident impulses.

6 A strange bonus happens. At times, without my insisting on it, my writings become coherent; the successive elements that occur to me are clearly related. They lead by themselves to new connections. Sometimes the language, even the syllables that happen along, may start a trend. Sometimes the materials alert me to something waiting in my mind, ready for sustained attention. At such times, I allow myself to be eloquent, or intentional, or for great swoops (treacherous! not to be trusted!) reasonable. But I do not insist on any of that; for I know that back of my activity there will be the coherence of my self, and that indulgence of my impulses will bring recurrent patterns and meanings again.

7 This attitude toward the process of writing creatively suggests a problem for me, in terms of what others say. They talk about "skills" in writing. Without denying that I do have experience, wide reading, automatic orthodoxies and maneuvers of various kinds, I still must insist that I am often baffled about what "skill" has to do with the precious little area of confusion when I do not know what I am going to say and then I find out what I am going to say. That precious interval I am unable to bridge by skill. What can I witness about it? It remains mysterious, just as all of us must feel puzzled about how we are so inventive as to be able to talk along through complexities with our friends, not needing to

plan what we are going to say, but never stalled for long in our confident forward progress. Skill? If so, it is the skill we all have, something we must have learned before the age of three or four.

8 A writer is one who has become accustomed to trusting that grace, or luck, or—skill.

9 Yet another attitude I find necessary: most of what I write, like most of what I say in casual conversation, will not amount to much. Even I will realize, and even at the time, that it is not negotiable. It will be like practice. In conversation I allow myself random remarks—in fact, as I recall, that is the way I learned to talk—so in writing I launch many expendable efforts. A result of this free way of writing is that I am not writing for others, mostly; they will not see the product at all unless the activity eventuates in something that later appears to be worthy. My guide is the self, and its adventuring in the language brings about communication.

10 This process-rather-than-substance view of writing invites a final, dual reflection:

1) Writers may not be special—sensitive or talented in any usual sense. They are simply engaged in sustained use of a language skill we all have. Their "creations" come about through confident reliance on stray impulses that will, with trust, find occasional patterns that are satisfying.

2) But writing itself is one of the great, free human activities. There is scope for individuality, and elation, and discovery, in writing. For the person who follows with trust and forgiveness what occurs to him, the world remains always ready and deep, an inexhaustible environment, with the combined vividness of an actuality and flexibility of a dream. Working back and forth between experience and thought, writers have more than space and time can offer. They have the whole unexplored realm of human vision.

Ideas and Meaning

1. What statements does Stafford make about writing that are similar to what Didion said in her essay?
2. What does Stafford mean when he says that skill is not part of his writing? Does he imply that writing "skills" cannot be taught? Explain.
3. What is the process Stafford goes through when he writes? What are his first two requirements for beginning? What time of day does he prefer? How does your process differ from or coincide with Stafford's?
4. How is writing "one of the great free human activities"?
5. Why is it important that Stafford not judge the value of what he writes as he is writing? Does he ever judge it? Explain.

6. Why doesn't he worry about coherence? What makes his writing coherent?

7. Why does Stafford say that writers may not be "special—sensitive or talented in any usual sense"? Do you agree or disagree? Why? If writers are not "special," how does Stafford define the writer?

8. How is it true that "writers have the whole unexplored realm of human vision"? Give examples.

9. Didion talks about *why* she writes and Stafford about *how* he writes; that is, he describes the process of his writing. From what Didion has written about her process of writing in "Why I Write" and in "On Keeping a Notebook," would you say that her process is similar to or different from Stafford's? Support your answer with reference to Didion's two essays.

Development and Style

1. How does Stafford get the reader's attention? What is his tone?

2. Who is his audience and what is his purpose?

3. What is Stafford's thesis, and how does he develop it?

4. What are the central ideas of paragraph 3 and 4? How does Stafford develop each of them?

5. Why is the comparison Stafford uses in paragraph 3 particularly appropriate?

6. What suggestions might you make to improve Stafford's development in paragraphs 4 and 6? What would help the reader better understand the central idea of each paragraph?

7. Analyze the transitions between paragraphs, beginning with paragraph 3 and ending with paragraph 8.

8. Identify the construction that begins each sentence in paragraph 6.

9. Like Didion, Stafford has also written a one-sentence paragraph for emphasis. Why would he want to emphasize this particular idea?

10. Exclamation marks are appropriately used after exclamations. They also tend to emphasize the words or statements they follow. However, most teachers of writing caution against the overuse of exclamation marks, especially as a means of achieving emphasis. Stafford has used an exclamation mark once in paragraphs 1, 3, and 4 and twice in paragraph 6. Analyze the effects of each use of this mark. Is each use of the mark justified in your opinion? Why? Why not? Rewrite each sentence using another appropriate

punctuation mark. Which sentence do you prefer—yours or Stafford's? Why?

11. Reconstruct all the sentences in paragraph 5. How does your revision alter the meaning of the original paragraph?

Celia's Two Responses

Reading Journal: "A Way of Writing" First Response

I am so glad that Stafford said, "Yet another attitude I find necessary: most of what I write, like most of what I say in casual conversation, will not amount to much." Many times I've strayed away from writing in my journal because I felt I had nothing worthwhile to say. But, now I realize a writer doesn't have to have anything worthwhile to say, especially when he writes to himself. It's okay to make small talk to yourself. I guess I heard others (those peers in my high school) criticize the writer. He was labeled dreamy, unproductive and basically weird. Weird & unproductive I don't want to be. I guess what others don't know is that writing is not unproductive or weird—also writing is not dreamy—writing is reality. Writing is reality! Writing is reality!! I want to be real. I want to be a writer. But most of all, I want to be free. Those who never taste the writer's freedom never understand this. I guess writers can be placed in the same category as runners. The more you run the more you want to run. The more you write the more you want to write. Both suffer under the same word—obsession. A runner becomes addicted to running because his body produces a chemical that gives him a natural high. A writer becomes addicted to writing because his mind is released & free! I've done both—run & write. I ran before I started writing. Both are lonely occupations. Both cause you to see the beautiful—but the world a writer enters far far exceeds a runner's world. A writer's world—forever alive, forever real, forever free!

Second Response

This is fun! I like this!—writing! I'm sitting here pigging out on a Mars bar (at 10:25 p.m.—an unheard of time to eat candy bars) & writing. And I don't have to worry what anyone thinks. Everyone's asleep & it's me & my pen. What a night. Failure doesn't even exist here—why? There's no right or wrong. There is just—now. (I'm eating another Mars!)

Failure used to bother me—especially before it ever happened. But once it happened the sting of the first time dulled the pain of the second time. I would lie if I said I didn't care if I failed or not. Every human doesn't want to fail. That's why we only do what we're good at. Most of us don't stick at those things we fail at. And who can fail at feeling, reacting. Who? Tell me, Who! No one. Everyone has the ability to write. Anyone can pig out on a Mars bar & love it. But—we must take the first step. We must take the first bite. If not, how will we ever know how writing tastes. How can we know its flavor. It's in the tasting, that we discover—it's in the tasting that we learn. It's in the tasting that we grow. We become fattened by our indulgence in writing. Once you've tasted a morsel, you'll want the whole meal! Take a bite with me. Won't anyone sit with me and pig out on Mars bars? If not—that's okay—I'm not alone.

In her responses, especially her second, Celia associates almost exclusively. Do you think that she has failed to engage in a dialogue with Stafford? What do you find particularly interesting about her second response? Do you think that writers "pig out" on writing? In her first response, Celia mentions the images of a writer held by her peers in high school. What are your images of the writer? Do you consider the writer an unproductive dreamer?

Speaking of unproductive dreamers, some students have accused E. B. White of being such a person after reading the following letter he wrote to his wife. Still other students have called him selfish, whereas some have said that he was courageous.

You can decide for yourself. As Mark Twain noted, it is a difference of opinion that makes horse races. One might also add that it is just such a difference that makes literary criticism.

E. B. WHITE

To Katharine S. White

[New York]
31 May [1937]

My dear Mrs. White:

1 It has occurred to me that perhaps I should attempt to clarify, for your benefit, the whole subject of my year of grace—or, as I call it, My Year. Whenever the subject has come up, I have noticed an ever so slight chill seize you, as though you felt a draught and wished someone would shut a door. I look upon this delicate spiritual tremor as completely natural, under the circumstances, and suggestive only of affectionate regard, tinged with womanly suspicion. In the world as now constituted, anybody who resigns a paying job is suspect; furthermore, in a well-ordered family, any departure from routine is cause for alarm. Having signified my intention to quit my accustomed ways, I shall do you the service of sketching, roughly, what is in my heart and mind—so that you

may know in a general way what to expect of me and what not to expect. It is much easier for me to do this in a letter, typing away, word after word, than to try to tell you over a cup of coffee, when I would only stutter and grow angry at myself for inexactitudes of meanings (and probably at you, too, for misinterpreting my muddy speech).

2 First, there is the question of *why* I am giving up my job. This is easy to answer. I am quitting partly because I am not satisfied with the use I am making of my talents, such as they are; partly because I am not having fun working at my job—and am in a rut there; partly because I long to recapture something which everyone loses when he agrees to perform certain creative miracles on specified dates for a particular sum. (I don't know whether you know what this thing is, but you'll just have to take my word that it is real. To you it may be just another Loch Ness monster, but to me it is as real as a dachshund.)

3 Now there comes the question of *what* I am going to do, having given up the job. I suppose this is a fair question—also the question of what I intend to use for money. These matters naturally concern you, and Esposito [grocer], and everybody. Dozens of people have asked: "What are you going to do?" so strong is their faith in the herb activity. I know better what I am *not* going to do. But I won't try to pretend (to you, anyway) that that is the whole story either. In the main, my plan is to have none. But everyone has secret projects, and I am no exception. Writing is a secret vice, like self abuse. A person afflicted with poetic longings of one sort or another searches for a kind of intellectual and spiritual privacy in which to indulge his strange excesses. To achieve this sort of privacy—this aerial suspension of the lyrical spirit— he does not necessarily have to wrench himself away, physically, from everybody and everything in his life (this, I suspect, often defeats him at his own game), but he *does* have to forswear certain easy rituals, such as earning a living and running the world's errands. That is what I intend to "do" in my year. I am quitting my job. In a sense, I am also quitting my family—which is a much more serious matter, and which is why I am taking the trouble to write this letter. For a long time I have been taking notes—sometimes on bits of paper, sometimes on the mind's disordered pad— on a theme which engrosses me. I intend to devote my year to assembling these notes, if I can, and possibly putting them on paper of the standard typewriter size. In short, a simple literary project. I am not particularly hopeful of it, but I am willing to meet it half way. If at the end of the year, I have nothing but a bowlful of cigarette stubs to show for my time, I shall not begrudge a moment of it and I hope you won't. They say a dirigible, after it has been in the air for a while, becomes charged with

static electricity, which is not discharged till the landing ropes touch the field and ground it. I have been storing up an inner turbulence, during my long apprenticeship in the weekly gaiety field, and it is time I came down to earth.

4 I am not telling people, when they ask, that I am proposing to write anything during My Year. As I said above, nothing may come of it, and it is easier to make a simple denial at the start, than to invent excuses and explanations at the end. I wish you would please do the same. Say I am taking a Sabbatical and doing nothing much of anything—which will come perilously near the truth, probably.

5 When I say I am quitting my family, I do not mean I am not going to be around. I simply mean that I shall invoke Man's ancient privilege of going and coming in a whimsical, rather than a reasonable, manner. I have some pilgrimages to make. To the zoo. To Mount Vernon. To Belgrade, and Bellport,[1] and other places where my spoor is still to be found. I shall probably spend a good deal of time in parks, libraries, and the waiting rooms of railway stations—which is where I hung out before I espoused this more congenial life. My attendance at meals may be a little spotty—for a twelvemonth I shall not adjust my steps to a soufflé. I hope this doesn't sound ungrateful, or like a declaration of independence— I intend it merely to inform you of a new allegiance—to a routine of my own spirit rather than to a fixed household & office routine. I seek the important privilege of not coming home to supper unless I happen to. I plan no absences, I plan no attendances. No plans.

6 The financial aspect of this escapade does not seem portentous, or ominous. I'm going to have Arty send me the money which comes in from my securities.[2] I'm going to sell the P.A. [Pierce Arrow], which should bring $2,000, of which you get $1500. My taxes are paid, and I have enough money in the bank to continue in the same fifty-fifty arrangement with you in all matters of maintenance, recreation, and love. My luncheons will be 50 centers, instead of the dollar and a quarter number, and I will be riding common carriers, not Sunshine cabs. Instead of keeping a car on service at a garage, I would like your permission to keep the Plymouth nearby at some cheap lodging. I don't anticipate laying in a cellar of wine, or buying any new broadloom carpets. I think if I pull in my ears and you watch your artichokes, we can still stay solvent. I think it is better to do it this way than to try some possibly abortive rearrangement of our way of living, such

1. Bellport, Long Island.

2. Arthur Illian, White's investment counselor.

as letting out the top floor to a Bingo society, or going to France to take advantage of the cheap wines. I notice Joe is already starting to sell his paintings.

7 Well, this about covers my Year. I urge you not to take it too seriously, or me. I am the same old fellow. I hope I shall give and receive the same old attentions and trifles. I don't want you tip-toeing around the halls telling people not to annoy me—the chances are I won't be doing anything anyway, except changing a bird's water. But I do want you to have some general conception of my internal processes during this odd term of grace. I want you to be able to face my departure for Bellport on a rainy Thursday afternoon with an equanimity of spirit bordering on coma.

Yrs with love and grace,
Mr. White

P.S. This letter is rather long, but I didn't have time to make it shorter, such are the many demands on me these days from so many points of the compass. I realize, too, that the whole plan sounds selfish and not much fun for you; but that's the way art goes. You let yourself in for this, marrying a man who is supposed to write something, even though he never does.

P.P.S. Unnecessary to answer this communication. Would be a drain on your valuable time. Just signify your good will with a package of Beemans—one if by land, two if by sea.

PPPPPS. Will be glad to answer any questions, or argue the whole matter out if it fails to meet with your approval or pleasure. I do not, however, want to discuss the literary nature of the project: for altho you are my b.f. and s.c.,[3] I will just have to do my own writing, as always.

Ideas and Meaning

1. If you had been in Katharine White's place, how would you have reacted to this letter?
2. Would you call White self-centered? Uncaring? Why? Why not?
3. Does White's letter reinforce the image of the writer as "dreamy and unproductive"? Why? Why not?
4. What are White's plans for "his year" and why does he call it a "term of grace"?
5. What sort of "project" does he have in mind, and why doesn't he want others to know about it?
6. Why does White write a letter to his wife rather than talk

---

3. "Best friend and severest critic."

to her? If you were in her place, would you rather have had this letter or would you rather have talked? Explain.

7. In his postscript White apologizes for the length of his letter. Explain the paradox that it would take more time to make the letter shorter than it does to make it longer.

8. What reasons does White give for leaving his job? Do they seem reasonable to you? Why? Why not.

9. Would you say that White is responsible or irresponsible? Explain.

10. What does White mean when he says that "writing is a secret vice, like self abuse"?

11. What has White done to prepare for his year? Would it be possible for you or other people you know to arrange a year off work, a year to do whatever you liked? Explain. Do you think it would be a good idea or a bad idea for everyone to have a year off at some point in his or her life? Explain.

Development and Style

1. Even though this is a personal letter, not an essay, what is White's main point? How does he support it?

2. What is his tone, and what is his purpose?

3. What are the central ideas of paragraphs 2, 3, 5, and 6? How does White develop each of them? Point out the specific details White uses in paragraphs 5 and 6.

4. To compare how he looks at his third reason for quitting his job with how his wife might view it, what two metaphors does White use? What are their connotations? Why is each particularly appropriate?

5. Besides the metaphors he uses in paragraph 2, White uses other metaphors to clarify his ideas. Identify them. What are the connotations of each? How is each appropriate?

6. In paragraph 5, why is the noun *spoor* a particularly appropriate word in the context White uses it?

7. Except for paragraph 6, White has used dashes in every paragraph. Substitute another appropriate punctuation mark in each example. Which is more effective—the dash or your substitution? Why?

8. Ordinarily a parenthetical phrase in the middle of a sentence is set off by a dash at the beginning of the phrase and one at the end of it. In the first sentence of his letter, White uses a dash at the beginning of his phrase and a comma at the end. Replace the comma with another dash. What is the difference in the effect of the two marks? Which do you prefer? Why?

9. In the second sentence of paragraph 2, why does White use

semicolons instead of comas to separate his series of dependent clauses beginning with the subordinate conjunction *because?*

10. In the two sentences below, what is the difference in effect, and which do you prefer? Why?

> . . . partly because I am not having fun working at my job—and am in a rut there; partly because . . . (White's sentence)
> . . . partly because I am not having fun working at my job (and am in a rut there); partly because . . .

11. Identify the means of transition between paragraphs, beginning with paragraph 2 and ending with paragraph 7.

12. In paragraph 5, White has used a series of intentional, parallel fragments. What are the effects? Replace the period in the sentence preceding the fragments, substituting in turn each of the three alternative marks—the comma, the colon, and the dash. Which is more effective, White's use of parallel fragments or one of the other options? Why?

13. Rearrange several consecutive sentences in paragraph 5 and discuss the difference in effect and meaning between White's original and your revisions.

Stan's Two Responses

Reading Journal: "To Katharine S. White" First Response

This letter exudes a charm not often found. I don't see how Katharine could say no or argue the point. It was that well written. White was extremely frank and honest, yet his word choices were such that Mrs. White could not react with feelings of resentment. This letter is a brilliant piece of marital diplomacy concerning a matter that has the possibility of becoming an open fray between partners, or at least a shock as daily routine is broken. the letter resembles a business correspondence due to the formality and the way that all facets of the situation are worked out. This gives credibility to White's decision. And barely submerged under this formality is the honesty and warmth of a mate asking the other for understanding.

Second Response

White is about to embark on a year-long vacation to the land of leisure and creativity. His intentions are to put together some thoughts that have been banging around his head, but he limits himself only to an attempt at this, and no more. I envy him for this. How I long for a substantial amount of time to tie together the many thoughts and ideas that constantly bludgeon my brain. But, as a student and a member of the proletariat, I find little if any time to devote to my artistic talents, whatever they may be. The hope of "next week I'll have some time" is dimming rapidly and becoming "next month." Time is illusory. It slows with anticipation, yet blinks away much as a mirage when we need it. Time has no friends, merely brief acquaintances. White made a pact with Time for one year to pursue his whims. I'll wager it was the fastest year of his life.

In his response Stan calls attention to the charm and business-like manner of White's letter. Another student wrote that White seemed to have planned this "sabbatical" for a while but that per-haps he thought of it only the day before. What clues are there that would negate White's having made his decision shortly be-fore writing the letter?

In contrast to the gentle and humorous persuasion of White's letter is Lawrence's serious and passionate essay on the novel as a mirror of Life, with a capital *L*. Although they differ in these respects, you will find that, like White's, Lawrence's style is both unique and unforgettable.

D. H. LAWRENCE

Why the Novel Matters

1 We have curious ideas of ourselves. We think of ourselves as a body with a spirit in it, or a body with a soul in it, or a body with a mind in it. *Mens sana in corpore sano.* The years drink up the wine, and at last throw the bottle away, the body, of course, being the bottle.

2 It is a funny sort of superstition. Why should I look at my hand, as it so cleverly writes these words, and decide that it is a mere nothing compared to the mind that directs it? Is there really any huge difference between my hand and my brain? Or my mind? My hand is alive, it flickers with a life of its own. It meets all the strange universe in touch, and learns a vast number of things, and knows a vast number of things. My hand, as it writes these words, slips gaily along, jumps like a grasshopper to dot an *i*, feels the table rather cold, gets a little bored if I write too long, has its own rudiments of thought, and is just as much *me* as is my brain, my mind, or my soul. Why should I imagine that there is a *me* which is more *me* than my hand is? Since my hand is absolutely alive, me alive.

3 Whereas, of course, as far as I am concerned, my pen isn't alive at all. My pen *isn't me* alive. Me alive ends at my fingertips.

4 Whatever is me alive is me. Every tiny bit of my hands is alive,

every little freckle and hair and fold of skin. And whatever is me alive is me. Only my fingernails, those ten little weapons between me an an inanimate universe, they cross the mysterious Rubicon between me alive and things like my pen, which are not alive, in my own sense.

5 So, seeing my hand is all live, and me alive, wherein is it just a bottle, or a jug, or a tin can, or a vessel of clay, or any of the rest of that nonsense? True, if I cut it it will bleed, like a can of cherries. But then the skin that is cut, and the veins that bleed, and the bones that should never be seen, they are all just as alive as the blood that flows. So the tin can business, or vessel of clay, is just bunk.

6 And that's what you learn, when you're a novelist. And that's what you are very liable *not* to know, if you're a parson, or a philosopher, or a scientist, or a stupid person. If you're a parson, you talk about souls in heaven. If you're a novelist, you know that paradise is in the palm of your hand, and on the end of your nose, because both are alive; and man alive, which is more than you can say, for certain, of paradise. Paradise is after life, and I for one am not keen on anything that is *after* life. If you are a philosopher, you talk about infinity, and the pure spirit which knows all things. But if you pick up a novel, you realize immediately that infinity is just a handle to this self-same jug of a body of mine; while as for knowing, if I find my finger in the fire, I know that fire burns, with a knowledge so emphatic and vital, it leaves Nirvana merely a conjecture. Oh, yes, my body, me alive, *knows*, and knows intensely. And as for the sum of all knowledge, it can't be anything more than an accumulation of all things I know in the body, and you, dear reader, know in the body.

7 These damned philosophers, they talk as if they suddenly went off in steam, and were then much more important than they are when they're in their shirts. It is nonsense. Every man, philosopher included, ends in his own finger-tips. That's the end of his man alive. As for the words and thoughts and sighs and aspirations that fly from him, they are so many tremulations in the ether, and not alive at all. But if the tremulations reach another man alive, he may receive them into his life, and his life may take on a new colour, like a chameleon creeping from a brown rock on to a green leaf. All very well and good. It still doesn't alter the fact that the so-called spirit, the message or teaching of the philosopher or the saint, isn't alive at all, but just a tremulation upon the ether, like a radio message. All this spirit stuff is just tremulations upon the ether. If you, as man alive, quiver from the tremulation of the ether into new life, that is because you are man alive, and you take sustenance and stimulation into your alive man in a myriad ways. But to say that the message, or the spirit which is communicated to you, is more important than your

living body, is nonsense. You might as well say that the potato at dinner was more important.

8 Nothing is important but life. And for myself, I can absolutely see life nowhere but in the living. Life with a capital L is only man alive. Even a cabbage in the rain is cabbage alive. All things that are alive are amazing. And all things that are dead are subsidiary to the living. Better a live dog than a dead lion. But better a live lion than a live dog. *C'est la vie!*

9 It seems impossible to get a saint, or a philosopher, or a scientist, to stick to this simple truth. They are all, in a sense, renegades. The saint wishes to offer himself up as spiritual food for the multitude. Even Francis of Assisi turns himself into a sort of angel-cake, of which anyone may take a slice. But an angel-cake is rather less than man alive. And poor St. Francis might well apologize to his body, when he is dying: "Oh, pardon me, my body, the wrong I did you through the years!" It was no wafer, for others to eat.

10 The philosopher, on the other hand, because he can think, decides that nothing but thoughts matter. It is as if a rabbit, because he can make little pills, should decide that nothing but little pills matter. As for the scientist, he has absolutely no use for me so long as I am man alive. To the scientist, I am dead. He puts under the microscope a bit of dead me, and calls it me. He takes me to pieces, and says first one piece, and then another piece, is me. My heart, my liver, my stomach have all been scientifically me, according to the scientist; and nowadays I am either a brain, or nerves, or glands, or something more up to-date in the tissue line.

11 Now I absolutely flatly deny that I am a soul, or a body, or a mind, or an intelligence, or a brain, or a nervous system, or a bunch of glands, or any of the rest of these bits of me. The whole is greater than the part. And therefore, I, who am man alive, am greater than my soul, or spirit, or body, or mind or consciousness, or anything else that is merely a part of me. I am a man, and alive. I am man alive, and as long as I can, I intend to go on being man alive.

12 For this reason I am a novelist. And being a novelist, I consider myself superior to the saint, the scientist, the philosopher, and the poet, who are all great masters of different bits of man alive, but never get the whole hog.

13 The novel is the one bright book of life. Books are not life. They are only tremulations on the ether. But the novel as a tremulation can make the whole man alive tremble. Which is more than poetry, philosophy, science, or any other book-tremulation can do.

14 The novel is the book of life. In this sense, the Bible is a great confused novel. You may say, it is about God. But it is really about man alive. Adam, Eve, Sarai, Abraham, Isaac, Jacob, Sam-

uel, David, Bath-Sheba, Ruth, Esther, Solomon, Job, Isaiah, Jesus, Mark, Judas, Paul, Peter: what is it but man alive, from start to finish? Man alive, not mere bits. Even the Lord is another man alive, in a burning bush, throwing the tablets of stone at Moses's head.

15 I do hope you begin to get my idea, why the novel is supremely important, as a tremulation on the ether. Plato makes the perfect ideal being tremble in me. But that's only a bit of me. Perfection is only a bit, in the strange make-up of man alive. The Sermon on the Mount makes the selfless spirit of me quiver. But that, too, is only a bit of me. The Ten Commandments set the old Adam shivering in me, warning me that I am a thief and a murderer, unless I watch it. But even the old Adam is only a bit of me.

16 I very much like all these bits of me to be set trembling with life and the wisdom of life. But I do ask that the whole of me shall tremble in its wholeness, some time or other.

17 And this, of course, must happen in me, living.

18 But as far as it can happen from a communication, it can only happen when a whole novel communicates itself to me. The Bible—but *all* the Bible—and Homer, and Shakespeare: these are the supreme old novels. These are all things to all men. Which means that in their wholeness they affect the whole man alive, which is the man himself, beyond any part of him. They set the whole tree trembling with a new access of life, they do not just stimulate growth in one direction.

19 I don't want to grow in any one direction any more. And, if I can help it, I don't want to stimulate anybody else into some particular direction. A particular direction ends in a *cul-de-sac*. We're in a *cul-de-sac* at present.

20 I don't believe in any dazzling revelation, or in any supreme Word. "The grass withereth, the flower fadeth, but the Word of the Lord shall stand for ever." That's the kind of stuff we've drugged ourselves with. As a matter of fact, the grass withereth, but comes up all the greener for that reason, after the rains. The flower fadeth, and therefore the bud opens. But the Word of the Lord, being man-uttered and a mere vibration on the ether, becomes staler and staler, more and more boring, till at last we turn a deaf ear and it ceases to exist, far more finally than any withered grass. It is grass that renews its youth like the eagle, not any Word.

21 We should ask for no absolutes, or absolute. Once and for all and for ever let us have done with the ugly imperialism of any absolute. There is no absolute good, there is nothing absolutely right. All things flow and change, and even change is not absolute. The whole is a strange assembly of apparently incongruous parts, slipping past one another.

22 Me, man alive, I am a very curious assembly of incongruous parts. My yea! of today is oddly different from my yea! of yester-

day. My tears of tomorrow will have nothing to do with my tears of a year ago. If the one I love remains unchanged and unchanging, I shall cease to love her. It is only because she changes and startles me into change and defies my inertia, and is herself staggered in her inertia by my changing, that I can continue to love her. If she stayed put, I might as well love the pepper-pot.

23 In all this change, I maintain a certain integrity. But woe betide me if I try to put my finger on it. If I say of myself, I am this, I am that!—then, if I stick to it, I turn into a stupid fixed thing like a lamp-post. I shall never know wherein lies my integrity, my individuality, my me. I *can* never know it. It is useless to talk about my ego. That only means that I have made up an *idea* of myself, and that I am trying to cut myself out to pattern. Which is no good. You can cut your cloth to fit your coat, but you can't clip bits off your living body, to trim it down to your idea. True, you can put yourself into ideal corsets. But even in ideal corsets, fashions change.

24 Let us learn from the novel. In the novel, the characters can do nothing but *live*. If they keep on being good, according to pattern, or bad, according to pattern, or even volatile, according to pattern, they cease to live, and the novel falls dead. A character in a novel has got to live, or it is nothing.

25 We, likewise, in life have got to live, or we are nothing.

26 What we mean by living is, of course, just as indescribable as what we mean by *being*. Men get ideas into their heads, of what they mean by Life, and they proceed to cut life out to pattern. Sometimes they go into the desert to seek God, sometimes they go into the desert to seek cash, sometimes it is wine, woman, and song, and again it is water, political reform, and votes. You never know what it will be next: from killing your neighbour with hideous bombs and gas that tears the lungs, to supporting a Foundlings Home and preaching infinite Love, and being co-respondent in a divorce.

27 In all this wild welter, we need some sort of guide. It's no good inventing Thou Shalt Nots!

28 What then? Turn truly, honourably to the novel, and see wherein you are man alive, and wherein you are dead man in life. You may love a woman as man alive, and you may be making love to a woman as sheer dead man in life. You may eat your dinner as man alive, or as a mere masticating corpse. As man alive you may have a shot at your enemy. But as a ghastly simulacrum of life you may be firing bombs into men who are neither your enemies nor your friends, but just things you are dead to. Which is criminal, when the things happen to be alive.

29 To be alive, to be man alive, to be whole man alive: that is the point. And at its best, the novel, and the novel supremely, can help you. It can help you not to be dead man in life. So much of

a man walks about dead and a carcass in the street and house, today: so much of women is merely dead. Like a pianoforte with half the notes mute.

30 But in the novel you can see, plainly, when the man goes dead, the woman goes inert. You can develop an instinct for life, if you will, instead of a theory of right and wrong, good and bad.

31 In life, there is right and wrong, good and bad, all the time. But what is right in one case is wrong in another. And in the novel you see one man becoming a corpse, because of his so-called goodness, another going dead because of his so-called wickedness. Right and wrong is an instinct: but an instinct of the whole consciousness in a man, bodily, mental, spiritual at once. And only in the novel are *all* things given full play, or at least, they may be given full play, when we realize that life itself, and not inert safety, is the reason for living. For out of the full play of all things emerges the only thing that is anything, the wholeness of a man, the wholeness of a woman, man alive, and live woman.

Ideas and Meaning

1. What seems to be Lawrence's definition of "man alive"?
2. What does he mean by the phrase "tremulations upon the ether"?
3. What is the most important thing to Lawrence?
4. Why does Lawrence say that the Bible must communicate itself wholly to him? What distinctions does Lawrence imply between the "Word of the Lord" and the whole Bible?
5. Why does Lawrence criticize saints such as St. Francis of Assisi? How do you feel about Lawrence's criticism? Explain.
6. Why does Lawrence criticize scientists? Do you agree or disagree with his point? Why?
7. Why does he criticize philosophers? Do you agree or disagree with him and why?
8. Why does Lawrence criticize the clergy? Do you agree or disagree and why?
9. According to Lawrence, why does the novel matter? How does he define the kind of novel he has in mind?
10. Why does Lawrence say that it is useless to talk of one's ego? Do you agree or disagree? Why?
11. In what way does Lawrence say that his hand has knowledge? Do you agree or disagree with his thinking? Why?
12. Do you agree or disagree that growth in one direction only ends in a cul-de-sac? Explain.
13. What statements did you find most puzzling or confusing?
14. What was the last novel you read? Did the characters seem alive to you, whole people, or were they "good according

to pattern, bad according to pattern, or even volatile according to pattern"? Explain.

15. How can novels help us to avoid being "dead in life"? Explain. Has a character in a novel ever illustrated deadness in life to you? If so, who? what caused this character to be dead in life?

16. Would you say that at present the film is a more important art form than the novel? Why? Why not?

17. Name one or more films you have seen that you think depicted "man alive," "woman alive," or both.

18. Name one or more films you've seen that showed deadness in life,·one-dimensional people who acted according to pattern. Explain.

19. Did this essay prompt you to want to read a novel by Lawrence? Why? Why not?

Development and Style

1. How does Lawrence get the reader's attention, and what is his tone?

2. From his voice, what image do you have of Lawrence?

3. Who is his audience? What is his purpose?

4. What is his thesis? How does he support it?

5. How does the first part of the essay pertain to the thesis?

6. What are the central ideas of paragraphs 7, 8, and 9? How does Lawrence support each of them?

7. Besides paragraphs that support his thesis, Lawrence has written paragraphs that provide transition and emphasis. Identify both the transitional paragraphs and the emphatic ones.

8. As you have learned, through repetition of key words or phrases, writers achieve both coherence and emphasis. What words and phrases does Lawrence repeat most? Is he unnecessarily repetitive? Why? Why not? If so, what words or phrases do you find tiresomely repetitive?

9. Analyze the transitions between paragraphs, beginning with paragraph 7 and ending with paragraph 14.

10. Analyze the constructions that begin each of the sentences in paragraphs 11 through 13.

11. Paragraph 13 ends with a dependent clause written alone as an intentional fragment. Why does this kind of fragment provide a particularly effective transition? Where else has Lawrence written a dependent clause alone intentionally?

12. Revise the sentence structure in paragraph 10. When you have finished, compare your version with Lawrence's. Which is more effective? Why?

13. Discuss the metaphors Lawrence uses in paragraphs 1, 2,

5, 7, and 23. What are their connotations? How are they appropriate?

14. In the third sentence of paragraph 23, Lawrence has violated the "rule" that only one mark of punctuation be used at a time. This is how the sentence would ordinarily be punctuated.

> If I say of myself, I am this, I am that, then, if I stick to it, I turn into a stupid fixed thing like a lamp-post.

Which version is more effective? Why? Would you punctuate the sentence another way? How?

15. In paragraph 18, Lawrence encloses a parenthetical phrase, "but *all* the Bible," in dashes. Substitute parentheses for the dashes. What is the difference in the effect of the two pairs of marks?

16. One characteristic of Lawrence's writing is its intensity. How does he achieve such intensity? Does it enervate or energize the reader? Explain.

17. Of the four professional essays in this chapter, which do you prefer? Why? Which essay contains the best writing? Why?

Monica's Two Responses

Reading Journal: "Why the Novel Matters" First Response

D. H. Lawrence says a lot of pretty bizarre stuff here, some of which I agree with. Sometimes people do try to pinpoint life so much that they are "dead" or blind to what, in reality, is the majority of life. I have a few friends who would probably fall into that category. One is a graduate student in biology and for him, the only interesting things are slides and PBS scientific programs. Believe it or not, he's still a likable person, but anyone who closes himself off from other things that much is missing a lot. (It's not pleasant to think of people you're friends with as being dead!)

His discussion of philosophers and the way that thought becomes all-important to them is a little confusing. I mean, he seems to be doing the same thing by writing this entire "philosophical" essay. Part of that, though, lies in the problem of having to pinpoint anything—when you try to define it—you lost it.

I'm not sure about Lawrence's assessment that the novel is the supreme form of man alive. Yes, I agree that novels probably encompass (if they attempt to) more of life as a whole; but I'm not sure that it's fair to say all poems can't, or other forms of art can't. A lot of my most meaningful experiences have been with novels, but I've also read poems that I've found very "alive"; nowadays, there are films that do this as well. While novels might be my personal favorite, I'm not sure that I could say they're the supreme form.

Second Response

After my second reading of this essay, I think it's interesting that Lawrence deals so much in the concrete. He counts only those things which show definite signs of being alive as of utmost importance—the physical body namely. He says that the sum of all knowledge is an accumulation of nothing more than all things he knows in the body. I wonder how far he really carries that—does he include his own interpretations? I guess he does, because the mind is in the body. Yet, he doesn't seem to include the philosopher's thoughts . . . well, that's not really true either though, because I think what he was getting at there was that because the philosopher says that thought (abstract) is of utmost importance, he becomes dead because he's only considering part of the whole.

I would like to believe that the physical being, what is seen to be alive is the most important thing. We strive so much to keep this body going, although we probably abuse it equally as much, that someone watching our society would probably think that it was true. But, there are so many other things in my head right now, that I don't really think the body is the most important thing (I'd probably change my mind if I got sick tomorrow!).

I noticed this time that Lawrence included Shakespeare among those that make the whole man alive tremble. I guess this means he includes plays along with novels as a superior form. Well, I like that, but just as I said in my other response, I still feel like that might be leaving out some important things. Yes, the novel gives a lot more time to develop, convince, and characterize (among other things), but I'm not sure it's fair to hold it supreme for everyone. For me, the best novel or play would probably be the most effective, but others would disagree. I guess it's just in how you perceive things.

Conclusion

It would be hard to find four professionals whose styles differ more than the four writers you have just read. It would also be hard to find writers you can learn more from about the art of writing than you can learn from Didion, White, and Lawrence.

Perhaps in the essay you write explaining a way that you differ from most people, you can mingle Lawrence's passion and intensity with Didion's clarity and honesty and, last, with White's extraordinary charm. Such a combination, however, might be asking too much of any writer. But at least in the next chapter you will be given the chance to try your wings once more as a fledgling writer of exposition. Who knows, you may find that you soar much higher than you ever thought possible. In any event, besides practicing all the writing skills you have acquired thus far, you will learn more about writing introductions and conclusions—new ways to get your essay off the ground and into flight and new ways to land more safely, more smoothly, and more satisfactorily.

Through the Looking-Glass: Writing about Your Differences from Others

12

In the last chapter, Joan Didion discussed the reasons she is a writer; William Stafford described his particular process of writing; in a letter to his wife, E. B. White explained why he was taking a year off work; and D. H. Lawrence explained why the novel is important. Basically, all four writers explained the ways their beliefs or actions differ from those of others. Therefore, like the professional writers in Chapter 9, these writers wrote expository essays. In this chapter you will again have the opportunity to write exposition, this time to explain how you too, differ from other people.

Finding a Topic

For you, as for almost everyone, it should be a relatively easy matter to think of the things you do, the beliefs you have, or the ways you do things that make you different from others. You have probably observed, for example, that no two people study alike; no two people wash dishes alike; no two people write alike; you could go on and on. But to aid your creative juices, you might use the following headings for brainstorming.

Attitudes I Have

Things I Like to Do

Things I Do Not Like to Do

Habits I Have

Why I _____

A Way of _____

Why _____ Matters

People I'd Like to Write

Under the last heading you could list anyone who did not understand something you did in the past or does not understand something you plan to do. You could also list anyone who does not understand something about you—a habit, a personality trait, and so on. In addition, you could list anyone to whom you'd like to write a letter because what you have to say is easier said in writing than in a face-to-face conversation. (Also, you probably don't need reminding at this point, but don't forget to check your reading responses and journal for interesting and appropriate ideas.)

The following is a sample of Sara's listing.

Attitudes I Have

that God is in man
that parents aren't always right
that life is not always fair
that instant everything stinks

Habits I Have

listening to old rock
insanity for the sake of levity
writing strange stories
worrying

Why _____ Matters

nothing
sex
money
love
everything

People I'd Like to Write

Mom—re: religion, politics, movies, life—why we differ
Dad—re: my six months in Myrtle Beach and why it was important
Robert Heinlein—why I think his sci-fi is junk
Joan Didion—about why I think we have a lot in common

A Way of _____

worrying
writing
loving
looking
living

After you have listed under these headings or others, reread your lists and put a checkmark by the habits, attitudes, or activities that differ most from those of others. For instance, suppose you listed procrastination as a habit. A great many people procrastinate and generally for similar reasons. However, one interesting way to handle this subject would be to describe the *ways* you procrastinate because people certainly differ in that regard.

To further stimulate your creative juices, you might like to read the final drafts of Sara's classmates Susan and Gretta.

Susan's Final Draft

Letter to Sylvia Plath

To Sylvia Plath:

1 I'm writing this letter to say that your novel The Bell Jar frightened the hell out of me. Reading the novel is like reading a novel about myself; for like you, I suffered a breakdown. Your descriptions of things that took place during your illness brought vivid memories that sent chills down my spine. Never had I felt that someone else could understand the pain of mental illness. This understanding brought relief . . . and fear. I recovered, as you did, but years after you recovered, you committed suicide.

2 Suicide—even the word brings terrifying thoughts. I often wonder why you decided to fill your lungs with gas and leave the world shortly after the birth of your second child. With your awards for poetry, your children and extensive education were you still not satisfied? I know it's useless to ponder questions that will never be answered, but I can't help it because, Sylvia, I'm afraid that someday I may choose death as well.

3 Why shouldn't I be afraid? My sickness was just like yours. It started off with insomnia. I remember those sleepness nights with the sounds of night flooding my room; the rustling of sheets driving me mad. Sleep—all I wanted was sleep, but yet, I was mystified by not feeling sleepy, just bored. In your novel, you were amused by your wakefulness after thirty days without sleep. My insomnia only lasted a week. Tranquilizers came to my "rescue" as they did yours. We were both turned into zombies, marking the beginning of mental decay. Losing your mind is such a slow process.

4 I wanted to cry when I read you had lost all sense of time and locked yourself away from the world. I did the same thing; never talked or socialized with anyone. I had to be reminded what day it was, as if I cared. Like you, I stopped bath-

ing. My oily hair matted to my scalp, permeating the air with a sickening sweet stench. The clothes I never changed were faded jeans and a flannel shirt unlike your white dress with blue cornflowers. I suppose one must be comfortable while depressed.

5 When we were healthy we sought comfort in the same things—hot baths and poetry. It's funny how the things you enjoy are the things you deprive yourself of when you are sick. Once you said you could remember every fixture and ceiling of all the tubs you bathed in, so can I. Taking a bath is like a ritual. You fill the tub with hot water, then ease yourself in very slowly. The steam rises taking the dirt and pain; making you pure again. Poetry does much the same thing. It lifts the pain and refreshes the mind. Your descriptions of bathing and poetry appear to be much the same. They both can take away bad things, like being deceived, for example.

6 Do you remember the deception by those who said they were your friends? Your doctor friends promised no more shock treatments, as my friend said "no more drugs." Anger filled my heart and eyes as I read of your unannounced shock treatments. I felt anger when more drugs were forced on me. Those doctors were such good friends that they even made more promises. Did you laugh at the promises they made you? Everything will be "fine" on your way to a "healthy" state of mind. I don't know about you, but a "healthy" state of mind was bizarre.

7 Your novel stops talking about illness after your first supposed recovery. Depression did follow you though. It follows me. That frightens me.

8 If our sicknesses were so similar, as were our recoveries, plus our spells of depression, who's to say our similarities end there? You said you often wondered if the bell jar would descend again, distorting your view. Several years later the bell jar did descend, suffocating you.

9 It would be nice to talk over coffee and cigarettes, but you have made that impossible. I only hope that someday I can find the answers that you did not. Until then dreams will do.

10 I have the image of walking on the beach with footprints stretched out . . . off into the water. Looking closer, I see you in spirit form—blowing sand along the shore, covering the steps you've taken. This vision brings answers because I can imagine that you are giving me a sign not to give up. It brings sadness, because I realize you must regret your choice.

As I remain,

Susan

Ideas and Meaning

1. How was Susan's illness similar to Plath's?
2. What is Susan's fear? Do you think that she has cause to be afraid? Why? Why not?
3. Are people who have mental breakdowns crazy? Why? Why not?
4. Why doesn't Susan mention the cause or causes of her breakdown?
5. What is Susan's occasional vision of Plath? How does she interpret this vision? How would you interpret it? Explain.
6. Why were poetry and bathing important to Plath and Susan?
7. How does Susan feel about her doctors? Would you feel the same? Why? Why not?
8. How does the image of a bell jar descending over one describe the commencement of mental illness?
9. What were the results of Susan's drug therapy? Plath's shock treatments?
10. In the second paragraph Susan asks why Plath committed suicide, why she was not satisfied with what she had. Is being satisfied with one's life a deterrent to suicide? Explain. Do you know anyone personally or anyone famous who committed suicide and who had also achieved a great deal? Who? What had this person achieved? Why do you think that this person committed suicide? Why do you think people commit suicide?
11. What does the image of the descent of the bell jar imply about a person's control over his or her mental illness? Do you think a person has control over whether or not he or she has a mental breakdown? Explain.
12. If you had been Susan, would you have written this letter for the assignment? Explain. Do you admire her or not for doing so? Explain?
13. Read the following poem by Emily Dickinson. What connections do you see between it and one or more of the ideas Susan expresses in her essay?

Much Madness is divinest Sense

Much Madness is divinest Sense—
To a discerning Eye—
Much Sense—the starkest Madness—
'Tis the Majority
In this, as All, prevail—
Assent—and you are sane—

> Demure—you're straightway danger-
> ous—
> And handled with a Chain—

Can you relate this poem to your own or other people's current, or past, personal, social, or political lives?

Development and Style

1. Even though this is not an essay, how does the first sentence get your attention?
2. What is the point of Susan's letter? How does she support it?
3. What is Susan's purpose?
4. What is her tone? From her voice, what image do you have of Susan?
5. How does she support the generalization ending paragraph 9, "Until then dreams will do"?
6. How does she support the central ideas of paragraphs 3, 4, 5, and 6?
7. What are some of the concrete/specific words and phrases Susan uses? Point out the general or abstract words or phrases that need to be made more specific.
8. Analyze the transitions between paragraphs from paragraph 2 to the end of the essay. Are there any weak transitions? If so, supply stronger ones.
9. What are the connotations of the metaphor of the bell jar?
10. Analyze the sentence structure in paragraph 6. Would you revise any of the sentences? If so, why? How?
11. In paragraphs 2, 3, and 5, Susan uses dashes to set off words and phrases. What is the effect of each use? Would you have used another mark of punctuation? If so, what and why?
12. In the second sentence of paragraph 1, in the fourth sentence of paragraph 3, and in the sixth sentence of paragraph 5, Susan has used semicolons. In paragraphs 3 and 5 her usage is nonstandard. What is the effect of her use of the semicolon where ordinarily a comma would be used? In each sentence, which mark is more effective—the semicolon or the comma? Why? What would be the effect of a dash in place of the semicolon? In each sentence, which is most effective—the comma, the semicolon, or the dash? Why?
13. Of the professional women writers you have read so far, does Susan's voice or style resemble any one of them? Explain.

Gretta's Final Draft

Floats and Sinkers

1 There is something about a lazy, racing river that is both attractive and terrifying. Staring up at me as I glance along the water is a reflection, my reflection; my image blending in perfectly with nature. But if I look too intently, the image is gone, leaving behind the tossing pebbles and white foam of a swift current rushing downstream. I've always wanted to be close to nature, to blend in, but more and more often it seems that pavement and shelter form an insurmountable wall between the two of us. Should I walk barefoot through the woods, stickers prick my feet, thorns slice through my flesh, and I bleed. It has been too long since I roamed barefoot along the riverbank, and now a boat must separate us. But that's okay, because the distance is not so great, and there's a new joy to be found in lazily floating along and dangling a line in the water.

2 I guess I don't really fish to catch anything; I fish to be close to the river. Cares seem to drift away as I lean against the side of the boat, while the sun sinks past the skin, past the muscle, past the bone, into the very marrow. Warm all over. Nowhere do I find that warmth more comforting than in Laceyville, Pennsylvania, when the snow begins to melt, forming crystal streams that drip slowly down the mountains. Amid all this moisture that is spring, the town hold its annual fish float along the Susquehanna River. Neglecting their responsibilities, the people come with boats, poles, beer and bait to search out the elusive fish. I come too, dropping all obligations, to float down the river.

3 Although I always have a lot of fun floating down that river, there is a darker element as well. Whenever I fish, be it alone or with others, a weathered old man casts his line beside me. He smiles but there is no warmth; he laughs, but it isn't genuine. He was my first and best fishing partner, and to this day I try to decide if I ever really made any pathways into his world. If so, he never gave any indications. I remember one Christmas Eve that we spent fishing on the frozen Susquehanna. A beautiful blue light filled the skies, reflecting off the new snow, giving everything a milky white appearance. Complete silence. Neither of us said a word the entire time. Even the river was silent, trapped beneath a thick layer of ice. We were trapped too—I couldn't tell him how painful it was to love him, and he couldn't tell me why he had to be such a bastard—we could only watch as the water roared downstream.

4 Gramps could be found downstream in nearly everything he did. He'd worked on the railroad all his life and was anxious to reach that magic age when he'd be free of his chains, could claim his retirement money, and fish on the river full time. Well, that's not exactly true; he already fished on the river full time. And I pattered up behind him, dropping my line next to his, hoping he would let me in on the secrets of the world, which I was convinced that he alone possessed. He was the eternal fisherman, above and beyond anything else.

5 Unfortunately, the railroad was always calling Grandma to find out where the eternal fisherman was, and she, knowing full well that he was shirking his responsibilities out on that river, always replied that she didn't know. Knowledge is painful, and it was especially painful for me then because my grandfather blew his image. I saw the bottle more and more; I saw the anger more and more. Grandma knew she came third, behind the fishing and behind the alcohol. I wonder how she felt about that. She has cried twice that I know of, once after he hit her, and the second time after he died.

6 There's a very ugly filial line that connects that man to me; it surfaces when I drink, and it surfaces as I cast my line, ignoring all other responsibilities. I choose to remember him as he most often was; with a boat, pole, and bottle—alone. Many a Sunday morning burst forth brilliantly from the east to discover a crumpled old man curled up in the corner of a boat with his bottle, downstream once again.

7 I guess that when I participate in the Laceyville fish float, part of me does it for him. Since Gramp's death, I've entered with four old guys from town, and looking into their faces I feel I'm seeing his. Sunken, watery eyes, sagging skin that folds into a million wrinkles like so many criss-crossing roads on a map, and brown teeth darkened from too much smoking and too little cleaning, these are all signs of age, and they're signs of him, and they're signs of what I will become. Just another person found sleeping in my boat downstream.

8 I don't fish with these men only because they're old though. I fish with them because they're fun. Just last year as we were nearing the finish line, and all of my partners were passed out in the boat, one of their poles bent nearly in half. I grabbed that pole and began a fight that lasted fifteen minutes. A magnificent glistening channel cat unwillingly surfaced, and I proudly laid him down with the rest of our catch. Amazingly enough, when that fish won the tournament, all four of those drunken old men claimed to have caught it.

"She was rough; took a full twenty minutes to bring her in." . . .

"Nope, nope, took a half hour of playing with her 'till I got
her landed." . . .

"Boys, dream on, when I caught this beauty I was in control
. . . she came up in five minutes!"

One time when we were all out on the river again, I suggested
that I caught the fish. They all laughed and laughed, tears
flowed through the crevices in their faces, and the boat rocked
frighteningly.

9 As we cast our lines out into the water, the sun reflects off
the liquid droplets that cling to it, making wonderful spider-
webs of brilliant colors. Watching the shimmering droplets
slip slowly down the line and disappear mysteriously into the
river, I realize that I'll always come to fish. It's hereditary.
When I'm fishing, a mean, desperate old man fishes with me;
his face reminds me that unfortunately, there's something
about love that goes beyond the bad that a person does. Fishing also reminds me that while I'll always be separate from
the water, the mountains, and the sky, at least I can come as
close to being one with everything as the distance between the
boat and my body allows. Then I can just sit back, toss out a
line, and quit fighting, allowing myself to drift downstream
where eventually, we all end up.

Ideas and Meaning

1. What is the metaphorical significance of Gretta's title? Who
   or what are the floats? The sinkers?
2. Gretta discovered this topic by listing under "Why _____
   Matters." Why does this event matter to Gretta? Besides
   the event, what else matters to her?
3. Why was Gretta's grandfather an important person in her
   life? From her description, would you call him a "mean,
   desperate old man"? Why was he "desperate"?
4. Why does Gretta fish now with several old men? How are
   they similar to her grandfather?
5. What kind of relationship does Gretta have with nature?
   What kind of relationship does she want? What prevents
   her from having such a relationship?
6. How does Gretta use the phrase "drift downstream" met-
   aphorically? How is it that we all eventually "drift downstream"? What was the cause of her grandfather's "drifting
   downstream"?
7. What particular images from Gretta's essay remain in your
   mind?
8. If you enjoy any particular ritual involving nature, what is
   it? How do you feel about it? If you once enjoyed an activ-

ity similar to Gretta's, but no longer do, why did you give it up?

9. Is there a relative towards whom you have ambivalent feelings, such as Gretta's towards her grandfather? Explain. Do you have the sense that Gretta has or has not resolved her feelings? Explain. Have you resolved yours? Explain.

10. Does Gretta imply that she might become "a mean, desperate" drunkard? Explain.

11. Would you describe this essay as positive or negative, or would you use some other term? Explain.

Development and Style

1. How does Gretta get the reader's attention? What is her tone?

2. Who is her audience? What is her purpose?

3. What is her thesis? How does she support it?

4. What are the central ideas of paragraphs 3, 4, 5, and 6? How does Gretta develop each one?

5. What are the connotations of the phrase "Floats and Sinkers"? What are the connotations of the phrase "drifting downstream"?

6. Although Gretta's essay is filled with concrete words and phrases, which ones were most effective in your opinion? What are the connotations of each?

7. Analyze the transitions between paragraphs, beginning with paragraph 2 and ending with 9. Are there any weak transitions? If so, supply stronger ones.

8. Are there any sentences in Gretta's essay that you would revise? If so, which ones? Why would you revise them? How would you rewrite them?

9. In the second sentences of paragraphs 1 and 6, Gretta uses a semicolon where either a comma or a dash would be the preferred mark. Which mark—the semicolon, the comma, or the dash—is most effective in these two sentences? Why?

10. In paragraph 8, why does Gretta indent the entire dialogue between her and the old fishermen? Write the dialogue using the standard form. Which do you prefer? Why?

11. How would you describe the differences between Gretta's voice and Susan's? Between their styles? Does Gretta's voice or style resemble the voice or style of any one of the professional women writers you have read in this text? If so, explain the resemblances as specifically as you can.

Sara's Draft for Criticism

As you will see in the following draft that Sara brought to class for criticism, she became a very good writer, even though she was a good one to begin with.

Why I Worry

Could you think of a more interesting specific title?

1 I worry habitually about whatever is available for worry. The scope of availability is endless; it ranges from the sublime to the ridiculous. And it's a senseless, perpetual, losing battle: I worry, so I smoke cigarettes, then I worry that I'll contract emphysema or lung cancer and die a long and lingering death. Cancer, emphysema—one's as fatal as the other—nothing to worry about there.

Maybe this could be more attention getting?

good

What are some specific examples of what you worry about?

2 My boyfriend, who has not worried a single moment in the four years I've known him, chides me endlessly for my worries. He tells me I'm pathological, that I'll go crazy, develop ulcers, or die young if I don't change my ways. It's only his joking concern, but of course, it simply makes my situation worse. It maddens me, drives me to the limits of my patience, his brazen air of insouciance in the face of all this potential material for worry. But he is a classic nonworrier: he sleeps soundly every night, spends money without agonizing over bills and debts, goes to work and leaves it behind. I am the quintessential worrier, with all the telltale signs: the chewed fingernails, the frazzled morning looks and bloodshot eyes from sleepless nights, the bromides in the medicine chest. It's a minor miracle we've survived together.

nice phrase

What? If you give examples above, this will work

good use of details

maybe a transitional phrase like "In Contrast"

3 Those who do not worry cannot fathom the workings of a worried mind. They find no rationale in the grievous mornings (the worst time for hardened worriers) when one jars bolt upright out of a hindered sleep. But the fears and night demons are there, real or not. The phobias are no less troublesome, being contrived. I think I can sympathize with Joan Didion and her migraines,* particularly in regard to the unsympathetic nonsufferers. All the "don't worry about its" in the world do nothing to abate our cares any more than the offhand prescription of a couple of aspirin can do to cure a migraine. They just don't know, having nothing to gauge it by. When all is said and done, however, I don't particularly envy the non worrier. I know, intrinsically, that I am far more sensitive, somehow more worthy than he is. I pay my dues every day, while I like to think that, in the end, his will be extracted in one lump sum for all his carelessness. No one says worriers have to be completely benign.

the chronic worrier's

who? There's no reference.

ref?

I'd choose another word because of the connotations

4 They say it dissipates with age, this malaise of the overconcerned. In a way I hope not. What do you do with your time, free from worry, after years of self-indulgence in the habit? My mother, a chronic worrier for fifty years, grey well before

* Sara, who became enamored of Didion's style, had read "In Bed," an essay Didion wrote about her migraines.

thirty, with fingernails bitten always to the quick, decided one day, out of the blue, to give it up. She stopped worrying, grew the nails of a ring model, and painted them red. The sight of the sun rising out of the western sky could not have surprised me more than did this vision of my mother sporting those elegantly tapered and lacquered fingernails. The red, I suppose, was her flag of freedom, a sign of victory over worry, but in my eyes, she somehow lost a lot of character in that gesture. I began to worry about her state of mind, having nothing better to do, it seemed, than file and paint her nails. Worrying seemed to me less a waste of time. My great aunt Alice, on the other hand (on whom, in her twilight years, we were heartles, or perhaps just plain exasperated enough to pin the disrespectful moniker "Alice in Wonderland"), went to the grave a veteran worrier at ninety-two. When, for all intent and purposes, Alice had nothing in the world left to worry about, she felt compelled to invent for herself new trauma. And create it she did, with the flair that only a mind burdened by too many years of too much worry can do. She worried about places, persons, events that, except in her mind, had ceased to exist: her home, her family, and oddly enough, the Civil War (or the War of Northern Agression, as she preferred to call it). On warm days towards winter's end, she worried that her house (long since abandoned and then razed for the planting of pulpwood timbers) needed its annual spring cleaning. She worried every evening, without fail, about Papa (dead for forty years) and what he was having for supper. And, much to the dismay of us all, she was given to occasional agonized speculations as to whether General Sherman was apt to make another blazing march through the hallowed South. These harried ruminations, and more, plagued her till her dying day.

5 While I doubt that I'll ever give up worrying completely, I hope I'll never carry it to the extremes my illustrious aunt did. But who knows, I might. All I know right now is that I'd rather be in wonderland with aunt Alice than somewhere else filing my nails.

I would break this paragraph somewhere. Perhaps where I suggested.

excellent details, Sara

You have a nice style I think, an interesting way of writing. You also have some good details. One problem I noticed was your using pronouns when I wasn't sure what they referred to.

The following is the guide Sara's reviewers used.

The Critic's Guide

1. Does the writer have an interesting title?
2. Does the first sentence get the reader's attention?
3. What is the writer's tone? Are there any words, phrases, or

metaphors with connotations that are inconsistent with the tone?

4. What is the thesis?
5. Is the thesis adequately developed with supportive statements?
6. Are the supportive statements ordered logically with the stronger points near the end of the essay?
7. Are supportive paragraphs adequately developed? Do any central ideas of paragraphs need examples, descriptive details, and so forth, for further development? Do any examples, descriptive details, and so on, need to be improved?
8. Are there any words or phrases that could be more concrete or specific?
9. Are sentence beginnings and lengths varied?
10. Are stronger transitions needed between any two sentences or paragraphs?

Critical Analysis

Sara's vocabulary is extensive, and as a result, she uses words precisely most of the time. As her critic pointed out, however, the one instance in this essay that perhaps she does not is when she uses the word *benign*, which means "kindly," a meaning that Sara intends here. Nevertheless, we now see the term used most often in connection with tumors, so that its associations are somewhat negative, though its denotation is certainly *not*. Besides this minor problem, Sara's reviewers also suggested that she try to improve her first sentence and her title, which could certainly be both more original and more specific. "Why I Worry" doesn't make me (or anyone else I imagine) particularly want to read this essay.

And even though Sara is generally very good at using specific details, she does need some examples to support the second sentence of her first paragraph.

Last, although Sara has the beginnings of a good introduction, as with almost any writing, she could improve it. Later you will see that after Sara learned more about the introductions and conclusions of expository/persuasive essays, she improved both paragraphs in her final draft.

Writing Introductions

Sometimes rudimentary introductions come to writers when they begin to write. Other times, writers begin writing the body of their essays first and wait until later to write an introduction. Ideas for an introduction may come to a writer while he or she is writing a first, second, or later draft of an essay. *When* a writer composes an introduction is both arbitrary and unimportant. However, that an essay have an introduction *is* important. Despite the importance of this paragraph, you should not stew and worry over it early in the process of writing. If you did, you might never get a word down. Concern for a good introduction comes later in the writing process. For one thing, as the body of an essay is revised, it changes, and as it changes, in all likelihood, so too will the introduction to it. But once the body of an essay is more or less in final-draft form, a writer can work on polishing the introduction to it. Ironically, the beginning of your essay may be the last part of it you write.

The Functions of an Introduction

You already know one purpose of an introduction: to get the reader's attention. In the third chapter you learned various ways of capturing the reader's interest in the first sentence. Besides accomplishing this important purpose, introductions accomplish several others as well.

After getting your readers' attention, you need to keep their interest, and therefore you may need to give your readers enough information about your subject for them to understand what you write. For example, if you were writing an essay on the Conrail disputes for a general audience, you would need to explain briefly what these disputes have entailed in order to maintain the interest of your readers, many of whom might be unfamiliar with the subject. On the other hand, if you were writing about the stockpiling of nuclear weapons, the majority of your audience would not need a lengthy explanation of the situation.

Besides explaining the background of a subject, an introduction lets readers know your particular focus on the subject. If you are talking about nuclear stockpiling, for instance, what specifically are you focusing on? Why we should discontinue it? Ways we can reduce the dangers? However, informing readers of your focus *does not* mean that you must state your thesis in your introduction.

Last, in addition to letting your reader know your focus (not necessarily your thesis), your introduction lets readers know your attitude toward your subject. That is, you establish a tone of voice here at the beginning of your essay.

To recapitulate: introductions to essays accomplish these functions:

1. They get the reader's attention.
2. They provide information readers may not have.
3. They let readers know the writer's particular focus on the subject.
4. They let readers know the writer's attitude towards his or her subject.

Ways to Accomplish the Aims of an Introduction

While accomplishing these four aims of an introduction, you may do a number of things:

1. Use an *illustration* of your thesis.
2. Use a very *descriptive example* of your thesis.
3. Use an *anecdote* that supports your thesis.
4. *Define* any *terms* that your audience is unlikely to be familiar with. Or, if you are using a familiar term in an unusual way, define it.
5. *Discuss* the *implications of a quotation* you began with.
6. Either *extend* or *discuss* the *significance of a metaphor or analogy* you began with.

These are but a few ideas of what you can do after you get your readers' attention. And to illustrate several of these ideas, suppose that your subject were nuclear stockpiling. You might begin with a vivid description of the horrifying effects of a nuclear blast. Or, suppose that I began an essay with this metaphorical statement: "A coherent essay is like a freight train." I could extend the metaphor and explain the significance of the comparison: "Every paragraph is connected to the one before and after it. Furthermore, the beginning and ending paragraphs of an essay are similar to the engine and caboose of a train. Like the engine of a freight train, the introduction of an essay makes it go, and like the caboose, the conclusion signals the end of it."

After you have read the professional and student examples in this chapter, you will have a much clearer idea of the many and varied ways there are to write interesting and satisfying introductions.

A Final Note about Introductions

In the past, you may have heard that you should always write your thesis at the end of your introductory paragraph. It is important for you to know that you certainly need not do so, and, in fact, you most certainly should not mechanically end every introduction you write with a thesis.

As you have seen in the professional writing you have read, some writers do not state a thesis explicitly anywhere in their essays. Furthermore, you have seen that if writers do state a thesis explicitly, it may come near the beginning, in the middle, or near the end of their essays. And even if a thesis comes near the end of an introduction, it may not come there in every essay a writer composes.

It is difficult to think of any statement that is *always true* about writing or the way writers compose. But if there were one at all, it might be this: To write by formula is to kill the life of your essay. An essay is a living organism to which you give birth. During its composition you follow its own genetic coding, allowing it to shape itself accordingly. To make it fit the Procrustean bed of formula is to make it what it was not meant to be. To cut off its legs or arms to make it conform to a preconceived shape is to cut off its life. No two children of the *same parents* have identical genetic coding or identical shapes. Neither will any two of your essays. Certainly, your essays will not have shapes identical to those other writers compose. Thus, rid yourself of the notion that introductions must end with a thesis. If you do anything, try hard *not* to put your thesis there.

One other point is that even though writers' attitudes towards their subjects do not change, their tones certainly can alter. For example, in her essay, Judith Viorst's attitude towards her subject is serious, although her tone is certainly light sometimes, especially in paragraph 13 when she pokes fun at herself for caring about her makeup. Also, you might consider E. B. White's letter to his wife, which is also serious and yet, in the sixth paragraph, his tone is humorous when he says that he and his wife can get by if he "pulls in his ears" and she "watches her artichokes." Despite the injunctions of Aristotle, who insisted on unity of genre, great writers have continually disobeyed him—William Shakespeare, for one, who consistently mixed the comic with the tragic. The point is this: you may find that a shift in tone helps you achieve your purpose. Furthermore, you will find that professional writers do it all the time for that very reason.

One last important fact: The introduction of an essay may consist of one, two, three, or more paragraphs. The following professional examples show not only varying lengths but also varying approaches.

Professional Examples

In this excerpt from her essay "God's Tooth," Annie Dillard begins by describing the event that prompted her writing.

1 Into this world falls a plane.
2 The earth is a mineral speckle planted in trees. The plane snagged its wing on a tree, fluttered in a tiny arc, and struggled down.
3 I heard it go. The cat looked up. There was no reason: the plane's engine simply stilled after takeoff, and the light plane failed to clear the firs. It fell easily; one wing snapped on a fir top; the metal fell down the air and smashed in the thin woods where cattle browse; the fuel exploded; and Julie Norwich seven years old burnt off her face.

4 Little Julie mute in some room at St. Joe's now, drugs dissolving into the sheets. Little Julie with her eyes naked and spherical, baffled. Can you scream without lips? Yes. But do children in long pain scream?

5 It is November 19 and no wind, and no hope of heaven, and no wish for heaven, since the meanest of people show more mercy than hounding and terrorist gods.

After this five-paragraph introduction, Dillard skips several extra spaces before continuing the next section of her essay. In this particular introduction, Dillard has indented her first sentence even more spaces than she does succeeding paragraphs. Thus, she gets the reader's attention several ways: Her first sentence is inverted, descriptive, and short. In addition it is written alone as a paragraph and indented farther than the second paragraph. By the end of this introduction, readers know both Dillard's focus and her tone, and they also have the information they need—knowledge of the occasion that prompted her essay. You might note further that Dillard gives you this information in a beautifully concrete description that keeps your attention as surely as the "glittering eye" of Coleridge's Ancient Mariner held the attention of the departing wedding guests.

Now here is another one you may remember, Judith Viorst's three-paragraph introduction to "Friends, Good Friends—And Such Good Friends," which ends with an explicitly stated thesis.

1 Women are friends, I once would have said, when they totally love and support and trust each other, and bare to each other the secrets of their souls, and run—no questions asked—to help each other, and tell harsh truths to each other (no, you can't wear that dress unless you lose ten pounds first) when harsh truths must be told.

2 Women are friends, I once would have said, when they share the same affection for Ingmar Bergman, plus train rides, cats, warm rain, charades, Camus, and hate with equal ardor Newark and Brussel sprouts and Lawrence Welk and camping.

3 In other words, I once would have said that a friend is a friend all the way, but now I believe that's a narrow point of view. For the friendships I have and the friendships I see are conducted at many levels of intensity, serve many different functions, meet different needs and range from those all-the-way as the friendship of the soul sisters mentioned above to that of the most nonchalant and casual playmates.

At the end of these paragraphs, the reader knows not only Ms. Viorst's focus and tone, but her thesis as well.

This last example comes from John Ciardi's essay entitled "Is Everybody Happy?" which is printed in the next chapter.

1 The right to pursue happiness is issued to Americans with their birth certificates, but no one seems quite sure which way it ran. It may be we are issued a hunting license but offered no game. Jonathan Swift seemed to think so when he attacked the idea of happiness as "the possession of being well-deceived," the felicity of being "a fool among knaves." For Swift saw society as Vanity Fair, the land of false goals.

2 It is, of course, un-American to think in terms of fools and knaves. We do, however, seem to be dedicated to the idea of buying our way to happiness. We shall all have made it to Heaven when we possess enough.

In his initial sentence Ciardi gets his readers' attention with his humorous personification of happiness, and he keeps it with the ensuing analogy and the quotation from Swift. At the end of the second paragraph, readers know his particular focus and his tone, an ironic blend of humor and seriousness.

Practice Revising Introductions

The following are Laura's and Gretta's original and revised introductions.

Laura's Original Introduction

It's difficult to change people. We all know that. But let me tell you how you can do it.

Laura's Revised Introduction

At 11:00 a.m. on November 15, 1968, I married my husband.

By 11:00 p.m. I knew that I had not found the perfect mate. I suspected it that evening when our best man showed up at the kitchen door with a six-pack and a toothpick-eating grin. I knew it when they dealt the cards. It was then that I learned that five card stud had nothing to do with sex, that Walt Disney had lied, and that the perfect husband was a fantasy. But it became my favorite fantasy and now, fifteen years later, I can tell you exactly how to mold yourself a mate to fit your fantasy.

Gretta's Original Introduction

Every spring when the snow begins to melt and form little streams dripping down the mountains and the sun bites into the cool nip in the air, Laceyville, Pennsylvania, holds its annual fish float. The float itself is a bit of a curiosity, because while it isn't recognized by the town as an "official event" involving the closing of businesses, the heads of those businesses seem to look the other way when no one shows up for work. Old and young men and some women all flock to the Susquehanna River with boats, poles, beer and bait in search of those elusive fish. I too manage to find myself up on that river in the cool nip when the streams drip down the mountains, having dropped everything I was doing to join the search for the fish. Normally I don't allow myself these deviations from the norm, but I'm always compelled to return to that river.

Gretta's Revised Introduction

There is something about a lazy, racing river that is both attractive and terrifying. Staring up at me as I glance along the water is a reflection, my reflection; my image blending in perfectly with nature. But if I look too intently, the image is gone, leaving behind the tossing pebbles and white foam of a swift current rushing downstream. I've always wanted to be close to nature, to blend in, but more and more often it seems that pavement and shelter form an insurmountable wall between the two of us. Should I walk barefoot through the woods, stickers prick my feet, thorns slice through my flesh, and I bleed. It has been too long since I roamed barefoot along the riverbank, and now a boat must separate us. But that's okay, because the distance is not so great, and there's a new joy to be found in lazily floating along and dangling a line in the water.

I guess I don't really fish to catch anything; I fish to be close to the river. Cares seem to drift away as I lean against the side of the boat, while the sun sinks past the skin, past the muscle, past the bone, into the very marrow. Warm all over. Nowhere do I find that warmth more comforting than in Laceyville, Pennsylvania, when the snow begins to melt, forming crystal streams that drip slowly down the mountains. Amid all this moisture that is spring, the town holds its annual fish float along the Susquehanna River. Neglecting their responsibilities, the people come with boats, poles, beer and bait to search out the elusive fish. I come too, dropping all obligations, to float down the river.

Both Laura and Gretta improved their introductions when they revised. Although Gretta's original introduction was effectively concrete and descriptive, she has lengthened her revision to two paragraphs that are also very effective and that allow her more space to describe and clarify her focus. In her revision Laura tried writing her first sentence alone, an effective device for getting the reader's attention, as you saw in Dillard's writing. In her second paragraph she has given her readers the information they need to know her focus.

As you have seen, introductions perform four important functions in your essays. Sometimes they are difficult to write, but for beginning writers, conclusions can often present an even more difficult problem.

Writing Conclusions

Perhaps during the course of this semester you have edited an essay that just stopped. You were left hanging and leafing through sheets of paper, looking for the conclusion. Had you or the writer gotten the pages out of order? No. Then, there you were, left dangling in mid-air, so to speak. No ground beneath you, no conclusion. Unlike a cartoon, your essay has no Porky Pig to announce to your readers: "Well, th–th–th–that's all, folks."

But, indeed, that message is precisely what a writer must convey in such a way that readers feel that the author's point has been effectively made and supported. Readers must feel that all has been said that needs to be. If you have had trouble writing conclusions, the following list of ideas should help you compose more effective final paragraphs for your essays.

Ways to Conclude an Essay

1. Give a last, good example that supports your thesis.
2. State your thesis.
3. Predict the future as a result of your thesis.
4. State one or more implications of your thesis.
5. State one or more consequences of your thesis.
6. Demand action (particularly useful in a persuasive essay).
7. Ask a thought-provoking question pertinent to your thesis.
8. Refer to something you wrote earlier in your essay.
9. Use a quotation pertinent to your thesis.

Often writers use these methods in combination—for example, by stating the thesis with one last strong illustration of it, or by using a quotation together with a prediction. Of course, referring to something you have said earlier in your essay, especially something in your introduction, gives a nice sense of the whole, the completion of a circle.

To illustrate, again suppose that you wrote an essay on nuclear stockpiling that began with a very descriptive example of the effects of a nuclear blast. In your conclusion you could refer to this example, perhaps by asking a question. In addition, you could call for action and write yet another vivid description of nuclear devastation.

Finally, like introductions, conclusions may consist of more than one paragraph, as you will see in the conclusions written by Dillard, Viorst, and Ciardi.

Professional Examples

Even though you may have some trouble understanding the following conclusion to Dillard's essay, you should have no trouble seeing that she has used a combination of several of the ideas for writing conclusions that you were given earlier.

33 And now outside the window, deep on the horizon, a new thing appears, as if we needed a new thing. It is a new land blue beyond islands, hitherto hidden by haze and now revealed, and as dumb as the rest. I check my chart, my amateur penciled sketch of the skyline. Yes, this land is new, this spread blue spark beyond yesterday's new wrinkled line, beyond the blue veil a sailor said was Salt Spring Island. How long can this go on? But let us by all means extend the scope of our charts.

34 I draw it as I seem to see it, a blue chunk fitted just so beyond islands, a wag of graphite rising just here above another anonymous line, and here meeting the slope of Salt Spring: though whether this be headland I see or heartland, or the distance—blurred bluffs of a hundred bays, I have no way of knowing, or if it be island or main. I call it Thule, O Julialand, Time's Bad News; I name it Terror, the Farthest Limb of the Day, God's Tooth.

Because you do not have her text before you, you cannot tell that Dillard has separated her two concluding paragraphs from the previous section of her essay with extra spacing, just as she did her introduction. In this two-paragraph conclusion, Dillard states part of her thesis in the last sentence of paragraph 33, and in paragraph 34 she also states part of her point: she has no way of knowing the answers to unfathomable mysteries but she will extend the scope of her charts. And what she has no way of knowing, she envisions as a blurred island or part of the main, to which she gives names that refer to the inexplicable tragedy she has written about.

Now, the following is Judith Viorst's conclusion, which, like Dillard's, consists of two paragraphs.

30 The best of friends, I still believe, totally love and support and trust each other, and bare to each other the secrets of their souls, and run—no questions asked—to help each other, and tell harsh truths to each other when they must be told.

31 But we needn't agree about everything (only 12-year-old girl friends agree about *everything*) to tolerate each other's point of

view. To accept without judgment. To give and to take without ever keeping score. And to *be* there, as I am for them and as they are for me, to comfort our sorrows, to celebrate our joys.

Here Viorst refers to what she said in her first two paragraphs concerning her original idea of friendships between women. Thus, her circular conclusion gives a nice sense of completion.

Last, here is Ciardi's conclusion, also two paragraphs, although it would be possible, perhaps, to consider his final paragraph alone his conclusion.

14 Happiness is never more than partial. There are no pure states of mankind. Whatever else happiness may be, it is neither in having nor in being, but in becoming. What the Founding Fathers declared for us as an inherent right, we should do well to remember, was not happiness but the *pursuit* of happiness. What they might have underlined, could they have foreseen the happiness-market, is the cardinal fact that happiness is in the pursuit itself, in the meaningful pursuit of what is life-engaging and life-revealing, which is to say, in the idea of *becoming*. A nation is not measured by what it possesses or wants to possess, but by what it wants to become.

15 By all means let the happiness-market sell us minor satisfactions and even mirror follies so long as we keep them in scale and buy them out of spiritual change. I am no customer for either puritanism or asceticism. But drop any real spiritual capital at those bazaars, and what you come home to will be your own poorhouse.

In paragraph 14 of this conclusion, Ciardi states his thesis that happiness is the pursuit of what is "life-engaging and life-revealing." And in his last paragraph, Ciardi ends with a prediction of the rather dire consequences should his readers refuse to accept his idea that true happiness is not to be bought. He predicts that those who continue to think that it can will find themselves spiritually bankrupt.

Even though all three of these conclusions written by professional writers consisted of two paragraphs, you should not get the idea that all conclusions must have two paragraphs. These writers' works were chosen for various reasons, and it was merely coincidental that all had two-paragraph conclusions. Also, as I pointed out previously, you could certainly consider Ciardi's final paragraph alone his conclusion.

As you can now see, Laura and Gretta, who successfully revised their introductions, were equally successful when they tackled their conclusions.

Practice Revising Conclusions

Laura's Original Conclusion

Thus you can see that with patience and perseverance, you too can have your ideal mate.

Laura's Revised Conclusion

My fantasy man sustained me through some very trying times in my marriage. In the deepest despair, I sometimes saw his image reflected in soap bubbles at the sink or staring back at me from water rings on the coffee table. Now, of course, I see him in my husband's face. Is this possible? Yes. And if you have perseverance and patience, you too can be married to your fantasy.

Laura's one-sentence prediction based on her thesis ends her essay. Also, her revision is more satisfying now because she has referred to statements made earlier in her essay.

Gretta's Original Conclusion

As we cast our lines, I just sit back, quit fighting, and allow myself to drift downstream where eventually, we all end up.

Gretta's Revised Conclusion

As we cast our lines out into the water, the sun reflects off the liquid droplets that cling to it, making wonderful spider-webs of brilliant colors. Watching the shimmering droplets slip slowly down the line and disappear mysteriously into the river, I realize that I'll always come to fish. It's hereditary. When I'm fishing, a mean, desperate old man fishes with me; his face reminds me that unfortunately, there's something about love that goes beyond the bad that a person does. Fishing also reminds me that while I'll always be separate from the water, the mountains, and the sky, at least I can come as close to being one with everything as the distance between the boat and my body allows. Then I can just sit back, toss out a line, and quit fighting, allowing myself to drift downstream where eventually, we all end up.

Like Laura's original paragraph, Gretta's original conclusion is also satisfying. However, also like Laura's, her revision is much better. In her revision Gretta refers to something she mentioned earlier in her essay, her grandfather ("a mean, desperate old man"), the person who first took her fishing on the river. Also, she has added more descriptive details, while retaining the statement that ended her original conclusion, a kind of metaphor that simultaneously makes her point and predicts the future for all of us.

To both students one can only exclaim "Bravo!"

Sara's Final Draft

In her final draft Sara has added some examples where she needed them in her first paragraph, and she has also improved her first sentence. In addition, she has added some material to her very nice conclusion. Last, you will note that Sara has a new title, which caused her a great deal of trouble. Some of the titles she thought of were "Alice in Wonderland: or Why Worry?" "In Wonderland with Aunt Alice: Or Why Worry?" and "The Confessions of a Chronic Worrier." Finally, she decided to combine the last two and admitted that she did not really like this title either. If it were your essay, what would you call it?

In Wonderland with Aunt Alice:
Or The Confessions of a Chronic Worrier

1 Some people have it and some people don't: that knack for getting through their lives, day to day, or at whatever adopted pace, with never a worry, care, or troubled moment. Not me. I'm one of the have-nots, in this case. I worry habitually about whatever is available for worry—grades, health, money, houseplants, full-scale nuclear war. The scope of availability is endless; it ranges from the sublime to the ridiculous. And it's a senseless, perpetual, losing battle: I worry, so I smoke cigarettes, then I worry that I'll contract emphysema or lung cancer and die a long and lingering death. Cancer, emphysema—one's as fatal as the other—nothing to worry about there.

2 My boyfriend, who has not worried a single moment in the four years I've known him, chides me endlessly for my worries. He tells me that I'm pathological, that I'll go crazy, develop ulcers, or die young if I don't change my ways. It's only his joking concern, but of course, it simply makes my situation worse. It maddens me, drives me to the limits of my patience, his brazen air of insouciance in the face of all this potential material for worry. But he is a classic nonworrier: he sleeps soundly every night, spends money without agonizing over bills and debts, goes to work and leaves it behind at the end of the day. On the other hand, I am the quintessential worrier, with all the telltale signs: the chewed fingernails, the frazzled morning looks and bloodshot eyes from sleepless nights, the bromides in the medicine chest. It's a minor miracle we've survived together.

3 Those who do not worry cannot fathom the workings of a worried mind. They find no rationale in the grievous morn-

ings (the worst time for hardened worriers) when one jars bolt upright out of a hindered sleep. But the fears and night demons are there, real or not. The phobias are no less trouble-some, being contrived. I think I can sympathize with Joan Di-dion and her migraines, particularly in regard to the unsym-pathetic nonsuffers. All the "don't worry about its" in the world do nothing to abate the chronic worrier's causes any more than the off-hand prescription of a couple of aspirin can do to cure a migraine. Nonsuffers of both ills just don't know, having nothing to gauge the pain by. When all is said and done, however, I don't particularly envy the nonworrier. I know, intrinsically, that I am far more sensitive, somehow more worthy than he is. I pay my dues every day, while I like to think that, in the end, his will be extracted in one lump sum for all his carelessness. (No one says worriers have to be completely unvengeful souls.)

4 They say it dissipates with age, this malaise of the overcon-cerned. In a way I hope not. What do you do with your time, free from worry, after years of self-indulgence in the habit? My mother, a chronic worrier for fifty years, grey well before thirty, with fingernails bitten always to the quick, decided one day, out of the blue, to give it up. She stopped worrying, grew the nails of a ring model, and painted them red. The sight of the sun rising out of the western sky could not have surprised me more than did this vision of my mother sporting those ele-gantly tapered and lacquered fingernails. The red, I suppose, was her flag of freedom, a sign of victory over worry, but in my eyes, she somehow lost a lot of character in that gesture. I began to worry about her state of mind, having nothing better to do, it seemed, than file and paint her nails. Worrying seemed to me less a waste of time.

5 My great aunt Alice, on the other hand (on whom, in her twilight years, we were heartless, or perhaps just plain exas-perated, enough to pin the disrespectful moniker "Alice in Wonderland"), went to the grave a veteran worrier at ninety-two. When, for all intent and purposes, Alice had nothing in the world left to worry about, she felt compelled to invent for herself new trauma. And create it she did, with the flair that only a mind burdened by too many years of too much worry can do. She worried about places, persons, events that, except in her mind, had ceased to exist: her home, her family, and oddly enough, the Civil War (or the War of Northern Agres-sion, as she preferred to call it). On warm days towards win-ter's end, she worried that her house (long since abandoned and then razed for the planting of pulpwood timbers) needed its annual spring cleaning. She worried every evening, with-out fail, about Papa (dead for forty years) and what he was

having for supper. And, much to the dismay of us all, she was given to occasional agonized speculations as to whether or not General Sherman was apt to make another blazing march through the hallowed South. These harried ruminations, and more, plagued her till her dying day.

6 While I doubt that I'll ever give up worrying completely, I hope I'll never carry it to the extremes my illustrious aunt did. Alice was, after all, a bit of an eccentric, and hers was a bizarre case in point. (It was, I might add, only after Alice left us that my mother grew her nails long.) I haven't quite decided what I'll do with my habit. I think I'd be at a loss without it. What to do with all that time and unchannelled energy? Maybe when I retire from social work, I'll offer a community minicourse in Creative Worrying, assured that aunt Alice is somewhere in Wonderland, smiling—and worrying.

Conclusion

Of the three student essays in this chapter, which had the most significant thesis? The most developed thesis? The most developed paragraphs? Which writer wrote the best introduction? The best conclusion? Be sure to give the reasons for your answer to each question.

If you enjoyed writing the kind of essay you wrote in this chapter, you should enjoy even more the kind you will write in the last chapter. Like the professional writers you will read in the next chapter, you will be allowed to do what we all love to do— vent our criticisms of the world we live in.

Proofreading Tip: The Run-On Sentence

Unlike the comma fault, which may be acceptable in certain constructions, the run-on sentence, one with no punctuation between two or more complete thoughts, is not acceptable except when an author is attempting to duplicate stream of consciousness, such as James Joyce does in his novel *Ulysses* or William Faulkner in his novel *The Sound and the Fury*.

However, your essays do not duplicate stream of consciousness since they represent ordered thought, and the run-on only causes confusion and misreading. For example, consider this sentence:

> I was really snowed under exams came at a really bad time for me.

Did you misread this the first time? This is an example of the confusion that can result from a run-on sentence.

When the two sentences are separated with an appropriate punctuation mark, the reader is not confused.

I was really snowed under; exams came at a really bad time for me.
I was really snowed under. Exams came at a really bad time for me.

As you may remember, the colon is also used to separate complete sentences; however, it is commonly used between two sentences when the second is a result or an effect of the first, when the second restates or interprets the first, or when the second is in apposition to a word in the first. In this pair of sentences, none of these relationships exists; thus, the colon is not a good choice.

Here's one further example:

The truth was difficult to accept I had lost my best friend.

Can this run-on be corrected using each one of three marks—the period, the semicolon, and the colon?

The truth was difficult to accept. I had lost my best friend.
The truth was difficult to accept; I had lost my best friend.
The truth was difficult to accept: I had lost my best friend.

Evidently, all three marks work, but which do you prefer? Most likely, you and your classmates prefer the colon because the second sentence is in apposition to the noun *truth* in the first sentence. That is, the second sentence renames or identifies the noun *truth*.

To recapitulate the differences among these marks:

1. Use the period between sentences if they express unrelated ideas.
2. Use the semicolon if they express related ideas.
3. Use the colon if the second sentence is an effect or a result of the first sentence, if the second is in apposition to a noun in the first sentence, or if the second restates or interprets the first sentence.

Exercise: Recognizing and Correcting the Run-on Sentence

Now read the following sentences, and if there are any run-on sentences, correct them in the space provided, using an appropriate punctuation mark between the sentences.

1. I couldn't believe it I had three final exams scheduled on the same day.

2. When Linda came home from work, her husband had already prepared their dinner.

3. In the middle of the night I awoke there was a strange sound coming from the kitchen.

4. Jake detested contact sports he disliked football most of all.

5. After studying awhile you should take a break studying too long at a time reduces your concentration.

6. Because it was late, Susan quit reading although she found it difficult to put the novel down.

7. After picking strawberries, the boys made a pie that they topped with whipped cream.

8. Driving home was no fun the trip was long, hot, and boring.

9. Since it was raining, Glenda couldn't play tennis.

10. Learning to play tennis is hard it's harder than learning to play racquetball.

When you proofread your final draft, look especially for run-on sentences, but don't forget the previous proofreading tips on the comma fault, the unintentional fragment, the dangling modifier, and the semicolon.

Suggestions for Further Writing

1. Like Joan Didion, we all have images of people or places that "shimmer around the edges" and that remain in our minds oftentimes for reasons we are not aware of, that is, unless or until we write about them. Let your mind go now until you have a picture that has recurred for reasons you are unaware of. Write a descriptive narrative of the particular occasion that resulted in this image, and afterwards try to write why this particular image is one that has remained in your mind. For example, when I did this assignment with my students, I wrote about a particular image I got whenever I thought of my days as a student at the University of Texas. It was of a specific day in my composition class, and I never knew *why* this particular image always occurred to me until I wrote about it. If you like, you may use this assignment as a journal entry headed "A Recurring Image" or something similar and more specific that you think of yourself.

2. Choose any one of your previous essays and revise the introduction and conclusion.

3. Write about an activity you enjoy in the outdoors—fishing, hiking, boating, whatever. Use good, concrete description so that your reader gets clear images of your experience. You should limit your writing to one particular occasion that you remember vividly.

4. Write about a person close to you towards whom you have ambivalent feelings.

5. Write a letter to any writer you admire. It can be someone you have read in this text or elsewhere. Like Susan's, your letter may be to a writer no longer living.

6. Write a letter to any one of the three student writers in this chapter—Sara, Susan, or Gretta. You may write a response to a particular statement or statements or to her entire essay. Or you might write to ask questions or to give advice.

7. Write a response to this question: Which student essay— Sara's, Susan's, or Gretta's—did you prefer? Why? Be specific about the writer's composition skills, commenting on such accomplishments as development, concreteness, coherence, and sentence structure.

8. Assume that you are Katharine White. Write a letter to your husband in response to his.

9. Write a letter to D. H. Lawrence telling him what you liked or disliked about his essay and why. If you prefer, you may write both what you liked and disliked and why.

10. You are going on a two-week cruise, and you must take one of these writers with you—Joan Didion, E. B. White, William Stafford, or D. H. Lawrence. Whom would you choose and why? Write your response, giving as many reasons as you can think of. Option: Whom wouldn't you take, and why?

11. List ideas to fill in the blank in this heading: "Why _____ Doesn't Matter." Choose one of your ideas and write a first draft.

12. Of the professional writers you have read thus far in this text, which one do you admire most? Why? Consider voice, style, and development of ideas. Write a first draft of your analysis.

13. Write a first draft on the following topic: "A Way of Enjoying Myself."

14. Fill in the blank and write a first draft on the following topic: "Why I Admire _____."

15. Write a letter to someone who disapproved of a particular action you took or a decision you made in the past. Explain your action or the reasons for your decision as convincingly and persuasively as you can.

Reading
and Writing
Persuasion

CHAPTER

The Critical "I": Reading about What's Wrong with Our World

13

ubi saeva indignatio ulterius cor lacerare nequit.
> Jonathan Swift's epitaph (1667–1745)

Translated, Swift's epitaph reads: "Where savage indignation can lacerate (tear) his heart no more." This inscription marks Jonathan Swift's tombstone on the floor of St. Patrick's Cathedral in Dublin, Ireland. Probably more than any other writer in the history of English literature, Swift devoted the energies of his mind and pen to the elucidation of the faults he found in mankind—us Yahoos.*

In American literature there have been many writers who have criticized American institutions and values—Samuel Clemens, the nineteenth-century author of *Huckleberry Finn*; Woody Allen, contemporary filmmaker and essayist; Joan Didion, journalist and novelist; and Ellen Goodman, newspaper columnist, to name but a few.

Although Swift, Clemens, and Allen use satire, a special kind of literature that blends humor with criticism, writers need not be satirists in order to illuminate the faults they see in people or in their social customs and institutions. As a matter of fact, probably you and others you know engage almost daily in conversations that concern social criticism of one kind or another. Because we are imperfect, despite our rationality, we continue not only to exhibit irrational, "Yahoo" behavior, but to found "Yahoo" institutions as well. What is more irrational than men at war, killing each other for no other reason than that their governments told them to do so? As nineteenth-century British poet and

---

* As you may know, Yahoos are the disgusting, irrational creatures who are representatives of humanity in Swift's *Gulliver's Travels*.

novelist Thomas Hardy wrote in his satirical poem entitled, "The Man He Killed,"

> Yes; quaint and curious war is!
> You shoot a fellow down
> You'd treat if met where any bar is,
> Or help to half-a-crown.
>
> (11.17–20)

And speaking of Yahoo institutions, Swift would no doubt be appalled at our obsession with drive-throughs, from fast-food places to funeral homes. Unfortunately, there is ample material in our world to excite any writer's "savage indignation."

In this chapter, for example, four professional writers use their pens to criticize certain aspects of our society. First, Amitai Etzioni, a professor of sociology at George Washington University and author of several books on war and its effects, presents his views on individual rights versus the common good. Next, Neil Postman, a professor at New York University who has written a great deal about language and educational theory, presents his criticism of television. More lighthearted, Lewis Thomas, noted medical researcher and acclaimed essayist, criticizes "operant conditioning" in his own inimitable style. Last, in his essay, poet John Ciardi criticizes our commercialistic society for the notion that we can buy happiness. These four writers have distinctly different voices and styles, but they all have one thing in common: "savage (or not so savage) indignation" aroused by our society's attitudes, values, or institutions.

AMITAI ETZIONI

When Rights Collide

1 The viewpoint, now gaining momentum, that would allow individuals to "make up their own minds" about smoking, air bags, safety helmets, Laetrile, and the like ignores some elementary social realities. The ill-informed nature of this viewpoint is camouflaged by the appeal to values that are dear to most Americans. The essence of the argument is that what individuals wish to do with their lives and limbs, foolhardy though it might be, is their own business, and that any interference would abridge their rights.

2 Mr. Gene Wirwahn, the legislative director of the American Motorcyclist Association, which is lobbying against laws requiring riders to wear helmets, put it squarely: "The issue that we're speaking about is not the voluntary use of helmets. It's the question of whether or not there should be laws telling people to wear them." State representative Anne Miller, a liberal Democrat in Illinois, favors legalization of Laetrile. She explains that she is aware that this apricot-pit extract is useless, but insists that "the

government shouldn't protect people from bad judgment. They might as well bar holy water."

3 U.S. representative Louis Wyman recently invoked much the same argument in leading the brigade that won adoption in the House of a resolution making seat belts voluntary. The 1974-model cars had been engineered not to start unless the seat belt was buckled. Wyman, a New Hampshire Republican, called the buckle-up system un-American, saying it made the government a Big Brother to auto drivers. Representative Abraham Kazen, Texas Democrat, summed it all up: "It is wrong to tell the individual what is good for him. . . . These are some of the things that the American people want to judge for themselves. Give them the equipment if they so desire, *and if they do not, let them do whatever they want.*"

4 No civil society can survive if it permits each person to maximize his or her freedoms without concern for the consequences of one's act on others. If I choose to drive without a seat belt or air bag, I am greatly increasing my chances, in case of accident, of being impaled on the steering wheel or exiting via the windshield. It is not just my body that is jeopardized; my careening auto, which I cannot get back under control, will be more likely to injure people in other autos, pedestrians, or riders in my car. (Yes, my passengers choose their own fate when they decide to ride with me, but what about the infants who are killed and injured because they are not properly protected?)

5 American institutions were fashioned in an era of vast unoccupied spaces and preindustrial technology. In those days, collisions between public needs and individual rights may have been minimal. But increased density, scarcity of resources, and interlocking technologies have now heightened the concern for "public goods," which belong to no one in particular but to all of us jointly. Polluting a lake or river or the air may not directly damage any one person's private property or living space. But it destroys a good that all of us—including future generations—benefit from and have a title to. Our public goods are entitled to a measure of protection.

6 The individual who chooses to act irresponsibly is playing a game of heads I win, tails the public loses. All too often, the unbelted drivers, the smokers, the unvaccinated, the users of quack remedies draw on public funds to pay for the consequences of their unrestrained freedom of choice. Their rugged individualism rapidly becomes dependency when cancer strikes, or when the car overturns, sending the occupants to hospitals for treatment paid for at least in part by the public, through subsidies for hospitals and medical training. But the public till is not bottomless, and paying for these irresponsible acts leaves other public needs without funds.

7 True, totalitarian regimes often defend their invasions of individual liberties by citing public need or "national interest." One difference is that they are less concerned with protecting public goods than they are with building national power or new world orders. Instead of insisting on protection for *some* public rights, such regimes seek to put the national interest above all individual rights. The lesson is that we must not allow any claim of public or national need to go unexplained. But at the same time, we cannot allow simpleminded sloganeering (from "creeping Communism" to "Big Brother") to blind us to the fact that there are needs all of us share as a community.

8 Last but not least, we must face the truth about ourselves. Are we the independent, self-reliant individuals the politicians like to tell us we are? Or are we a human combination of urges and self-controls, impulses and rational judgments? Can we trust ourselves to make wise judgments routinely, or do we at times have to rely on the laws our elected representatives have fashioned, with our consent, to help guide us? The fact is that driving slowly saves lives, lots of lives; but until we are *required* to do so, most of us drive too fast. The same holds true for buckling our seat belts, buying air bags, and so on. Similarly, we need protection from quack cures. It sounds very libertarian to argue that each person can make up his or her own mind about Laetrile. But the fact is that when confronted with cancer and fearful of surgery, thousands of Americans are tempted to try a "painless medication" first, often delaying surgery until it is too late.

9 All in all, it is high time the oversimplifications about individual freedom versus Big Brother government were replaced by a social philosophy that calls for a balance among the rights of *various* individuals, between individual rights and *some* public rights, and that acknowledges the support we fallible individuals need from the law.

Ideas and Meaning

1. What is Etzioni criticizing?
2. In paragraphs 2 and 3, why does he quote the remarks of his opponents?
3. How does failure to "buckle up" invade the rights of others?
4. How do "unbelted drivers, smokers, the unvaccinated, and the users of quack remedies" cost the public money? Do you agree that these people are "irresponsible"? Explain.
5. How does Etzioni answer the charge that laws such as those he recommends are suggestive of totalitarian regimes?
6. What is the point Etzioni makes in paragraph 8? Do you agree or disagree? Explain.
7. Has your state passed a seat-belt law? If so, how do you

feel about it? Has your state repealed a seat-belt law? If so, how do you feel about the repeal? If your state does not have a seat-belt law, would you like one? Why? Why not?

8. With what point does Etzioni conclude his essay? Is this point convincing? Why? Why not? Is this his strongest point? If not, where does he state his strongest point?

9. Do you believe that useless drugs like Laetrile should be legalized because "the government shouldn't protect the people from bad judgment"? Explain your answer.

10. In paragraph 5, Etzioni contrasts the America we live in now with the one that existed when our Constitution was framed. Why does he do this? What is his point?

11. Are there any laws that you feel are invasions of a person's individual rights? If so, explain why you feel as you do.

12. Are you for or against the federal government's testing its employees for drug use? Explain your answer. Do you think private industry has the right to use such tests on its employees? Explain.

13. If you were face to face with Etzioni, what questions would you ask him?

Development and Style

1. How does Etzioni get the reader's attention? How could he improve his beginning sentence?

2. How many paragraphs comprise his introduction? Is his introduction effective? Why? Why not?

3. What is his tone?

4. What is his thesis? Does he state it explicitly? If so, where? Is the arrangement of his essay inductive, deductive, or both?

5. How does Etzioni support his thesis? Is his support adequate? Why? Why not? If not, what additional support would you suggest?

6. Which paragraph in the essay does not clearly support Etzioni's thesis? What is the point of this paragraph? Could he shift this paragraph somewhere else in the essay with better results? Explain.

7. Point out several words and phrases with negative connotations. In their contexts, how do these negative connotations help Etzioni achieve his purpose?

8. Where in his essay does Etzioni need stronger transitions? Suggest transitions that you would use. [Hint: one weak transition occurs between two sentences in paragraph 2.]

9. What is the transition in the first sentence of paragraph 4 that connects it with paragraph 3? How could you make the transition between the two paragraphs stronger? Between which paragraphs does Etzioni have strong transitions?

10. Where does Etzioni use italics for emphasis? Do you agree
    that such emphasis is necessary in these statements? Ex-
    plain.
11. Analyze Etzioni's means of development in paragraphs 6,
    7, and 8. Are there any paragraphs in the essay that need
    further development? If so, what would you suggest?
12. Analyze sentence beginnings and lengths in paragraph 8.
    Are there any sentences that you would rearrange? If so,
    how would you reconstruct them? Compare your revision
    with Etzioni's. Which is more effective? Why?
13. What means of conclusion does Etzioni use? Is his conclu-
    sion effective? Why? Why not? If not, how would you im-
    prove it?
14. From his writer's voice, how do you picture Etzioni? Is his
    voice similar to that of any other professional writer in this
    text? If so, who, and how are the styles alike?
15. Of the professional writers in this text, whose style con-
    trasts most with Etzioni's? Which style do you prefer? Why?

Mike's Two Responses

Reading Journal: "When Rights Collide" First Response

Etzioni sees the tip of the iceberg in this essay but misses
the bulk that lies under the waterline. The concluding paragraph is the basic definition of government or who gets what,
when, and where. He should have expanded his essay on this
definition because the bottom line has always been individual
versus public rights. Another shortcoming is that the Constitution and the Bill of Rights are never mentioned. How can individual rights be discussed without citing these documents
when the essay deals with governmental regulations over personal liberties? How can Etzioni imply that an individual is
violating another person's rights by not wearing a motorcycle
helmet or by taking Laetrile? I fail to see the connection. The
public is already controlled by too much government interference now. I agree with Ronald Reagan on his philosophy regarding keeping the federal government out of the public's
business. After all, the Constitution was written from the
point of view of limiting government and only legislating and
regulating public affairs with the powers granted to government by the people.

Second Response

The people of the state of North Carolina were blackmailed
by the federal government into a mandatory seat-belt law. In
order to satisfy the special-interest groups in Detroit, the fed-

eral government has threatened to cut off federal highway funds to states who do not pass seat-belt laws. These laws relieve the automobile industry of its commitment to develop the air-bag system by 1987. The federal government missed the mark by limiting the public's freedom of choice. Instead of repealing the requirement for air bags, our Big Brother eliminated choice regarding the wearing of a seat belt. It is much easier to restrict individual freedom rather than to have to tackle the well-organized auto industry or consumer-protection advocates. The federal government was in a no-win situation, so it stepped on the public, again. Freedom of choice could have been spared if the auto industry, the consumer advocates, and the federal government had truly considered the public good when deciding the seat-belt issue. Seat belts are standard equipment that let you exercise your option of whether or not to use them. Why couldn't air bags have been an option on automobiles?

Now, on an entirely different subject, Neil Postman offers a very perceptive, if somewhat gloomy, analysis of the devastating effects of television on our society.

NEIL POSTMAN

The Day Our Children Disappear

1 I am aware that in addressing the question of the future of education, one can write either a "good news" or a "bad news" essay. Typically, a good news essay presents readers with a problem, then proceeds to solve it (more or less). Readers usually find such essays agreeable, as well they should. A good news essay gives us a sense of potency and control, and a really *good* "good news" essay shows us how to employ our imaginations in confronting professional issues. Although I have not yet seen the other essays in this special *Kappan*, I feel sure that most of them are of the good news type, solid and constructive.

2 A bad news essay, on the other hand, presents readers with a problem—and ends (more or less). Naturally, readers find such essays disagreeable, since they engender a sense of confusion and sometimes hopelessness. Still, they have their uses. They may, for example, help us understand some things that need explaining. Let me tell you, then, that while I hope my remarks will be illuminating, you must prepare yourself for an orthodox—even classical—bad news essay. I wish it could be otherwise, because I know my temperament to be more suited to optimism than to gloom and doom. But I write as a person whose academic interests go by the name of media ecology. Media ecology is the study

of the effects of communications technology on culture. We study how media affect people's cognitive habits, their social relations, their political biases, and their personal values. And in this capacity I have almost nothing optimistic to write about, for, if I am to respect the evidence as I understand it, I am bound to say that the effects of modern media—especially television—have been and will probably continue to be disastrous, especially for our youth. What I intend to do here is describe in some detail one important respect in which this is the case and explain how it occurred. As is the custom in bad news essays, I shall offer no solution to this problem—mainly because I know of none.

3 Before proceeding, I must express one bit of "good news" about what I shall be saying. It is to be understood that when I speak of some development as "disastrous," I mean that it is disastrous from my very limited point of view. Obviously, what appears disastrous to me may be regarded as marvelous by others. After all, I am a New Yorker, and most things appear to me disastrous. But even more to the point, what may appear disastrous at one historical moment may turn out to be marvelous in a later age. There are, in fact, many historical instances of someone's correctly predicting negative effects of a medium of communication but where, in the end, what appeared to be a disaster turned out to be a great advance.

4 The best example I know of concerns the great Athenian teacher, Socrates, who feared and mocked the written word, which in his time was beginning to be used for many purposes and with great frequency. But not by him. As you know, Socrates wrote no books, and had it not been for Plato and Xenophon, who did, we would know almost nothing about him. In one of his most enduring conversations, called the *Phaedrus*, Socrates gives three reasons why he does not like writing. Writing, he says, will deprive Athenians of their powerful memories, for if everything is written down there will be no need to memorize. Second, he says that writing will change the form of education. In particular, it will destroy the dialectic process, for writing forces students to follow an argument rather than participate in it. And third, Socrates warns that writing will change concepts of privacy and the meaning of public discourse, for once you write something down you never know whose eyes will fall upon it—those for whom it is intended, perhaps, but just as likely those for whom it is not intended. Thus, for Socrates, the widespread use of writing was, and would be, a cultural disaster. In a sense it was. For all of Socrates' predictions were correct, and there is no doubt that writing undermined the oral tradition that Socrates believed to be the most suitable mode for expressing serious ideas, beautiful poetry, and authentic piety. But Socrates did not see what his student, Plato, did: that writing would create new modes of thought altogether and provide new

and wonderful uses for the intellect—most especially what today we call *science*.

5   So without intending to suggest an unsupportable comparison, I write as a Socrates-like character, prophesying that the advent of the television age will have the direst outcome. I hope that among you there is a Plato-like character who will be able to see the television age as a blessing.

6   In order for me to get to the center of my argument as quickly as possible, I am going to resist the temptation to discuss some of the fairly obvious effects of television, such as its role in shortening our students' attention span, in eroding their capacity to handle linguistic and mathematical symbolism, and in causing them to become increasingly impatient with deferred gratification. The evidence for these effects exists in a variety of forms— from declining SAT scores to astronomical budgets for remedial writing classes to the everyday observations of teachers and parents. But I will not take the time to review any of the evidence for the intellectually incapacitating effects of television. Instead, I want to focus on what I regard as the most astonishing and serious effect of television. It is simply this: Television is causing the rapid decline of our concept of childhood. I choose to discuss this because I can think of nothing that is bound to have a more profound effect on our work as educators than that our children should disappear. I do not mean, of course, that they will physically disappear. I mean that the *idea* of children will disappear.

7   If this pronouncement, on first hearing, seems implausible, let me hasten to tell you that the idea of childhood is not very old. In fact, in the Western world the idea of childhood hardly existed prior to the 16th century. Up until that time children as young as 6 and 7 were not regarded as fundamentally different from adults. As far as historians can tell, the language of children, their dress, their games, their labor, and their legal rights were the same as those of adults. It was recognized, of course, that children tended to be smaller than adults, but this fact did not confer upon them any special status; there were certainly no special institutions for the nurturing of children. Prior to the 16th century, for example, there were no books on child rearing or, indeed, any books about women in their role as mothers. Children, to take another example, were always included in funeral processions, there being no reason anyone could think of to shield them from knowledge of death. Neither did it occur to anyone to keep a picture of a child if that child lived to grow to adulthood or had died in infancy. Nor are there any references to children's speech or jargon prior to the 17th century, after which they are found in abundance. If you have ever seen 13th- or 14th-century paintings of children, you will have noticed that they are always depicted as small adults. Except for size, they are devoid of any of the physical character-

istics we associate with childhood, and they are never shown on canvas alone—that is, isolated from adults. Such paintings are entirely accurate representations of the psychological and social perceptions of children prior to the 16th century. Here is how the historian J. H. Plumb puts it:

> There was no separate world of childhood. Children shared the same games with adults, the same toys, the same fairy stories. They lived their lives together, never apart. The coarse village festivals depicted by Breughel, showing men and women besotted with drink, groping for each other with unbridled lust, have children eating and drinking with the adults. Even in the soberer pictures of wedding feasts and dances, the children are enjoying themselves alongside their elders, doing the same things.

8 Barbara Tuchman, in her marvelous book about the 14th century titled *A Distant Mirror*, puts it more succinctly: "If children survived to age 7, their recognized life began, more or less as miniature adults. Childhood was already over."

9 Now the reasons for this are fairly complicated. For one thing, most children did *not* survive; their mortality rate was extraordinarily high, and it is not until the late 14th century that children are even mentioned in wills and testaments—an indication that adults did not expect them to be around very long. In fact, probably because of this, in some parts of Europe children were treated as neuter genders. In 14th-century Italy, for example, the sex of a child who had died was never recorded.

10 Certainly, adults did not have the emotional commitment to children that *we* accept as normal. Phillipe Aries, in his great book titled *Centuries of Childhood*, remarks that the prevailing view was to have several children in order to keep a few; people could not allow themselves to become too attached to something that was regarded as a probable loss. Aries quotes from a document that records a remark made by the neighbor of a distraught mother of five young children. In order to comfort the mother, the neighbor says, "Before they are old enough to bother you, you will have lost half of them, or perhaps all of them."

11 We must also not forget that in a feudal society children were often regarded as mere economic utilities, adults being less interested in the character and intelligence of children than in their capacity for work. But I think the most powerful reason for the absence of the idea of childhood is to be found in the communication environment of the Dark and Middle Ages. Since most people did not know how to read, or did not *need* to know how to read, a child became an adult—a fully participating adult—when he or she learned how to speak. Since all important social transactions involved face-to-face oral communication, full competence to speak and hear—which is usually achieved by age 7—

was the dividing line between infancy and adulthood. There was no intervening stage, because none was needed—until the middle of the 15th century. At that point an extraordinary event occurred that not only changed the religious, economic, and political face of Europe but also created our modern idea of childhood. I am referring, of course, to the invention of the printing press. And because in a few minutes you will, perhaps, be thinking that I am claiming too much for the power of modern media, especially TV, it is worth saying now that no one had the slightest inkling in 1450 that the printing press would have such powerful effects on our society as it did. When Gutenberg announced that he could manufacture books, as he put it, "without the help of reed, stylus, or pen but by wondrous agreement, proportion, and harmony of punches and types," he did not imagine that his invention would undermine the authority of the Catholic Church. Yet less than 80 years later Martin Luther was in effect claiming that, with the Word of God on everyone's kitchen table, Christians did not require the Papacy to interpret it for them. Nor did Gutenberg have any inkling that his invention would create a new class of people: namely, children. Or more specifically, male children, for there is no doubt that boys were the first class of specialized children.

12 How was this accomplished? Simply by the fact that, less than a hundred years after Gutenberg's invention, European culture became a reading culture; i.e., adulthood was redefined. One could not become an adult unless he or she knew how to read. In order to experience God, one had to be able, obviously, to read the Bible, which is why Luther himself translated the Bible into German. In order to experience literature, one had to be able to read novels and personal essays, forms of literature that were wholly created by the printing press. Our earliest novelists—for example, Richardson and Defoe—were themselves printers. Montaigne, who invented the essay, worked hand in hand with a printer, as did Thomas More when he produced what may be called our first science fiction novel—his *Utopia.* Of course, in order to learn science one not only had to know how to read but, by the beginning of the 17th century, one could read science in the vernacular— that is, in one's own language. Sir Francis Bacon's *The Advancement of Learning,* published in 1605, was the first scientific tract an Englishman could read in English. And of course one must not forget the great Dutch humanist, Erasmus, who, understanding the meaning of the printing press as well as anyone, wrote one of the first books of etiquette for the instruction of young men. He said of his book, "As Socrates brought philosophy from heaven to earth, so I have led philosophy to games and banquets." (By the way, Erasmus dedicated the book to his publisher's son, and the book includes advice and guidance on how to convert prostitutes to a moral life.)

13 The importance of books on etiquette should not be over-looked. As Norbert Elias shows in his book titled *The Civilizing Process,* the sudden emergence in the 16th century of etiquette books signifies that one could no longer assume that children knew everything adults knew—in other words, the separation of child-hood from adulthood was under way.

14 Alongside of this, Europeans rediscovered what Plato had known about learning to read: namely, that it is best done at an early age. Since reading is, among other things, an unconscious reflex as well as an act of recognition, the habit of reading must be formed in that period when the brain is still engaged in the task of ac-quiring oral language. The adult who learns to read after his or her oral vocabulary is completed rarely becomes a fluent reader.

15 What this came to mean in the 16th century is that the young had to be separated from the rest of the community to be taught how to read—that is, to be taught how to function as an adult. This meant that they had to go to school. And going to school was the essential event in creating childhood. The printing press, in other words, created the idea of school. In fact, school classes originated to separate students according to their capacities as readers, not to separate them according to age. That came later. In any event, once all of this occurred it was inevitable that the young would be viewed as a special class of people whose minds and character were qualitatively different from those of adults. As any semanticist can tell you, once you categorize people for a par-ticular purpose, you will soon discover many other reasons why they should be regarded as different. We began, in short, to see human development as a series of stages, with childhood as a bridge between infancy and adulthood. For the past 350 years we have been developing and refining our concept of childhood, this with particular intensity in the 18th, 19th, and 20th centuries. We have been developing and refining institutions for the nurturing of children; and we have conferred upon children a preferred status, reflected in the special ways we expect them to think, talk, dress, play, and learn.

16 All of this, I believe, is now coming to an end. And it is coming to an end because our communication environment has been rad-ically altered once again—this time by electronic media, espe-cially television. Television has a transforming power at least equal to that of the printing press and possibly as great as that of the alphabet itself. It is my contention that, with the assistance of other media such as radio, film, and records, television has the power to lead us to childhood's end.

17 Here is how the transformation is happening. To begin with, television presents information mostly in visual images. Al-though human speech is heard on TV and sometimes assumes importance, people mostly *watch* television. What they watch are

rapidly changing visual images—as many as 1,200 different shots every hour. This requires very little conceptual thinking or analytic decoding. TV watching is wholly a matter of pattern recognition. The *symbolic form* of television does not require any special instruction or learning. In America, TV viewing begins at about the age of 18 months; by 30 months, according to studies by Daniel Anderson of the University of Massachusetts, children begin to understand and respond to TV imagery. Thus there is no need for any preparation or prerequisite training for watching TV. Television needs no analogue to the McGuffey *Reader*. And, as you must know, there is no such thing, in reality, as children's programming on TV. Everything is for everybody. So far as symbolic form is concerned, "Charlie's Angels" is as sophisticated or as simple to grasp as "Sesame Street." Unlike books, which vary greatly in syntactical and lexical complexity and which may be scaled according to the ability of the reader, TV presents information in a form that is undifferentiated in its accessibility. And that is why adults and children tend to watch the same programs. I might add, in case you are thinking that children and adults at least watch at different times, that according to Frank Mankiewicz's *Remote Control*, approximately 600,000 children watch TV between midnight and two in the morning.

18 To summarize: TV erases the dividing line between childhood and adulthood for two reasons: first, because it requires no instruction to grasp its form; second, because it does not segregate its audience. It communicates the same information to everyone simultaneously, regardless of age, sex, race, or level of education.

19 But it erases the dividing line in other ways as well. One might say that the main difference between an adult and a child is that the adult knows about certain facets of life—its mysteries, its contradictions, its violence, its tragedies—that are not considered suitable for children to know. As children move toward adulthood we reveal these secrets to them in what we believe to be a psychologically assimilable way. But television makes this arrangement quite impossible. Because television operates virtually around the clock—it would not be economically feasible for it to do otherwise—it requires a constant supply of novel and interesting information. This means that all adult secrets—social, sexual, physical, and the like—must be revealed. Television forces the entire culture to come out of the closet. In its quest for new and sensational information to hold its audience, TV must tap every existing taboo in the culture: homosexuality, incest, divorce, promiscuity, corruption, adultery, sadism. Each is now merely a theme for one or another television show. In the process each loses its role as an exclusively adult secret.

20 Some time ago, while watching a TV program called "The Vidal Sassoon Show," I came across the quintessential example of

what I am talking about. Vidal Sassoon is a famous hairdresser whose TV show is a mixture of beauty hints, diet information, health suggestions, and popular psychology. As he came to the end of one segment of the show in which an attractive woman had demonstrated how to cook vegetables, the theme music came up and Sassoon just had time enough to say, "Don't go away. We'll be back with a marvelous new diet and, then, a quick look at incest." Now, this is more—much more—than demystification. It is even more than the revelation of secrets. It is the ultimate trivialization of culture. Television is relentless in both revealing and trivializing all things private and shameful, and therefore it undermines the moral basis of culture. The subject matter of the confessional box and the psychiatrist's office is now in the public domain. I have it on good authority that, shortly, we and our children will have the opportunity to see commercial TV's first experiments with presenting nudity, which will probably not be shocking to anyone, since TV commercials have been offering a form of soft-core pornography for years. And on the subject of commercials—the 700,000 of them that American youths will see in the first 18 years of their lives—they too contribute toward opening to youth all the secrets that once were the province of adults—everything from vaginal sprays to life insurance to the causes of marital conflict. And we must not omit the contributions of news shows, those curious entertainments that daily provide the young with vivid images of adult failure and even madness.

21 As a consequence of all of this, childhood innocence and specialness are impossible to sustain, which is why children have disappeared from television. Have you noticed that all the children on television shows are depicted as merely small adults, in the manner of 13th- or 14th-century paintings? Watch "The Love Boat" or any of the soap operas or family shows or situation comedies. You will see children whose language, dress, sexuality, and interests are not different from those of the adults on the same shows. Like the paintings of Breughel, the children *do* everything the adults do and are shielded from nothing.

22 And yet, as TV begins to render invisible the traditional concept of childhood, it would not be quite accurate to say that it immerses us in an adult world. Rather, it uses the material of the adult world as the basis for projecting a new kind of person altogether. We might call this person the adult-child. For reasons that have partly to do with TV's capacity to reach everyone, partly to do with the accessibility of its symbolic form, and partly to do with its commercial base, TV promotes as desirable many of the attitudes that we associate with childishness: for example, an obsessive need for immediate gratification, a lack of concern for consequences, an almost promiscuous preoccupation with con-

sumption. TV seems to favor a population that consists of three age groups: on the one end, infancy; on the other, senility; and in between, a group of indeterminate age where everyone is somewhere between 20 and 30 and remains that way until dotage descends. In *A Distant Mirror*, Tuchman asks the question, Why was childishness so noticeable in medieval behavior, with its marked inability to restrain any kind of impulse? Her answer is that so large a proportion of society was in fact very young in years. Half the population was under 21; a third under 14. If we ask the same question about our own society, we must give a different answer, for about 65 percent of our population is over 21. We are a nation of chronological grown-ups. But TV will have none of it. It is biased toward the behavior of the child-adult.

23 In this connection, I want to remind you of a TV commercial that sells hand lotion. In it we are shown a mother and daughter and challenged to tell which is which. I find this to be a revealing piece of sociological evidence, for it tells us that in our culture it is considered desirable that a mother should not look older than her daughter, or that a daughter should not look younger than her mother. Whether this means that childhood is gone or adulthood is gone amounts to the same thing, for if there is no clear concept of what it means to be an adult, there can be no concept of what it means to be a child.

24 In any case, however you wish to phrase the transformation that is taking place, it is clear that the behavior, attitudes, desires, and even physical appearance of adults and children are becoming increasingly indistinguishable. There is now virtually no difference, for example, between adult crimes and children's crimes; in many states the punishments are becoming the same. There is also very little difference in dress. The children's clothing industry has undergone a virtual revolution within the past 10 years, so that there no longer exists what we once unambiguously recognized as children's clothing. Eleven-year-olds wear three-piece suits to birthday parties; 61-year-old men wear jeans to birthday parties. Twelve-year-old girls wear high heels; 42-year-old men wear sneakers. On the streets of New York and Chicago you can see grown women wearing little white socks and imitation Mary Janes. Indeed, among the highest-paid models in America are 12- and 13-year-old girls who are presented as adults. To take another case: Children's games, once so imaginatively rich and varied and so emphatically inappropriate for adults, are rapidly disappearing. Little League baseball and Peewee football, for example, are not only supervised by adults but are modeled in their organization and emotional style on big league sports. The language of children and adults has also been transformed so that, for example, the idea that there may be words that adults ought not to use in the presence of children now seems faintly ridiculous. With TV's re-

lentless revelation of all adult secrets, language secrets are difficult to guard, and it is not inconceivable to me that in the near
future we shall return to the 13th- and 14th-century situation in
which no words were unfit for a youthful ear. Of course, with the
assistance of modern contraceptives, the sexual appetite of both
adults and children can be satisfied without serious restraint and
without mature understanding of its meaning. Here TV has played
an enormous role, since it not only keeps the entire population in
a condition of high sexual excitement but stresses a kind of egalitarianism of sexual fulfillment: Sex is transformed from a dark
and profound mystery to a product that is available to everyone—
like mouthwash or underarm deodorant.

25 In the 2 November 1980 *New York Times Magazine,* Tuchman
offered still another example of the homogenization of childhood
and adulthood. She spoke of the declining concept of quality—in
literature, in art, in food, in work. Her point was that, with the
emergence of egalitarianism as a political and social philosophy,
there has followed a diminution of the idea of excellence in all
human tasks and modes of expression. The point is that adults
are *supposed* to have different tastes and standards from those of
children, but through the agency of television and other modern
media the differences have largely disappeared. Junk food, once
suited only to the undiscriminating palates and iron stomachs of
the young, is now common fare for adults. Junk literature, junk
music, junk conversation are shared equally by children and adults,
so that it is now difficult to find adults who can clarify and articulate for youth the differences between quality and schlock. It
remains for me to mention that there has been a growing movement to recast the legal rights of children so that they are more
or less the same as those of adults. The heart of this movement—
which, for example, is opposed to compulsory schooling—resides
in the claim that what has been thought to be a preferred status
for children is instead only an oppression that keeps them from
fully participating in the society.

26 All of this means, I think, that our culture is providing fewer
reasons and opportunities for childhood. I am not so single-minded
to think that TV alone is responsible for this transformation. The
decline of the family, the loss of a sense of roots (40 million
Americans change residence every year), and the elimination,
through technology, of any significance in adult work are other
factors. But I believe that television creates a communication
context which encourages the idea that childhood is neither desirable nor necessary—indeed, that we do not need children. I said
earlier, in talking about childhood's end, that I did not mean the
physical disappearance of children. But in fact that, too, is happening. The birthrate in America is declining and has been for a

decade, which is why schools are being closed all over the country.

27 This brings me to the final characteristic of TV that needs mentioning. The *idea* of children implies a vision of the future. They are the living messages we send to a time we will not see. But television cannot communicate a sense of the future or, for that matter, a sense of the past. It is a present-centered medium, a speed-of-light medium. Everything we see on television is experienced as happening *now*, which is why we must be told, in language, that a videotape we are seeing was made months before. The grammar of television has no analogue to the past and future tenses in language. Thus it amplifies the present out of all proportion and transforms the childish need for immediate gratification into a way of life. And we end up with what Christopher Lasch calls "the culture of narcissism"—no future, no children, everyone fixed at an age somewhere between 20 and 30.

28 Of course I cannot know what all of this means to you, but my own position, I'm sure, is clear. I believe that what I have been describing is disastrous—partly because I value the charm, curiosity, malleability, and innocence of childhood, which is what first drew me to a career in education, and partly because I believe that adults need, first, to be children before they can be grown-ups. For otherwise they remain like TV's adult-child all their lives, with no sense of belonging, no capacity for lasting relationships, no respect for limits, and no grasp of the future. But mainly I think it is disastrous because it makes problematic the future of school, which is one of the few institutions still based on the assumption that there are significant differences between children and adults and that adults therefore have something of value to teach children.

29 So my bad news essay comes down to these questions: In a world in which children are adults and adults children, what need is there for people like ourselves? Are the issues we are devoting our careers to solving being rendered irrelevant by the transforming power of our television culture? I devoutly hope your answers to these questions are more satisfactory than mine.

Ideas and Meaning

1. Do you accept or reject the idea that television has contributed to the decline of the concept of childhood in our culture? Why?

2. According to Postman, what other societal influences have contributed to the loss of distinction between adults and children?

3. In his introduction Postman warns that his is a "bad news"

essay. How does he define such an essay? *Is* this a bad news essay? Explain. What ideas did you find especially gloomy?

4. From your own experience with young children, give an example of how their language, dress, or knowledge of "life's mysteries" is adultlike. Do you find their adultlike behavior, dress, or knowledge upsetting? Explain.

5. Do you see any difference between yourself at the age of ten and the ten-year-olds you observe now? Explain.

6. How do you feel about organized competitive sports for children, like Little League baseball and football? If you participated in either, was your experience good or bad? Explain.

7. Do you believe in compulsory education? Why? Why not?

8. What legal rights do you think children should have?

9. How are Socrates and his student Plato pertinent to Postman's essay?

10. Why was the invention of the printing press one of the primary factors in the emergence of the distinction between childhood and adulthood?

11. According to Postman, what are the two primary reasons that television erases the dividing line between adulthood and childhood?

12. Explain what Postman means by the "adult-child." Do you agree or disagree that television is aimed at an audience of adult-children? Why?

13. In addition to those Postman gives, can you supply further examples of commercials that emphasize the loss of distinction between adults and children?

14. Give examples of your own to support Postman's statement that television "reveals and trivializes all things private and shameful and therefore it undermines the moral basis of culture."

15. At the end of the fifth paragraph, Postman suggests that there might be a Plato somewhere to counter his Socratic stance. Do you see the television age as a blessing? Explain.

16. Do you agree or disagree with Barbara Tuchman (paragraph 25) that egalitarianism is responsible for the declining concept of quality in literature, art, food, and work? Why?

17. Have you seen any television shows that contained material that was inappropriate for young viewers? Explain.

18. In addition to those Postman provides, can you give further examples of the similarity between adults' and children's clothing?

19. What "secrets of adulthood" did you learn from watching television?

20. Can you provide any solutions to the problems posed by Postman's "bad news" essay?

Development and Style

1. How does Postman get the reader's attention?
2. How does he introduce his essay? How many paragraphs comprise the introduction? What is his tone?
3. Who is his audience, and what is his purpose?
4. What is Postman's thesis, and how does he support it?
5. Are you convinced of his thesis by the end of the essay? Why? Why not? What is Postman's strongest point in support of his thesis? Where does it come in his essay?
6. The essay is divided into four sections: paragraphs 1 through 5, 6 through 11, 12 through 17, and 18 through 29. What purpose does each section accomplish? Why does Postman break between paragraphs 17 and 18?
7. What generalization does Postman support with the example of Socrates?
8. Why does Postman include a historical account of the emergence of the distinction between childhood and adulthood?
9. What is the central idea of paragraph 22? How does Postman support it?
10. In paragraph 22, does Postman need examples for his statement that "television promotes an obsessive need for immediate gratification, a lack of concern for consequences, and an almost promiscuous preoccupation with consumption"? Why? Why not? Can you supply specific examples for each of these "childish" attitudes? What are the connotations of the adjectives *obsessive* and *promiscuous?*
11. What is the function of paragraph 23?
12. What is the central idea of paragraph 24? How does Postman support it? Are there any statements that need support not provided by Postman? If so, which one or ones? Can you provide the examples you would like to have?
13. Analyze the transitions between paragraphs, beginning with paragraph 12 and ending with paragraph 17.
14. Are there any sentences that you would rearrange? If so, rewrite them and analyze the difference between the effects of your sentences and Postman's.
15. Are there any statements that you would emphasize by using a one-sentence paragraph? Which one or ones?
16. Are there any paragraphs that you would break into more than one paragraph? If so, why would you do so, and where would you break them?

17. Discuss the effects of Postman's use of the dash and the colon. Are there any uses of either that you would replace with other appropriate marks of punctuation? If so, what marks would you use and why? What is the difference between the effect of your choice of punctuation and Postman's?

18. What word in paragraph 28 is a repetition of a word Postman used in his introduction? What is the effect of his repetition? What is the effect of the repetition of this word within this paragraph? What are the connotations of this word?

19. How does Postman's last paragraph refer to his introduction? What other means of concluding does he use?

Claire's Two Responses

Reading Journal: "The Day Our Children Disappear"
First Response

I think Neil Postman has a well thought out point in his essay. Children are definitely losing their shy, cute, sometimes gregarious personalities. They are becoming small adults with the bitterness, vocabulary, and outlook that is enforced by watching television.

I have noticed in my small cousin's play that she includes adult-type problems. One time when I was babysitting Kim, she was playing dolls on the floor. Ken was having an affair with Skipper so Barbie poisoned Skipper. Barbie is in jail but the judge likes her a lot, so she's set free. Not only was she talking like this, but right in front of me like nothing was wrong. It is natural for an eight-year-old to speak of adultery and murder in play these days. That's not all—she cleared her toys away in time for "Dynasty." What is the world coming to?

Second Response

I find myself at a standstill by this essay. I agree with what Postman is saying but I'm not sure what to do about it. There is censorship but where do you draw the line there? Not only is censorship a sticky subject but there is the old argument "They'll just learn it somewhere else." Well I guess somewhere else would be better at times.

I don't know, you read articles all the time where children commit crimes and say they watched them on television. What can a person do? I wish Postman had given some ideas of his own about such a problem, because I agree it is a problem. Children are disappearing and we watch it happen. Television isn't the only criminal either—toys, candy (chewing tobacco, gum), and comic books all portray these adult images that seem to hurry adulthood. Has television corrupted society, or has society corrupted television?

Claire asks some good questions at the end of her second response: Is television merely a reflection of society, or does society reflect the image of itself portrayed on television? Although Claire wishes that Postman had given some suggestions for a solution, she herself recognizes the impossibility when she mentions the problems inherent in censorship and the fact that children are faced with other sources of corruption in our society in addition to television. However, do you agree or disagree with her that children could learn "elsewhere" what they learn from viewing television?

Whereas Postman criticizes television, an outgrowth of media technology, in the following essay, Lewis Thomas criticizes operant conditioning, an outgrowth of advanced medical technology.

LEWIS THOMAS

Autonomy

1 Working a typewriter by touch, like riding a bicycle or strolling on a path, is best done by not giving it a glancing thought. Once you do, your fingers fumble and hit the wrong keys. To do things involving practiced skills, you need to turn loose the systems of muscles and nerves responsible for each maneuver, place them on their own, and stay out of it. There is no real loss of authority in this, since you get to decide whether to do the thing or not, and you can intervene and embellish the technique any time you like; if you want to ride a bicycle backward, or walk with an eccentric loping gait giving a little skip every fourth step, whistling at the same time, you can do that. But if you concentrate your attention on the details, keeping in touch with each muscle, thrusting yourself into a free fall with each step and catching yourself at the last moment by sticking out the other foot in time to break the fall, you will end up immobilized, vibrating with fatigue.

2 It is a blessing to have options for choice and change in the learning of such unconsciously coordinated acts. If we were born with all these knacks inbuilt, automated like ants, we would surely miss the variety. It would be a less interesting world if we all walked and skipped alike, and never fell from bicycles. If we were all genetically programmed to play the piano deftly from birth, we might never learn to understand music.

3 The rules are different for the complicated, coordinated, fantastically skilled manipulations we perform with our insides. We do not have to learn anything. Our smooth-muscle cells are born

with complete instructions, in need of no help from us, and they work away on their own schedules, modulating the lumen of blood vessels, moving things through intestines, opening and closing tubules according to the requirements of the entire system. Secretory cells elaborate their products in privacy; the heart contracts and relaxes; hormones are sent off to react silently with cell membranes, switching adenyl cyclase, prostaglandin, and other signals on and off; cells communicate with each other by simply touching; organelles send messages to other organelles; all this goes on continually, without ever a personal word from us. The arrangement is that of an ecosystem, with the operation of each part being governed by the state and function of all the other parts. When things are going well, as they generally are, it is an infallible mechanism.

4 But now the autonomy of this interior domain, long regarded as inviolate, is open to question. The experimental psychologists have recently found that visceral organs can be taught to do various things, as easily as a boy learns to ride a bicycle, by the instrumental techniques of operant conditioning. If a thing is done in the way the teacher wants, at a signal, and a suitable reward given immediately to reinforce the action, it becomes learned. Rats, rewarded by stimulation of their cerebral "pleasure centers," have been instructed to speed up or slow down their hearts at a signal, or to alter their blood pressures, or switch off certain waves in their electroencephalograms and switch on others.

5 The same technology has been applied to human beings, with other kinds of rewards, and the results have been startling. It is claimed that you can teach your kidneys to change the rate of urine formation, raise or lower your blood pressure, change your heart rate, write different brain waves, at will.

6 There is already talk of a breakthrough in the prevention and treatment of human disease. According to proponents, when the technology is perfected and extended it will surely lead to new possibilities for therapy. If a rat can be trained to dilate the blood vessels of one of his ears more than those of the other, as has been reported, what rich experiences in self-control and self-operation may lie just ahead for man? There are already cryptic advertisements in the Personal columns of literary magazines, urging the purchase of electronic headsets for the training and regulation of one's own brain waves, according to one's taste.

7 You can have it.

8 Not to downgrade it. It is extremely important, I know, and one ought to feel elated by the prospect of taking personal charge, calling the shots, running one's cells around like toy trains. Now that we know that viscera can be taught, the thought comes naturally that we've been neglecting them all these years, and by judicious application of human intelligence, these primitive

structures can be trained to whatever standards of behavior we wish to set for them.

9 My trouble, to be quite candid, is a lack of confidence in myself. If I were informed tomorrow that I was in direct communication with my liver, and could now take over, I would become deeply depressed. I'd sooner be told, forty thousand feet over Denver, that the 747 jet in which I had a coach seat was now mine to operate as I pleased; at least I would have the hope of bailing out, if I could find a parachute and discover quickly how to open a door. Nothing would save me and my liver, if I were in charge. For I am, to face the facts squarely, considerably less intelligent than my liver. I am, moreover, constitutionally unable to make hepatic decisions, and I prefer not to be obliged to, ever. I would not be able to think of the first thing to do.

10 I have the same feeling about the rest of my working parts. They are all better off without my intervention, in whatever they do. It might be something of a temptation to take over my brain, on paper, but I cannot imagine doing so in real life. I would lose track, get things mixed up, turn on wrong cells at wrong times, drop things. I doubt if I would ever be able to think up my own thoughts. My cells were born, or differentiated anyway, knowing how to do this kind of thing together. If I moved in to organize them they would resent it, perhaps become frightened, perhaps swarm out into my ventricles like bees.

11 Although it is, as I say, a temptation. I have never really been satisfied with the operation of my brain, and it might be fun to try running it myself, just once. There are several things I would change, given the opportunity: certain memories that tend to slip away unrecorded, others I've had enough of and would prefer to delete, certain notions I'd just as soon didn't keep popping in, trains of thought that go round and round without getting anywhere, rather like this one. I've always suspected that some of the cells in there are fluffing off much of the time, and I'd like to see a little more attention and real work. Also, while I'm about it, I could do with a bit more respect.

12 On balance, however, I think it best to stay out of this business. Once you began, there would be no end to the responsibilities. I'd rather leave all my automatic functions with as much autonomy as they please, and hope for the best. Imagine having to worry about running leukocytes, keeping track, herding them here and there, listening for signals. After the first flush of pride in ownership, it would be exhausting and debilitating, and there would be no time for anything else.

13 What to do, then? It cannot simply be left there. If we have learned anything at all in this century, it is that all new technologies will be put to use, sooner or later, for better or worse, as it is in our nature to do. We cannot expect an exception for the

instrumental conditioning of automatic functions. We will be driven to make use of it, trying to communicate with our internal environment, to meddle, and it will consume so much of our energy that we will end up even more cut off from things outside, missing the main sources of the sensation of living.

14 I have a suggestion for a way out. Given the capacity to control autonomic functions, modulate brain waves, run cells, why shouldn't it be possible to employ exactly the same technology to go in precisely the opposite direction? Instead of getting in there and taking things over, couldn't we learn to disconnect altogether, uncouple, detach, and float free? You would only need to be careful, if you tried it, that you let go of the right end.

15 Of course, people have been trying to do this sort of thing for a long time, by other techniques and with varying degrees of luck. This is what Zen archery seems to be about, come to think of it. You learn, after long months of study under a master, to release the arrow without releasing it yourself. Your fingers must do the releasing, on their own, remotely, like the opening of a flower. When you have learned this, no matter where the arrow goes, you have it made. You can step outside for a look around.

Ideas and Meaning

1. What is Thomas's primary objection to operant conditioning? Do you agree or disagree with his position? Why?

2. What are Thomas's reasons for not wanting to be in charge of his liver? What is humorous about this example?

3. How does Thomas suggest that we use our knowledge of operant conditioning? How does Zen archery illustrate what he means?

4. Thomas says that if we have learned anything in this century, it is that "all new technologies will be put to use, sooner or later, for better or worse." Can you give some examples of new technology used for the worse? The better?

5. Can you give some examples of how the ability to control autonomic functions might be beneficial?

6. Would D. H. Lawrence agree or disagree with Thomas's suggestion that we become like Zen archers, letting our bodies operate on their own? Explain.

7. From what we know about the human brain, is Thomas's suspicion that some of his brain cells are "fluffing off" likely to be true or untrue?

8. What are the things Thomas would change if he could control his brain? Would you want to change the same things? Are there any additional changes you would make in the way your brain operates, given the opportunity?

9. At the end of paragraph 11, Thomas says that he could "do with a bit more respect." What does he mean? What are the implications? Can you give a personal example of a time you felt that your brain didn't respect you very much?
10. If you could learn to control your autonomic functions, what would you want to control? Why? What would you not want to control? Why?
11. Do you believe that scientists will use this knowledge the way that Thomas suggests? Explain.
12. Would you call Thomas's position antiscientific or antiprogressive? Why? Why not? Considering that Thomas is both a doctor and a medical researcher, does his position surprise you? Explain.

Development and Style

1. How does Thomas get the reader's attention?
2. How does he introduce his essay, and how many paragraphs comprise his introduction?
3. What is Thomas's tone?
4. What is his purpose, and who is his audience?
5. What is Thomas's thesis? Does he state it explicitly? If so, where?
6. How does he support his thesis? Is his support convincing? Why? Why not? What is Thomas's strongest point in support of his thesis? Where does it come in his essay?
7. What are the central ideas of paragraphs 4, 5, 9, and 10? How is each idea developed? Is each paragraph developed adequately? Why? Why not?
8. Analyze the transitions between paragraphs, beginning with paragraph 4 and ending with paragraph 12.
9. Point out the comparisons Thomas has used. How is each one appropriate? What are the connotations of each?
10. What statement has Thomas indented alone for emphasis? Why this particular one?
11. How do the intentional fragments that begin paragraphs 8 and 11 provide both emphasis and transition?
12. In the third sentence of paragraph 11, Thomas uses a colon to separate several appositives from the sentence. Why does the colon work better than the dash there? What is the difference in effect between the two marks?
13. In this same sentence from paragraph 11, instead of commas, use semicolons to separate the series of appositives. Which mark do you prefer? Why?
14. Are there any sentences that you would rearrange or punctuate differently? If so, rewrite them. Why did you revise the construction or the punctuation? What are the differ-

ences in meaning and effect between your sentences and Thomas's?

15. How does Thomas conclude? What is the connection between the example he uses here and the ones he used in his first paragraph?

16. Because Thomas is a doctor and a scientist, you might expect his style to be more difficult and his vocabulary more technical than it is. Point out phrases or statements in which he uses the common vernacular.

17. Of the professional writers you have read in this text, whose style does Thomas's most resemble? What characteristics do the two writers share? Which do you prefer and why?

Jan's Two Responses

Reading Journal: "Autonomy" First Response

I found "Autonomy" pretty interesting. For years, gurus over in India and other Asian and European countries have been controlling their own heart rate, perspiration rate, blood pressure, etc. It always seems so strange to watch programs where all of our great doctors attach electrodes to these thin old men and then sit back and watch in awe as they actually do control their bodies. It seems that doctors and scientists are always trying to come up with ways to make us a little more invincible—to beat the odds and live forever.

I tend to agree with Lewis Thomas though. I don't really think I would want the responsibility of controlling my liver, brain, stomach and whatever. I imagine that being able to do this correctly would entail years and years of medical study and training, and I for one am not up to that. If it's possible though, someone's going to go for it, and I guess that in a way, that's good. People have the need, I think to test their bounds and go as far as they possibly can. We've attacked ourselves from the outside in an attempt to control our minds with every kind of drug conceivable, and the next logical step is to try attacking from the inside.

This idea of controlling the brain is really interesting though. I always like to look at the negative side of things first, and therefore I can just envision all of these mental robots or vacancies walking around. The majority of people would probably stimulate their pleasure centers a lot, and we'd have millions of euphoric people walking around all the time. Others would experiment with depression areas and probably get in so deep that they couldn't get back out. People would have ten million different things wrong with them because they gave the wrong command up in the big room. Good things could probably happen too: people might be able to cure their own depression and perhaps women could prevent symptoms of PMS.

Second Response

After my second reading of Thomas's article, his next to last paragraph has reminded me of something really strange. It doesn't really have a whole lot to do with this essay, but I'll put it down anyway. I read a book a long time ago—one of those "B" horror novels—about these people who went around killing others by leaving their bodies and getting into stuffed animals and the like that belonged to the people they wanted to kill. At any given time you could just be sitting in your room and suddenly your teddy bear would jump up and hack you to death. Now, imagine if everyone in the world was able to leave his body; this would come to no good at all. People would probably want to switch bodies, and we'd never know who we were really talking to.

I like the idea of the mind being able to cure all illness rather than some machine. It would be great to know that no one would have to be hooked up to a machine ever again. This would seem to imply that people could control their lives and deaths though. What a can of worms that would open up. Suddenly we'd have zillions of people who were a thousand years old refusing to die—refusing to make room for all the new people showing up. This is getting a little too sci-fi for me.

Jan doesn't exactly change her mind, having seen both the advantages and disadvantages of operant conditioning in her first response, but she does project a great many negative results should we develop the ability to control our brains. Do you think that people will someday be able to "shout their thoughts" or to use their brains to live thousands of years?

Although Thomas's view of his subject is negative, John Ciardi, author of the following essay, presents an even more negative view of his subject—Americans' misconception of the meaning of happiness.

John Ciardi

Is Everybody Happy?

1 The right to pursue happiness is issued to Americans with their birth certificates, but no one seems quite sure which way it ran. It may be we are issued a hunting license but offered no game. Jonathan Swift seemed to think so when he attacked the idea of happiness as "the possession of being well-deceived," the felicity

of being "a fool among knaves." For Swift saw society as Vanity
Fair, the land of false goals.

2 It is, of course, un-American to think in terms of fools and
knaves. We do, however, seem to be dedicated to the idea of buying our way to happiness. We shall all have made it to Heaven
when we possess enough.

3 And at the same time the forces of American commercialism
are hugely dedicated to making us deliberately unhappy. Advertising is one of our major industries, and advertising exists not to
satisfy desires but to create them—and to create them faster than
any man's budget can satisfy them. For that matter, our whole
economy is based on a dedicated insatiability. We are taught that
to possess is to be happy, and then we are made to want. We are
even told it is our duty to want. It was only a few years ago, to
cite a single example, that car dealers across the country were
flying banners that read "You Auto Buy Now." They were calling
upon Americans, as an act approaching patriotism, to buy at once,
with money they did not have, automobiles they did not really
need, and which they would be required to grow tired of by the
time the next year's models were released.

4 Or look at any of the women's magazines. There, as Bernard
DeVoto once pointed out, advertising begins as poetry in the front
pages and ends as pharmacopoeia and therapy in the back pages.
The poetry of the front matter is the dream of perfect beauty.
This is the baby skin that must be hers. These, the flawless teeth.
This, the perfumed breath she must exhale. This, the sixteen-year-
old figure she must display at forty, at fifty, at sixty, and forever.

5 Once past the vaguely uplifting fiction and feature articles, the
reader finds the other face of the dream in the back matter. This
is the harness into which Mother must strap herself in order to
display that perfect figure. These, the chin straps she must sleep
in. This is the salve that restores all, this is her laxative, these are
the tablets that melt away fat, these are the hormones of perpetual youth, these are the stockings that hide varicose veins.

6 Obviously no half-sane person can be completely persuaded
either by such poetry or by such pharmacopoeia and orthopedics.
Yet someone is obviously trying to buy the dream as offered and
spending billions every year in the attempt. Clearly the happiness-
market is not running out of customers, but what is it trying to
buy?

7 The idea "happiness," to be sure, will not sit still for easy definition: the best one can do is try to set some extremes to the
idea and then work in toward the middle. To think of happiness
as acquisitive and competitive will do to set the materialistic extreme. To think of it as the idea one senses in, say, a holy man of
India will do to set the spiritual extreme. That holy man's idea of
happiness is in needing nothing from outside himself. In wanting

nothing, he lacks nothing. He sits immobile, rapt in contemplation, free even of his own body. Or nearly free of it. If devout admirers bring him food he eats it; if not, he starves indifferently. Why be concerned? What is physical is an illusion to him. Contemplation is his joy and he achieves it through a fantastically demanding discipline, the accomplishment of which is itself a joy within him.

8 Is he a happy man? Perhaps his happiness is only another sort of illusion. But who can take it from him? And who will dare say it is more illusory than happiness on the installment plan.

9 But, perhaps because I am Western, I doubt such catatonic happiness, as I doubt the dreams of the happiness-market. What is certain is that his way of happiness would be torture to almost any Western man. Yet these extremes will still serve to frame the area within which all of us must find some sort of balance. Thoreau—a creature of both Eastern and Western thought—had his own firm sense of that balance. His aim was to save on the low levels in order to spend on the high.

10 Possession for its own sake or in competition with the rest of the neighborhood would have been Thoreau's idea of the low levels. The active discipline of heightening one's perception of what is enduring in nature would have been his idea of the high. What he saved from the low was time and effort he could spend on the high. Thoreau certainly disapproved of starvation, but he would put into feeding himself only as much effort as would keep him functioning for more important efforts.

11 Effort is the gist of it. There is no happiness except as we take on life-engaging difficulties. Short of the impossible, as Yeats put it, the satisfactions we get from a lifetime depend on how high we choose our difficulties. Robert Frost was thinking in something like the same terms when he spoke of "The pleasure of taking pains." The mortal flaw in the advertised version of happiness is in the fact that it purports to be effortless.

12 We demand difficulty even in our games. We demand it because without difficulty there can be no game. A game is a way of making something hard for the fun of it. The rules of the game are an arbitrary imposition of difficulty. When the spoilsport ruins the fun, he always does so by refusing to play by the rules. It is easier to win at chess if you are free, at your pleasure, to change the wholly arbitrary rules, but the fun is in winning within the rules. No difficulty, no fun.

13 The buyers and sellers at the happiness-market seem too often to have lost their sense of the pleasure of difficulty. Heaven knows what they are playing, but it seems a dull game. And the Indian holy man seems dull to us, I suppose, because he seems to be refusing to play anything at all. The Western weakness may be in the illusion that happiness can be bought. Perhaps the Eastern

weakness is in the idea that there is such a thing as perfect (and therefore static) happiness.

14 Happiness is never more than partial. There are no pure states of mankind. Whatever else happiness may be, it is neither in having nor in being, but in becoming. What the Founding Fathers declared for us as an inherent right, we should do well to remember, was not happiness but the *pursuit* of happiness. What they might have underlined, could they have foreseen the happiness-market, is the cardinal fact that happiness is in the pursuit itself, in the meaningful pursuit of what is life-engaging and life-revealing, which is to say, in the idea of *becoming*. A nation is not measured by what it possesses or wants to possess, but by what it wants to become.

15 By all means let the happiness-market sell us minor satisfactions and even minor follies so long as we keep them in scale and buy them out of spiritual change. I am no customer for either puritanism or asceticism. But drop any real spiritual capital at those bazaars, and what you come home to will be your own poorhouse.

Ideas and Meaning

1. What is Ciardi criticizing in this essay? Do you agree or disagree with his position? Explain.
2. Although Ciardi says that happiness is a slippery word to define, how does he finally define it? Is his definition a good one? Explain. Is Swift's a good definition? Explain. How would you define happiness?
3. What connection do you see between Swift's definition of happiness and Ciardi's? What connection is there between Swift's definition and Ciardi's criticism of the idea that happiness is to be found in material possessions?
4. How does Thoreau illustrate Ciardi's idea that happiness consists in the effort to "take on life-engaging difficulties"?
5. Is it true that "the advertised version of happiness" is effortless? Explain. Can you give some specific examples? What are the examples that Ciardi gives?
6. What two definitional extremes of happiness does Ciardi give in order to find a balance? Do you agree with Ciardi that the happiness of the holy man of India is perhaps illusory? Why? Why not? How is "happiness on the installment plan" illusory? Explain.
7. Why is American advertising "dedicated to making us deliberately unhappy"? Give some specific examples of ads in magazines or on television that made you unhappy with yourself. Explain how and why they made you unhappy.

Did you buy anything as a result of your unhappiness? What did you buy? What effect did the purchase have on you?

8. In paragraph 3, where Ciardi criticizes the commercialism of automobile dealers, what other criticism is implied?
9. What material possessions do you have that have contributed to your happiness? Name them and explain how and why they have made you happy.
10. If the idea of happiness is in the pursuing, so that it is always the idea of becoming, does a person ever obtain happiness? What is Ciardi's answer to this question? Does his answer satisfy you? Why? Why not?
11. Name some activities you have engaged in that required a great deal of effort on your part. What was the result of your effort? Did you feel "happy"? Explain.
12. Do you agree with Ciardi that "the Indian holy man seems dull to us because he seems to be refusing to play anything at all"? Why? Why not? Is the Indian holy man pursuing anything that takes effort?
13. When Ciardi uses games to illustrate the pleasure one gets from efforts to win despite the rules, he implies that life is like a game with happiness the goal. Is this a good analogy? Why? Why not?
14. At the present time what are you pursuing that is "life-engaging" or "life-revealing"? What has been the effect of these pursuits? Have they made you happy? Explain.
15. Would you consider yourself happy at the present time? If so, why? If not, why not?
16. Think of a time in your life when you were extremely unhappy. What made you unhappy? What did you do about it?
17. Explain the meaning of Ciardi's last sentence: "But drop any real spiritual capital at those bazaars, and what you come home to will be your own poorhouse." What are "those bazaars"? And, specifically, how will you be the poorer?

Development and Style

1. How does Ciardi get the reader's attention?
2. What is his tone? From his writer's voice, how do you picture Ciardi?
3. What is his purpose, and who is his audience?
4. How does Ciardi introduce his essay? When do you know what his focus will be?
5. What is his thesis? If it is explicit, where is it stated? How

does Ciardi develop his thesis, and what is his strongest point in support of it?

6. How does he develop paragraphs 3, 4, 7, and 11?

7. What is the function of paragraph 8?

8. Analyze the transitions between paragraphs, beginning with paragraph 2 and ending with 14.

9. In paragraphs 4 and 5, what are the examples Ciardi uses to illustrate his central ideas? Should they have been more specific, naming actual products? Why? Why not?

10. Analyze the beginnings of sentences in paragraph 3. Would you reconstruct any of them? If so, rewrite the sentence(s) and compare your revision(s) with Ciardi's. Which is more effective—your sentence or Ciardi's? Why?

11. In the second sentence of the first paragraph, Ciardi uses an analogy. What are its implications and connotations? Is it effective? Why? Why not?

12. In the last paragraph, Ciardi uses the figure of speech "spiritual capital," and he uses the noun *poorhouse* in a figurative way also. Is each figure of speech effective? Explain.

13. In paragraph 7, Ciardi personifies (the attribution of human characteristics to inanimate objects or ideas) the noun *happiness.* Is this personification effective? Why? Why not?

14. The last sentence in paragraph 5 contains a series of parallel sentences separated by commas. Replace the commas with semicolons. What is the effect? Which mark do you prefer and why?

15. In the second sentence of paragraph 3, what are the effects of Ciardi's use of parallel structure ("not to satisfy desires but to create them") and his repetition of the infinitive phrase "to create"? In this same sentence Ciardi uses a dash where he could have used a comma. Replace the dash with a comma. Which mark is more effective? Why?

16. In the fourth and fifth sentences of paragraph 3, Ciardi repeats the infinitive phrase "to want." What is the effect of this repetition?

17. The last three sentences in paragraph 4 are intentional parallel fragments. What is the effect? Make all the fragments complete by adding the verbs *are, is,* and *is,* respectively. Which do you prefer, the fragments or the complete sentences? Why?

18. In the third sentence of paragraph 5, Ciardi has used a similarly constructed fragment. Make it a complete sentence by adding the verb *are.* Which do you prefer—the fragment or the complete sentence? Why?

19. In the second sentence of paragraph 4, what is the effect of the antithesis "begins as poetry in the front pages and ends

as pharmacopoeia and therapy in the back pages"? (Antithesis uses parallel structure to state opposing ideas.)

20. What are the connotations of the following words and phrases: *happiness-market, becoming, bazaar, acquisitive, competitive, commercialism,* and *pharmacopoeia?*

21. If you consider paragraphs 14 and 15 Ciardi's conclusion, what means of concluding does he use? If you consider only paragraph 15 his conclusion, what are his means of concluding?

22. Which of the four essayists, Postman, Ciardi, Thomas, and Etzioni, do you think you would like best as a person, judging by his writer's voice? Why? Which essay did you prefer? Why? Which essay did you like least? Which essayist was the best writer? Why?

Jamie's Two Responses

Reading Journal: "Is Everybody Happy?" First Response

Who is to say where happiness lies? Ciardi makes some pertinent observations about the American pursuit of happiness. If happiness rests solely with the acquisition of Money and the stuff it can buy, I think I'll create my own version of happiness.

I hate money for its absolute power over us in this society. Consider money for a minute. In examining a paper bill, one may see a foldable object with pictures of stuffy-looking forefathers on it whose faces are laced with red and blue threads. So, you say, it is symbolic of God. Consider gold in the same light you have just seen the dollar. It is a dull metallic object that somebody decided was valuable and is the reason for the wars we wage!

Yet money is the stuff that dreams are made of. If you have "enough," your freedom to live as you choose is nearly guaranteed. If not, no matter how deserving you are, you will be trapped into a possibly undesirable lifestyle. Maybe money wouldn't be such a frustrating subject if it were distributed fairly to those people who are truly deserving. Unfortunately, the only way that will happen is if God would appoint himself secretary of the treasury. Until then, Mr. Ciardi, everybody may not be happy.

Second Response

I am very wary of American commercialism for its ability to make us "deliberately unhappy." The advertising business does its public few favors by creating desires at a faster rate than we can possibly satisfy them. I can remember a time in my life, somewhere between puberty and middle adolescence, when the media helped me to make self-loathing a way of life. Coincidentally, this is also around the same time that I temporarily traded in my worthwhile reading material for the glossy pages of Glamour, Vogue, and Cosmopolitan. Like many other impressionable young girls, I became somewhat obsessed with the "dream of perfect beauty." I inflicted an enormous amount of pressure (and aerobics) on myself to fulfill that now ridiculous dream. That mercifully short phase in my life took place years ago, but I won't soon forget the pain of such an empty dream. Adolescent awkwardness and self-consciousness, combined with the media's pressure to be perfect, can be pretty deadly to a young woman's developing self-image, especially if she's impressionable enough to take the "dream" seriously. Fortunately, I escaped from this stage unscathed, but there are those women who are not fortunate. These combined factors are not only damaging to one's self-image, but they have also been blamed for the increasing numbers of women who suffer from self-destructive eating disorders and other strange behavior patterns. I wonder if the advertising agencies will ever take into consideration some of the social impacts of the desires that they implant in the American public.

Conclusion

Having read the professional essays in this chapter, you probably already have a number of ideas for an essay of your own criticizing this various, beautiful, and occasionally (frequently?) absurd world we live in. In the next chapter you will have the opportunity to excoriate or gently criticize some aspect of our society. In addition, you will be shown ways to emphasize your points, many of which you have already observed in the professional and student writing in preceding chapters.

C H A P T E R

The Critical "I": Writing about What's Wrong with Our World

14

In the last chapter you read the essays of four professional writers who expressed varying degrees of "savage indignation" as a result of several aspects of our society. All four writers' purposes were similar: they wanted their audience not only to understand their views but to accept them as their own. In other words, these writers saw a *change* they would like to make in our society, and they all hoped *to persuade* their audiences to make those changes. Thus, these professional essays are examples of *persuasion,* one of the four rhetorical modes defined for you in Chapter 3. Although the writers of these essays occasionally used exposition, or even description, their primary purpose was to persuade their audiences to accept their views.

Now it is your turn to persuade an audience that the change you would like to make in our society or its institutions is one that we need to make. Whether you are "savagely" indignant like Ciardi or mildly indignant like Thomas does not matter. The most important consideration is that you find a subject that matters to you a great deal.

Finding a Topic

If you do not have several ideas in mind already for a persuasive essay criticizng some aspect of our society, you might begin by reviewing your responses to the essays you read in the last chapter. It is quite likely that you have one or more ideas that could form the nucleus of a persuasive essay. For example, perhaps you wrote a number of reasons that you opposed Etzioni's stance, or perhaps Postman's essay prompted you to write a number of criticisms of certain television shows or commercials. And, although you probably don't need reminding at this point, don't forget to review your personal journal for ideas!

After you have reread your responses and scanned your personal journal for ideas, you might use the following suggested headings for listing. Or, if you prefer, you could use one or more as a heading for a focused freewrite. One other suggestion: you might form small groups and brainstorm together, using the suggested headings or ones you think of yourselves. This kind of sharing can be helpful because someone in your group might mention an idea that is new and appealing to you. Whether you list on your own or brainstorm in a group, you might begin by writing down other headings that you or your groupmates think of. The following are headings that served as the basis for one group's brainstorming. (These abbreviated headings represent the attitudes, actions, and so on, of society that you would like to criticize.)

Attitudes And Values

selfishness	beauty is good	all prejudice—against
uncaring	wealth	blacks, clerks, women
success	instant gratification	
impatience	our generation's apathy	

Actions or Behavior

child abuse	infidelity
laws like seat-belt laws	taking dope
violence	being two-faced
neglect of elderly	TV watching
cheating	laziness
	fads

Institutions

living together	Christmas	the welfare
marriage	advertisements	system
sororities	drive-thru everything	fraternities
fancy weddings	religious TV programs	garage sales
funerals	Cabbage Patch dolls	
MTV		

Groups of People

doctors	bargain hunters
lawyers	dope-heads
TV addicts	conformists
professional athletes	militant vegetarians
Christmas shoppers	

In order to further stimulate your thinking, you might read Sophie's and Meg's final drafts, which follow.

Sophie's Final Draft

Will the Real Miss America Please Stand Up?

1 Do Americans believe that beauty is only skin deep? Not really. Yet, we are a nation obsessed with physical beauty. We balance it on three-inch heels and send it strutting down a runway for grading and approval. We applaud it. We reward it. And then—we sell it. Sell it to the public as Miss America.

2 And the public buys it—skin and all.

3 This year they bought Vanessa Williams. But when they found out just how much skin came with the bargain, they wanted to trade her in for a little less seductive model. So, for appearing nude in Penthouse magazine, Vanessa Williams lost her title—a title that she won by selling those same glossy attributes to a panel of judges.

4 True, she wore clothes—clothes that covered much more than anatomy. Clothes that concealed the real image of the entire contest: that the American woman's role is to be physically beautiful, sexually pleasing—and stupid.

5 Supporters of the pageant argue that this is untrue: that entrants are judged not on beauty alone but on talents and accomplishments as well. I suppose one could consider a tap dancer standing on her head, clacking her heels against a plank held above her feet a talent. And wasn't it impressive when Miss Hawaii announced her greatest accomplishment—breakfast with Marcus Allen in front of the L.A. Raiders' locker room?

6 It is time that America examined the worth of such an institution—a degrading institution that fosters ambiguous values in our youth. From infancy, our children are taught the importance of beauty. They see it on television; they see it in magazines. The message is loud and clear: To be beautiful is to be loved.

7 To be beautiful has, somehow in our society, become equivalent to being superior. Children in school know it. Adults in the job market know it—looks count.

8 I worry.

9 I worry because little girls barely out of diapers are toddling across stages all over our country selling their smiles and dimples for plastic crowns and brass trophies. I worry because their parents think nothing of entering them, like poodles in a dog show, in contests that define and decide their worth by physical appearance. What happens to the five-year-

old who doesn't win the "Little Miss Canned Corn" pageant? Does an hour's cry on Mother's shoulder erase the damage? Unfortunately not.

10 The damage of these pageants go far beyond the individual. They affect every woman in America. We have fought long and hard to be taken seriously. But can we be taken seriously while teetering down a runway in a swimsuit and three-inch heels? I think not. I <u>know</u> not! Women must support each other if we are to achieve and maintain equality. A contest that leads to hatred and rivalry is an impediment to that mutual support and to our advancement.

11 And rivalry does exist. Those who participate sometimes will do anything to win. They smear lipstick on opponents' swimsuits. They pour soft drinks onto evening gowns. And they perpetuate the image of silliness and vanity that has inappropriately been assigned to women throughout history.

12 It is difficult enough to take insults from the opposite sex, but slurs from our own sex are inexcusable. And slurs are what we sometimes get. For example, Marguerite Piazza, a 1983 Miss America judge, stated, "You can't have somebody with short legs and a big behind be Miss America. . . . No way!"

13 "And why <u>not</u>?" I ask.

14 And just <u>how</u> close does Miss America come to representing the American woman? We are a nation of diversity. Different colors. Different nationalities. Different religions. Very few of us, if any, are physically perfect. And to achieve such perfection, how many of us would have a nose job or starve on six hundred calories a day? Not many. However, many of us do achieve success in careers, in families, and in being decent, warm human beings. Yet each year, one woman—judged by physical beauty—represents us all. Miss America? She surely does.

15 By a mile!

Ideas and Meaning

1. What is Sophie's main objection to the Miss America contest? Do you agree or disagree with her? Why?
2. How do you feel about contest judge Marguerite Piazza's statement that "you can't have somebody with short legs and a big behind be Miss America"?
3. Sophie points out that parents enter their small children in beauty contests. How would being entered in beauty contests harm a child? Have you ever known a child contestant? If so, how did the child feel about it? If you had a child, would you enter her in a beauty contest? Why? Why not?

4. How old were you when you realized that being good-looking was important in this society? Was there any particular incident involved in your awareness? Explain. If not, how were you made aware of this particular cultural value?

5. Would putting an end to beauty contests of all kinds help to change Americans' emphasis on physical beauty? Explain.

6. Would putting an end to such contests promote a better image of women? Explain. Do you think that beauty contests exploit and degrade women? Explain.

7. Do you believe that the Vanessa Williams scandal damaged the image of both the contest and the winner? Explain.

8. If Sophie were designing a Miss America pageant, on what bases do you imagine the winner would be chosen?

9. Would you like to see an end to beauty contests? Why? Why not?

10. Did Sophie's essay change your opinion of the Miss America contest? Explain.

Development and Style

1. How does Sophie get the reader's attention? How many paragraphs comprise her introduction?

2. What is her tone? Who is her audience, and what is her purpose?

3. What is her thesis, and how does she support it?

4. What are the central ideas of paragraphs 5, 6, 7, 9, 10, 11, and 12? How is each idea developed? Does any one or more of these ideas need additional support? If so, what is needed?

5. Point out examples of concrete/specific words and phrases. What general words or phrases could be replaced with more specific ones?

6. Analyze the transitions between paragraphs in the essay. Are there any weak transitions? If so, how would you improve them?

7. Are there any sentences you would rearrange? If so, rewrite them and compare your revisions with Sophie's original sentences: which is more effective and why?

8. What means of concluding does Sophie use? How many paragraphs comprise her conclusion? Is her conclusion effective? Why? Why not?

Meg's Final Draft

Degeneration

1 "I don't much care about the people in China or wherever. I have everything that I want." This comment was made by an

American teenage boy who was being interviewed on a television news broadcast concerning the effects war has had on
children in various parts of the world. This young man, probably only a few years my junior, as American-looking as apple
pie, with wind-tossled hair and rosy cheeks, uttered one of the
most frightening statements I have ever heard in my life. Why
is this statement so frightening? Because it reflects the attitudes of many of the young people in America today. Because
it shows the selfishness of a generation that has been pampered and protected from reality. Because it rings in my ears
like a message of destruction—the destruction of my own generation.

2   Indeed, "destruction" is a very harsh term to use in order to
describe the fate of my own generation. Is it, perhaps, too
harsh? I don't think so. By "destruction" I don't necessarily
mean that we are all going to kill ourselves physically. Maybe
we will. But more specifically, we are going to kill ourselves
mentally and emotionally because of our attitudes. These attitudes are the ropes with which we are going to hang ourselves. These attitudes are the anchors that are dragging us to
the bottom of a muddy swamp of destruction where our minds
will stagnate and our emotions will cease to function. What attitudes am I speaking of?

3   The foremost attitude which threatens my generation is selfishness. Like the young boy on the news broadcast, my generation "doesn't much care" as long as we get what we want.
And what does this generation want? The words of a recent
top-40 song sum this question up in a nutshell—this generation "just wants to have fun." Fun. This is the major focus on
high school and college campuses today. Fun. Fun. Fun. Who
cares about anything else? Mommy and Daddy will pack up
the nice little Porsche they bought with surfboards, skate-
boards, pom-poms, and footballs, pat little Junior on the head,
and tell him or her to "study hard." Junior can't wait to roar
off to school, cruise around in pink plastic sunglasses (minus
the Mickey Mouse), and have fun.

4   There is certainly nothing wrong with having fun, but there
should be a time and place to do so. That's what weekends are
for. But this does not apply to many young people today. Monday and Wednesday nights are favorite "free draft" nights at
the university that I attend. Students squirm in their seats
during my evening history class because the class is taking up
valuable party time. Frequent moans, sighs, and whines are
voiced until the instructor announces the end of the class. At
this time it would not be wise to be standing in the pathway
toward the door for fear of being trampled. Is this college or is
this kindergarten? Sometimes I wonder. My generation is

much too concerned with <u>self</u> pleasures to be worried about trivial matters such as writing, reading, and science. That is why Junior doesn't <u>want</u> to write. That is why our high schools and colleges <u>offer</u> low-level English courses and Basket Weaving 101. Because Junior is too busy having fun.

5 Fun can be a very self-destructive thing. Especially when it spawns laziness. And I am afraid that is another thorny weed that has wrapped itself around my generation. Laziness. Junior has been so busy having fun he or she doesn't know how to <u>work</u>. About a month ago, one of my classes was discussing the worst job anyone could possibly have. Three-fourths of the class had <u>never</u> had a job. One girl spoke up and said, "Well, I've never <u>really</u> had a job, but one time Daddy made me and my brother take the water hose and spray slugs off of our lawn chairs before our lawn party. It was yucky and horrible!" Of course the class agreed.

6 This is really sad. My generation doesn't know how to work because my generation has never <u>had</u> to work. Except for maybe an occasional Burger King job for party money, many young people just don't have to work. Why? Because good old Mom and Dad are standing nearby with open hearts and open wallets.

7 Laziness has made my generation not only physically and mentally weak but also politically weak. How many young Americans today could tell you what's going on in the news? How many really care? How many care about the E.R.A., civil rights, or the situation in Nicaragua? Why should this generation care about Vietnam or the incident at My Lai? <u>We've</u> never had to go to war. How many political protests, demonstrations, or community organizations do young people participate in? Very few. Whatever happened to the youth revolution of the 1960s that was going to change the world? They tried. We haven't. How many times do you hear anything positive about this generation in the news? The last time I heard <u>anything</u> concerning this generation in the news was the fact that approximately 1,000 college students in America committed suicide last year. And the number is steadily increasing.

8 The situation at hand is frightening. The future of this nation will one day be in <u>our</u> hands. Will we know how to handle the terrifying realities <u>that</u> are in store for us? I hope so. I am not saying that <u>every single</u> person in this generation is selfish, lazy, or irresponsible. Some are not, many are. Maybe we will grow and mature. Maybe we will learn to care for and love those other than ourselves. I hope so. If not, our minds will congeal, our eyes will collect dust, and our idle hands will begin to fidget angrily with the war toys our forefathers built.

9 The result?

10 The end of fun, of laziness—
11 Of Everything.

Ideas and Meaning

1. What are Meg's criticisms of her generation? Do you agree or disagree? Why?
2. Would you agree that many of the people your age are self-centered? Fun-seeking? Lazy? Unaware of world problems? Explain.
3. Do you read a newspaper or a weekly news magazine like *Time* or *Newsweek?* Why? Why not? If you do, what current national or international problems concern you?
4. Have you ever participated in a political demonstration? Explain. If you have not, are there any current political issues you feel strongly enough about that you would like to demonstrate your beliefs? Explain.
5. Meg says that 1,000 college students committed suicide last year (1984). Did this figure surprise you? Explain. Could there be a connection between the attitudes of her generation, according to Meg, and this statistic?
6. Should children of wealthy parents have to work for more than "party" money? Explain.
7. The implication of Meg's position is that working for necessities such as clothing, shelter, or food is good for a person. Do you agree or disagree? Why?
8. Are many or most of your college classmates and acquaintances primarily interested in fun and secondarily interested in their college courses? Explain.
9. What is your own hierarchy of values? Indicate the importance of the following ten phrases by numbering them from 1 (most important) to 10 (least important).

   world oppression
   poverty in America
   studying
   the problems of the elderly
   attending class
   having fun
   world hunger
   earning money
   keeping abreast of current national and international affairs
   turning in assignments on time

   Explain your hierarchy. Are several items of equal value to you?
10. If you could change one attitude you have observed in those of your generation, what would it be? Explain.

11. What seems to be the predominant attitude of your parents' generation? Explain. What adjectives would you use to describe your parents' generation? What adjectives would you use to describe your own?
12. In paragraph 8, does Meg's qualification of her indictment of her generation make her position more or less convincing? Why?

Development and Style

1. How does Meg get the reader's attention? How does she introduce her subject? What is her tone?
2. Who is her audience, and what is her purpose?
3. What is her thesis, and how does she support it?
4. What are the central ideas of paragraphs 2 through 7? How is each idea developed? Are any of these ideas in need of further support? If so, what is needed?
5. What are the metaphors Meg uses in paragraph 2? What are the connotations of each? How is each appropriate? Does it ruin her effectiveness to use two different comparisons? Explain. How are the two comparisons related?
6. What is the metaphor Meg uses in paragraph 5? What are the connotations? How is it appropriate?
7. Point out the concrete/specific words and phrases in paragraphs 3 and 4. Are there any general words or phrases that could be replaced with more specific ones?
8. Analyze the transitions between paragraphs throughout the essay.
9. Would you change the construction of any of Meg's sentences? If so, rewrite them and compare your revisions with Meg's original versions: Which is more effective? Why?
10. Where has Meg written a permissible comma fault? Why is it permissible?
11. What is the effect of paragraphs 9, 10, and 11? If Meg had written these paragraphs as the last statements of paragraph 8, would the effect be the same? Explain. Which arrangement do you prefer? Why?
12. In paragraph 8, what is the effect of Meg's repetition of the statement "I hope so"?
13. How does Meg conclude her essay? How many paragraphs comprise her conclusion? Is her conclusion effective? Why? Why not?

Margo's Two Focused Freewrites

After you have listed alone, brainstormed with a group, or free-written under several headings, put checkmarks by two or more ideas that appeal to you. Then, like Margo you might choose two subjects and freewrite drafts of each topic. The following are her two focused freewrites, one on radical vegetarians and the other on unfair discrimination against smokers.

Radical Vegetarians

I don't care what anyone eats, or what else they do with their bodies, if it doesn't affect me. I have nothing against vegetarians either, as long as they don't try to push their views off on me. I just don't like the ones who are always condemning others for what they eat and how they live.

I tried vegetarian once myself, but it didn't last too long, and it wasn't just because I missed having meat to eat. I joined a food co-op in which most of the members were vegetarians and holistic-lifestyle-oriented types. It was attractive and interesting enough at first, but it soon turned out to be one big bore. These people were totally out of touch with reality, for the most part. They had nothing to talk about but food, meat, and anyone who consumed it was anathema to them. I felt out of place and gave it up.

Not long ago I saw an old militant from the co-op in the grocery store. She was, naturally, checking out the produce dept., and I tried to avoid her on my way to the meat counter, but I was caught. We chatted briefly and she told me she was expecting a baby some months in the future. I was shocked. The assumed father was a known jerk and both seemed unprepared for parenthood. She must have caught on, because she admitted that her natural contraceptive method had failed. The father had just gone north to live at a Yoga retreat where she would later join him and give birth (of course) by the natural method. I was getting hungrier by the minute and wanted only to get away from this bore, but it seems I'm always stuck in situations where I must be polite. But, just when I thought I could get away, came the clencher: Vegetarians always have to know what you're eating, so she asked, "What are you buying here?"

"We're cooking out tonight and I just came in to pick up a few things for the grill," I answered uncomfortably.

"Still eating MEAT, eh?" she demanded with disgust and disapproval. "I still never touch it, of course."

I felt like screaming, "Great! And I'll bet you still don't shave your legs and you still fart like a cart horse from that weird stuff you call food!"

But, of course, I had to be polite, so I managed only to say, "That's wonderful. You'll probably live longer than me, but at least I'll have more fun!"

On the Side of the Underdogs

I've always been one to take the side of the underdog, and, in this case, you might say I'm on my own side, being an underdog myself. What I'm talking about is smoking versus nonsmoking, and it's hands-down who's the black sheep in this contest. In this age of fitness fever and striving for tip-top physical condition, smoking has become about as popular as cannibalism or pederasty. And that's not stretching it much.

One has to be a pretty tough cookie to smoke these days what with all the heavy warnings from the American Lung Association and the flak from nonsmokers. Not only do you have to worry about possible damages you may be causing yourself, you've got your self-esteem to worry about as well. Nonsmokers have a way of undermining that for you right away. No wonder smokers and nonsmokers tend to be such cliquish lots. They can't stand one another, and a few billows of smoke from burning tobacco isn't the main culprit here. They pose a serious threat to one another, and I don't mean physical. Witness the way nonsmokers behave in the company of a smoker. Not only do they recoil in disgust and near horror, they've got to make a good show out of it, too. They fake coughing attacks, fan their hands wildly, open windows at the most inopportune times and places, do anything to get out of range of the tiniest wisp of smoke. And the ever-present bit of advice: "Don't you know smoking's bad for your health?" (How astute!) To which there are but two acceptable replies: (1) "Yes, but there's something worse for your health—not minding your own damn business," or (2) "Sure, I know it'll probably kill me, but I'd hate to die thinking there's nothing wrong with me." That gets 'em every time.

As you can tell from her two freewrites, Margo, a twenty-five year-old who returned to school to finish a degree begun some years earlier, was a very witty, articulate person. It is evident also that, because of her sense of humor, Margo has the makings of a satirical essay in both of these freewrites. Since she was truly more "indignant" over militant vegetarians than she was over the "victimization" (as she put it) of smokers by nonsmokers, Margo decided on that topic. Another factor in her decision was that what she disclosed in her freewrite was really true: she had recently encountered one of the "militants" whom she formerly knew, and, as a result, her ire had been freshly aroused. Her groupmates also preferred this topic, but they suggested that she replace the slang word *fart*, which the dictionary also lists as a "vulgarism" (a word or phrase used only in common, colloquial, and coarse speech).

Would you have made the same suggestion? Are there any reasons that her use of the word might be acceptable here?

In her next draft you will see what Margo decided to do, but before she prepared another draft for peer criticism, she cubed her subject and afterwards answered the seven questions she had learned to ask about the subjects of expository or persuasive essays. You may read the following results.

Margo's Cubing: Militant Vegetarians

Describe: A militant vegetarian, as the term no doubt implies, is one who goes well beyond the bounds of merely excluding the flesh of dead animals from the daily dietary intake. Not only does the militant "veg" steadfastly abstain from anything remotely related to the animal kingdom, such as eggs and any form of dairy offering, (some even refuse to wear anything made of leather or fur, or so much as a feather in a cap) but is also seemingly compelled to recoil in horror from all who do not likewise abstain.

Compare: Militant vegetarians are not at all unlike any of a number of religious fanatics who seem to exist solely for the purpose of ramming their own piety down the throat of any hapless soul unfortunate enough to wander within arm's (or ear's) reach of them. Like the fanatic, they cling to their half-baked convictions with all the tenacity of a pit dog going for the kill. And, like the fanatic, militant vegs usually smell—the former of mothballs and hair tonic; the latter of garlic and from an acute lack of personal hygiene.

Associate: Whenever I think of rampant vegetarians (which is as seldom as possible) a number of associations come readily to mind. The strongest is of the now somewhat hackneyed terms "bubble head" or "space case"—references, of course, to one who is wholly out of touch with "the real world." Rampant vegs operate under the constant delusion that proper diet, a more "laid-back" lifestyle, and a daily herbal enema are the solution to the world's social, economical, and political melee. With little exception, they seem to be caught in a sort of temporal and cultural time warp, with flower power, incense, sitar music and "make love, not war" the order of the day.

Analyze: Rampant vegetarianism, as should now be quite evident, far exceeds the mere choice of diet. Any true rampant veg must evidence strict adherence to several standards of appearance and behavior. First, a certain clear-cut visual image must be upheld at all times. The subject must, without fail, appear transfixed by some point just beyond the normal human being's field of vision. That is, he never appears to look at a thing, but through or around it, as if it didn't exist. Second, personal appearance and dress are of optimum importance to the concept of rampant vegetarianism. The male veg must look as if he has not shaved, showered, or had a haircut since (as they themselves so aptly put it) "Dylan went electric." The females are, without exception of the "earth mother" ilk—long hair, worn loose or braided; cotton garments, preferably imported from India; a total lack of cosmetic enhancement; and always, always unshaven legs and armpits. Rampant vegs of either gender must come off as sincere ad nauseum and, of course, more than just a trifle self-righteous. In short, the total concept of militant vegetarianism is as much form as content, wherein a precarious balance of just the right look and the right thing to say (always in a stylized Richard Brautiganish—1960ish jargon) must be maintained.

Apply: This one's the stumper for, as much as I've tried, I can't determine any real, legitimate use for militant vegetarianism, but, as usual, my suspicions border on the paranoid. My guess is that, like fanatics of any bent, the rampant vegs are out to transform the world. They have a plan: they want to change our way of eating and, thereby, our ways of thinking and living, and they go about it with the combined tact of a third-rate used-car salesman and a white-supremacist party campaigner. With a zeal as sinister as any hard-core Marxist's, they're out to convert the pariahs of the meat-eating world into whole-wheat, bean-sprout, and tofu-full automatons. Their world vision of an eternal Rainbow Rally just outside the Denver City limits is as nightmarish to us carnivores as a People's Social and Economic State is to the quintessential capitalists of Wall Street.

> *Argue:*   No problem! Let's face it, anyone who is as glar-
> ingly repulsed by the sight of a perfectly pre-
> pared Chateaubriand or rack of lamb as by the
> discovery of a fresh road kill has something ba-
> sically <u>wrong</u> with him. I am intrinsically a tol-
> erant <u>individual</u>. I have nothing in the world
> against vegetarians (and here I mean those who
> simply don't eat meat), but rampant, radical, mil-
> itant vegs are another thing altogether. One's di-
> etary choice is (or God knows, <u>should</u> be) as per-
> sonal a matter as religious, political, and sexual
> preferences. You know—you go your way and I'll
> go mine. It's the "I don't eat meat—I'm OK; you
> eat meat—you're not OK" attitude that turns me
> off.

It is evident from her writing here that Margo was being truthful when she said that she had had "a really good time" cubing
her subject. Now, here are her responses to the list of seven questions, which she also seems to have enjoyed writing.

Margo's Responses to Seven Questions

1. What are the causes of militant vegetarians?

   Lord knows, but I can say what the causes of my dislike of
   them are. But, let me see . . . Causes . . . Well, militant
   vegs can come from any walk of life, and their parents
   never figure out where they went wrong. However, for the
   most part, mature, rampant vegs can trace their roots to
   pampered, upper-middle-class families. As with nearly all
   radicals, an intricately interwoven sense of rebellion and
   sacrifice is necessary. They seem to think that if they reject their elders' standards, they can somehow atone for
   the familial guilt incurred by the ingestion of all those
   cold-bloodedly murdered Sunday dinner entrees. Heaven
   help the meat-packing mogul who harbors a young militant veg-in-the-making.

2. What are the effects of militant vegetarians?

   Rampant vegs are a blatantly homogeneous bunch. A sea-
   soned observer can spot one a mile away. They all look
   like throwbacks from the Flower Generation, which seems
   to point out their basic insecurities and inability to cope
   with a changing world. Any one of them could be a character right out of Tom Robbin's <u>Another Roadside Attrac-
   tion</u> or <u>anything</u> by Richard Brautigan—i.e., the kind of
   people Your Parents Warned You About. Also, they are ob-

viously paranoid and distrustful of all meat eaters. (They're always worried that some enterprising carnivore is going to lace their texturized vegetable protein lasagna with ground chuck.) And they're the most boring conversationalists—they have nothing to talk about but food, the benefits of breastfeeding, and their latest trip to the Hatha Yoga retreat in the Catskills. Last, but not least, they smell bad.

3. What are the types of militant vegetarians?

Basically, male and female, with few instances of middle ground (although its not unheard of). In many cases, it's difficult, if not impossible, to tell one from the other by plain sight alone. Other than that, they're all alike.

4. How do militant vegetarians compare with others like them?

This is a difficult proposition for, as far as I can tell, there are no others like them. However, they are (thank God) a minority, and therefore, subject to the same speculation as other dissimilar factions—for instance, hippies, the now (nearly) lost breed of oddballs of the previous generation. Both are similar in appearance and lifestyle but, of course, not all hippies are vegetarians. Rampant vegetarians are, for the most part, most certainly hippies and, while many ex-hippies are now stockbrokers, executives, and generally regular people, I can't even conceive of an ex-rampant veg. They're just not subject to change.

5. How do rampant vegetarians contrast with others like them?

There is as little to contrast rampant vegs with as to compare. I suspect the most obvious opposite of the rampant veg would be the Yuppie, the latest breed of anything-but-oddball of the present generation. No rampant veg could ever be a Yuppie and vice versa. The mere notion of a rampant veg/Yuppie would be as blatantly oxymoronish* as that of an ethical loan shark or a sweet Medusa.

6. What is the process of becoming a militant vegetarian?

If what you're looking for is a method to the madness, forget it. They are the way they are because that's the way they are and they want everybody else to be just like them.

---

* An oxymoron is a figure of speech that is self-contradictory, such as "a frenzied calm," "a cold passion," and, of course, a "veg/Yuppie."

7. Who are some examples of militant vegetarians?

> I know a lot of vegetarians since I used to be one, but I don't know any famous ones that others would know. Unless—is Jane Fonda a veg? If she isn't, she ought to be. Of those I know, there's Syl (a pseudonym), the one I wrote about in my freewrite. She really ticked me off with her disgusting self-righteousness. Then there's this woman whom I had the misfortune to have to wait on in the restaurant the other day. I think I'll begin my essay with her. Paranoid, that's what she was. A perfect example of the veg's paranoia.

There is a great deal of good material here, as a result of Margo's use of both these invention techniques. As you have just read, she even thought of a new way to begin her essay—with an example of a radical vegetarian that she waited on in the restaurant where she works. But one obvious thing worth noting, in addition, is that her writing certainly illustrates something I said earlier when I cautioned you against continuing to write about *any* subject that you had lost interest in. If you're bored, your reader will be bored. On the other hand, if you're having a good time, such as Margo admittedly had when she cubed, then your reader will also. One last comment: Margo's occasional use of the adjective *rampant* in place of *militant* is especially interesting because of both its denotation and connotation. Denotatively, *rampant* is not really synonymous with either *militant* or *radical*, but the imagery it evokes is absolutely perfect for conveying Margo's attitude towards radical vegetarians.

Now that Margo has a great deal of material, she needs to write another draft, organizing the ideas that she decides to use.

Organizing Persuasive Essays

In Chapter 10 you were told that you should put your stronger points near the end of expository essays. The same arrangement is best for persuasive essays because readers remember most vividly what they read last. Since Margo is planning to write a satirical essay in which she will use examples of at least two vegetarians in order to support her thesis, she will put last the vegetarian who illustrates the quality she dislikes most (her strongest point against them, in other words), which is their self-righteous condemnation of people who are not in their camp. Margo's organizational task is a fairly simple one since almost all of us would readily agree that self-righteousness is a much more distasteful characteristic than paranoia, the characteristic illustrated by the other vegetarian that Margo plans to use as an example.

However, as you perhaps noted when you answered the questions at the end of the readings in the last chapter, determining the strongest point in an essay is often difficult and arbitrary. Nevertheless, if you list the supportive points you plan to make, it is fairly easy to see which ones are relatively weak and which are relatively strong. You recall, for instance, that Sophie's thesis was that beauty pageants are damaging to our society, especially to women and young children. The main points she made were presented in this order:

1. We are a nation obsessed with physical beauty.
2. Beauty contests foster ambiguous values in our youth.
3. The damage of beauty pageants affects every woman in America.
4. Miss America, for example, does not represent the American woman because we are a nation of diverse nationalities and few women are physically perfect.

You would probably agree that the last two points are stronger than the first two, although their strength derives in part from Sophie's having made the first two points. That is, because of the inductive order of Sophie's persuasion, she needs to make the first two points in order to give support to her specific denouncement of the Miss America pageant.

If you have any trouble deciding which of your points to put last in your essay, ask a classmate. If you ask several people, there will most likely be some disagreement, especially over which *one* point is the strongest. But determining the one strongest point will always be arbitrary. The only necessity is that the *relatively stronger points* come near the end of expository or persuasive essays.

The following is the guide that Margo's reviewer used to make suggestions for improvement when he read a further draft of her essay.

The Critic's Guide

1. Does the writer have an interesting title indicative of his or her slant on the subject?
2. Does the writer's introduction begin with an attention-getting sentence? Does it establish the writer's tone? Does it let the reader know the focus?
3. Does the writer have a thesis, either implicit or explicit?
4. Is the thesis adequately supported? Could you suggest additional supportive statements? Could any of the supportive statements be stronger?

5. Are the stronger supportive statements near the end of the essay?
6. Are the central ideas of paragraphs adequately supported with examples, descriptive details, and so forth? Could any of this supportive material be improved: better examples, better description, and so on?
7. Are there strong transitions between sentences and paragraphs? Are the means of transition varied?
8. Are sentence beginnings and lengths varied?
9. Are the connotations of words, phrases, and metaphors consistent with the writer's attitude toward his/her subject?
10. Does the conclusion leave the reader satisfied that the writer has proven his point? Could the writer improve his/her conclusion by using other means?

Margo's Draft for In-class Criticism

Meat into the Eater: A Satirical Look at Militant Vegetarianism*

Great beginning

1 She looked at me with crystal-clear china-blue eyes set in a face with a flawless complexion and announced, almost defensively, "I don't eat MEAT."
2 "So what!" I wanted to shout. "I eat it three times a day, preferably raw, and I like to suck eggs out of their shells for dessert!"
3 But I was working, and, of course, one must always be courteous to the customer who (it goes without saying) is always right, no matter how far they make you want to stick your finger down your throat. It was a typical harried Friday night at the local restaurant where I work, and the last thing I felt like dealing with at that hour was a rampant vegetarian. But I told myself to take it easy, it would be over with before I knew it.

Why not put in the specific name of it?

4 "Well, then, perhaps you'd like to try our guacamole salad or the vegetarian sample platter," I suggested amicably enough.
5 "Well, I don't know. It doesn't have MEAT on it does it? I don't eat MEAT." (They always pronounce the word as if a fair-sized clump of barnyard offal had just been deposited in their mouth.)

? Wouldn't this be plural to agree with they?

This is funny!

6 "Hey," I thought to myself, "this one's stupid, too," but managed to explain congenially that it contained no meat, hence

* Margo's title is a parody of the sermon "Meat Out of the Eater" by the colonial American minister Michael Wigglesworth.

the name Vegetarian Sampler Platter. She finally settled, after what seemed like hours of deliberation, on the Guacamole Salad (probably still not quite sure as to the exact nature of the Sample Platter), drank a few after-dinner drinks with her friend, smoked a few cigarettes, and left. I always find it highly ironic that some of your most militant meat shunners will consume alcohol by the barrels and smoke cigarettes by the barnsful. They probably do drugs, too, in vast quantities, as long as they're organic and contain no animal fats.

nice humor—so true, too!

7 Actually, I don't particularly care what any one puts in his or her own body, or how they go about it. And I don't have a thing in the world against vegetarians, as long as they don't castigate me for my choice of a diet somewhat different from theirs. It's the ones who are always on the defensive, always ready to condemn others for what they see as a less than wholesome and "natural" lifestyle that rub me the wrong way. I even tried vegetarianism myself once, but for a variety of reasons, eventually reverted back to my old ways. I had, for a couple of years, become fairly actively involved in a local natural foods cooperative, in which a large percentage of the members are vegetarians with holistically oriented lifestyles. The basic concept of the cooperative and many of the dietary doctrines promoted there seemed (and still seem) sensible, even attractive.

into?

I think this is redundant with revert

Tense shift — were

8 But through this venture, I soon found that the majority of the hard-core vegetarians and "naturalists" were disappointingly shallow and one-dimensional. Their whole life's interest seemed to be consumed wholly by food: the nature, the procurement, and the preparation of it. Trying to broach a topic of conversation with them that was not centered around some aspect of natural foods was like asking a tree for the time of day. Meat was anathema to them, and anyone who ate it worthy of consignment to the ninth circle of hell. Naturally, I soon began to feel grossly out of place with this bunch and eventually dropped out.

the ironic use of this word is great

9 Recently, I ran into Syl, an old acquaintance, one of the militants from the co-op (at the grocery store.) I noticed her perusing the produce stand as I hurried past on my way to the meat counter to pick up some pork chops for the grill. She flagged me down and, after the customary exchanges, announced that she was expecting her first child some months down the road. I was somewhat shocked, as she was still single and seemed wholly unprepared for motherhood and childrearing. Evidently my surprise must have made itself obvious, for she intimated, as she selected a heftly cabbage, that her natural contraceptive method had proved somewhat less than effective. The father, another rampant veg (of course) and

awkward also why not be more specific & name the grocery store?

general self-righteous jerk had recently gone north to take up residence at a retreat. She would join him there later where the baby would be born (of course) by the natural method. As the pork chops and grill beckoned to my gnawing stomach, I began to sicken of this entire little scenario. I must admit I had to quell the urge to extend my most sincere wish that Mr. and Ms. Natural's natural issue emerge, appropriately enough, as a tofu baby with alfalfa sprouts for hair. Clearly, this was no occasion for such hostile levity. Just when I thought I could make a clean getaway came the inevitable dreaded question "What are you buying here, Margo?" (They always have to know what you're eating)

I believe the period goes inside here, since the entire sentence is parenthetical.

10 "Well, we're cooking out tonight. I just thought I'd pick up a few things for the grill," I found myself answering sheepishly.
11 "Still eating MEAT?" she demanded disgustedly, that familiar glint of disapproval in her eye. "I still never touch it."
12 "Great!" I wanted to scream. "And I bet you still don't shave your legs or armpits, and I bet you still <u>pass gas</u> all the time from eating garbanzo paste and dried figs!"

This isn't as funny as "fart" is it?

13 But, ever the diplomat, I managed to choke back my exasperation and only say with a smile, "That's wonderful. You'll probably live longer than me, but I bet I'll enjoy it more."

This is a great essay, Margo. It's so funny! I wish I could write like this. P.S. I think you better ask Dr. S. about "fart." I think it's better than "pass gas."

Critical Analysis

As her reviewer points out, Margo has written an extremely successful satirical essay. It's amazing how satire, a kind of humorous harpoon, takes the edge off the sting when it hits its mark. For that reason, satire is probably the most effective way to criticize any aspect of humanity or its institutions. It just doesn't hurt as much if we can laugh. Even though Margo's satire is so well written, her reviewer did make a few suggestions for revision: that Margo replace the general nouns *restaurant* and *grocery store* with the specific names of these places and that she make a few changes in sentence structure. Not only is Margo's essay well developed and coherent, but her word choice is remarkably precise and effective.

In reference to her word choice, however, Margo's critic noted that the euphemism "pass gas" is not nearly as funny in this particular context as the slang word Margo had used originally. Do you know why? Because the slang expression *fart* is a shift in level of diction (and, as you no doubt noticed, this is not the only instance of Margo's shift in level of diction for the sake of humor). Remember that you were cautioned *not* to shift levels of diction *unless* you wanted to be humorous. And, of course, Margo *does* want to be funny here. For one thing, she is writing satire, a blend of seriousness and humor for the purpose of criticism; for another, she is setting up a contrast here between what she *says* to Syl and what she's really thinking that she'd *like to say,* a marked contrast for her, as for most of us in similar situations. Thus, there are really two reasons that Margo could use the slang word *fart* here: she *wants* to be funny and the word also appears in dialogue of a kind—a dialogue that Margo is having with herself. As a result, I think you can see that Margo's use of the slang term here coincides with the guidelines concerning diction that you were given in Chapter 4.

Even though Margo has written an extraordinarily effective satire on radical vegetarians, she might want to revise some of her sentence structure or punctuation in order to help her emphasize certain statements more.

Using Emphasis

You have read the works of a number of professional writers who have used various punctuation marks, various kinds of sentence structure, and various arrangements of sentences to help them emphasize their points. Since you are writing an essay now that presents your criticism of some aspect of our lives, you might especially want to emphasize some of your most important points.

Using Punctuation to Emphasize

The Dash

Many of the writers you have read have used dashes to set off one or more items in apposition to another word.

> One might say that the main difference between an adult and a child is that the adult knows about certain facets of life—its mysteries, its contradictions, its violence, its tragedies—that are not considered suitable for children to know.
>
> (Postman, paragraph 19)

The dash may also be used in place of parentheses to enclose a parenthetical expression. The result is that the expression is emphasized.

> Evelyn's friend is her mother's age—but I share so much more than I ever could with my mother"—a woman she talks to of music, of books and of life.
>
> (Viorst, paragraph 20)

The Colon

Colons can also be used to set off words, phrases, or sentences in apposition to another word. Unlike the dash, however, a pair of colons cannot enclose a series of appositives or a parenthetical expression in the middle of a sentence. More formal than the dash, the colon also causes a reader to pause and thus whatever comes after the colon is emphasized.

> So my bad news essay comes down to these questions: In a world in which children are adults and adults children, what need is there for people like ourselves?
>
> (Postman, paragraph 29)

Italics

In handwritten or typewritten essays, italics are indicated by underlining the word, phrase, or sentence you wish to italicize. You should use this means of emphasizing very sparingly, as a great many underlined words give the impression that the writer is gushy or overwrought.

> "The party was *not* for you, the spider was *not* a black widow, *it wasn't that way at all.*"
>
> (Didion, "On Keeping a Notebook," paragraph 7)

The Exclamation Mark

The exclamation mark can emphasize what it follows, but like italics, this mark should be used sparingly. If it is overused, the writer comes off rather like an overly effusive high school cheerleader.

> But can we be taken seriously while teetering down a runway in a swimsuit and three-inch heels? I think not. I *know* not!
>
> (student essay)

Using Sentence Structure to Emphasize

1. Begin with a phrase stating that something important follows: *by all means, above all, most of all, most important*(ly), *most significant*(ly), *of primary importance, of utmost importance, of utmost concern,* to name some examples.

   > *By all means* let the happiness-market sell us minor satisfactions and even minor follies so long as we keep them in scale and buy them out of spiritual change.
   >
   > (Ciardi, paragraph 15)

2. Repeat key words or phrases.

   > *These attitudes* are the ropes with which we are going to hang ourselves. *These attitudes* are the anchors that are dragging us to the bottom of a muddy swamp of destruction.
   >
   > (student essay)

3. Use intentional fragments.

> This is the baby skin that must be hers. *These the flawless teeth. This the perfumed breath she must exhale.*
> (Ciardi, paragraph 4)

4. Use a series of two or more parallel phrases or sentences.

> For otherwise they remain like TV's adult-child all their lives, *with no sense of belonging, no capacity for lasting relationships, no respect for limits,* and *no grasp of the future.*
> (Postman, paragraph 28)

5. Use a series of two or more parallel fragments.

> "Which means," says Elaine, "that I'll talk about being overweight but not about being depressed. Which means I'll admit being mad but not blind with rage. Which means that I might say that we're pinched this month but never that I'm worried sick over money."
> (Viorst, paragraph 7)

6. Begin a sentence with a coordinate conjunction. (This construction emphasizes through surprise—we expect coordinate conjunctions to join, not separate, two or more parallel constructions.)

> This meant that they had to go to school. *And* going to school was the essential event in creating childhood.
> (Postman, paragraph 4)

7. Use inversion. (Also emphatic through surprise.)

> Into this world falls a plane.
> (Dillard, "God's Tooth," paragraph 1)

Using Arrangement to Emphasize

1. Use a short sentence or a fragment after a moderately long or very long sentence.

> But we needn't agree about everything (only 12-year-old girl friends agree about *everything*) to tolerate each other's point of view. *To accept without judgment.*
> (Viorst, paragraph 31)

2. Ask a question. This is especially effective if the question is short and the preceding sentence is relatively long.

> After the first flush of pride in ownership, it would be exhausting and debilitating, and there would be no time for anything else.
> *What to do then?*
> (Thomas, paragraph 13)

3. Ask a question and answer it. This can be especially emphatic if the answer is a command or a call for action.

> What then? Turn truly, honourably to the novel, and see wherein you are man alive, and wherein you are dead man in life.
>
> (Lawrence, paragraph 28)

4. Indent one statement alone as a paragraph.

> There are already cryptic advertisements in the Personal columns of literary magazines, urging the purchase of electronic headsets for the training and regulation of one's own brain waves, according to one's taste.
> *You can have it.*
>
> (Thomas, paragraph 7)

This is also an example of emphasis as a result of a short sentence following a long one.

5. Indent an intentional fragment alone as a paragraph.

> All I knew then was what I wasn't, and it took me some years to discover what I was.
> *Which was a writer.*
>
> (Didion, "Why I Write," paragraph 6)

Of all these ways to achieve emphasis, the two used most frequently by the professional writers in this text are the intentional fragment and the one-sentence paragraph.

Practice Using Emphasis

If you want to practice using emphasis, you might revise the introduction, the conclusion, and one other paragraph in your essay, preferably one in which you make a really important point.

You will find that using some of these emphatic constructions and arrangements will have another beneficial effect on your writing—you will actually generate more ideas as a result. For example, just look at the additional ideas in Sophie's and Meg's revised paragraphs, which follow.

Sophie's Original and Revised Paragraphs

Original Introduction

Because Vanessa Williams appeared nude in *Penthouse* magazine prior to winning the Miss America pageant, she lost her title—a title that she won by selling those same glossy attributes to a panel of judges.

Revised Introduction

Do Americans believe that beauty is only skin deep? Not really. Yet, we are a nation obsessed with physical beauty. We balance it on three-inch heels and send it strutting down a runway for grading and approval. We applaud it. We reward it. And then—we sell it. Sell it to the public as Miss America.

And Americans buy it—skin and all.

Original Middle Paragraph

The damage of these pageants go far beyond the individual. They affect every woman in America. We have fought long and hard to be taken seriously, but we cannot be taken seriously while strutting down a runway in a swimsuit and three-inch heels. Women must support each other if we are to achieve equality.

Revised Middle Paragraph

The damage of these pageants go far beyond the individual. They affect every woman in America. We have fought long and hard to be taken seriously. But can we be taken seriously while teetering down a runway in a swimsuit and three-inch heels? I think not. I _know_ not! Women must support each other if we are to achieve equality.

Original Conclusion

We are a nation of diversity. A nation of different colors, different nationalities and different religious beliefs. Very few of us are physically perfect, and most of us would never dream of having a nose job or existing on six hundred calories a day to win a contest. Yet we are often successful in careers in spite of the image perpetuated by these pageants.

Miss America? By a mile!

Revised Conclusion

We are a nation of diversity. Different colors. Different nationalities. Different religions. Very few of us, if any, are physically perfect. And to achieve such perfection, how many of us would have a nose job or starve on six hundred calories a day? Not many. However, many of us do achieve success in careers, in families, and in being decent and warm human beings. Yet each year, one woman—judged by physical appearance—represents us all. Miss America? She surely does.

By a mile!

Meg's Original and Revised Paragraphs

Original Introduction

A comment made on national television by an Amerian teenage boy rang in my ears. "I don't care much about the people in China or wherever. I have everything that I want." This young man, probably only a few years my junior, as American-looking as apple pie, uttered one of the most frightening statements I have ever heard in my life because it reflects the attitudes of many of the young people in America today.

Revised Introduction

"I don't much care about the people in China or wherever. I have everything that I want." This comment was made by an American teenage boy who was being interviewed on a television news broadcast concerning the effects war had had on children in various parts of the world. This young man, probably only a few years my junior, as American-looking as apple pie, with wind-tossled hair and rosy cheeks, uttered one of the most frightening statements I have ever heard in my life. Why is this statement so frightening? Because it reflects the attitudes of many of the young people in America today. Because it shows the selfishness of a generation that has been pampered and protected from reality. Because it rings in my ears like a message of destruction—the destruction of my own generation.

Original Middle Paragraph

Not only has laziness made my generation weak physically as well as mentally, but it has also made us weak politically. Young Amerians today are not concerned with the news. There are hardly any political activists under thirty. There is nothing positive about my generation in the news. The last time I heard anything concerning this generation in the news was the fact that approximately 1,000 college students in America committed suicide last year.

Revised Middle Paragraph

Laziness has made my generation not only physically and mentally weak, but also politically weak. How many young

Americans today could tell you what's going on in the news? How many really care? How many care about the E.R.A., civil rights, or the situation in Nicaragua? Why should this generation care about Vietnam or the incident at My Lai? We've never had to go to war. How many political activists are under the age of thirty? How many political protests, demonstrations, or community organizations do young people participate in? Very few. Whatever happened to the youth revolution of the 1960s that was going to change the world? They tried. We haven't. How many times do you hear anything positive about this generation in the news? The last time I heard anything concerning this generation in the news was the fact that approximately 1,000 college students in America committed suicide last year. And the number is steadily increasing.

Original Conclusion

The situation at hand is frightening. The future of this nation will one day be in our hands. Will we know how to handle the terrifying realities that are in store for us? Only if we grow and mature. Only if we learn to care for and love those other than ourselves.

Revised Conclusion

The situation at hand is frightening. The future of this nation will one day be in our hands. Will we know how to handle the terrifying realities that are in store for us? I hope so. I am not saying that every single person in this generation is selfish, lazy, or irresponsible. Some are not, many are. Maybe we will grow and mature. Maybe we will learn to care for and love those other than ourselves. I hope so. If not, our minds will congeal, our eyes will collect dust, and our idle hands will begin to fidget angrily with the war toys our forefathers built.
The result?
The end of fun, of laziness—
Of everything.

Both Sophie and Meg improved the effectiveness of their paragraphs a great deal, and they generated more ideas in addition to making these ideas more forceful by using emphasis. In your opinion, which writer was more successful? Why? At this point, you might want to reread both their final drafts, identifying the various kinds of emphasis each of them uses throughout their essays.

Margo's Final Draft

Meat into the Eater: A Satirical Look at Militant Vegetarians

1 She looked at me with crystal-clear china-blue eyes set in a face with a flawless complexion and announced almost defensively, "I don't eat MEAT."

2 "So what!" I wanted to shout. "I eat it three times a day, preferably raw, and I like to suck eggs out of their shells for dessert!"

3 But I was working and, of course, one must always be courteous to the customer who (it goes without saying) is always right, no matter how far they might make you want to stick your finger down your throat. It was a typical harried Friday night at Burrito Bob's, where I work, and the last thing I felt like dealing with at that hour was a rampant vegetarian. But I told myself to take it easy, it would all be over before I knew it.

4 "Well, then, perhaps you'd like to try our Guacamole Salad or the Vegetarian Sample Platter," I suggested amicably enough.

5 "Well, I don't know. It doesn't have any MEAT on it does it? I don't eat MEAT." (They always pronounce the word as if a large clump of barnyard offal had just been deposited in their mouths.)

6 "Hey," I thought to myself, "this one's stupid, too," but managed to explain congenially that it contained no meat, hence the name <u>Vegetarian</u> Sample Platter. She finally settled, after what seemed like hours of deliberation, on the Guacamole Salad (probably still not quite sure as to the exact nature of the Sample Platter), drank a few after-dinner drinks with her friend, smoked a few cigarettes, and left. I always find it highly ironic that some of your most militant meat shunners will consume alcohol by the barrels and smoke cigarettes by the barnsful. They probably do drugs, too, in vast quantities, as long as they're organic and contain no animal fat.

7 Actually, I don't particularly care what anyone puts into his or her own body, or how they go about it. And I don't have a thing in the world against vegetarians, as long as they don't castigate me for my choice of a diet somewhat different from theirs. It's the ones who are always on the defensive, always ready to condemn others for what they see as a less than wholesome or "natural" lifestyle that rub me the wrong way.

8 I even tried vegetarianism once myself, but for a variety of reasons, eventually reverted to my old ways. I had, for a couple of years, become fairly actively involved in a local natural foods cooperative in which a large percentage of the members

were vegetarians with holistically oriented lifestyles. The basic concept of the cooperative, and many of the dietary doctrines promoted there, seemed (and still seem) sensible, even attractive. But through this venture, I soon found that the majority of the hard-core vegetarians and "naturalists" were disappointingly shallow and one-dimensional. Their whole life's interests seemed to be consumed wholly by food: the nature, procurement, and preparation of it. Trying to broach a topic of conversation with them that was not centered around natural foods or some other aspect of holistic life was like asking a tree for the time of day. Meat was anathema to them, and anyone who ate it or even <u>thought</u> of eating it was worthy of consignment to the ninth circle of Hell. Naturally, I soon began to feel grossly out of place with this bunch and eventually dropped out.

9 Recently at Krogers, I ran into Syl, an old acquaintance, one of the militants from the co-op. I noticed her perusing the produce stand as I hurried past on my way to the meat counter to pick up some pork chops for the grill. She flagged me down and, after the customary exchanges, announced that she was expecting her first child some months down the road. I was somewhat shocked, as she was still single and seemed wholly unprepared for motherhood and child-rearing. Evidently my surprise must have made itself obvious, for she intimated, as she selected a hefty cabbage, that her natural contraceptive had proven somewhat less than effective. The father, another rampant veg (of course) and general self-righteous jerk, had recently gone north to take up residence at a Yoga retreat. She would join him there later where the baby would be born (of course) by the natural method.

10 By now, the pork chops and grill were beckoning to my gnawing stomach, and I was beginning to sicken of this entire little scenario. I must admit I had to quell the urge to extend my most sincere wish that Mr. and Ms. Natural's natural issue emerge, appropriately enough, as a tofu baby with alfalfa sprouts for hair. But clearly this was not the occasion for such hostile levity. Just when I thought I could make a clean getaway came the inevitable dreaded question: "What are you buying here, Margo?" (They always have to know what you're eating.)

11 "Oh, well, we're cooking out tonight, and I just thought I'd pick up a few things for the grill," I found myself answering sheepishly.

12 "Still eating MEAT?" she demanded disgustedly, that familiar glint of disapproval in her eye. "I still never touch it, of course."

13 "Great!" I wanted to scream. "And I bet you still don't shave

your legs or armpits or use deodorant, and I bet you still fart all the time from eating garbanzo paste and dried figs!"

14 But, ever the diplomat, I managed to choke back my exasperation and only say with a condescending smile, "How wonderful. You'll probably live longer than me, but I bet I'll enjoy it more."

Conclusion

Of the three student essays—Margo's, Sophie's, and Meg's—which do you prefer? Why? Which one contains the best writing, judged on these bases: the significance of the thesis, development, coherence, and style? Of these student essays and the professional ones in the last chapter, which do you like best? Why? Which is the best written? Which essay do you like least? Why?

From this text and your first-semester course in composition, you have learned a great deal about writing, so that you probably have much more to say about why you prefer one essay over another. Also as a result of what you have learned about writing, you have undoubtedly become a more astute critic of your classmates' writing and of your own as well.

In addition to becoming a better writer and a better critic of writing, I hope you have also become convinced that writing is a way of seeing and knowing and that it is, therefore, a way of living, a way of being truly alive. Above all, I hope that you continue to write as a way to make meaning of your own world and the world we all live in.

Proofreading Tip: Subject/Verb Agreement

Agreement between subject and verb simply means that a singular subject takes a singular verb and a plural subject takes a plural verb.

Steve reads the newspaper daily.
Several *students read* the newspaper daily.

However, in certain constructions, students have trouble with agreement. For example, when a prepositional phrase intervenes between subject and verb, writers will sometimes make the verb agree with the object of the preposition, not the subject of the sentence. Following is an example, which you may have noticed when you read Sophie's essay in this chapter.

The *damage* of these pageants *go* far beyond the individual.

Since the noun *damage* is the singular subject, the verb must also be singular.

> The *damage* of these pageants *goes* far beyond the individual.

Another construction that causes trouble is a sentence that begins with one of the expletives, *there* or *here*. In such a construction the subject comes after the verb, and the inclination is to use a singular verb without checking the subject beforehand.

> Here *is* your *books.*
> There *is* several *bookcases* in my room.

The subjects of both these sentences, *books* and *bookcases*, are plural. Thus, the following sentences are correct.

> Here *are* your *books.*
> There *are* several *bookcases* in my room.

Another construction sometimes causing trouble is a compound subject joined by *either/or, neither/nor*. When both subjects are singular, the verb is singular; if both are plural, the verb is plural.

> Neither the *dog* nor the *cat likes* to go to the vet's.
> Neither the *dogs* nor the *cats like* to go to the vet's.

However, the trouble occurs when one subject is singular and the other is plural. Like the rule involving compound subjects with *here* and *there*, the verb agrees in number with the subject nearer it.

> Neither the dog nor the *cats like* to go to the vet's.
> Neither the cats nor the *dog likes* to go to the vet's.

If one or both of the subjects are personal pronouns, the verb agrees in number with the subject nearer it, and only the pronouns *he, she* and *it* take a singular verb. For example, in this sentence, would the auxilary verb be *has* or *have?*

> Both Maria and Jim play tennis, but neither she nor he _____ taken lessons.

What about the verb in this sentence?

> Maria and I (play, plays) tennis occasionally, but neither she nor I (likes, like) to play doubles.

In the first sentence the verb *has* is correct because singular subjects joined by *either/or, neither/nor* take a singular verb. In the second sentence, the first verb should be the plural verb *play* because compound subjects joined by *and* are plural. The second verb should also be the plural verb *like* because the personal pronoun closer to the verb is the pronoun *I*, which takes a plural verb.

One final construction causing trouble involves collective nouns that designate a group of people, such as *team, class, faculty, committee,* and *jury,* to name a few. When the sentence indicates that such subjects are *acting as one,* as a unit, the verb is *singular.* On the other hand, if the sentence indicates that the subject *acts individually* with a *plurality of actions,* the verb is *plural.* For example, the following sentences are correct.

> The jury *have* not *agreed* on the verdict.
> The jury *has agreed* on the verdict.

Now consider this sentence:

> The faculty *has* not *voted* on the new grading system yet.

Why should the verb be the plural *have* instead of the singular *has?* Individual members cast individual votes.

> The faculty *have* not *voted* on the new grading system yet.

What about these sentences?

> The committee *adjourns* at three o'clock.

Because the noun *committee* is acting as a unit here, the singular verb *adjourns* is correct.

> The committee *eat* at various nearby restaurants.

Here, because the sentence indicates a plurality of action, the plural verb *eat* is correct.

Exercise: Recognizing and Correcting Errors in Subject/Verb Agreement

Read the following sentences and cross out any incorrect verbs. Rewrite the sentence in the space provided if the verb needs to be corrected.

  1. When either Sue or I go shopping, we always spend too much.

  2. Brett, along with his friends Jamie and Clara, like to jog in the early morning.

  3. The dean and the faculty has decided to revise the grading system.

  4. There is several reasons why students and faculty needs a fall break.

  5. Either Rebecca or Juanita is planning a surprise party for Laura.

6. Lana and Phillip like to water-ski, but neither she nor her friend like to drive the boat.

7. Today the jury vote for or against the defendant.

8. The class meet at eight o'clock on Monday and Wednesday evenings.

9. Neither rain nor snow keep the postman from his appointed rounds.

10. Here is some new topics for you to write about.

If you are using the present tense in your essay, you will need to be more careful about agreement than if you are using the past tense because only the verb *to be* makes a distinction between singular and plural number in the past tense. *(I, he, she,* or *it was; we, you,* or *they were).*

Proofread carefully and try not to let any lack of agreement between subject and verb escape your attention.

Suggestions for Further Writing

1. Make a survey of students on your campus, asking why they think that the Miss America contest is, or is not, a good idea. Then write an essay supporting your own position, and cite one or more of the students you interviewed as support for one or more of your statements.

2. Take a poll of classmates or dormmates about their reading habits. Ask if they read a weekly news magazine or a newspaper regularly. Ask which magazine or newspaper they read and which sections interest them most. Write a report of your findings.

3. Write an essay in which you discuss what you like about the attitudes or other characteristics of your generation.

4. Write a letter to Meg stating why you agree or disagree with her thesis. Be sure to give examples or other data to support your generalizations. (If you have done the second suggestion, you might use statistical data or quotations from your interviews.)

5. Write a letter to Margo stating why you agree or disagree with her thesis. Be sure to support your reasons with examples or other means of development.

6. Write a letter to John Ciardi stating why you agree or disagree with his thesis. Be sure to give support for your reasons.

7. What is the most disturbing aspect of television in your opinion? Respond in a freewrite.

8. Write a private journal entry exploring a prejudice that you wish you did not have. State what the prejudice is, how long you have had it, the reasons you think you developed it, how it makes you feel about yourself, and what you might do to eliminate it.

9. Write a letter to Lewis Thomas stating why you agree or disagree with his thesis. Be sure you give support for your reasons.

10. Write a letter to Amitai Etzioni stating why you agree or disagree with his thesis. Be sure to give support for your reasons.

11. What attitudes and characteristics do you find most disturbing in people eight to ten years younger than yourself? Respond in a freewrite.

12. Assume the role of Plato to Postman's Socrates. Write a letter to Postman in which you point out the positive aspects of television. You might also consider possible future developments in its use.

13. Other than racial prejudice, make a list of prejudices that you find particularly annoying in other people. Choose one and write an essay in which you explain why this particular prejudice is so annoying to you.

14. Suppose that you were a visitor to America from a highly evolved culture on another planet. Write an essay in which you criticize one or more of the attitudes, actions, or institutions of Earthlings that you consider especially barbaric in the light of your advanced morality and consciousness. (You might entitle the essay "Letter to Earth" or something similar.)

Ways to Combine Sentences

Part I: Sentence Combining Using Adverb and Adjective Clauses

The Adverb Clause

If you write two simple sentences that have a temporal or causal relationship, you can combine them using an adverb clause introduced by a subordinate conjunction that indicates time or cause. For example, consider these two simple sentences:

Joan played golf. Her husband went shopping.

As they are written now, the precise causal or temporal relationship between these two sentences is not explicit. However, if we combine them, using various subordinate conjunctions, we can show the many precise causal or temporal relationships that are possible between the two.

When Joan played golf, her husband went shopping. (time)
Whenever Joan played golf, her husband went shopping. (time)
After Joan played golf, her husband went shopping. (time)
While Joan played golf, her husband went shopping. (time)
Before Joan played golf, her husband went shopping. (time)
Until Joan played golf, her husband went shopping. (time)
As Joan played golf, her husband went shopping. (time or cause)
Because Joan played golf, her husband went shopping. (cause)
Since Joan played golf, her husband went shopping. (cause)

As you can see, combining sentences that have a causal or temporal relationship allows you to show that relationship explicitly through the use of various subordinate conjunctions. For example, here are some other possible relationships between these two sentences.

Joan played golf when her husband went shopping.
Joan played golf whenever her husband went shopping.

Joan played golf after her husband went shopping.
Joan played golf while her husband went shopping.
Joan played golf before her husband went shopping.
Joan played golf until her husband went shopping.
Joan played golf as her husband went shopping.
Joan played golf because her husband went shopping.
Joan played golf since her husband went shopping.

In this set of sentences the causal or temporal relationships have shifted from those shown in the first set. In both sets, however, the relationship will remain the same in each sentence whether the adverb clause comes first or last.

Joan played golf after her husband went shopping.
After her husband went shopping, Joan played golf.

The meaning of both sentences is the same: the husband goes shopping, and afterwards, Joan plays golf. The beauty of this particular syntactic (pertaining to the order of words in a sentence) feature of adverb clauses is that if you need to vary the beginning of a sentence because you have too many starting with the subject, you can choose the second option just discussed.

Now let's look at two sentences similar to ones you might write in an essay.

Jennifer came home after midnight. I didn't get a wink of sleep.

The implied relationship is causal; thus, we could use *because, since,* or *as.*

Because Jennifer came home after midnight, I didn't get a wink of sleep.
I didn't get a wink of sleep because Jennifer came home after midnight.

You should note that there is a comma after the introductory adverb clause, but that there is no comma before the conjunction when the clause ends the sentence. This is the general rule, but if the introductory clause is very short, you may *sometimes* omit the comma. Whether or not you omit the comma depends on the sentence. Look at this sentence, for example.

When it rains it pours.

Now read this one:

When it rains cats and dogs usually go indoors.

Did you misread this sentence the first time? Look at the difference when a comma is placed after the introductory clause.

When it rains, cats and dogs usually go indoors.

You should not have had any trouble this time. Just keep in mind that when you punctuate sentences, your punctuation should be an aid to the reader's understanding.

Last, in addition to the ones just listed, there are other subordinate conjunctions that introduce adverb clauses, such as *although, even though, whereas, as if, as long as, as soon as, as though, if, unless,* and *than.* However, it is unlikely that you would construct two sentences that could be combined using one of these conjunctions. Because of the particular kinds or relationships expressed by these conjunctions, you would use them in one sentence, not in two, to express your thought. For example, would you write the following two sentences?

> I will not go to the party. I will not go to the party unless you come, too.

You see, it is impossible to express the relationship shown by the conjunction *unless* without using it.

Exercise I: Using Adverb Clauses to Combine Sentences

Combine the following pairs of sentences by using adverb clauses, and be sure to write each combination twice, using both of your syntactical options.

1. Yesterday was sunny and warm. My son and I flew kites in the park.
2. Christmas was a cold, blustery day. We sat before a fire, eating walnuts and roasted marshmallows.
3. Tuesday, Barry partied almost all night. Wednesday morning he failed his calculus exam.
4. Mother came home late. I had already done the dishes.
5. Sonny wanted a job for the summer. He had large bills at several department stores.

The Adjective Clause

Besides using the adverb clause, you can also use the adjective clause to combine two sentences when one sentence adds information about a noun or pronoun in the other one. For example, consider these two sentences:

> My daughter lives in Greensboro. She is a student at UNCG.

When we combine these sentences, we have two textual options in the adjective clause.

> My daughter, who lives in Greensboro, is a student at UNCG.
> My daughter, who is a student at UNCG, lives in Greensboro.

Which sentence is preferable? We cannot truly say because we do not know the context in which the two sentences appear. However, as a general rule, the more important information should be written in the independent clause. Only if we knew the context would we know which sentence contained the more important information, but out of context, most people would probably agree that the first sentence is preferable because what a person does is usually considered more important than where he or she lives.

Now let's look at sentences we can combine using *whom*, the objective case of the pronoun *who*. Consider these two sentences and the combination beneath them.

> Thea Elvsted paid a call on George and Hedda.
> Hedda did not like her.

> Thea Elvsted, whom Hedda did not like, paid a call on George and Hedda.

If you have trouble telling which case of the relative pronoun to use, the subjective *who* or the objective *whom*, look at the case of the pronoun in the sentence you replace with the adjective clause. In the second of the preceding sentences, "Hedda did not like her," the pronoun *her* is in the objective case; therefore, you will use the objective relative pronoun *whom* when you replace the sentence with the adjective clause. Of course, you can also analyze the sentence elements in the adjective clause to determine which case you should use:

> s v v *d.o.*
> Hedda did not like whom.

To test this hint, let's look at one more example.

> Mr. Sweet died while Alice Walker was in graduate school. Alice Walker's family really loved him.

Before we combine these sentences, what is the case of the pronoun *him?* Since it is the objective case, we will use the objective case relative pronoun *whom* in the adjective clause that replaces this sentence.

> Mr. Sweet, whom Alice Walker's family really loved, died while Alice Walker was in graduate school.

Now here are two sentences that can be combined by using the relative pronoun *whose*, the possessive case of the relative pronoun *who*.

> My daughter is biking across the country. Her friend Amy is accompanying her.
> My daughter, whose friend Amy is accompanying her, is biking across the country.

Note that the pronoun *her* which is both the objective and possessive form of the feminine personal pronoun, is replaced in the adjective clause by the possessive relative pronoun *whose.*

Here is another example:

I know a wealthy woman. Her poodle has a diamond collar.
I know a wealthy woman whose poodle has a diamond collar.

You have probably noticed that the preceding sentence differs from all the previous examples in one respect: there is no comma separating the adjective clause from the rest of the sentence. The reason is that the adjective clause in the sentence is needed to identify the noun *woman.* Thus, because it is needed in the sentence, it is not separated from it by a comma. This kind of clause is called an *essential* adjective clause. As you might expect, adjective clauses that are *not needed* to further identify the nouns they modify are called *nonessential.* In the other examples in this section, the adjective clauses were nonessential because they were not needed to further identify the nouns that they modified.

If a nonessential clause comes in the middle of a sentence, there is a comma before it and one after it, as you saw in the other examples. If the clause comes at the end of the sentence, there is a comma before it. For example, if we change the earlier sentences, we can make the adjective clause nonessential, and we can write it at the end of the sentence or in the middle.

Amelia Jones is a very wealthy woman. Her poodle has a diamond collar.
Amelia Jones is a very wealthy woman, whose poodle has a diamond collar.

or

Amelia Jones, whose poodle has a diamond collar, is a very wealthy woman.

Remember that if the adjective clause is not needed (nonessential) to further identify a noun, it is separated from the sentence by commas. On the other hand, if the clause is needed (essential) for further identification of a noun, there are no commas separating it from the sentence.

Besides the relative pronouns *who, whose,* and *whom,* you can also use the relative pronouns *that* and *which* to introduce adjective clauses. However, as a general rule, the pronoun *that* is used to introduce *essential* clauses, whereas the pronoun *which* is used to introduce *nonessential* clauses. There is also one other distinction made among these pronouns: the pronouns *who, whom,* and *whose* are used to *refer only to people,* not to animals or objects; the pronoun *which* is used to *refer only to animals or objects,* never to people; last, the pronoun *that* is used to *refer to people, animals,* or *objects.*

Now let's look at two sentences that we can combine by using one of the relative pronouns *which* or *that*.

A dog appeared at my door. It was emaciated and dirty.

It appears that we have two textual options in the adjective clause, but which pronoun would be better? Let's see.

A dog that was emaciated and dirty appeared at my door.
A dog that appeared at my door was emaciated and dirty.
A dog which appeared at my door was emaciated and dirty.
A dog which was emaciated and dirty appeared at my door.

Since both clauses are essential, the relative pronoun *that* is preferred. Now let's look at the following sentences and possible combinations.

The day was almost over. It had been cold and dreary.
The day, which was almost over, had been cold and dreary.
The day, which had been cold and dreary, was almost over.

Why is the pronoun *which* preferred here? In both sentences, "The day had been cold and dreary" and "The day was almost over," the noun *day* is sufficiently identified so that the additional information in the adjective clause is nonessential. Consider these two sentences and the combinations that follow them.

My neighbors have gone on vacation. They asked me to mow their grass.
My neighbors, which have gone on vacation, asked me to mow their grass.
My neighbors, which asked me to mow their grass, have gone on vacation.

What's wrong with these two combined sentences? The adjective clause is nonessential, so why not use the pronoun *which?* As you should recall, we need to use the pronouns *who* or *that* because the noun *neighbors* refers to people. Of these two pronouns, *who* is preferable because the pronoun *who* is preferred when an adjective clause modifies a person or people. Also, the clause is nonessential, and the pronoun *that* is preferred in essential clauses.

My neighbors, who have gone on vacation, asked me to mow their grass.
My neighbors, who asked me to mow their grass, have gone on vacation.

Here is one last example, followed by two possible combinations.

A silver necklace lay on the table. It was covered with dust and mold.
A silver necklace that was covered with dust and mold lay on the table.
A silver necklace that lay on the table was covered with dust and mold.

Exercise II: Using Adjective Clauses to Combine Sentences

Now, combine these pairs of sentences and use all your textual and/or syntactical options. Then put a checkmark by the combinations you prefer because the more important information comes in the independent clause, because the rhythm is better, or because the more important or concrete words come at the end. Keep in mind that you are making these judgments out of context.

1. Joe's father is a butcher. He has worked at the A&P store for twenty years.
2. A. R. Ammons is a well-known poet. He was born in Whiteville, North Carolina.
3. A young girl stood by the entrance to the library. She had a wistful look on her face.
4. Fred Chappell lives in Greensboro, North Carolina. In 1985 he won the Bollingen Prize for poetry.
5. My grandfather visited us last summer. I did not remember him.

Exercise III: Using Adverb and Adjective Clauses to Combine Sentences

In order for you to practice combining sentences using both adjective and adverb clauses, combine the following pairs of sentences. If you can combine any pair using both kinds of clauses in two different sentences, do so. Also, if you can combine two sentences using more than one adjective or adverb clause, use all your textual and/or syntactical options.

1. Jennifer broke her leg at the senior prom. She had to be carried up and down stairs for two weeks.
2. Hedda Gabler is the heroine of one of Henrik Ibsen's most famous dramas. She is a manipulative and frustrated woman.
3. My neighbor is a very good criminal lawyer. Her husband tends to the house and the children.
4. Shakespeare's tragedy *King Lear* is one of his most difficult plays. It is, perhaps, his greatest drama.
5. Behind the house there was a barn. It was old and vine-covered.
6. The Jenkinses won the New Jersey lottery. They went on a tour of Europe last summer.
7. Othello is a well-known tragic hero. He was viciously deceived by Iago.
8. D. H. Lawrence wrote the play *The Widowing of Mrs. Holroyd*. Then he wrote a story similar to it entitled "Odour of Chrysanthemums."
9. Mike was an excellent quarterback throughout his high

school years. He won an athletic scholarship to Washington State University.

10. Virginia Woolf has received a great deal of acclaim from feminist critics. Her novels *Mrs. Dalloway* and *To the Lighthouse* are particularly interesting.

Exercise IV: Sentence Combining in the Context of Your Own Writing

Read through the essays you have written so far, and look for sentences that could be combined by using either adverb or adjective clauses. Copy these sentences on a piece of paper and beneath them write the combination having the syntactical and textual option that best suits your needs and purpose at that particular point in your essay.

Part II: Sentence Combining Using Appositive, Prepositional, Participial, Infinitive, and Absolute Phrases

The Nonessential Appositive Phrase

The appositive phrase is a noun phrase that renames a noun either before or after it. Nearly all sentences with nonessential adjective clauses can be rewritten by using a nonessential appositive phrase in place of the adjective clause. Like the nonessential adjective clause, the nonessential appositive phrase is separated from the sentence by commas. For example, consider these sentences from Part I:

Joe's father is a butcher. He has worked at the A&P store for twenty years.

Instead of combining these sentences with the adjective clause "who is a butcher," we can use the appositive phrase:

Joe's father, a butcher, has worked at the A&P store for twenty years.
A butcher, Joe's father has worked at the A&P store for twenty years.

We can also construct an appositive phrase from the second optional adjective clause "who has worked at the A&P store for twenty years."

Joe's father, an employee of the A&P store for twenty years, is a butcher.
An employee of the A&P store for twenty years, Joe's father is a butcher.

Even though the appositive phrase may be placed before or after the noun it renames, you probably noticed that one or the other position sounds better, depending on the length or construction of the phrase itself or on the noun it renames. For instance, in the first pair of sentences, the second arrangement beginning with the appositive *a butcher* sounds awkward. The reason may be that the noun it renames, *father*, is preceded by the possessive noun *Joe's*. If we remove the possessive and substitute a name for the noun *father*, the awkwardness diminishes somewhat.

A butcher, Bob Jones has worked at the A&P store for twenty years.

On the other hand, in the second pair of sentences, the appositive phrase placed at the beginning of the sentence works better than it does placed after the noun *father*. The reason is that the appositive phrase is quite long, so that it causes a lengthy separation between the subject *father* and the verb *is*. Thus, even though you have one more syntactical option using the nonessential appositive phrase than you have using the nonessential adjective clause to combine any two sentences, your options will sometimes be reduced because of the awkwardness of one of the constructions.

Let's look at two more sentences from Part I. Perhaps with these sentences, all four combinations will work well.

Fred Chappell won the Bollingen Prize for poetry in 1985. He lives in Greensboro, North Carolina.
Fred Chappell, a resident of Greensboro, North Carolina, won the Bollingen Prize for poetry in 1985.
A resident of Greensboro, North Carolina, Fred Chappell won the Bollingen Prize for poetry in 1985.
Fred Chappell, winner of the Bollingen Prize for poetry in 1985, lives in Greensboro, North Carolina.
Winner of the Bollingen Prize for poetry in 1985, Fred Chappell lives in Greensboro, North Carolina.

Which sentences do you prefer? They all read fairly well, with the exception, perhaps, of the third combination in which the appositive phrase causes too long a separation between subject and verb. However, if we keep in mind that the most important information should be written in the independent clause and that it should also come at the end of a sentence, then one of the first two sentences would be best, and since both of these sentences read well, your final choice would depend on your context. For example, perhaps you need a sentence that does not begin with the subject. If so, you would choose the second sentence. Or, perhaps, you would choose the first sentence because it provided a better transition.

The Essential Appositive Phrase

When you combine sentences by using the essential appositive phrase, you will have neither the textual nor the syntactical options that you have when you use nonessential phrases. There will be only one textual possibility, and the phrase will always come after the noun it renames. In addition, like the essential adjective clause, there will be no commas to separate it from the rest of the sentence. Let's look at two sentences that can be combined by using an essential appositive phrase.

Jane's roommate is named Miranda. She is from Burbank, California.
Jane's roommate Miranda is from Burbank, California.

In this combination the proper noun *Miranda* is the essential appositive that identifies Jane's roommate. Now here is a further example:

Hemingway wrote a novel called *For Whom the Bell Tolls*. It takes its title from one of John Donne's "Meditations."
Hemingway's novel *For Whom the Bell Tolls* takes its title from one of John Donne's "Meditations."

Obviously, we need the essential appositive *For Whom the Bell Tolls* in order to identify which Hemingway novel the sentence refers to. Let's look at one more example.

One of Annie Dillard's essays is entitled "God's Tooth." It is about an inexplicable tragedy involving a young girl.
Annie Dillard's essay "God's Tooth" is about an inexplicable tragedy involving a young girl.

You should note that if you reverse the order of these noun phrases, the appositive phrase will become nonessential. Can you analyze why this happens?

Miranda, Jane's roommate, is from Burbank.

For Whom the Bell Tolls, a novel by Hemingway, takes its title from one of John Donne's "Meditations."

"God's Tooth," an essay by Annie Dillard, is about an inexplicable tragedy involving a young girl.

The difference is that the essential information is now contained in the sentence. Hence, the appositive phrase is not needed.

Exercise I: Using Appositive Phrases to Combine Sentences

Now, to practice using the appositive phrase to combine sentences, try combining the following pairs of sentences. When you use nonessential phrases, remember to use all your textual and syntactical options, even though one or more may result in an awkward sentence. At this point, you want to learn all the options you have for constructing and combining sentences. Later, when you are writing an essay, you can reject those options that result in awkward constructions. When you must use an essential appositive phrase to combine two sentences, you will have only one option. The following is an example of what you should do with combinations that use nonessential phrases.

Susan is a very energetic person. She is majoring in engineering.

Susan, an energetic person, is majoring in engineering.

An energetic person, Susan is majoring in engineering.

Susan, an engineering major, is a very energetic person.

An engineering major, Susan is a very energetic person.

1. Shakespeare wrote a tragedy called *Hamlet.* It takes place in Denmark.
2. My sister Gail was a star athlete. She was a member of the varsity basketball squads in junior high and high school.
3. Josie is a very talented and unselfish person. She is an excellent student and a volunteer worker in a convalescent home.
4. Virginia Woolf wrote a novel called *To the Lighthouse.* It describes the fascinating character Mrs. Ramsay.
5. Mrs. Dalloway is the heroine of one of Virginia Woolf's novels. She is an unforgettable character.

The Prepositional Phrase

In addition to using appositive phrases, you may combine two or more sentences by using one or more prepositional phrases. Although prepositions are too numerous to mention them all, some that you might use are the following: *besides, in addition to, in, on, upon, with, despite, between, among,* and *during.*

For example, consider these two sentences.

Dr. Stephens is the chairman of the English department. He is also a member of the board of trustees.

Besides being chairman of the English department, Dr. Stephens is also a member of the board of trustees.

Besides being a member of the board of trustees, Dr. Stephens is also chairman of the English department.

Here is another example:

A young man strolled down the lane past my house. He had a red beard.

A young man with a red beard strolled down the lane past my house.

Exercise II: Using Prepositional Phrases to Combine Sentences

Now try using prepositional phrases to combine the following sentences and remember to use all the options you have. After you have finished combining by using prepositional phrases, whenever you can do so, combine each set of sentences by using an appositive phrase. Be sure to use all textual and syntactical options even though one option results in an awkward sentence.

1. Mother stood by the kitchen sink. She had a sad look on her face.
2. Gregory played the last half of the game. He was in terrible pain from a broken ankle.
3. Frieda is pre-med major. She is also president of the student council and a member of the debate team.
4. Ann's father is mayor of Centerville. He is also a partner in an automobile dealership and an alderman of his church.
5. Jean's mother is very intelligent and caring. She is also a very busy pediatrician.

The Participial Phrase

Now let's look at how you can combine sentences using participial phrases. There are two participles in English—the present participle, which ends in *-ing* and the past participle, which ends in *-ed* in regular verbs. In irregular verbs there is a vowel change. For example, *wearing* and *worn* are the present and past participles, respectively, of the verb *to wear*, whereas the present and past participles of the regular verb *to dress* are *dressing* and *dressed*. Both of these participial forms, which must add a form of the verb *to be* in order to become finite verbs, can be used alone as adjectives. Look at the following example.

The water *is running*. (finite verb)
Running water gets on my nerves. (adjective)
I *was dressed* for the dance. (finite verb)
Dressed for the dance, I was ready to go. (adjective)

As you see in the last example, participles may also have modifiers. In this sentence the prepositional phrase *for the dance* modifies the participle *dressed*.

Now consider these two sentences. How could you combine them using a present or past participial phrase?

A. R. Ammons was born in Whiteville, North Carolina. He is a well-known poet.

A. R. Ammons, born in Whiteville, North Carolina, is a well-known poet.

Born in Whiteville, North Carolina, A. R. Ammons is a well-known poet.

As you see in these two sentences, the past participial phrase may come either before or after the word it modifies. In addition to these two positions, the present participial phrase may sometimes also take a position at the end of a sentence. Occasionally, however, the terminal position causes ambiguity in regard to the word the phrase modifies, as you will see when we combine the following two sentences, using all the options we have.

> The young executive scurried up the stairs. She was carrying her briefcase.

> Carrying her briefcase, the young executive scurried up the stairs.

> The young executive, carrying her briefcase, scurried up the stairs.

> The young executive scurried up the stairs, carrying her briefcase.

> Scurrying up the stairs, the young executive carried her briefcase.

> The young executive, scurrying up the stairs, carried her briefcase.

> The young executive carried her briefcase, scurrying up the stairs. (!)

Strange briefcase, huh? So we lost one option. Nevertheless, we have created *five* sentences that will work by using the participial phrase to combine two sentences. Also, since the participial phrase allows you at least two, and sometimes three, syntactical options, it is a handy construction to know.

Now let's look at two sentences that will not allow you the number of options you had with the two sentences we just combined.

> I got dressed too hurriedly. I forgot to tie my shoelaces.
> Dressing too hurriedly, I forgot to tie my shoelaces.
> I, dressing too hurriedly, forgot to tie my shoelaces.
> I forgot to tie my shoelaces, dressing too hurriedly.

It appears that with pronouns, the participial phrase must come *before* it. Now, let's see what happens when we try the other optional participial phrase.

> Forgetting to tie my shoelaces, I dressed too hurriedly.
> I, forgetting to tie my shoelaces, dressed too hurriedly.
> I dressed too hurriedly, forgetting to tie my shoelaces.

The first sentence in this set does not work because it reverses the logical cause-effect sequence. That is, the cause is dressing too quickly; the effect is untied shoelaces. The second sentence won't work because it appears that you cannot put a participial phrase *after* the pronoun it modifies. But what about the last sentence? How is it different from the last sentence in the first set? The difference is that in the last sentence of the first set, the word preceding the phrase is the noun *shoelaces*, whereas in the last sentence of the second set, the word preceding the phrase is the adverb *hurriedly*. Therefore, it appears that we must amend the rule we previously formulated to read like this: A participial phrase must precede the pronoun it modifies unless it is a present participial phrase. If it is, the phrase may come at the end of the sentence as long as it does not follow a noun that it seems to modify in addition to the pronoun.

Exercise III: Using Participial Phrases to Combine Sentences

Now try combining the following sets of sentences using present or past participial phrases. Use all *the options you have that follow the syntactical rules for participial phrases. Also, if you can use either the appositive phrase or the prepositional phrase, or both, to combine each set of sentences, by all means do so after you have first exhausted all your options using the participial phrase.*

1. Dr. Jones, my energetic math instructor, strode into the classroom. He carried a book satchel over his left shoulder.
2. The young doctor hurried to her car. She was running very fast.
3. I worked from 9:00 A.M. to 9:00 P.M. for two weeks during Christmas. I earned enough money to pay half my tuition this semester.
4. Mary looked a sight. She was dressed in a pair of her father's old army fatigues.
5. Jenny stopped talking when she saw the decorated room. She was shocked. She was also delighted.

The Infinitive Phrase as a Modifier

In addition to the present and past participles of verbs, you can also use the infinitive form of verbs to combine sentences. Like the two participial forms, an infinitive alone or an infinitive phrase can be used as an adjective. However, besides being used as adjectives, infinitive phrases can also be used as adverbs and as nouns. Another difference between participial phrases and infinitive phrases is that the infinitive phrase should be placed only at the beginning or end of a sentence. Unlike the participial phrase, which may be placed after a noun it modifies, the infinitive phrase should not come between the subject and verb. For example, look at these two sentences and the combinations that follow them.

Ann quit her job. She wanted to devote more time to mothering.
To devote more time to mothering, Ann quit her job.
Ann, to devote more time to mothering, quit her job.

In the second combination you can readily see the awkwardness that results from putting an infinitive phrase between the subject and verb. Also illustrated by the first and third sentences is the sometimes arbitrary definition of an infinitive phrase as an adjective or an adverb. For instance, in the last sentence, the infinitive phrase might be considered an adverb, modifying the verb *quit* because it answers *why* Ann quit her job. On the other hand, in the first combined sentence, the phrase appears to act as an adjective, modifying the proper noun *Ann* although it might still be seen as a modifier of the verb *quit.* However, the reason for considering the phrase an adjective is that if an infinitive begins a sentence, it must modify the first noun or pronoun after it. If it does not, the result is the error known as the dangling modifier, which is discussed at greater length in the proofreading tip in Chapter 8. Look at this sentence, for example:

To be a good student, many hours of study are necessary.

What is wrong here? The noun that follows the infinitive phrase is *hours,* and *hours* cannot be good students. Thus, we need to correct the sentence with a noun or pronoun that refers to a person.

To be a good student Jan had to study for hours.
or
To be a good student, one must study for hours.

The same problem exists even if the infinitive phrase comes at the end of the sentence. There is still no noun or pronoun for the phrase to modify.

Many hours of study are necessary to be a good student.
A person must study many hours to be a good student.

Thus, when you combine sentences using an infinitive phrase as a modifier, remember this: If the phrase begins the sentence, make sure that the first noun or pronoun following it is appropriate; and if the phrase ends the sentence, be sure that there is an appropriate noun or pronoun in the sentence for the phrase to modify.

Now let's combine these two sentences:

Beth began playing racquetball several years ago. She wanted to get into better shape.

To get into better shape, Beth began playing racquetball several years ago.

Beth began playing racquetball several years ago to get into better shape.

Exercise IV: Using Infinitive Phrases as Modifiers to Combine Sentences

Before you learn how to combine sentences using the infinitive phrase as a noun, you need to practice combining sentences by using the infinitive phrase as a modifier. Combine the following sets of sentences using infinitive phrases as modifiers, and use both syntactical options in each combination. Once you have finished combining these sentences using infinitive phrases, whenever it is possible to do so, combine each set by using the other phrasal constructions you have learned to use—the appositive, the prepositional, and the participial. When you use these other constructions, be sure that you also use all the textual and/or syntactical options afforded by each.

1. My mother learned how to use a word processor. She wanted to get a better job. She also wanted to make more money.
2. Last year I took up jogging. I wanted to improve my health.
3. Sarah decided to major in special education. She wanted to help children with learning disabilities.
4. Steve sunbathed daily. He wanted to get a good tan.
5. The horses came close to the fence. They wanted the sugar cubes we held in our hands.

The Infinitive Phrase as a Noun

Last, unlike the participial phrase, the infinitive alone or the infinitive phrase may be used as a noun. Thus, you could combine two sentences using an infinitive phrase as the subject of a sentence or as the predicate noun. For example, look at these two sentences and the following combinations.

The reason I came to college was that I wanted to get a good education. I also wanted to improve my social skills.
To get a good education and to improve my social skills were the reasons I came to college. (subject)
The reasons I came to college were to get a good education and to improve my social skills. (predicate noun)

Before you try your hand at combining sentences by using infinitive phrases as nouns, here is one more example. How would you combine these three sentences?

Jill had two goals in life. She wanted to become an ichthyologist. She also wanted to raise horses.

There are two combinations possible, as you saw previously: one uses the infinitive phrase as the subject, the other uses it as the predicate noun.

To become an ichthyologist and to raise horses were Jill's two goals in life.

Jill's two goals in life were to become an ichthyologist and to raise horses.

Exercise V: Using Infinitive Phrases Both as Modifiers and Nouns to Combine Sentences

The following are five sets of sentences that you may combine using infinitive phrases as modifiers, as nouns, or as both. Whenever possible, combine them by using the infinitive phrase both as a modifier and as a noun. Also be sure to use all textual and/or syntactical options. Here is an example.

Mary went to New York. She wanted to get away from home. She also wanted to become an actress.

To get away from home and to become an actress, Mary went to New York.

Mary went to New York to get away from home and to become an actress.

To get away from home and to become an actress were the reasons Mary went to New York.

The reasons Mary went to New York were to get away from home and to become an actress.

1. Linda decided to go to a community college. She wanted to be near her home and family. She also wanted to keep her job.
2. I agreed to work two months without pay. I wanted to get some job experience. I also wanted to make some contacts.
3. Competing in a swim meet takes a lot of practice. I had to swim three hours every day.
4. Bill's aims were many. He wanted money. He also wanted recognition.
5. My roommate John did a lot of things he didn't really want to do. He did them because he wanted acceptance and popularity.

The Absolute Phrase

One last phrasal construction that you might use to combine sentences is the absolute phrase. This phrase consists of a noun and modifiers. It is called absolute because it seems to convey a separate (absolute) thought although it may appear to modify either a noun in the sentence or the whole sentence that it is attached to. Like the infinitive phrase used as a modifier, the absolute phrase may be placed at the beginning or the end of a sentence. Look at these two sentences, for example.

Melinda gazed into space. Her book lay open before her.

We can combine these two sentences by using the absolute phrase in either of two positions—at the beginning or at the end of the sentence.

Her book lying open before her, Melinda gazed into space.
Melinda gazed into space, her book lying open before her.

Now, how could you use the absolute phrase to combine these two sentences?

The rain was falling in huge drops. Jeremy dashed toward the barn.

These are the possibilities:

The rain falling in huge drops, Jeremy dashed toward the barn.
Jeremy dashed toward the barn, the rain falling in huge drops.

Like the other phrasal constructions you have read about, the absolute phrase offers you syntactical options. As a result, it, too, can be very useful to you as a writer. If you need a sentence that begins with a construction other than the subject, you could write a sentence using an absolute phrase at the beginning of it. Or you could write a sentence that began with an appositive, prepositional, participial, or infinitive phrase. Of course, you also need to keep in mind other factors such as rhythm and coherence. In addition, you need to keep in mind that the emphatic position in a sentence is at the end. Consequently, you put your most important information or your most concrete images there. As with everything else in writing, your final choice of one sentence over another depends on the entire writing context, and, above all, on your purpose.

Exercise VI: Using Absolute Phrases to Combine Sentences

Now, combine the following pairs of sentences, and be sure to use both syntactical options in each combination you think of. After you have combined these sentences using the absolute phrase, read the sentences again and use any of the other phrasal constructions (appositive, prepositional, participial, or infinitive) that you can. Again, use all the textual and/or syntactical options you have with each combination.

1. Mother anxiously paced the floor by the telephone. The screen door flapped open and shut in the wind.
2. Jake waited for the ambulance. His arms were in a makeshift sling.
3. The sky was a deep purple. Julie walked the beach, thinking about her problems.
4. I told the coach that I had to quit the team. My mother's advice reverberated in my mind.

5. Ms. Jones explained the Pythagorean theorem. Her voice was as shrill as a bird's.

Exercise VII: Sentence Combining in the Context of Your Own Writing

Read through the essays you have written thus far, and look for two or more sentences that you could combine using appositive, prepositional, participial, infinitive, or absolute phrases. Copy the sentences and beneath them write the combination with the syntactical and textual option that best suits your needs and purposes at that particular point in your essay.

When you have finished this exercise, you should complete the following one.

Exercise VIII: Final Sentence-Combining Exercise Using Clauses and Phrases

Combine the following pairs or sets of sentences using as many of your options as possible: the adverb clause, the adjective clause, or the appositive, prepositional, participial, infinitive, and absolute phrases. For each construction that you are able to use, be sure to use all your syntactical and/or textual options.

1. It rained all day Saturday. Jake and I went to see *Out of Africa.*
2. My favorite professor was a middle-aged neoclassicist. He taught a course in Pope, Johnson, and Swift.
3. My friend Mary is a novelist. She is from Pennsylvania.
4. Sam slithered into the classroom. His bookbag was slung over his shoulder.
5. A weird-looking man was standing in the hallway. He had a bushy black beard.
6. John's car disappeared. He vanished around the bend into the clouds of smoke ahead.
7. My favorite professor has a great sense of humor. He graduated from Michigan State University.
8. I stayed up all night studying. The next morning I had a terrible headache.
9. Louise is a political science major. She is also interested in geriatrics and aviation.
10. I got up at six o'clock this morning. I wanted to get a good schedule for next fall.
11. I could not remain on the swim team. I hated to give it up, but I work too many hours.
12. The elephant's enormous body leveled the underbrush. He headed straight towards us.

13. My cousin Gary is a journalist. He lives in Los Angeles.
14. Matt's trip to New Orleans was cancelled. He decided to treat himself to the movies and a big dinner.
15. The car broke down. Sam and I left the others to search for help.
16. The ostrich was enormous. It had a long neck and long, spindly legs.
17. An old book lay on the table. It was covered with dust and mold.
18. I missed my final exam on Wednesday. Tuesday night I got sick with the flu.
19. Dana's father is very wealthy. She drives a brand new Mercedes.
20. The land where I live is very pretty. It has rolling green hills and lots of elm and oak trees.

INDEX